# EUROPEAN WARFARE, 1494–1660

The start of the Italian Wars in 1494, subsequently seen as the onset of 'modern warfare', provides the starting point for this impressive survey of European warfare. In addition to conflict in early modern Europe, this book covers trans-oceanic expansion which led to interaction with extra-European forms of military might. Jeremy Black looks at technological aspects of war as well as social and political developments and consequences during this key period of military history. This sharp and compact analysis contextualises European developments, as well as establishing the global significance of events in Europe.

Black departs from recent work on military history in this period in giving due weight to the operational character and military dynamic of war alongside the social context. This text, handling a long chronological period with a broad geographical range, not only offers an excellent summary of early-modern European warfare, but is a thought-provoking survey that will interest anyone studying this period of military history.

**Jeremy Black** is Professor of History at the University of Exeter. His numerous publications include *European Warfare, 1660–1815* (1994) and *Western Warfare 1775–1882* (2001).

# WARFARE AND HISTORY
## General Editor, Jeremy Black
*Professor of History, University of Exeter*

# EUROPEAN WARFARE, 1494–1660

*Jeremy Black*

London and New York

First published 2002
by Routledge
2 Park Square, Milton Park, Abingdon, Oxon, OX14 4RN

Simultaneously published in the USA and Canada
by Routledge
711 Third Avenue, New York, NY 10017

*Routledge is an imprint of the Taylor & Francis Group*

© 2002 Jeremy Black

Typeset in Bembo by Taylor & Francis Books Ltd

*British Library Cataloguing in Publication Data*
A catalogue record for this book is available from the British Library

*Library of Congress Cataloging in Publication Data*
A catalog record for this book has been requested

ISBN 0–415–27531–8 (hbk)
ISBN 0–415–27532–6 (pbk)

FOR CHRISTOPHER DUFFY

# CONTENTS

# PREFACE

This book is intended as a 'prequel' to my *European Warfare 1660–1815* (London and New Haven, 1994), and is aimed for the same broad readership, contributing both to scholarly debate and serving as a good text for under-graduate courses and for the general military history reading public. The book offers a mix of thematic and chronologically organised chapters with start and end dates which are not regarded as absolute 'turning points' but as indicative of more general shifts. I have tried to emulate the distinctive features of *European Warfare 1660–1815* by devoting considerable attention to Europe's military profile and activities outside Europe. This is seen as an important contextualisation for European developments and also a way to establish the global significance of developments within Europe. There is also an inclusion of naval developments and warfare. This contributes to an understanding of the global impact of Western warfare and opens the possibility of comparing land and sea developments. The book combines operational history with an analysis of structures and long-term change, and with cultural, social and political contexts.

Throughout the book, I have tried to emphasise the diversity of force structures and military developments within Europe, not least by giving due weight to changes in Eastern Europe. This helps undermine the determinism implicit in any 'meta-narrative' or overarching schematic analysis. In partic-ular, it is important to avoid allowing the technology of weaponry to drive the interpretation and, instead, to give due weight to social and political contexts. This argument relates to the still current debate on the 'military revolution' in early modern Europe, a concept that has entered the main-stream of work on the period. Unlike studies that give too much weight to selected conflicts, particularly the Dutch Revolt and the first phase of the Thirty Years' War, in order to emphasise military innovations and support the thesis of a military revolution, this book offers a wider ranging coverage, of major wars, local conflicts and rebellions, in order to demonstrate the continued role of cavalry and of traditional weapons systems and tactical formations, the non-revolutionary character of military changes, and the rela-tive capability of armed forces. The study of a variety of conflicts helps to aid appreciation of the role and consequences of leadership, individual decisions, alliances and the political context of war, the multiple commitments of states and the social, economic and environmental constraints of warfare.

The book will begin in the 1490s for two reasons. The onset of the Italian Wars in 1494 was subsequently seen as the onset of 'modern warfare' and was certainly important in terms of sixteenth-century developments. In addition, the voyages of Columbus to the West Indies and of Vasco da Gama to India marked the beginning of a new global relationship between Europe and the world. However, at the same time, there is need for a degree of 'backward looking', not least to include the fall of Constantinople in 1453 and the advance of the Ottoman Turks in South-east Europe.

The book will close in 1660. 1659–60 saw the end of a twenty-four year conflict between the Bourbon kings of France and the Habsburg rulers of Spain, as well as the end of the Nordic War of 1655–60 and, with it, of Swedish expansion, and of the republican interregnum in the British Isles. 1660 also marks the end of the military revolution originally discerned by Michael Roberts. Although it is a valuable closing date, the conclusions will probe continuities. The choice of dates is not novel,[1] and is adopted without any suggestion that the period was either radically different to what had come before or crucial to the development of modern warfare.

Although this work is not written with reference to any particular approach to military history, it is worth noting its position. In contrast to the usual emphasis of works that are written in terms of the 'New Military History', with its emphasis on 'war and society', there is an attempt to give due weight to the operational character and military dynamic of war. All too often, the 'war and society' approach almost demilitarises military history, and also provides no clues to relative capability or to success in combat and conflict. In the limited space available, this study seeks to give due weight to operational factors and to issues of relative capability. There is also an engagement with the leading concept employed to discuss the period, the Military Revolution, although, to prevent that from overly dominating the book, it is not placed first. The subject deserves several volumes, but if this book serves as a helpful introduction it will have amply fulfilled its purpose.

Nomenclature poses a major problem. Terms like Turkish and Spanish provide ready identification for modern students, but have only limited value as a description of multi-ethnic polities, not least because the Safavid dynasty in Persia (Iran) and the Uzbeks also recruited among the Turkmen tribes. In the sixteenth and seventeenth centuries, members of the Ottoman elite did not use the term Turk, which meant rustic peasant or country bumpkin, to describe themselves. To label this multinational, multiethnic, multilingual policy as Turkish imposes a Western ethnolinguistic rubric upon a multiethnic empire which was by no means a nation-state. In the case of the Habsburgs, Austria and Spain are used to designate the two branches of the family after the abdication of Charles V.

It is a great pleasure to dedicate this book to one of the two military historians who has most influenced my work, a friend who years ago over a glass of whisky in my office in Durham gave me the best advice on how to write that I have ever received. I owe much to the work of other scholars, including those academics with whom I have discussed this subject for a quarter-century and also to students I have taught. I would particularly like to thank Gabor Ágoston, Christopher Duffy, Jan Glete, Richard Harding and Gervase Phillips for commenting on an earlier draft in its entirety, Brian Davies, Mark Fissel, Steve Gunn, Mack Holt, Rhoads Murphey and Mark Stevens for commenting on groups of chapters, and Derek Croxton, David Goodman, Alan James, Bob Knecht and David Parrott for commenting on individual chapters. None are responsible for any individual chapters that remain. I am most grateful for the skill and patience of the production editor, Lauren Dallinger and copy-editor, Morgen Witzel. I would also like to thank Sarah for agreeing to visit military sites on holidays to Austria, Denmark, Belgium, France, Germany, Italy, the Netherlands and Spain.

# 1

# INTRODUCTION

War, its conduct, cost, consequences and preparations for conflict, were all central to history in the early modern period. As European exploration and trade linked hitherto separated regions, so force played a crucial role in these new relationships and in their consequences. Conflict was also crucial to the history of relations between European states, as well as to their internal histories.

Warfare throughout the period was affected by social and physical conditions very different to those of today. The relatively low level of technology in even the most developed societies subjected all warfare to serious constraints. The limited nature of industrial activity, combined with low agricultural productivity and the absence of any real understanding of infectious diseases, ensured that population figures were low everywhere and that the potential pool of warriors was restricted. Most labour was exerted by generally malnourished human or animal muscle, and other power sources were natural and fixed: water and wind power and the burning of wood. There were no rapid communications on land or sea. This affected the movement of soldiers, supplies and messages.

These constraints affected the scope and conduct of warfare at every turn, but, nevertheless, in the period of this book, Europe's position in the world dramatically changed. This was not simply because, as states based on settled agrarian societies, those of Europe were able to call on what were, by the standards of the age, relatively large populations and the resources to support armed forces and developed governmental structures. This was as, or even more, true of some non-European societies, especially Ming China. Instead, it is necessary to consider the growing global reach capability of the states of Atlantic Europe.

This capability is a reminder of the military diversity of the period. Rather than thinking in terms of one pattern of military development that spread more or less effectively across Europe, for example the Military Revolution discussed in Chapter 3, it is more helpful to think of multi-centred developments. In addition to the changes in land warfare in Western Europe that are the subject of the Military Revolution theory, it is also possible to discuss an

Atlantic naval revolution, as well as changes in land warfare in Eastern Europe that owed much to the stimulus provided by conflict with the Ottomans and their Tatar allies, and a separate, albeit not independent, process of change in Gaelic warfare in parts of the British Isles.[1]

As well as the example provided by inter-European conflict, adaptation to an external threat was important. In place of the Hungarian cavalry destroyed by the Ottomans at Mohács on 29 August 1526, and in response to Ottoman infantry and cannon, the Austrian Habsburgs, later in the century, deployed infantry and cannon in positional warfare that entailed support from field fortifications. The Russians also developed the infantry–cannon–fortification combination, in part in response to the challenge from Islamic powers. The widespread borrowing of military methods from the Ottomans included the Venetian use in Italy of Albanian and Greek *stradiots* (light cavalry) who had initially been employed to fight the Ottomans in Greece and Friuli.[2] The Ottomans influenced the force structure and tactics the Russian army developed in the mid-sixteenth century, with the new *streltsy* infantry drawing on the example of the janissaries. The Ottomans also benefited from renegades and adventurers who brought expertise in land and naval warfare from Christian Europe. Mutinies of mercenaries and their defection to the Ottomans were an important source of expertise.[3]

Alongside the reminder of military variety within Christian Europe and of influences from outside Western Europe, it is also appropriate to note the spread of tactics, techniques and technology within Christian Europe. For example, sixteenth-century Russia was influenced by developments including those in Italian military engineering and gun-casting. More generally, the development of artillery encouraged the recruitment of foreign specialists, for example from Germany, the Low Countries and France by the kings of Scotland in the late fifteenth and early sixteenth centuries.[4] In the early 1600s, Dutch shipbuilders were hired to help modernise the Swedish fleets, with Scottish shipbuilders coming to Denmark for the same reason, and in 1617 Venice recruited 4,000 Dutch troops to help in operations against Austria.[5]

Warfare mediated and encouraged the processes through which major changes occurred; and, in turn, was affected by developments within Europe's dynamic civilisation, including demographic expansion, transoceanic discovery, intellectual enquiry and the spread of printing. In the sixteenth century, a series of transformations had major impacts on political relations. These included the Protestant Reformation, the advance of the Ottomans, the creation of European empires in the New World, which led to a flow of bullion into Europe, and a profound socio–economic shift characterised both by a major rise in population, after nearly two centuries of decline or stagnation, and by inflation. The resulting strains affected social and political relations within states, helping to make them more volatile, and also interacted with developments in international relations. The distinction between the two is less than clear-cut, particularly in the Holy Roman Empire (essentially modern Germany and Austria), but also in states that won independence through rebellion (the United Provinces) and in those that failed to do so (Ireland, Wallachia). The interaction of 'international' and 'domestic' politics and warfare ensured the overthrow in the 1550s of the quasi-hegemonic position of the Habsburgs in Western and Central Europe created by the Emperor Charles V in the 1520s–1540s, and, in the 1590s, of the dominant position in Western Europe created in the 1560s–mid-1580s by his son, Philip II of Spain.

This stress on policy serves as a reminder that there is a 'problem of agency' in the discussion of military change:

> an impression is sometimes communicated that there was something automatic about the technology per se that changed wars, states, and societies...but a respectable proportion of military technological change has to do with problem solving...it is repetitive warfare fought over regional hegemony that has been most responsible for escalating army sizes, military costs, and military technology in Europe.[6]

This approach ensures that it is necessary to see technological change as an enabler of attitudes and policies, rather than as the driving force of modernity. Technology may have changed and developed because policy-makers were interested in this development and were willing to reward those who developed technology in their interests. Gunpowder had several uses, particularly in mining, but, for centuries, the main effort of using it was in the development of more reliable, more mobile and more efficient tubes made of metal, suitable for firing lethal missiles driven by gunpowder.

In so far as the impact of technology is concerned, it is necessary to be cautious about determinist assumptions[7] and to avoid using misleading modern criteria about effectiveness.[8] Instead, it is possible to point to other factors that encouraged the spread of new weaponry:

> the proliferation of portable firearms...was due to the lack of fundamental technological change. The continuously poor technical quality of portable firearms had to be compensated for by their deployment in large numbers, in well-ordered armies, under an ethics of self-constraint and a mechanistic aesthetics.[9]

It is more generally important to be cautious in discussing the nature of change. The twentieth century had a fascination not only with machines but also with the concept of revolution. When, in 1924, Charles Oman referred to 'the military revolution of the sixteenth century',[10] he was employing a term that had a particular resonance in the context of the thought of the period. It is unclear that that term is still pertinent.

# 2

# CULTURAL, SOCIAL AND POLITICAL CONTEXTS

## A bellicose society

The military reflected the nature of society, and its actions exemplified current attitudes towards human life. Killing was generally accepted as necessary, both for civil society – against crime, heresy and disorder – and in international relations. War itself seemed necessary. In modern terms, it was the inevitable product of an international system that lacked a hegemonic power. To contemporaries, it was natural as the best means by which to defend interests and achieve goals. The idea that such objectives might be better achieved through diplomacy enjoyed limited purchase in a society that took conflict for granted; although there was a long-standing Christian critique of unjust wars and a related call to fight the non-believer.

Warfulness encouraged war, and the frequency of conflict ensured that a fresh turn to force seemed natural. By modern standards, European society was bellicose. Furthermore, a habit of viewing international relations in terms of concepts such as glory and honour was a natural consequence of the dynastic commitments and personal direction that a monarchical society produced. This habit reflected traditional notions of kingship, and was the most plausible and acceptable way to discuss foreign policy in a courtly context. Such notions also matched the heroic conceptions of royal, princely and aristocratic conduct in wartime.

Past warrior-leaders were held up as models for their successors. The example of Henry V of England was powerful at the court of Henry VIII (r. 1509–46), and Edward III's victories over France were also a touchstone. Henry IV of France (r. 1589–1610) looked back to Hercules and to the French kings who had invaded Italy, not to the weak monarchs who had ruled in the meantime.[1] The Ottoman ruler Suleiman I, 'the Magnificent', (r. 1520–66) was presented as the second Alexander the Great. Glory could be won through war. Thus the future Emperor Maximilian II (r. 1564–76) served in his uncle Charles V's German campaign in 1546–7. He led a cavalry division at the siege of Ingolstadt in 1546 and enjoyed taking part in the battle of Mühlberg.

Similarly, aristocrats looked back to heroic members of their families who had won and defended nobility, and thus social position and role, through glorious and honourable acts of valour. These traditions were sustained, both by service in war and by a personal culture of violence in the form of duels, feuds and displays of courage, the same socio-cultural imperative affecting both the international and the domestic sphere. This imperative was far more powerful than the cultural resonances of the quest for peace: the peace-giver was generally seen as a successful warrior, not as a royal, aristocratic or clerical diplomat.

The pursuit of land and heiresses linked the monarch to his peasants. As wealth was primarily held in land and transmitted through blood inheritance, it was natural at all levels of society for conflict to centre on succession disputes. Peasants resorted to litigation, a method that was lengthy and expensive, but to which the alternative was largely closed by state disapproval of private violence. Monarchs resorted to negotiation, but the absence of an adjudicating body, and the need, in particular, for a speedy solution once a succession fell vacant, encouraged a decision to fight.

## Rulers

Most of the royal and aristocratic dynasties ruling and wielding power in 1660 owed their position to the willingness of past members of the family to fight to secure their succession claims. The Tudors defeated the Yorkists to win England in 1485, the Bourbons had had to fight to gain France in the 1590s, the Austrian Habsburgs 'Royal' Hungary in the 1520s and Bohemia in 1620, the Braganzas Portugal in 1640, and the Romanovs to force the Polish Vasas to renounce their claim to Russia in the 1630s. Battles such as the Tudor victory at Bosworth (1485) and the Habsburg triumph at White Mountain (1620) were crucial in this process. The Vasas fought to gain Sweden in the 1520s and, in the 1590s, to remove a Catholic Vasa. The Princes of Orange owed their position in the United Provinces (modern Netherlands) to the success of the Dutch Revolt, and their subsequent power and influence derived in large part from their subsequent role as commanders of the Dutch army. George II Rákóczy, Prince of Transylvania, invaded Poland in 1657 in an unsuccessful attempt to become the king of all or part of it. This was not only a matter of engaging in war. Many rulers also took a prominent role in command, and even combat. In 1487, Charles VIII of France led a royal army against a noble rebellion, and his presence helped lead rebel garrisons to surrender. He also fought on the battlefield at Fornovo (1495). His successor, Louis XII, took part in the successful cavalry attack on the Venetians at Agnadello (1509). His opponent Pope Julius II commanded his forces in person (wearing armour) at the siege of Mirandola in 1511. Henry IV of France led a crucial cavalry charge at Ivry (1590), although other royal figures on the battlefield did not take any comparable role. Ferdinand of Aragon led the force in 1500 that suppressed the Islamic rising in the Sierra Nevada that had began the previous year. In 1642, his descendant Philip IV of Spain joined the forces that unsuccessfully sought to suppress the Catalan rising.

Similarly, republics had to fight to assert their independence and defend their interests. Thus, Venice and Genoa fought off foreign assailants and took precautions against domestic insurrection, while the United Provinces abjured their obedience to Philip II, and Geneva its to the Dukes of Savoy. Other bodies tried but failed to do likewise – the Estates of Bohemia in 1619–20, and the Estates of Catalonia in 1640–52.

Although peaceful successions of new dynasties did take place, as in England when James VI of Scotland became James I in 1603, war and inheritance were often two sides of the same coin. This was a problem exacerbated by varying and disputed succession laws, and by the need, in marital diplomacy, to avoid morganatic marriages. The bellicist nature of court society and the fusion of *gloire* and dynasticism encouraged a resort to violence in the pursuit of such interests and claims. In his advance south towards Naples in 1494–5, Charles VIII of France entered Florence and Rome on horseback carrying his lance, an image of glorious power. Louis XII of France entered Genoa in 1507 in full armour carrying a naked sword. The Emperor Charles V challenged Francis I of France to personal combat in 1528 and Francis took up the challenge. Although nothing came of it, Charles's move, and the response, expressed the ideal values of the period.[2] In 1597, Henry IV of France made his entry into Amiens, on horseback, sceptre in hand, to watch the defeated Spanish garrison surrender. The revival of the Classical triumph and procession was not restricted to Christian Europe, but was also used by the Ottomans, for example in Suleiman's campaign of 1532. *Gloire* and dynasticism appear today to be irrational factors, but it is not a helpful approach to treat the values of the period as anachronistic. Instead, it is necessary to treat the rulers, ideologies and motives of the period on their own terms in order to understand the goals pursued through war.

In recent years, there has been a reaction against the earlier scholarly tendency to treat rulers and ministers (who were also of course courtiers) as if they were figures to be understood in modern terms with an emphasis on a supposed desire on their part to further state-building. Instead, there has been an emphasis on the persistence of chivalric and religious notions in the assumptions underlying policy and in the political culture of the period. Thus, Prince Henry 'The Navigator' (1394–1460), a crucial figure in the development of the Portuguese empire, has been repositioned in terms of Portuguese crusader and follower of both chivalry and astrology, rather than as a Renaissance Prince.[3] This is important, as Portuguese maritime expansion has been seen as the cutting edge of the modern world. Philip II of Spain (r. 1556–98) has been presented as thinking in terms of a 'messianic imperialism' that stemmed from his strong religious convictions and his beliefs that God would support his policies. This has led to an understanding of his imperial overreach, as well as specific policy failures, as played out in Philip's mind in terms of a cosmic struggle. There was no 'viable alternative strategic vision'.[4]

This interpretation is important as Spain, under Philip, was the leading power in the Christian world, and his policies helped frame the agenda of international politics throughout much of it. It can be argued, that, irrespective of such attitudes on the part of leaders, militaries operated as professional bodies and developed in a competitive process; in other words that the nature of military change was systemic and that the 'agency' of individual rulers was of limited importance. Such an interpretation, however, underrates the extent to which the policy choices (compulsions is a more appropriate term) of rulers determined military goals.

## The aristocracy

The overlapping groups variously described as aristocracy, nobility and traditional local elites had an advantage as military commanders because they had political leverage and patronage which might create the obedience and loyalty necessary to recruit junior officers and soldiers. The rise of a 'modern' officer corps in theory ensured that the state had to create an alternative structure through which the ruler could distribute patronage (rewards for loyalty and efficiency). In practice, this was to a large extent done by integrating the aristocracy and nobility with the 'state' and giving them access to royal patronage and combining it with the patronage and influence they had locally. Rulers could use the traditional influence of local elites, while the latter benefited from stronger rulers. The extent of this integration, however, varied greatly across Europe. For example, in Poland and Ireland major nobles remained semi-feudal warlords whose allegiance to central governments was limited.

War was seen as a source of glory for rulers and the officer class, much of which was made up from the nobility and, at sea, from both nobility and mercantile oligarchy. Social expectations and an absence of sustained social mobility at the level of military command affected the ability of rulers to select commanders. Louis XIII of France (r. 1610–43) and his leading minister from 1624 until his death in 1642, Cardinal Richelieu, were not alone in having to be very careful about the allocation of command among 'les grands'. Far from appointment to command reflecting any concept of professional aptitude, commanders who were personally loyal to Richelieu were selected, although this loyalty had more to do with predominantly personal and family ambitions and alignments amongst the *grands*, rather than with any shared sense of wider political objectives. The increase in the scale of French military activity from 1635 led, however, to commands being given to less than reliable or competent *grands*, while, at the same time, the need for success rose.[5] In all states, competition among senior commanders reflected their quest for prestige. Thus, in France in 1644, the Duc d'Enghien (from 1646, Prince of Condé) was furious that command was given to the king's uncle, the Duke of Orléans. More generally, aristocratic ambition and pride very much affected command decisions.

7

For social and political reasons, it was seen as important to appoint high-born commanders, only some of whom had relevant experience. Thus, the Dauphin, later Henry II, commanded the French forces against Charles V in Champagne in 1544, while Archduke Albert of Austria, a son of the Emperor Maximilian II, was appointed Captain-General of the Army of Flanders, in 1595, succeeding his brother Ernst. At the battle of Nördlingen in 1634, the Spaniards were commanded by the Cardinal-Infante of Spain, a son of Philip III, and the Austrians by his cousin the Emperor's heir, Ferdinand, King of Hungary and Bohemia, later Emperor Ferdinand III. Other forms of closeness to the monarch were also important. Charles V's bastard son, Don John of Austria, and Philip IV of Spain's bastard, another Don John, both held senior commands in Habsburg forces, those of the latter including one of the armies that advanced on Barcelona in 1651. Lautrec, the French commander in Italy in 1522, owed his position to his sister's relationship with Francis I. Henry III of France appointed his favourites, the Dukes of Épernon and Joyeuse, to commands in 1586, thus hopefully ensuring a measure of royal control in the war against the Huguenots.

Major nobles also played a key role in what can be seen in modern terms as revolutionary movements, in large part because they were not in fact revolutionary in intention, or, at least initially, social politics, but rather stemmed from the long-established role of nobles to counsel the monarch and, if apparently necessary, take this to the point of thwarting bad policies and evil ministers. Thus the house of Nassau was crucial to the struggle for an independent Low Countries (and the Walloon nobles to the return of the southern provinces to their allegiance to Philip II), while in France nobles acted as the military leaders of the Huguenot cause. The 'Estates-General of the Provinces of the said Union' established by the Huguenots in 1575 had a Protector with command of military affairs. Initially, the Prince of Condé, he was followed by Henry Montmorency-Damville, Governor of Languedoc, and then Henry of Navarre, later Henry IV. In the English Civil War of 1642–6, the nobility was divided, with the Third Earl of Essex commanding the Parliamentary army that fought the Royalists at Edgehill in 1642.

Aristocratic leadership could cause tension when conflicts were radicalised. Thus, in Paris in November 1591, Catholic radicals in the Council of Ten seized power, provoking a show of force by the Duke of Mayenne, the leader of the Catholic League. The anti-radical response included the takeover of the Paris bourgeois militia, the largest military body in Paris not under royal or aristocratic control. Officers loyal to Mayenne were appointed and soldiers of humble status, and not therefore entitled to belong to the militia, were disarmed. More generally, civil wars led to a degree of social fluidity in officership that in particular allowed low-ranking nobles and clients of nobles to rise to positions of greater military power than they would otherwise have done, as with the rise of Oliver Cromwell during the English Civil War.

The role of prominent nobles reflected not only their position as natural commanders in societies deeply imbued with hierarchical values, but also their importance in raising troops. Whether the authority in question was 'public' (for example the noble as provincial governor) or 'private' (the noble as landowner and prominent figure in the locality), this ability to raise troops reflected the strength and range of clientage. It reached out through kinship, sociability, deference, and the culture of benefits and respect that bound landed society together. Within this system, the ability of leading families to increase their wealth and influence in the sixteenth and early seventeenth century, in part through receiving and using royal offices, including military commands, ensured that they could wield considerable power. At the centre of their military power, leading aristocrats had military retinues, but these could be readily expanded with kinsmen, clients and tenants.

Socially exalted commanders had another consequence for the economics of war in that they made it viable to seek ransoms. Like other aspects of prize money, this is a reminder of the extent to which military units were entrepreneurial. Their employers, the rulers of the period, benefited from the resulting ability to transfer some of the costs of war to whoever these units could get money or supplies from, principally the areas in which they campaigned.

More generally, the monarch was the war leader, the head of a socio-political hierarchy and a related economic system based on property rights that were in large part predicated or originally based on war and military prowess. As the war leader, the monarch played a crucial role not only in international conflict but also in suppressing, or attempting to suppress, opposition, rebellion or disorder. Thus, Charles I commanded his armies as a symbol of legitimacy against the Scots in 1639 and during the English Civil War, for example at Edgehill (1642) and Naseby (1645), while Henry IV in 1605–6, Louis XIII in 1614, 1620–2, and 1627–8, and Louis XIV in 1650 accompanied armies sent to overawe or suppress opposition. Yet, not all monarchs discharged these roles. Philip II, in particular, failed to match his father's peripatetic military leadership, and did not command operations in the Iberian peninsula, neither the occupation of Portugal in 1580 nor the suppression of the Morisco (1568–70) and Aragonese (1591) rebellions.

The nobility justified their special status by drawing attention to such service, but command was seen as fun as well as duty, and was, with its analogue, hunting, the major activity and recreation for the landed orders. For example, the captains of the *compagnies d'ordonnance*, the heavy cavalry established in 1445 that was the key element in the French army, were leading nobles, and the other members of the companies were lesser nobles and others drawn together as clients of the captains. Each captain selected them and they wore his livery. Captains were appointed by the king, but, in practice, many captaincies passed from father to son. The French crown provided pay out of taxation, especially the *taillon* introduced in 1549, but this was often in arrears and the captains frequently had to call on their personal credit.

The captains of the French infantry were also nobles, although of a lesser rank than their cavalry counterparts: the superior social prestige of cavalry was a key element in the social politics of the military, and this affected moves to lessen the role of cavalry. As with other periods of military history, it is necessary to appreciate the political drive of the organisational dimension, rather than to adopt a weapons-centred approach. Despite the distinction between noble commanders and ships' captains, there was no comparable social politics at sea. The infantry in France and elsewhere was mostly recruited from the peasantry, the social group that the nobility were accustomed to directing.

The hierarchy and collective discipline of officership 'worked' and was made effective in large part because it rested on a definition of aristocratic honour and function in terms of military service. This was not incompatible with professionalism. A recent study of military honour in early modern England has concluded that it was professional, rather than primarily an expression of machismo or romantic chivalry.[6] At the same time, the fusion of professionalism with aristocratic honour did not really accord with the notion of military modernisation in terms of the development of state-controlled armies and navies imbued with bureaucratic values as well as obedience to the state. Instead, the relevant ideas and ideologies were more complex. Obedience to the monarch was personal and conditional, and, in many senses, effective direction of armies and navies meant employing the culture and economy of honour, rather than of command. The continued impact of earlier ideas were seen in the reputation of chivalric orders, especially in Catholic Europe. The Knights Hospitallers of Saint John of Jerusalem represented an ideal of honourable service to many, and they were followed by the Tuscan Order of Santo Stefano, established in 1562, and the Piedmontese Order of the Knights of Saints Maurizio and Lazzaro, established in 1573.

The importance of military prowess for honour, status and wealth explained the pressure to acquire such prowess. Nobles were proud of the frontal wounds they bore and death in battle exalted lineage. It was common for boys to be given the names of military saints or other figures noted for their bravery. The rising popularity of the duel was a pointed expression of the association of personal and family honour with conflict,[7] and also a product of the familiarity of the well-born with hand-to-hand combat. This knowledge was spread by family, friends, masters of arms, and manuals, and was an aspect of a society that was not only familiarised with violence but also did not regard it as separate from leisure.[8] Gambling, with its stress on risk and loss nobly borne, was another facet of aristocratic culture that contributed to bellicosity.

Partly as a result of this culture, military service was a desirable choice for many, although other factors also encouraged service. Promotion to boyar rank in sixteenth-century Russia depended in part upon service in the field army, and Ivan IV's Decree on Service (1556) held all nobles liable for lifelong service, including the most powerful boyars and princes with allodial estates. This was part of a social politics that bent the nobility to military service while compensating them with the enserfment of their peasant tenants.[9] Further west, the Thirty Years' War (1618–48) led to the grant of large expropriated estates to commanders. Thus, the estates of Protestant nobles in Bohemia were distributed to Habsburg commanders, while the Swedes gave their officers lands in their Baltic conquests. Ottavio Piccolomini's service to the Habsburgs in the 1630s and 1640s led to his being created Duke of Amalfi by Philip IV of Spain and to his being raised to the dignity of an imperial prince by the Emperor Ferdinand III. The grant of estates and titles helped create a new ruling order, but was also a way to reimburse military entrepreneurs for their costs in raising and supporting units; although this was more commonly done by giving them permission to raise 'contributions' from the enemy territory in which they were operating.[10] Entrepreneurs who were already socially prominent in the territories of rulers for which they were raising troops could hope to receive privileges such as jurisdictional rights. In some states, for example Sweden, warfare helped create new elite groups, which were rewarded with the traditional titles and privileges of the nobility, as well as, at least in part, the modern titles and salaries of civil and military bureaucracies.

More generally, the active interaction of aristocratic lifestyle and military needs was seen in aristocratic leisure activities such as hunting, which was characterised by an increasingly organised structure in this period, for example with a major ordinance in France in 1516. These activities responded to new military needs, as professionalisation operated within a world defined by the assumptions of aristocratic hegemony; as military skill and command had for long done. Tournaments remained important, as with those sponsored by James IV of Scotland in 1507–8, but also changed with the phasing-out of the joust, the invention of new forms using handguns, and the introduction of combat on foot.[11] There was a great interest in the military arts in the upbringing of aristocrats. The Jesuit college founded by Duke Ranuccio of Parma in 1601 included in its curriculum training in weaponry, horsemanship and movement in formation. The Jesuit-run Colegio Imperial, founded in Madrid in 1625 to educate the sons of nobles, sought to train them in military arts.

Professionalisation, or at least a more self-conscious professionalism,[12] was provided by the development of an officer corps responsive to new weaponry, tactics and systems, and increasingly trained, at least in part, in a formal fashion, with an emphasis on specific skills that could not be gained in combat conditions. Nobles did not give up war because of the gun. Instead, they retained their desire for mounted prominence, both in the cavalry and in command positions in the infantry. This helped account for the emphasis on noble steeds, and thus for the importance of the trade in war-horses, as horses of the necessary quality were not bred throughout Europe.

The role of traditional concepts of military behaviour and renown was seen in the literature and art of the period. The books nobles had in their libraries reflected their interest in war. Instead of responding to the machinisation of war by focusing on gunpowder weaponry, with its characteristics of impersonal and long-range fighting, captured best in volley fire, there was a focus in literature and art on hand-to-hand combat, valour, cavalry and infantry charges, and leadership from the front. For naval warfare, there was also an interest in heroic deeds, especially in boarding other ships.[13]

These cultural imperatives contributed to the idea that it was dishonourable to fight with firearms, and that they were unchivalrous, if not diabolical. As service in war was an expression of honour and designed to contribute to that end, it is not surprising that there was considerable ambivalence, not to say hostility, towards firearms, and this was revealed by participants as well as commentators. However, as this book shows, there were also good reasons why the use of firearms faced limitations. Technical specialists, such as master shipwrights, gunfounders, artillery officers and military engineers, had an ambiguous position. They were usually non-nobles, and they were regarded as socially inferior persons compared to aristocrats, but they were reasonably well-paid and would often serve the ruler who paid them best. Their ambiguous social position, however, was linked to the ambivalence about the use of firearms.

## The soldiery

The social dimension of war included an assumption that soldiers and sailors would serve at the behest and under the control of their social superiors, whether as feudal levies, militia, mercenaries or permanent armed forces, recruited voluntarily or by conscription. Although there was dissatisfaction and mutinies, the soldiery were not consulted about their conditions or instructions. A willingness to accept pain and privation was part of ordinary labour, and military service was another aspect of it. Levels of violence could also be very high for ordinary people. Furthermore, throughout society, violence was seen as the way to defend personal worth, in the form of honour, and thus seemed more acceptable.[14] Far from declining before the power of the state, the willingness to use violence was given fresh encouragement and direction by the tensions arising from the Reformation,[15] and from the socio-economic changes of the period. Both, but especially the former, required the purging of those deemed evil, and thus encouraged individual and collective violence.

At the same time, soldiers were not reduced to unthinking ciphers[16] and officers had to take steps to maintain morale. Aside from ensuring pay and supplies, there were particular efforts at moments of conflict. Thus, when attempts were made to storm fortresses, the soldiers were promised spoils, and there were often offers of money for the first to storm the walls. Morale and fighting spirit could also be linked to religious zeal, as with the Austrian and Bavarian forces in 1620, many of whom were willing to see their conflict with the Bohemian and Palatine forces in terms of a crusade against icono-clastic Calvinists who had desecrated images of the Virgin.

## Recruitment

Armed forces were raised by a variety of (sometimes overlapping) methods. A major distinction divided volunteers from conscripts, but in truth there were gradations of both volunteering and conscription. Contemporaries were also interested in the distinction between mercenaries who fought for any master and troops who only fought for their own territory. Mercenaries can be regarded both as an aspect of 'late' or 'sub' feudal warfare and as evidence of the onset of capitalism. In the former case, they reflected the ability of promi-nent individuals (and most leaders of mercenary forces were from the social elite) to recruit troops. Indeed, the distinction between such units and those raised by members of the social elite for the service of their sovereign was not always as clear as the use of the term mercenary might apply. Similarly, the fact that soldiers (and their commanders) were serving for money was not inher-ently incompatible with feudalism. Far from being static, the latter had proved an adaptable system that had responded to the spread of the money economy in the medieval period. Feudal concepts of position in return for service continued to influence aristocratic attitudes, although the formal character of feudal military service declined. The notion of reciprocal relationship was akin to that of the mercenary. The common result was that entrepreneurs were contracted to raise and maintain units and could also take a role in directing policy. As far as the troops were concerned, payment itself did not determine military status, as troops raised by a variety of means were paid.

A recent study of English and Welsh mercenaries serving with the army of the States General in the Dutch Revolt has led to the conclusion that 'contrary to the impression given by most historians, the majority of the rank and file...were not press-ganged criminals, vagabonds', but instead, were raised by gentlemen and drawn 'from their traditional connections – from clients, retainers, and tenants'.[17]

Mercenary forces had for long played a major role in Italy. They made contracts (*condotte*) with Italian cities and the *condottiere* who came to head these forces, especially the Sforza, played a major role in the politics of the period. Francesco Sforza became Duke of Milan in 1450. Their German counterpart, the bands of *Landsknechte*, were originally raised for Emperor Maximilian I, but swiftly showed a willingness to sell themselves to all bidders. This remained the case throughout the period.[18] In 1515, Francis I found it difficult to recruit arquebusiers (handgunners) in France and there-fore recruited 2,000 in Germany. In late 1521, there were Swiss units in the rival armies of France and the Pope, leading the Swiss Diet to order both to come home. Earlier, in 1499 they had served in the rival armies of France and Milan, but in 1500 the Swiss Confederation ordered the units in these armies not to fight each other.

Although discussion of mercenaries in this period focuses on German and Swiss troops, they came from across Europe. The Italian states, for example, were an important source, with Italians serving not only in the forces of the Habsburg rulers and overlords of much of Italy, but also for non-Habsburg rulers.[19] Expertise played an important role. Thus, having provided cross-bowmen for the rulers of France in the fourteenth century, the Italians sent arquebusiers in the sixteenth. The reluctance of the French to serve as arque-busiers and their preference for shock combat ensured that large sums had to be spent to hire foreign firepower, a measure that helped drive up the royal debt.

There was considerable variety in the mercenary trade. When units were provided by princes, the emphasis was not only on financial gain but also on political benefits, especially the pursuit of dynastic and territorial ambitions. In such cases, the provision of mercenary units can be seen as an aspect of alliance diplomacy.

The loyalty of mercenary units frequently led to concern, although the 'changing of sides' has to take note of the porosity and mutability of the 'sides'. For example, Danish-born Heinrich Holk (1599–1633) served Christian IV of Denmark and held Stralsund against Wallenstein in 1628, only to change over to the Austrian army when Christian left the war and to fight under Wallenstein. Mercenary units could be unreliable both politically and on the battlefield. Swiss mercenaries were unwilling to undertake the dangerous task of storming breaches. Moreover, mercenaries were frequently recruited at a distance from the zone of hostilities, which caused delay in starting operations and also created the problem of having to fight their way through, both facets of their role in the French Wars of Religion. As in 1587, they also showed a reluctance to move sufficiently far into France to make a return to Germany difficult. A spectacular and decisive example of betrayal by mercenaries switching sides in mid-battle occurred at Klushino in 1610 when Tsar Vasilii Shuiskii was betrayed by De la Gardie's Swedes, whose pay was in arrears. This threw open the road to Moscow to the Poles.

It is important also to note the loyal service that could be provided by mercenaries. In the Wars of Religion, for example the Dutch Revolt, the soldiers on both sides appear to have displayed a considerable degree of iden-tification with the confessional issues. Furthermore, when considering mutinies it is necessary to appreciate the extent to which they could be formulaic and formal; aspects of negotiation, indeed part of the process of consensus searching that characterised early modern government, rather than irreparable breakdowns in military systems, although the latter also occurred.

The habit of hiring troops from units that were being disbanded helped ensure a supply of men. However, such troops expected better pay than new recruits. The latter were 'trained' by a process of osmosis: being exposed to more experienced men. Aside from inexperience, new recruits also deserted more readily than experienced soldiers, although desertion was a serious problem at every stage. It became more serious when campaigning began. Desertion was particularly serious among the unpaid and lowly paid, but it was exacerbated by a willingness by other recruiters to sign up deserters. This reflected the desire of many deserters to get a recruitment bounty, and also the difficulty of readjusting to civilian society. For armies, signing up deserters at least ensured experienced men; although the practice certainly qualifies any suggestion that recruitment indicated a 'modernity' in military practice. Mercenaries also tended to have a fearsome reputation for depredations on civilians. In France, this was particularly true of German mercenaries, while in Transylvania in 1599–1606, the German, Bohemian, Italian, Hungarian and Walloon mercenaries of the Emperor Rudolf II, the Wallachian and Serbian mercenaries of Prince Michael of Wallachia, and the Ottomans and Tatars all inflicted terrible damage. Mercenaries were also responsible for considerable cruelty to civilians during the Thirty Years' War. Yet mercenaries were accustomed to war and had the group cohesion and experience that was crucial to combat success. It required training to employ a pike or an arquebus effectively.[20]

In contrast, militias and other forces recruited at the outbreak of hostilities were regarded as less combat-ready, in terms of both experience and training. Niccolò Machiavelli (1469–1527), a Florentine official and writer, advocated the use of militia in large part because they seemed to offer the republican virtue he saw in the Roman republic and thus a replacement to the unreliability of mercenaries. However, at the siege of Prato in 1512, the Florentine militia failed and with it both the Florentine government and Machiavelli's career.[21]

Militia were, nevertheless, particularly valuable in defending their area of recruitment from attack. Thus, in 1567, the Paris militia made up a large part of the army that defeated the Huguenots at nearby Saint-Denis. In Sweden, the long-established legal obligation for all able-bodied men to take part in defence had often been used as an instrument of power by the peasant communities. In the early 1540s, the king began making musters of the earlier informal, intermittent and locally-controlled militia forces, and preparing lists of (young able-bodied) men who should serve as soldiers in wartime. In 1544, the Council of the Realm approved this initiative. The men were increasingly given peace-time training by the king's officers, paid by the king and armed by the king, becoming a royal militia under royal control. By the 1550s, this militia had become an operational army which could defend any part of the country, as was shown in 1555 when they were rapidly deployed to eastern Finland for war with Russia.

This helped in securing the manpower for the series of wars that Sweden engaged in from 1563 and enabled Erik XIV to deploy larger forces than his Danish rival, Frederick II, who relied on professionals; although the traditional obligation to serve only in defence of the homeland posed a serious difficulty for successive Swedish monarchs. The conscription system was very important to Swedish effectiveness in the seventeenth century. The soldiers raised were less expensive than mercenaries (which may help account for the initiative of the 1540s), although it proved necessary to use the latter for offensive operations, such as Gustavus Adolphus's invasion of Germany in 1630. Aside from cost factors, the conscripts also proved better motivated.[22] In Spain, the Ordinance of Valladolid of 1496 had established that one man in twelve between the ages of 20 and 45 was obliged to serve.

Social and ethnic politics could also be involved in attempts to raise troops from throughout the population. In Transylvania, the pressure of superior Ottoman numbers in 1595 led the Prince, Sigismund Bátory, to call on the hitherto oppressed Székeleys, and they helped the princely troops and the army of the Estates to victory, only to be suppressed the following year, not least because the nobles did not wish to lose their serfs.

In France, the absence of a tradition of arming the peasantry affected the quality of the native infantry. In 1503, Pierre de Gié, one of the two Marshals in the army, persuaded Louis XII to agree to create a French infantry of 20,000 archers and pikemen, but this plan was abandoned when he was disgraced in 1504. This also ended Gié's largely unsuccessful attempt to establish the potential size of the feudal levy by carrying out a census.[23]

In 1534, cost and reliability, the disadvantages of relying on Swiss mercenaries for his elite infantry, led Louis's successor, Francis I, to order the raising of seven 'legions' of infantry, the title a conscious throwback to the ancient world, as was the practice of awarding a gold ring to particularly brave legionnaires. Each legion was designed to be 6,000 strong and to consist of volunteers from a particular region. Thus, the regional dimension of militia was retained, although these legions were explicitly intended to be long-service volunteers. The regional dimension was also seen in differences between the legions in the ratios of arquebusiers to other infantry. The legions, however, did not compensate for France's weakness in infantry, and certainly did not match the Spanish *tercios*, although this may have reflected a lack of commitment by the crown to infantry, rather than any inherent flaws in the legion concept.

The regional dimension of forces reflected the way in which troops were raised in particular localities. This could have both a 'private' and a 'public' aspect, underlining the often unhelpful nature of modern definitions. Thus, for example, prominent French aristocrats were often governors of provinces where they had the centre of their landholdings and affinities. This gave them a number of mutually supporting ways in which to raise troops, as was shown by Henry, Third Duke of Guise, in Champagne in the 1570s and 1580s, and by his brother Charles, Duke of Mayenne, in Burgundy.

What might be termed feudal means of raising forces remained important. In response to the Pilgrimage of Grace in 1536, the Duke of Norfolk mobilised his tenants for Henry VIII.[24] In 1625, Charles Emmanuel I of Savoy-Piedmont summoned a feudal levy. The following decade, both France and Spain sought to raise feudal levies. These, however, were an unreliable expedient, generally lacking in discipline, equipment and training.

Rulers, instead, sought to move towards professional standing armies that combined the experience of mercenaries with the reliability of subjects; although, in wartime, these armies tended to be supplemented by both militia and foreign mercenaries. The administrative capability (in terms of information, local officials, and police enforcement) that systems of conscription could call on with considerable success from the late seventeenth and eighteenth centuries were less in evidence earlier on, and rulers tended to create standing forces by drawing on mercenaries as well as by using the 'sub-feudal' pattern of encouraging aristocratic officers to recruit from their own connections and tenants. Rulers also had their own military retinues, especially guards, which served as the basis of wartime armies.

The convicts and slaves that were used at sea, for the galley fleets of the Mediterranean, lacked an equivalent on land. It was not possible to control soldiers in the manner that galley slaves were chained to their benches.

It would be mistaken to adopt too schematic an approach to recruitment, not least because armed forces varied greatly, not only between peace and war, but also within individual years of peace or war. A complex interaction of opportunity and motivation, involving factors such as the reliability of pay, the season, and the proximity of the harvest, encouraged recruitment or desertion, and the size of units could vary very greatly. This dominated operational effectiveness, not only because numbers were needed for campaigning, but also because desertion hit unit cohesion and lessened the reservoir of trained and experienced soldiers. The need for soldiers was such that most armies were willing to accept recruits irrespective of their religious belief.[25]

The political context was also important. Suspicious of much of his aristocracy, some of whom he blamed for an alleged plot in 1611, Duke Ranuccio of Parma (r. 1593–1628) built up a substantial peasant militia officered by aristocrats he was willing to trust. Similarly, a large peasant militia was developed in Savoy-Piedmont after Duke Emanuel Philibert was restored at the close of the Italian Wars. Such militias were far more under royal control than the feudal levies provided by aristocrats. In the kingdom of Naples, the *battaglione*, a large peasant militia, acted as a local security force, but the government relied rather on a Spanish *tercio* for its military force. Venice relied on professional troops, but also had a peasant militia. Like other militias, this could be introduced to new weaponry. In the early 1490s, steps were taken to teach some of the new recruits how to use the arquebus.[26] In 1516, Cardinal Cisneros, the regent of Castile, raised a militia to forestall aristocratic opposition, while, in 1596, a militia under crown appointees was created in the kingdom of Valencia, in order to offset dependence on the nobility. The same year, a militia was created in Bavaria.

Military service could bring peasants valuable status. In Savoy-Piedmont, militiamen gained legal and other privileges as a result of service, while wealthy peasants who could provide their own horses were allowed to fight duels and to hunt like nobles.

Urban militias provided a way to gain and affirm status. They also had a military and political value. The two could combine as in 1650 when Amsterdam made preparations against a siege planned by William II of Orange. In wartime, cities could not rely on the regular armed forces of the central government to provide defence, and nor did they wish to do so. Instead, the militia provided at least a layer of defence to all cities and frequently the sole defence. This was particularly important in resisting the requisitioning of opposing forces. It ensured that in order to obtain contributions, these forces would have to be able to overawe the cities.

Militia systems were also used in civil wars. In 1562, as France slipped into the first of its Wars of Religion, individual Protestant parishes and colloquies were set a quota of troops. Thus, the structure of the church was to become the structure of the army. However, as was common with other militia systems, aristocrats and their affinities were important to the military strength of the Huguenots: the clientage system ensured that greater nobles could bring lesser nobles with them. These different ways of raising troops corresponded to a functional contrast: the nobility were responsible for the heavy cavalry, the churches for the infantry. The church also helped raise money to recruit 7,000 mercenaries from Germany. The militias which Prince Dmitrii Pozharskii and Prokopii Liapunov formed in 1610–11 to drive the Poles from Moscow were a significant example of the effectiveness of militia in a civil war. In the French Wars of Religion, the civilian population was involved in the fighting, as perpetrators as well as victims. Local militias made up of town residents rather than professional soldiers were pivotal in both the St Bartholomew's massacres (1572) as well as the wars of the Catholic League (1584–95). Indeed, in the Parisian and provincial massacres of 1572, nearly the whole of the killing of 6,000 to 8,000 people was done by civilians rather than professional soldiers. The civilian Catholic population (especially local magistrates) was also vital in rejecting all the peace treaties granting legal rights and privileges to Huguenots before 1598 – one reason the wars dragged on so long. Ultimately, it was pressure from the Catholic population and public opinion, not just soldiers of the League, that forced Henry IV to abjure Protestantism in 1593 and become a Catholic once more, bringing about a possible solution and end to the wars.

In contrast to militias, money was required to pay regular, professional soldiers in order to prevent mutinies. Their impact on the most prominent army in Christian Europe, that of Philip II, has been ably studied by Geoffrey Parker.[27] These mutinies usually wrecked operations, but they could also create a new military requirement. Thus, a mutiny that began in September 1602 led to the exaction of contributions from a large part of the Spanish

Netherlands, and helped to determine military operations in 1603, leading to the Spanish siege of mutineers in Hoogstraeten. Archduke Albert had to agree their terms in May 1604 in order to restore his army's strength. Other armies also mutinied as well. For example, Maximilian II's attempt to besiege Ottoman-held Esztergom in 1566 collapsed when troops refused to move: they had mutinied over lack of pay and their leaders were opposed to the siege. In his war with Sweden in the 1560s, Frederick II of Denmark repeatedly had to face opposition from his troops to his plans that arose from his failure to pay and supply them. When, in 1641, the new Elector of Brandenburg, Frederick William, decided to cease hostilities in the Thirty Years' War and to disband the army most of which was composed of mercenaries, he faced opposition from their officers. Many were unwilling to swear allegiance to the new Elector, while they argued that, as the troops had sworn to serve both his predecessor and the Emperor, Ferdinand III, they remained in Imperial service.

The substantial arrears owed by Parliament to the New Model Army played a major role in English politics after the First Civil War (1642–6). Agitators or delegates appointed by regiments pressed Parliament for arrears, and in August 1647 the army occupied London. After the Second Civil War in 1648, the army leaders purged Parliament in order to stop it negotiating with the king, in a move (Pride's Purge, 6 December 1648) appropriately named after an officer, and then pushed through the trial and execution of Charles I for treason against the people. The leaders were determined to punish Charles as a 'Man of Blood' who had killed the Lord's People. The execution made compromise with the Royalists highly unlikely, and entrenched the ideological position of the new regime. The confiscation of land in conquered Ireland was used to help pay the arrears of soldiers' wages.

## The treatment of civilians

The conduct of troops frequently pressed hard on civilians. Especially if unpaid, they were apt to seize property from civilians and frequently to treat them with great brutality. This is particularly associated with Germany during the Thirty Years' War, most spectacularly in the sack of Magdeburg in 1631; but was in fact far more widespread. A recent study of the situation in Germany during the war has argued that harshness towards civilians was a matter not only of the ambiguous nature or laxness of the rules of war towards enemies and a brutal competition for resources, but also of animosity between troops and civilians and the extent to which soldiers protected and enforced their status and honour by a harsh treatment of others.[28] It was therefore an aspect of the increasing differentiation of soldiers as a military group that owed much to the prominence of mercenaries.

Devastation was not limited to the Thirty Years' War. In the Thirteen Years' War of 1593–1606 between Austria and the Ottomans, military operations, attacks on civilians, epidemics and civilian flight nearly depopulated large parts of the Hungarian plain.

The harsh treatment of civilians across Europe in part reflected that which soldiers could mete out to each other. High death rates in battle habituated soldiers to killing, and at very close quarters. Furthermore, the slaughter of prisoners was widespread. The killing of the Swiss garrison at Mondavi in 1543 led the Swiss and French infantry at the battle of Ceresole the following year to kill the *Landsknechte* who surrendered.

Military practice was frequently devastating for civilian society. Thus, the destruction of crops in order to intimidate and weaken opposing rulers, forces and towns had very harmful short-term effects on rural society. Civilians were particularly vulnerable when towns were stormed. It was then conventional for troops to sack them, as much as an expression of anger and power as in search for loot. The heavy casualties the French took in storming Brescia in 1512 led them to inflict a brutal sacking in which thousands were killed. Commanders sometimes favoured sacking as a warning to other towns to surrender when besieged and offered terms, but at other times they regretted the destruction of *matériel* and were concerned about the political repercussions. These could be very serious. In 1640, troops sacked Santa Coloma de Farnés in Catalonia, where a royal official had been killed, but this only led the peasantry of the surrounding countryside to rise in rebellion, setting in motion the collapse of royal authority through Catalonia.

However, it proved difficult to restrain troops. In 1562, the commanders of the French royal army tried to prevent a sack of Rouen when it was stormed, but the troops ignored the offer of a bonus and inflicted three days of torment on the city. More generally, rulers and generals who could not afford to pay their forces transferred the cost of supporting them to the regions in which they operated, an important aspect of war's characteristic as, at once, destructive[29] and an aspect of a different tempo of state activity. Looting and enforced 'contributions' removed coin and precious metals from areas, gravely hindering their economy.

Armies also caused much unintentional hardship. They were particularly important as spreaders of disease. Thus, in 1629, the French and Austrian armies took the plague with them into Italy. Possibly it would have spread anyway, but the armies certainly sped it up, and with devastating effects. Venereal disease was also spread by soldiers, and the intervention of outside powers in the Italian Wars (1494–1559) appears to have been especially significant in this respect. In particular circumstances, armies could also use disease, for example by preventing the inhabitants of a besieged city afflicted by plague from fleeing, as happened in the Austrian siege of Mantua in 1630.

At the same time, the relationship between military and society was far more complex and varied than one of simple animosity. In some respects, violence was the product of breakdown in a multifaceted set of links that encompassed recruitment, billeting, logistics and sexual links.[30] For example, the presence of a garrison led to an increase in the rate of illegitimate births in the area. This was disruptive and also put pressure on social welfare, as extended families, poor relief, charity and orphanages had to cope with the bastards; but the relationships should not simply be seen as adversarial. The military acted and interacted as part of a complex social network; not as something outside society.

## War and society

Wars could bring a degree of association between people and cause. This was an aspect of the degree to which warfare created 'states'; while the rivalries between them were in some fashion inherent to their very existence. War was very important not only in determining which dynasties controlled which lands, or where boundaries should be drawn, but also in creating the sense of 'us' and 'them' which was, and is, so important to the growth of any kind of patriotism. The idea of 'statehood' (as opposed to the earlier *natio* in its original meaning of people of a common descent) led to a territorialisation that was related to the development of a sense of political community separate from the monarch. The construction and territorialisation of identity was not restricted to the political elite.

As a result, a framework and ideology able to raise forces and to persuade people to fight emerged as an alternative to those summarised by the term feudalism. The martial configurations of these new political communities remained under monarchical control and direction. Indeed, the phenomenon of *gloire*, whether focused on the ruler or on a more diffuse sense of community, was part of a code which served to integrate heterogeneous groups into the gradually emergent 'states'.

In Europe, as elsewhere in the world, explanations of military success focused on leadership, individual bravery and collective prowess in the use of weaponry and discipline. An emphasis on technology as the motor of military change and success developed most of all in Europe, although other factors continued to be seen as important and the emphasis on technology did not match that to be shown from the nineteenth century. Furthermore, the skills involved in employing the firearms of the period were rather those of a repetitive industrial process (and not therefore seen by contemporaries as praiseworthy) than those requiring intellectual effort or the understanding of a complex technology:

> In the days of the matchlock arquebus the soldier had first to dismount and secure his match; then to blow any sparks from his firing pan; then to prime the pan with special fine gunpowder, remembering to shake any excess from the pan and to tamp the pan with his finger; then to recharge his piece with regular gunpowder and to reload it with wadding and shot, drawing out his ramrod and

tamping the powder and ball with just the right amount of pressure. He was then ready to cock his mechanism, blow his match to life, fix it in the matchlock's jaws, present his piece, and give fire.[31]

Military success did not only focus on conflict with other sovereign states. Troops were also involved in a range of internal tasks, and indeed all significant policing operations involved troops. Military operations took place along a continuum stretching from formal war to actions against smugglers. Given the severity of some rebellions, formal war did not necessarily entail greater commitments or problems than domestic action, although it generally did so. Nevertheless, although domestic conflict could be a serious problem, it was a matter of rebellion, not war, in the eyes of the rulers concerned and in that of most other monarchs. Commentators were generally able to differentiate between the policing and war functions of armed forces. There was also a relatively clear distinction in the *mentalités* of courtly society. Glory and honour could be gained through suppressing domestic discord, but it was primarily a function of defeating foreign rivals, and certainly not crushing peasants.

Just as war between rulers was encouraged by the bellicist culture, so also was civil conflict. Alongside the cultural factors encouraging conflict, there were also specific military and political characteristics and circumstances. These included the widespread distribution of weapons; the possibility of inflicting defeat on regular forces whose military superiority was limited, not least because of logistical, manpower and financial problems; ideological traditions justifying, but in turn constraining, rebellion, not least the contractual nature of authority; the employment of violence as part of a form of mass demonstration; and the degree to which 'states' had only a limited ability to integrate, or interest in integrating, the often disparate communities, groups and territories that composed them. The consequent limitations on the ability of 'states' to unite and to assimilate increased the possibilities of rebellion. Violence and warfare were endemic to society.

As with international conflict, issues of honour and reputation played a major role in encouraging civil conflict: they were central to much lawlessness and, in particular, to aristocratic and other feuds. Such feuding was assumed to be a part of noble privilege. In the late Middle Ages, warfare was the continuation of litigation by other means, not an incompatible alternative; and feuds have been seen as playing a major role in state-building by princes: there was an overlap between noble office-holding and participation in feuds.[32]

In France, private wars were banned in 1367, and in the Empire feuds were outlawed in 1495. This step was not immediately successful, but in the long run there was a decline in feuding. The last noble to organise a traditional feud, Wilhelm von Grumbach, was executed in 1567, and his patron, Duke John Frederick of Saxony, became the Emperor's prisoner. Long in dispute with the bishops of Würzburg over territorial claims, Grumbach had attacked Würzburg in 1563 and been placed under the imperial ban. Concern about

Grumbach's relationship to the rivalry between the Elector and the Duke of Saxony, and about possible links between Grumbach, John Frederick, the Calvinists and France, led the Emperor and the Elector of Saxony to action.

The distinction between feuds and 'high politics' was not clearcut, especially in regions of divided sovereignty. Albert Alcibiades, Margrave of Brandenburg-Kulmbach, allied with Henry II of France and Maurice, Elector of Saxony, against the Emperor Charles V in January 1552, but that April he abandoned the alliance after a quarrel with his former friend Maurice. That summer, he could only keep his army in being by ravaging and enforced contributions, which led to his being placed under the imperial ban. He regained favour by supporting Charles against Henry II, only to fight Maurice in 1553. Such patterns of behaviour and conflicts became less common in Germany during the second half of the century, but they revived during the Thirty Years' War. As with so many commanders, Albert, born in 1522, was young. The Cardinal-Infante, Spain's commander at Nördlingen (1634) was born in 1609.

Earlier, in the Knights' War of 1522, the Swabian League, in concert with the rulers of Hesse, the Palatinate and Trier, had suppressed the Imperial Free Knights who had risen against attempts to curtail them. The Rhineland Knights were led by Franz von Sickingen, a Lutheran with a long-standing feud with the Archbishop-Elector of Trier. However, his siege of Trier was unsuccessful. Sickingen was forced to raise the siege and retreat to his castle at Landstuhl, and, in April 1523, his fortress succumbed to bombardment. Sickingen suffered a mortal wound from a stone splinter. In England, the Tudors limited the affinities of nobles, which had served as the basis of their military potential. The execution of the Duke of Buckingham in 1521, in part because he was building a castle at Thornbury, discouraged others from the same course.

In Italy, in contrast, for example in the Veneto and Lombardy, there was a rise in violence and a revival of feuds at the close of the sixteenth century. Brigandage, frequently associated with the social elite, remained a marked feature of Sicilian society. Elsewhere in the dominions of the rulers of Spain, there were serious feuds in the kingdom of Aragon, including that in the 1570s and 1580s between the Count of Chinchón, a leading minister, and the Duke of Villahermosa, the most prominent noble, a struggle that encompassed rivalry at court and fighting in the localities.

Another example of civil conflict was provided by the suppression of heterodox opinion. Clerical bodies, such as the Inquisition, played a major role in this, but they were dependent on the support of secular authorities.[33] The language of religious struggle often mirrored that of war. This was accentuated when the two were conflated as a consequence of the Reformation. The combination led to new institutions that employed force to stamp out dissent, for example the Council of Troubles in the Low Countries (1567–76). The Roman Inquisition was founded in 1542. The righteous and heretics provided the soldiers in the resulting sacred struggle, and the violent but praiseworthy end of martyrdom was the fate of some of the former.[34] The treatment of alleged witches was another aspect of the violence of the age, and specifically, of the linkage of popular tensions with the strategies of official bodies. The suppression of heterodox opinion was not limited to Christian powers. For example, the Ottomans tried to suppress the kizilbash, (Shi'a) Turkmen tribes in eastern Anatolia which were natural allies of the Safavids.

While many nobilities and nobles derived their importance and sense of identity in large part from warfare, that did not ensure that internal conflict was incessant. Many disputes between nobles did not escalate into warfare. Instead, civil warfare had much to do with the balance of power and authority between larger political entities – states and kingdoms – and smaller entities, such as provinces, with their own identity and liberties.

It was easier than is the case today to sustain both war and a viable society. War was less destructive. Peasants knew how to hide the movable wealth of a village when an army was passing through, although, aside from the direct damage caused by conflict and soldiers, higher taxes pressed hard on both society and economy. Resources were destroyed and investment opportunities were lost. The use of relatively inefficient guns was such that the serious killing effects of firearms had not yet been realised; but the limited ability of medical knowledge to cope with wounds, particularly with subsequent infections, ensured that a higher percentage of the wounded died than in twentieth-century conflicts.

## War and state-building

The difficulty of defining the character and impact of war was accentuated by the limited extent to which the state monopolised organised violence. Authorised non-state violence, for example by mercantile companies with territorial power, was important, and unauthorised violence, for example feuds and piracy, were frequently large-scale. Attempts to limit either were hindered by the widespread nature of military entrepreneurship: the practice of hiring military services, particularly mercenaries.

The prevalence of this practice serves as a reminder of the need for caution before assuming any modern definition of state-building. The latter focuses on bureaucratisation, the rise of the 'tax state' and the development of state-controlled permanent forces.[35] Elements of these can indeed be noted, and linked to them was the attempt to ensure state control of arms that had a battlefield capability, especially cannon, a process facilitated by regalian rights over metals. It has been repeatedly argued that state control over cannon enabled central governments to dominate other centres of power – nobility and towns – and to overawe or destroy opposition.[36]

The fate of many castles was striking. In England, there was an extensive abandonment of castles, in some cases from the 1470s and, far more actively, in the Tudor period. Dunstanburgh Castle was already much ruined in 1538 and Dunster Castle in 1542, as a consequence of a lack of maintenance for decades. In 1597, a survey found that Melbourne Castle, a Duchy of Lancaster possession in Derbyshire, was being used as a pound for trespassing cattle. The castle itself was demolished for stone in the 1610s by its new owner, the Earl of Huntingdon. Warkworth Castle was neglected and, when James I visited it in 1617, he found sheep and goats in most of the rooms. By then, Bramber Castle, formerly a Sussex stronghold of the Howards, was in ruins. It is less clear what this was a potent demonstration of. Rather than seeing this shift as a simple product of the impact of royal artillery strength, it is worth noting that many declining castles (including those of the Duchy of Lancaster) were royal possessions, and that the nature of fortifications was such that as needs changed there were always redundant castles, and that this had always been true. When James VI of Scotland became James I of England there was less need for fortifications and James sold Dunstanburgh Castle in 1604. In addition, the more peaceful nature of the kingdom was such that Windsor Castle was now a palace whose fortified character was not central to its role. Painters captured decayed castles as potent symbols of mutability, as in Jan van der Croos's *Landscape with Ruined Castle of Brederode and Distant View of Haarlem* (1655).

In France, Francis I created a royal monopoly for saltpetre. In 1606, French artillery played a major role in persuading the rebel Duke of Bouillon to surrender his fortified town of Sedan rather than face a siege. The artillery was seen as sufficiently important by Henry IV's leading minister, Sully, for him to retain the post of *Grand Maître de l'Artillerie*. Yet, as so often with discussion of both military capability and technological advance, the stress on cannon as the enabler of a new military order is conceptually a misleading approach because it is monocausal. In addition, this specific argument is unhelpful because the shift towards stronger government was long-term, complex and only partial, and in none of those respects does it fit with the gunpowder explanation.[37]

The effectiveness of force was dependent on the political context. Thus, in 1594, Sigismund Bátory, Prince of Transylvania, abdicated when the Estates refused to support his declaration of war on the Ottomans, only to return at the head of the army and with the support of some leading figures. The Diet had the opposition leaders arrested and they were executed or murdered in prison. The following January, Transylvania's membership of the Holy League was confirmed. Ferdinand of Bavaria, Prince-Bishop of Liège (r.1612–50) clashed with the city of Liège over his attempts to control it. He turned to Austria and Spain for military assistance, only for their opponents, France and the Dutch, to provide counter-pressure. It was not until 1649 that Ferdinand was able to deploy about 3,000 troops in order to enforce his will. James VI of Scotland's succession to the English throne was followed by a firm campaign of repression against the border reivers or moss-troopers who dominated the Anglo-Scottish border lands. Many were killed and one of the most persistently troublesome clans, the Grahams, were forcibly transplanted to Ireland in 1606. Conversely, a lack of co-operation between France and Spain helped keep the border zone lawless and made it difficult to counter the smugglers of the region, whose bands were often led by nobles.

Governmental military capability could face serious weaknesses if there was a lack of social support. Aside from an absence of necessary backing for raising and supporting forces on the part of the powerful local social elite, there could also be an active political rivalry. This was shown clearly in mid-seventeenth-century Britain. The English Civil War of 1642–6 had revealed the military redundancy of the traditional centres of landed power in the face of a determined opponent. Garrisoned stately homes, such as Burghley House, Compton Wynyates, Coughton Court and Basing House, fell to siege and storming. In 1655, Oliver Cromwell entrusted authority in the localities to eleven Major-Generals, who were instructed to preserve security and to create a godly and efficient state. The division of the country among the Major-Generals created a new geography of military rule. They were ordered to take control over the Justices of the Peace, the local gentry who had traditionally governed the localities, and to take charge of the militia. Compared to the former Lords Lieutenants, the Major-Generals, however, lacked the local social weight to lend traditional patterns of obedience and deference to their instructions. No other regime sought to replicate this method, and Cromwell soon found it necessary to abandon the unpopular system of rule by Major-Generals.

It is important to note the prevalence of a different political course, one that centred on the search for a new consensus with the socially powerful, rather than on bureaucratic control and centralisation. The pursuit of this consensus was centralising – in that it focused the attention of regional elites on the centre – but not centralised, and it sought to accommodate the wide dispersal of rights and powers that characterised early modern society. The power of the 'state' has therefore to be understood in terms of consent as well as coercion. If government at one level was a means of extorting resources for the pursuit of policies that reflected the interests of rulers, the willingness to contribute resources was also important. Furthermore, the vitality of intermediate bodies, such as town councils, was important. They mediated between and reconciled the interests of central government and localities in a way that could not be done by centralised bureaucracies and their local agents.

Such consensual elements were also important in territorial expansion. A study of French expansion in Picardy, on her most vulnerable frontier, emphasises the domestic compromises necessary to advance French interests in a region of contradictory loyalties. Alongside the role of force, the winning over of a wide range of regional notables was also crucial. Their continued local power was complemented by the extension of the royal 'affinity' into the region.[38] The Austrian Habsburgs pursued the same approach in Bohemia and Hungary.

Yet consensus was not the same as allowing aristocratic families to do as they wished. Furthermore, there was a shift from the royal weakness and civil violence seen in many states in the mid-fifteenth century to, at least apparently, stronger governments in the early sixteenth century, certainly in England, France and, from the 1520s, Spain. Charles, Duke of Bourbon, the Constable of France, appeared an anachronistic figure in 1523 when, in response to attempts by the royal family to gain his lands, he asked Charles V for his sister in marriage and offered to support him with 8,500 troops in an invasion of France. The plan miscarried. Yet, before too much is made of this shift, it is worth noting that in the *Frondes* in the early 1650s leading French nobles felt able to defy the crown. Furthermore, the continued ability of 'overmighty subjects' to succeed, albeit against a vulnerable overlord, was shown in the Papal States in 1526 by the Colonna family who intimidated Pope Clement VII before occupying Rome.

## Military capability

If the emphasis in military capability is to be placed on such issues, rather than on weaponry, then military history becomes an aspect of general history. This is appropriate. Competing rulers directed clashing systems, and therefore the potential for, and impact of, war were strongly influenced by administrative and social practices and systems. These interacted with circumstances such that in some states impressive (at least by earlier standards) levels of organisation sustained far-ranging patterns of activity and action, although, elsewhere, war could trigger a reversion to apparently more primitive arrangements, with private entrepreneurs organising and local populations paying. Early and mid-seventeenth-century military structures were frequently unable to meet the demands for the financing, supply and control of armies in the lengthy wars of the period.[39] This situation was accentuated in civil conflicts, such as the French Wars of Religion (1562–98), when political and administrative practices and structures collapsed or, at least, were put under strain. Logistics posed a particular problem.[40]

The phrase 'apparently more primitive arrangements' employed in the previous paragraph serves to highlight the point that the confidence that might have been expressed half a century ago that public provision and state organisation were necessarily better, and therefore the goal of military development in the past, is now seen as a projection of a particular set of values. It is, instead, now possible to draw attention to the weaknesses of public provision, not least of state structures focused on clientage, and to the weaknesses of governments, for example the difficulties of obtaining adequate information and necessary skills. As a result, the value of private provision can be stressed. Indeed, 'progressive' forces, such as the New Model Army, relied on such provision.[41]

Increases in the size of armies and navies, and new fortifications and weaponry, combined to push up the cost of war, and also helped ensure that peacetime levels of preparedness were generally well below wartime strength. Standing armies did become more prominent compared to the previous century, but they remained small in peacetime. This lessened wartime effectiveness, and ensured that mercenaries played a major role in helping create larger wartime forces that had the necessary training, experience and weaponry. They were also important in enhancing peacetime strength. Thus, in 1567, Charles IX of France recruited 6,000 Swiss, a major increase in military capability that helped to touch off the Second French War of Religion. In most of these French Wars of Religion, the Protestants hired large numbers of German cavalry, and the Crown also recruited German cavalry. The hiring of such forces was an important aspect of the international dimension of armies. Aside from such units, it was common to hire foreign experts, especially artillerymen and cannon founders, as well as to be served by foreign officers. However, the very concept of foreignness is of only limited value, given the emphasis on personal links and service in the dynastic monarchies of the period. Across the Christian–Islamic divide, it was common to hire renegades, and this was an important means of transmitting expertise.

During war, resources had to be sustained. The Duke of Anjou captured Cambrai in 1581, but his unpaid army then disintegrated, compromising his attempt to wage war on Philip II of Spain. The difficulty of sustaining military activity itself contributed to the range of demands on the military, generally with foraging and other means of securing supplies, and, on occasion, as peasant risings against military depredations created a new challenge. This was true for example of France in 1593–4, and of England in 1644–5 during the Civil War. The *Tard-Avisés* of the former and the Clubmen of the latter were able to field considerable forces, although they were vulnerable to the professionalism and weaponry of regulars. The Clubmen in the Welsh Marches and the West Country sought to keep troops out of their areas. These unsuccessful risings were a determined attempt to restore local control and to limit the demands of garrisons such as Hereford and Langport. In addition, in December 1631, there was armed local resistance in the Meuse Valley to attempts by Spanish troops to take up winter quarters. The importance of obtaining supplies in the field also encouraged the devastation of potential supply sources, as, by both sides, in the war between Denmark and Sweden in 1563–70.

By global standards, European military administration was reasonably well developed.[42] Furthermore, deficiencies in army administration were not matched to the same extent at sea: the introduction of numbers of specialist warships led to a development of admiralties. The Spanish bureaucracy of the 1620s showed great agility and dedication in keeping the fleet supplied. Private contractors and public officials worked fruitfully together, forest legislation sought to conserve timber stocks, efforts were made to provide sailors and soldiers with nutritious food and good medical care, and severe discipline was enforced on erring fleet commanders and bureaucrats.[43] Russian military provisioning offers an example of the development of military administration by the mid-seventeenth century.

More generally, the practices of European military conduct depended heavily on clerks. However, the ethos of European warriordom was different, while bureaucratic processes were mediated through societies that were still dominated by the landed orders, specifically the aristocracy. Yet these also changed their attitudes. Although the process varied by individual, martial elite culture was transformed as knights became officers (although the distinction between the two should not be exaggerated). This helped ensure a continuation of ancestral political and social privilege, but one that was adapted to battlefield roles that required disciplined responses; although the number of occasions on which cavalry, once they had charged, lost order and disappeared from the battlefield in order to loot the opponent's baggage train suggests that this should not be exaggerated.

For both officers and soldiers alike, there was an emphasis on preparedness, specifically the training that was crucial to the effective use of weapons. It was only thanks to training and discipline, that different types of troops could combine effectively in battle tactics. Vulnerable handgunners needed to co-operate with pikemen to ensure protection and this required particular formations and tactics that posed demands on both officers and men.

At the same time, training was of scant value without experience and morale, both of which were more valuable sources of unit cohesion, and it is probable that the role of training has been exaggerated. Furthermore, the shift in recent scholarship towards devoting more attention to warfare in Eastern Europe and the Celtic lands suggests that a narrative and analysis of preparedness based on Western European models of training can be questioned. A shift in the current analysis of tactical proficiency in the period away from an emphasis on training towards one on experience helps explain the continued appeal of mercenaries, even though their demands for ready money posed a major problem.

This appeal can also be approached from a different angle. If state systems are anatomised in order to show that their effectiveness depended on consent, and that this could involve difficult constraints on royal policy and patronage, then there was no necessary antithesis of commission and contract warfare, or public versus private, to employ a later vocabulary, but, instead, two different forms of public–private partnership. Furthermore, these partnerships were not so much contrasting, but rather similar in form. In part, they reflected the different opportunities present for nobles and others in territories whose rulers were able to offer military employment (for example France and the Spanish empire) to those whose rulers could not provide such opportunities. Subjects of the latter sold their services further afield.

The responsiveness of rulers to the possibilities created by entrepreneurship has been discussed in a number of cases, including France and Spain, but it was not restricted to them. Furthermore, this responsiveness was apparent on both land and sea. It also extended to institutional forms, as with the Order of Santo Stefano, established by Duke Cosimo I of Florence. Having failed to sustain a galley squadron, the Duke used the model of the Order of Malta to create a crusading order that tapped the zeal, enthusiasm and resources of the Tuscan nobility in order to produce an effective, small-scale fleet. The use of Croatian and other irregulars on the 'military frontier' against the Ottomans developed by the Austrians was another instance of tapping into the various societies and economies that were willing to provide military service.[44] The Venetians also used Croatian irregulars to protect their position in Dalmatia.

These irregulars were not organised to fight as would be expected between professional forces in northern Italy. This is a reminder of the extent to which there was a variety in military organisation as well as fighting method. Notions of fitness for purpose, interacting with particular military cultures, ensured that there was no attempt to produce a uniform military system. As another instance of the comparison between 'private' and 'public' forces, the former frequently relied on enforced 'contributions' in order to obtain supplies, but so also did the latter. The failure of the provinces to pay the money owed for the Dutch war effort led in 1604 and 1605 to the dispatch of forces to the provinces of Drenthe and Groningen in order to make them pay.

It is important to draw explicit attention to the problems of evaluating evidence. To take the example of the production of saltpetre, an important constituent of gunpowder, it is possible to use it as an example of modernising tendencies, specifically the growth of the role of the state and the global impact as Europeans searched for foreign sources. In Sweden, farmers were forced to deliver the material to produce saltpetre to works run by the government. In 1612, the supervision of production was transferred to the military and in 1616, a decree ordered each homestead near the works (twenty-six in 1624) to deliver set amounts of soil, sheep's dung, ashes, wood and straw. As this was inadequate, in 1642 this aid was changed into a national tax that was to be used to finance imports. In addition, by the end of the century, mobile saltpetre extractor teams were sent round the country. However, only in 1723 did the War College make an inventory of the saltpetre-rich soils and only in 1746 was a national organisation for production created.[45] It is pointless to stress the developments of the 1610s without drawing attention to this later history. In the 1640s, the Irish Confederates boiled down exhumed decomposing Protestant corpses to extract saltpetre.

For most Europeans, the state was more peripheral than the harvest or the conflict with disease. War, the damage it could create, and the need to support it, through finance, recruitment and supplies, were the most significant impact of politics and the state. All European societies were militarised, in the sense that armies were a significant government preoccupation, and their financing, both directly and indirectly, a major problem for both state and subject. The extent to which this activity and expenditure produced results is a subject of the following chapters. In war, armies and navies were capable of considerable achievements. However, their organisational and technological capabilities were limited, particularly in terms of resource availability, mobility and fire-power. Nor was there any fundamental alteration in the nature of war. As a result, successful military powers did not need to alter their economic system or develop a sophisticated industrial capability. Although war was important, pressure for economic, social and governmental change was limited.

# 3

# A MILITARY REVOLUTION?

## The Roberts thesis

The concept of an early modern European military revolution was not invented by Michael Roberts, but in his inaugural lecture of 1955 he gave it shape and prominence. Focusing on the period 1560–1660, but as part of a longer term process in military change, stemming from the introduction of portable firearms, Roberts drew connections between military technology and techniques and larger historical consequences. He specifically argued that innovations in tactics, drill and doctrine by the Dutch and Swedes, designed to maximise the benefit of firearms, led to a need for more trained troops and thus for permanent forces, with major political and social consequences.[1] Thus weapons (technology) was important because they were marshalled by doctrine and particular habits of use (technique). The essentials of Roberts's thesis was a mutually sustaining relationship between the professionalism required for tactical changes and the rise of larger and more permanent state military forces. Roberts argued that changes in tactics, strategy, the scale of warfare and its impact upon society, which had their origins in the United Provinces in the 1590s and 1600s, and culminated in the Sweden of Gustavus Adolphus (r. 1611–32), deserved the description 'revolutionary'. In 1988, Geoffrey Parker summarised the thesis:

> First came a 'revolution in tactics': the replacement of the lance and pike by the arrow and musket, as the feudal knights fell before the firepower of massed archers or gunners. Associated with this development were a marked growth in army size right across Europe (with the armed forces of several states increasing tenfold between 1500 and 1700), and the adoption of more ambitious and complex strategies designed to bring these larger armies into action. Fourth and finally, Roberts' military revolution dramatically accentuated the impact of war on society: the greater costs incurred, the greater damage inflicted, and the greater administrative challenge posed by the augmented armies made waging war far more of a burden and

far more of a problem than ever previously, both for the civilian population and for their rulers.[2]

In the short term, this led to Swedish triumph in 1631, reversing the run of victories hitherto in the Thirty Years' War (1618–48) by the forces of the Emperor Ferdinand II and the Catholic League and, in the long term, to the creation of armies that were an effective force of statecraft, domestically and externally. These are held to have facilitated the development of absolutist states by shifting the balance of domestic military power towards sovereigns and away from their subjects.

Roberts was able to fit many developments into his thesis. Firing by rank required both discipline and training, and this led to an increase in the number of officers and the production of detailed training manuals. More complex manoeuvres required more training and discipline, and this could best be ensured by maintaining permanent forces, rather than hastily hiring men at the outbreak of wars. According to Roberts, 'drill for the first time in modern history became the pre-condition for military success' in the Dutch army under Maurice of Nassau. The new armies turned infantry firepower into a manoeuvrable winning formula, allowing rulers to envisage victorious campaigns. This enhanced the value of larger armies rather than fortifications, but these more substantial forces, operating over considerable distances, required a level of administrative support, in the supply of money, men and provisions, that led to new governmental institutions and larger financial demands. The domestic strains thus created helped to cause a mid-seventeenth century crisis that challenged what was presented as an effective royal monopoly of power. This monopolisation furthered and was in turn strengthened by a militarisation of society that owed much to military service, including the growth of noble officership. Military requirements and their ethos integrated society and the state. Thus, the modern art of war, with its large professional armies, and concentrated yet mobile firepower, was created at the same time as – indeed made possible and necessary – the creation of the modern state.

Roberts's lecture was simultaneously bold and brief. It was Braudelian in its ability to link grand sweeps to particular developments, but Roberts did not pursue the theme at book length. Instead, it was developed and transformed in a number of fruitful directions by Parker, although he minimised the shift in interpretation by using the same term. He argued that Roberts was wrong to see only the Dutch and Swedes as progressive and that the Spanish army was one of the most important and innovative of the period; claimed that changes in fortification technique from the late fifteenth century, specifically the development of the *trace italienne* – 'low, thick walls punctuated by quadrilateral bastions' – were revolutionary in consequence; moved the chronology of the Military Revolution back to encompass these changes; and, most significantly, pressed the need to look at the global dimensions of this Revolution, while also applying it to naval warfare, as Roberts had not done.

As far as European land warfare was concerned, Parker wrote:

> the improvements in artillery in the fifteenth century, both qualitative and quantitative, eventually transformed fortress design...the increasing reliance on firepower in battle...led not only to the eclipse of cavalry by infantry in most armies, but to new tactical arrangements that maximized the opportunities of giving fire...these new ways in warfare were accompanied by a dramatic increase in army size...all the evidence for radical military change, whether in army size, fortifications, or firearms comes from the lands of the Habsburgs or of their neighbours: from Spain, Italy, the Netherlands, and France. That was the heartland of the military revolution.

In a footnote, Parker excluded 'most of Spain' from the revolution for the same reason that he argued it was limited outside the heartland: 'The key variable appears to have been the presence or absence of the *trace italienne* for where no bastions existed, wars of manoeuvre with smaller armies were still feasible. And, for a long time, outside the "heartland" there was a marked reluctance to introduce the new defensive systems'.[3] In 1979, when he had argued that 'European warfare was transformed between 1450 and 1530 by a number of basic changes', the first was 'improved fortifications'. The *trace italianne* helped date the Military Revolution for Parker, as the 1530s were an important decade for the spread of new-style fortifications with bastions. In addition, the change in fortification technique was important to his attempt to match Roberts in linking technological developments in warfare to wider socio-political consequences. Parker focused on the need to deploy larger armies in order to besiege the new more extensive and stronger fortification systems, protected as they were by cannon. In short, the strengthening of the defensive made possible by the *trace italienne*, by making it harder to capture fortresses, ensured that it was necessary to starve them into surrender, a time-consuming development, while the strengthening also ensured that weaker powers had less need to engage in battle and, therefore, took away the possibility of achieving a rapid victory that way. The net effect was that wars became longer, driving up the resource implications, and ensuring that war became a Darwinian-type struggle of the capacity of different political systems to raise resources.

The last may well have been true, although to demonstrate it would require a comparison with late-medieval states and wars that has not really been made. Irrespective of this, the empirical case has been challenged by work suggesting that garrisons and besieging armies did not grow in size.[4] The re-examination of army sizes, a very difficult task given the misleading nature of their paper strength, has suggested that in many cases these did not increase in the sixteenth century, and that the rise in the size of the Spanish Army of Flanders to 86,000 men in March 1574 was exceptional.

Particularly if the global span of Parker, rather than the narrower European focus of Roberts, is adopted, then European overseas conquest can be seen as the Military Revolution. It is indeed possible to suggest that this process of conquest was revolutionary in cause, course and consequence, and was the aspect of military development that was most important on the global scale (see Chapter 4).

Yet it is also important to recall Roberts's contribution, not least his argument that the use of firearms itself posed serious tactical problems for armies within Europe,[5] and that the military changes he focused on reflected the tactical challenge of overcoming the mid-sixteenth-century inheritance of the battlefield use of firearms and, more specifically, the problem posed by its most effective exponent, the Spanish *tercio*. Irrespective of the accuracy of the particular arguments of this approach, it has great value for its understanding of the adoption of gunpowder weaponry as a complex process that created problems, not least through the adoption of comparable tactics and technology by all the combatants. This limited the *relative* capability of forces armed with firearms within Europe; not the inherent deficiencies of the weapons. These problems were the very opposite of the focus, in the discussion of the global dimension of the revolution, in terms of conflict with powers that lacked such firepower.

## Criticisms of the thesis

The standard account of the Military Revolution has been challenged by much of the research and analysis produced over the last decade, although Parker has responded robustly to the criticism.[6] There has been an emphasis in the criticism on the variety of factors that contributed to European success, and the nature and extent of this success have been qualified, points discussed in Chapters 4 and 9. To turn to the situation within Europe, it is possible to focus on a number of points. First, it has been argued that many of the changes used to define the Military Revolution, or associated with it, such as larger armies, greater military expenditure, new tactics, innovations in weaponry and the *trace italienne*, all had medieval precedents, and that the role of gunpowder weapon technology in them was limited. For example, fifteenth-century sieges in Italy indicated the importance of the spirit and commitment of the combatants and the availability of good infantry for storming the breaches, rather than of infantry armed with gunpowder.[7]

Secondly, it is also possible to minimise the change during the Roberts–Parker period by stressing the earlier impact of gunpowder weaponry.[8] Indeed, if the fifteenth century is seen as the 'era of interpretive flexibility and "experimental" development in gunpowder weaponry', then also the sixteenth century can be seen 'as a period of stability and closure', not 'new beginnings'.[9] It is also important to appreciate that the adoption of firearms was not simply a case of a new technology replacing an unchanging old one. For example, crossbows, which required far less training and physical strength than longbows, gained more penetrative power in the fifteenth century as a result of the development of steel bows. However, as a reminder of the complex trade-off of characteristics, these were expensive, as tempered spring steel was a costly material to make and one that required much skill. This was not the case with longbows, but they required lengthy training for proficient use (and also did not improve their specifications as crossbows did). Arquebuses required no steel, only iron, and cost considerably less than crossbows. There was only limited change in firearms technology during the sixteenth century, although an increase in numbers was important.

In response, it can be argued that medieval precedents constitute a prehistory of the Military Revolution. Maybe so, but this can be reconceptualised to argue that the so-called Revolution was in fact another stage in the process by which medieval warfare developed. In particular, the latter displayed a considerable ability to innovate, not only in tactics and fortifications but also in the infrastructure of military preparedness.[10]

Thirdly, a focus on gunpowder weaponry leads to the question why, if the earlier introduction of gunpowder (as of printing) in China did not lead to revolutionary changes, the situation should have been different in Europe. Fourthly, gunpowder provided the basis for different forms of hand-held projectile weaponry and artillery, but the technique of massed projectile weaponry was not new.

Fifthly, there is a mono-causal quality to some of the writing about military developments and their impact, as well as a degree of technological determinism. In contrast, although the ability to harness chemical energy was important and cannon have been referred to as the first workable internal combustion engines, it is possible to regard gunpowder weaponry as an agent, not a cause, of changes in warfare. At the same time, it is necessary to appreciate that gunpowder itself posed serious problems if its potential as a source of energy was to be utilised effectively. For long, cannon were not strong enough to make proper use of gunpowder. This did not change until the fifteenth century, with the development around 1420 of 'corned' powder, which provided the necessary energy but without dangerously high peak pressures.[11] For long, handheld weapons were not self-evidently superior to longbows and crossbows. They were, variously, heavier, slower to fire, less accurate (and inconsistent in their inaccuracy), and less reliable. The nature of the projectile was a particular problem. Spherical shot generates a large amount of aerodynamic drag, essentially because its wake is disproportionate to its cross-sectional area. This ensured that the projectiles of the period lost speed at a high rate: on average about three times faster than modern bullets. Lower speed meant less kinetic energy on impact, and thus less penetrative power. In addition, effects arising from their spin lessened their accuracy as a result of the 'Magnus Effect', in which spinning spheres generate both a low pressure and a high pressure zone. This characteristic could not be counteracted by skill in firing.

Modern test results have been variously interpreted. Tests carried out in Britain in 1998 by staff from Vickers Defence Systems suggested a 'quite dramatic difference between them [bows] and the gunpowder weapons, in particular the early matchlock replica…shows how the development of gunpowder weapons gave the potential not for an incremental increase in velocity, as had earlier weapon development, but one of an order of magnitude'. However, these tests employed modern black powder and used a far smaller range of handguns than those carried out in 1988–9 by the staff of the Steiermärkisches Landeszeughaus in Graz. The latter were more detailed, were related more closely to the effectiveness of body armour, have been reported at greater length, and are more revealing about the limitations of the handguns of the period.[12]

Aside from problems rooted in the mechanical properties of the weapons and the chemical nature of the gunpowder reaction (for example the lacking of consistency in purity of the chemical reagents), there were also characteristics of the weaponry that interacted with poor use, especially poor shooting, for example a lack of steadiness in igniting or otherwise firing.

It might therefore be asked why the use of the arquebus, the first effective handheld firearm, spread from the 1460s. This appears to have been due not to an instant acceptance of overwhelming capability, but to the use of the arquebus in a particular niche and by a specific group: militia who guarded city walls, a protected role that compensated for their battlefield vulnerability. From this, the use of the arquebus spread, but it is no accident that the weapon was most effective in the Italian Wars when employed in concert with field fortifications, as at Cerignola (1503). Again, there was no automatic conviction of the value of the new weapon. It was adopted only slowly in France and the British Isles, and in the former case appeared less valuable than a pike-heavy cavalry combination. The French willingness to use cannon, but not arquebuses, is a reminder of the need to refer to the impact of gunpowder technology in a discriminating fashion. The experience of battle did not automatically encourage the use of firepower. The French battlefield success in Italy in 1494–6, campaigns in which they had very little small arms firepower, did not lead them to change force structure, and although battles from Cerignola on encouraged a shift, the French use of 500 arquebusiers at Novara (1513) made scant difference. Placed in the line without cover they were killed by the attacking Swiss pikemen: casualties from shot did not deter the Swiss from pressing home the attack.

New machines of war have often enjoyed an impact on the imagination greater than that on the battlefield, particularly if their use is accompanied by dramatic sounds and sights. Contemporaries were impressed by the impact of gunpowder weaponry, and a celebrated passage by the Florentine historian Francesco Guicciardini emphasised the impact of the horse-drawn cannon used by Charles VIII of France in 1494–5.[13] However, a detailed study of the campaign has indicated that some of the bolder claims on behalf of this enhanced capability have to be questioned. Thus in this period, in 1494, the key Tuscan frontier fortresses attacked by the French – Sarzana and Sarzanello – repulsed the attacks, and the French were able to advance only as a consequence of a treaty negotiated by Piero de' Medici. The following January, Montefortino near Valmontone was stormed and sacked, without any apparent use of cannon. A bombardment did make a crucial breach in the walls of Monte San Giovanni, permitting its storming that February, but the bombardment of the Castel Nuovo in Naples was not as effective. Ten days of cannon fire inflicted only limited damage, the French ran short of iron balls and gunpowder, and the surrender of the garrison reflected exhaustion and division rather than the inexorable pressure of cannon fire.[14] It is also important not to underestimate the role of mining (as opposed to cannon) in sieges.[15]

On the battlefield, the relative immobility of cannon restricted their usefulness, and the impact of handheld gunpowder firearms was lessened by the extent to which pikes commanded attention in the late fifteenth century. They were far more impressive, effective and intimidating than earlier infantry non-missile weaponry, whereas gunpowder firearms were not a comparable advance on longbows and crossbows. Thus, in this period, it was possible to see pikes, cavalry and bow weapons as the most effective tactical combination, and the one that had to be developed and recruited for.

In the sixteenth century, firearms replaced bow weapons as their potential was grasped, but this learning curve also entailed learning to appreciate the limitations of firearms, both as weapons and tactically. Interlinked problems with range, accuracy and killing power helped guide their tactical use: effectiveness was seen to depend on volume of fire, not individual accuracy, and, therefore musketeers were grouped together, creating serious problems of vulnerability. The advantage of gunpowder weaponry rested initially in large part not on the specifications of the firearms, but on their ease of use. They were relatively inexpensive but, more significantly, required less training than longbows. The need for training was further lessened by the characteristics of the weapon and its use for volume fire rather than single-shot accuracy.

## The impact of the pike

Whereas the specifications and potential of firearms depended on technological development, there was no need for any comparable change in order to explain the spread of pikes, the infantry weapon of preference in much of Western Europe for much of the sixteenth century. Instead, pikes were a long-established weapon (searching for classical roots, writers referred back to Macedonian phalanxes), and their adoption depended on organisational factors: the existence of disciplined units able to use pikes effectively in attack, and on the conscious decision to employ the pike. The Classical roots of pikes helped encourage contemporaries to applaud them, but it is as well not to treat this preference as foolish. It was also a lesson that could be derived from observation of current warfare. Niccolò Machiavelli in his *Art of War* (1521) tried to update the seminal text, Vegetius's *Military Institutions of the Romans*, and was in part able to do so by focusing on the pike and treating the arquebus as similar to the missile weaponry of Rome's auxiliaries, an analysis that did not seem unrealistic. Indeed, the problem in comparing Renaissance with Classical warfare was set by the major role of French heavy cavalry, rather than by that of arquebusiers. The *Art of War* was frequently reprinted.

As with firearms, the use of pikes had a lengthy genesis in the later medieval period. Furthermore, rather than seeing an abrupt shift in terms of weaponry and tactics from earlier weapons, it is possible to note continuities with the spears used by the Flemings, as at Courtrai (1302), and the Scots, as at Bannockburn (1314), and with the halberds employed by the Swiss in the fourteenth century. The halberd was shorter than the pike, but the tactics employed were similar. As a reminder of the extent to which weaponry did not dictate tactics, the pike was originally employed as an offensive weapon, and therefore with a deployment in column. By the second half of the sixteenth century, however, the pike was primarily used in a defensive fashion, with a deployment linked to protecting arquebusiers; although this did not preclude attacks by the pikemen.[16] Discussion of the pike offers a valuable analogy for consideration of firearms, not least because both weapons were to be used most effectively in combined arms operations, but also because the discussion serves as a pointed reminder of the danger of basing an analysis of effectiveness on a reading of technical specifications. As with firearms, the development and changing use of polearms and staff weapons can more appropriately be seen in terms of adaptation rather than revolution; although there was no equivalent for such weapons to the role of artillery in siegecraft or naval warfare, and in both those cases the change in capability was more striking than any resulting from polearms and staff weapons.

The particular value of pikemen related not only to their role in attack but also to their ability to sustain a defence. They could provide protection against cavalry, as the pike outreached the lance. Furthermore, they provided arquebusiers with the defensive strength otherwise offered by walls or field entrenchments. Other infantry weapons were less able to do so. The combination of pike and cavalry was such that the percentage of troops in any army and of expenditure in any military budget devoted to firepower was lower than the usual stress on gunpowder weaponry might suggest.

At the same time, the effectiveness of pike units did not prevent a continued use of other stabbing or cutting weapons. These did not require the formations and training of pikemen, and also had a value in the irregular warfare of the period. In response to the fighting of the 1490s, Gonzalo de Córdoba had his Spanish infantry adopt sword and buckler weaponry and tactics to confront pike, although, from the 1510s, the Spaniards came to conform with the pike/firepower force structure. The French royal army did not dispense with the halberd until 1568, while swords and daggers are the most underrated weapons of the age. This is even more the case as arquebusiers usually also carried such weapons. An analysis of wounds suffered by the French army in the 1560s and 1570s suggests that 54 per cent were from sword injuries; a figure that in part reflected the important role of cavalry in the Wars of Religion.[17] More generally, weapons co-existed, in both different roles and also in essentially the same role, for longer than is generally appreciated. There was no abrupt shift from one weapon to another.

The development of firearms did not only occur against a background of changes in other infantry weapons. There were also important shifts in the use and armament of cavalry, as indeed there were to be throughout the period covered by this book. In the fifteenth century, heavy cavalry benefited from improvements in armour and also from the development of the lance rest. As a result of supporting the lance's weight on a prong attached to the breast-plate, it was possible to absorb recoil and to maintain momentum.[18] In the following century, cavalry were to employ firearms, although shock action, with lance or sword, continued to be important.

## Gunpowder and modernity

The debate about the impact of gunpowder can be located in terms of discussion about modernity and modernisation, and, specifically, about the existence of an early modern period. This is a Eurocentric notion that also reflects the Cronos tendency in European intellectual culture from the Renaissance to abandon the practice of viewing past ages as golden and, instead, to disparage the past, or at least to regard the present as better than the past, and a graspable future as likely to be better than both. The Renaissance was understood as a recovery of the Classical period, but this energy and vision was directed at surpassing what was presented as an inadequate intervening period. In short, the Middle Ages could be defined in order to be castigated and to serve as a counterpoint to what came before and after. Furthermore, the Classical period was sufficiently distant and obscure not to serve as a real model for a tendency that was not, in fact, conservative.

The concept of the early modern can be located in terms of the primitivisation of what came before and the foundation myth of the modern world. For long the latter was seen as depending on a rejection of what had come before, rather than as representing a development of, or from, it. The force of this rejection created the turning point.

This intellectual thesis was important to the public cultures of the Europeanised Western world. Whether commentators looked to the Renaissance, the Reformation or both, these developments, as generally understood, were taken to mark a dramatic break, and this break was then read into other contexts: economic, social, political, cultural and military. At one level, the narrative and theory of military revolution is the counterpart of humanism, printing, European exploration, Renaissance, Reformation and a new mental world.

However, if this early modern perspective is questioned, it becomes possible both to disaggregate its components, and to scrutinise particular developments, without employing an explanatory framework that relies, in part, on a possibly misleading general theory of the early modern period. Specifically, it is possible to query the notion of modernisation and also the idea that changes, at least in part, are to be explained by a process of emulation and of diffusion from other spheres. Thus, the positioning of the military history of the period, of military change, and of the 'Military Revolution' (which were far from co-terminous), depends in large part upon the notion and analysis of the early modern period, and specifically upon concepts of post-medievalism, modernity and modernisation.

These concepts are challenged by arguments that the onset of modernity and modernisation should be dated far later, either to the second half of the eighteenth century, with its Enlightenment cult of secular progress, or to the nineteenth, with the astonishing transformation of the productive and organisational capability of the Western world in the Industrial Revolution.

It is also possible to re-examine the role of force in the established narrative of the early modern period. The idea of the transition from medievalism depends in part on an understanding of force as playing a crucial role, and on a presentation of the nature and use of force as novel. Thus, the idea of a Military Revolution takes a part akin to that of the transition from feudalism to capitalism in Marxist and Marxisant models. This helps account for the popularity of the idea of such a revolution, and also for the need for a theory to explain it. If the concept did not exist, it would be necessary to devise an alternative to explain what are seen as major shifts in state-formation within Europe and in the world structure of power; although both can, conversely, be used to help explain developments in the military.

## Force, politics and government

More generally, force can apparently both explain and be the *modus operandi* of what has been seen as a politics and culture of control and expropriation. Changes in the latter that are perceived therefore apparently have to be linked to military developments. From this perspective, the Military Revolution fulfils the need for an abrupt and violent close to medievalism, the Middle Ages, and for the beginning of a world in which Europeans were on a path towards global influence, if not dominance. It also moved attention on from the thesis of an early modern, more specifically mid-seventeenth century, 'General Crisis' that had enjoyed considerable attention in the 1960s and 1970s,[19] but that did not address the issue of Europe's global position so directly. This thesis focused on strains of transition, most generally from supposedly medieval patterns to a more commercial and global early modern economy that created losers as well as winners. The thesis of a General Crisis could be related to Marxist and class models of the rise of the bourgeoisie, and could also, more narrowly, be applied to the fiscal and political problems caused by imperial overreach, government policy and war, especially in the context of a seventeenth-century downturn in the European economy (and demography). The General Crisis theory was extensively used in discussion of the English Civil War(s), the *Frondes* in France, the rebellions in the Spanish empire in the 1640s, especially in Catalonia, Portugal, Naples and Sicily, and contemporaneous risings in Moscow, Constantinople and elsewhere, for example the Swiss Peasants' War of 1653.

The theory of the General Crisis could be related to that of the Military Revolution by arguing that the latter had led to larger militaries (and more extensive fortification systems), and that the cost of these helped to create political opposition and social hardship, if not disorder. Conversely it was possible to separate the two, by suggesting that, in so far that a General Crisis existed and had a military dimension, this was due not to the pressures of improved capability, whether or not seen as a Military Revolution, but rather to the specific burdens of lengthy conflict in the early seventeenth century. In the case of France and Spain, this was the protracted warfare the first had been continually involved in since 1635, and the second since 1621, while in the British Isles the political consequences of Charles I's failure to defeat Scotland in the Bishops' Wars (1639–40) precipitated political collapse. These two approaches are not necessarily dichotomous, but there is an important difference in emphasis.

From Roberts on, proponents of the thesis of the Military Revolution have argued that developments in the conduct of war had very large consequences, both for the European state structure and on the course of the evolution of the Western military system. In itself, this approach does not require an abrupt close to the Middle Ages, and, for Roberts, 'the' Military Revolution began in 1560, after the Middle Ages are generally seen as over. Nevertheless, gunpowder has been employed in much of the literature like printing: as a totem of a different world. It was seen as instrumental in the demise of medieval feudalism, and thus as crucial to the outset of modernity.[20]

Aside from the military aspect, there are serious conceptual problems with this thesis. In particular, it makes only very limited sense in terms of much revisionist work on sixteenth-century and seventeenth-century European history, and this work is important for an understanding of issues such as goals, command and recruitment. In place of the traditional notion of new monarchies employing cannon and professional forces to monopolise power, this work emphasises the continuing strength of the nobility.[21] Indeed, in light of this scholarship, it is scarcely surprising that cavalry and noble officership both remained important. Military roles and tasks played a major role in holding polities together, not least by linking landed elite and ruler. The local levies of the former, whether or not in a feudal form, were politically as well as militarily significant. Thus, aside from the discussion of military details, it is apparent, at least in terms of the revisionist approach, that the military history of the period that has to be explained is very different, in terms of cause, course and consequence, to that outlined by Roberts and required by his readers searching for causes of modernisation.

At the same time, it is correct to complement the revisionist perspective with an awareness of the extent to which force, including new military forms, was employed by rulers in order to advance their power and enforce their authority. Thus, Cosimo de' Medici, ruler of Tuscany from 1537–74, built three citadels around Florence, each under the command of a non-Florentine. This overawing of the city was important to the consolidation of his power, and in 1569 Cosimo became the first Grand Duke of Tuscany. After Pope Paul III had suppressed a salt tax revolt in Perugia in 1540, he had a citadel built there. Similarly, Pier Luigi, Duke of Parma (1545–7) built a citadel at Piacenza as part of a campaign to establish his power that also saw moves against the castles of the aristocracy. This campaign was unwelcome, and he was assassinated. Having regained Amiens from Spanish forces in 1597, Henry IV of France ordered that a citadel be built there in order to establish royal power; earlier in the year, the city had refused to accept a royal garrison as they claimed the right of relying on their militia for their defence. This helped the Spaniards seize the city.

Discussion of the role of force in domestic disputes, as in Perugia and Parma, serves as a reminder that it is not always possible readily to separate international conflict from other uses of force. This offers the prospect of employing discussion of internal policing as an analogue for the military revolution. In the case of Tuscany, a relatively small state where the possibilities for effective government were greater than in larger polities, it is possible to point to areas of government development,[22] but it is also clear that the term 'absolutism' is misleading and that compromise played a major role in the administration of criminal justice under the first three Medici Grand Dukes. Unwilling to meet the high costs of rigid enforcement and unable to control the poor, the Grand Dukes found that compromise secured acknowledgement of their power to administer justice. Local officials played a crucial role in the capture of fugitives and the reporting of crime, but local police forces were small, poorly paid and generally enmeshed in local networks of family alliances. The Medici sought to create loyalty among local elites by upholding their interests against those of their competitors. The scale and organisation of violence, though possibly not its incidence, seems to have been much greater outside than within Florence. Authority was more effective in the city, and there violence was committed mainly by individuals and small groups of close kin, rather than by the locally potent families and factions that feuded in the smaller cities and the countryside. The resulting system was neither modern nor 'absolutist' as the term is currently generally understood in works that stress the rise of the modern state and the emergence of bureaucratic organisations.[23]

To turn from the analogue of policing, to the finances necessary to support military capability, a study of the kingdom of Naples, which made an important contribution to Spanish finances, argues that 'the lack of a responsible civil service undermined the cause of kings'. In Picardy, although there were no estates to limit royal power institutionally, the taxation policies of the French crown in the first half of the sixteenth century 'should raise a question over the view of Absolute Monarchies as blindly predatory power machines'.[24]

There is a more general problem about the relationship between what is seen as military modernisation and its political equivalent. The former, in the shape of improved capability, could inhibit the latter, in the case of state-building and the development of more effective organisational structures. This was repeatedly true of the need for resources, the quest for which challenged governmental control and political stability. It was also the case that military effectiveness could prevent the consolidation of state authority. In part this could be due to rivalry by other states with effective forces, but there was also the challenge of less well-resourced polities that were able to contest state-building. John Casimir of the Palatinate, who invaded France on behalf of the Huguenots in 1575–6, unsuccessfully sought to seize the bishoprics of Metz, Toul and Verdun, a challenge to the consolidation of France's eastern border. The Covenanter rebellion in Scotland destroyed Charles I's attempt at British state-building.

This serves as a reminder of the ambiguity and porosity of the concept of state-building. It is more appropriate to think of malleable political relationships, and of senses of identity above the local level that did not amount to identification with states or, other than in loose terms, nations. Furthermore, the dynastic imperative ensured that the creation of states was subordinated to a patrimonial proprietorship that encouraged such practices as dividing inheritances among members of the ruling family. This was seen not only with the inheritance of Charles V, but also with subsequent divisions among the Austrian Habsburgs. More generally, the role of younger sons and other relatives was an important complication. This was particularly so in France. Thus François Duke of Alençon and then of Anjou (1554–84), the brother of Francis II, Charles IX and Henry III, followed not only an important role in France but also tried to marry Elizabeth I of England and to succeed Philip II in the Low Countries where, in 1578 he was appointed 'Defender of the Liberty of the Netherlands'. He led an army into Hainault that year, although it was very weak, his capture of Cambrai in 1581 proved short-lived, and in 1583 he failed to seize Antwerp. Gaston, Duke of Orléans (1608–60), brother of Louis XIII of France, was less wide-ranging in his ambitions, but, nevertheless an important and independent political figure, able to raise forces and willing to conspire against the crown.

Similar policies were adopted by prominent princely and aristocratic families, the interests of which frequently spanned 'states'. The houses of Orange and Guise were good examples. The dynastic diplomacy of the Guise led to a role in France, Lorraine and Scotland. This also led to a dynastic military policy. In 1581–2, the Duke of Guise prepared an expedition to help his cousin, Mary Queen of Scots, then a prisoner of Elizabeth I, although lack of funds and propitious circumstances forced its abandonment.[25]

To return to periodisation, there are signs of an increase in centralisation in some states in the period 1430–1530, which was also a period of empire building, most successfully with the Ottoman and Habsburg empires. After that, state formation and empire building within Europe encountered serious problems that culminated in the mid-seventeenth century General Crisis. The military part of the shift in 1430–1530 included, but was not defined by, the decreased efficiency of static defences (walls) when siege guns became more operationally useful. The siege train did not create the European state, but it made effective central rulers more important as providers of protection. Mobile forces became more important than walls in providing defence. The new organisations for defence offered opportunities to traditional elite groups willing to accept changes.

## Force and change

The debate over the Military Revolution is linked to differences over the nature of change. If the evolutionary theories of many recent historians of technology are employed as models, there is an emphasis on incremental change, not breakthroughs, and on users, not designers. Thus, it is possible to stress incremental improvements in cannon, handheld firearms and gunpowder, although it is necessary to caution against any assumption of an even and continuous process of growth and development. Rather than treating gunpowder as a literally explosive starting point to modern times, it is possible to see its impact in terms of a lengthy process of adaptation, not least with the introduction of corned powder which offered a more predictable explosive power. In addition, there were developments in particular parts of firearms that improved their specifications, such as accuracy, rate of fire, weight and durability. For example, the stock was shaped to lessen the impact of recoil. Technical changes in cannon and gunpowder, for example controlled-grain corning, improved the effectiveness of individual pieces.[26]

The idea of 'punctuated equilibrium' advanced by Clifford Rogers seeks to combine both incremental and revolutionary change. More specifically, Rogers sees major developments in the fifteenth century, with infantry able to defeat cavalry, thanks to the longbow or the pike, and a major improvement in the effectiveness of artillery.[27] Irrespective of such methodological or empirical points, it is unclear that the concept of a revolution lasting a century or longer is really helpful.

It is also necessary to focus not on initial 'discoveries', but on diffusion, the understanding and regularisation of usage, and, crucially, effective usage. It is

45

therefore appropriate to comment on the widespread dissemination of cannon and firearms in the sixteenth century. These weapons could be transported and used in a variety of environments. The cumulative firepower of European forces rose greatly, both on land and at sea, and both in Europe and overseas. A similar emphasis on sixteenth-century diffusion is appropriate for new-style fortifications employing the *trace italienne*.

It is also far from clear which technologies are of most importance. There is a tendency in writing on war to focus on the battlefield and therefore firepower, but this can lead to an underrating of changes in command and control as well as in logistics. Developments in the former were limited in this period, but there were changes in the latter. Most interestingly, the sixteenth century witnessed the development of mobile front-wheel axle units for the four-wheeled wagons that predominated in northern Europe. Yet, the course of campaigning at the close of the period suggested that persistent resource problems outweighed any improvement in logistical capability. Improvements in ship construction and specifications, mentioned in Chapter 8, were of greater value than simply for naval or amphibious operations, as the sea was an important sphere for the movement of *matériel*, especially of siege artillery, which was difficult to transport by land.

Yet, compared to the changes of the nineteenth century, when steam power was applied to sea and land transport, those in the period 1494–1660 were very limited. Vessels remained very dependent on sea conditions, specifically wind and tide. The seasonal contrast in travel on both land and sea was far greater than it was to be by the mid-nineteenth century, as was the contrast between good and poor weather. This added an important element of unpredictability to the movement of troops, munitions, supplies, funds and messages. This was a central problem in strategic planning and execution, and one that has to be put alongside the tendency to focus on resources. The application of resources was as important as their availability, but this application required an overcoming of space that was not made possible by technological or organisational change. Aside from a lack of any revolution in vehicles, there was no comparable change in road surfaces or even the availability of roads, or in other means of information transmission.

It was easier to move bulky goods by river, but there was no dramatic improvement in river transport or routes in this period. They remained affected by droughts, floods and weirs; and there was no major programme of canalisation. In France, the Briare Canal was begun in 1604 and the Orléans Canal followed in 1651, in order to link the Seine and Loire river systems, but these were small-scale compared with what was to follow. Despite major and costly efforts in 1626–9, the Spaniards failed to construct a canal between the Rhine and the Maas. This was seen as an economic weapon – to divert the river trade of Germany from the Dutch to the Spanish Netherlands, as well as a strategic tool, offering the possibility of drying up Dutch water defences, causing floods elsewhere, and creating a barrier to impede Dutch advances.

The project failed due to financial problems and the advance in 1629 of Dutch forces too close to the proposed canal system.[28]

Problems with transport exacerbated those of agricultural productivity, ensuring that attacking armies could not transport the food they required. As a consequence, it was necessary to obtain supplies in the area of campaign. This had consequences not only for the character of strategy and operations, but also for the type of warfare that was most feasible in particular parts of Europe. Where agricultural yields were high, as in northern Italy or the Low Countries, it was possible to obtain adequate supplies from a relatively concentrated area, and this therefore encouraged a more concentrated form of campaigning, and one in which rival armies could confront each other without disintegrating from lack of supplies. This was far less the case across much of northern and eastern Europe, as well as in forested and mountainous areas. In pastoral regions, there was also insufficient grain for large forces.

The net effect might be assumed to be to encourage a concentration of campaigning in particular regions around the nodal points of communication systems that were generally fortified, such as Maastricht on the Meuse. This structuralist, almost deterministic, resource-based analysis however, is only true in part, because, far from campaigning elsewhere being absent, it was very much present, but different in time–space ratios. There was an emphasis on smaller and more rapidly moving forces. Thus, in 1592, the weak state of the royal army led Henry IV of France to operate instead with a 'flying force' (*camp volant*) of 9,000 men. Furthermore, where supplies were not plentiful, this encouraged a focus on engagements rather than sieges. That did not mean, however, that fortified positions could not be attacked. Instead, there was a reliance on storming positions. It is unlikely that this situation justifies description in terms of a military revolution. Instead, it is more appropriate to focus on the adaptability of warfare to circumstances, and on its protean quality when compared with the more rigid formulations of some contemporary and subsequent commentators.

If we see the major technological innovations in Europe as occurring prior to 1500 and argue that in the sixteenth century there was essentially incremental change, it is still necessary to rank the relative importance of the two processes. The latter, for example, made gunpowder weapons normative, with drill, tactics and doctrine all focused in a particular way. It is still unclear whether these changes in European warfare, however dated, deserve the description 'revolutionary'. For example, the effectiveness of the new geometrical layout in fortification is open to question.

This is also true of the increase in the size of armies, an issue that has attracted much attention, although there are empirical and methodological problems in analysing it. First, it is very difficult to establish the size of armed forces, let alone the percentage of total populations that they represented. Aside from the absence of national censuses, it is also clear that figures for armies are unreliable. A recent study of the size of the French army in the early seventeenth century has referred to the weakness of calculations that 'accept administrative targets and objectives which were in practice overwhelmed by a vast process of recruitment and wastage characteristic of each campaign'. An instructive footnote, that is of more general value for its reference to the need for care in the relationship between scholarship and synoptic accounts, refers to the author's reluctance 'to try to commit the information on troop strengths to tabular form, which, while convenient for subsequent syntheses, would risk generating precisely the misleading assumptions about "average annual troop strength" which I have been concerned to avoid'.[29]

Given the difficulties in calculating army sizes, and losses through casualties and, in particular, desertion and disease during campaigns, it may then seem rash to comment on the issue. However, two general points seem appropriate. First, although there was clearly no consistent ratio, it is apparent that the actual size of armies was considerably lower than their theoretical strength, particularly in wartime, when the latter rose rapidly but proved impossible to sustain, due both to resource availability and to the friction of operations. Second, it appears that there was an expansion in army size in the first half of the sixteenth century, as rulers benefited from demographic and economic growth and a measure of political consensus and consolidation, but that it proved difficult to sustain, let alone surpass, this over the following century due to economic problems, resource difficulties and political division. Within this general model, there were differences between particular states, with the Dutch Republic, Sweden and, apparently, Spain able to increase their armed forces and to maintain this increase.

It is also worth noting that many of the accounts of conflict in the period do not readily support the notion of a Military Revolution, understood in terms of a significant increase in European military effectiveness. However, military commentators have always complained about deficiencies, while military equipment and forces are wasting assets, particularly in war.

Doubts about the appropriateness of the description revolutionary can be linked with the argument that the crucial changes that occurred later, whether, for example, with flintlock, bayonet and larger standing armies and navies in 1680–1730, or with the Revolutionary and Napoleonic period of 1792–1815, better deserve description in terms of a Military Revolution.

It is also unclear how best to evaluate the organisational changes of the period. Bold claims about the role of military preparedness and war in pushing forward the development of modern state forms have been made. Thus, Jan Lindegren has argued that the development of a large peacetime standing army by Louis XI of France (1461–83), and the similar response by other rulers, was crucial:

> The problem that confronted princes and states was how to raise, and maintain on a yearly basis, the necessary troops and, of course, how to finance military operations. To manage all these new administrative

and bureaucratic structures and new methods of political and financial control had to be created, and there were profound changes in
other areas of society. Together this amounted to no less than a
reshaping of the whole power structure or, in other words, the birth
of the early modern state.[30]

However, it is unclear that terms such as 'bureaucratisation' are appropriate.
For example, it was not until after the mid-seventeenth century that the
growing role of the European state gradually replaced the semi-independent
military entrepreneurs of early days. On the other hand, Spain in the sixteenth
century and the United Provinces in the seventeenth were well advanced in
the field of international finance, and able to finance their activities, in part,
through a well-developed international credit network, while in the early
seventeenth century the Spanish government successfully implemented
timber conservation policies for the navy. Yet, in the eighteenth century
governments were to be better able to sustain wars in which reasonably well-
supplied armies could be directed to obtain particular goals, rather than to
have to search for food.

Indeed, the circumstances of war in 1494–1660 frequently made coherent
planning impractical and joint operations by different armies and allies difficult. For example, in 1634–5, Maximilian of Bavaria quarrelled with his ally
the Emperor Ferdinand II over troop quarters, the disposition of booty and
ransoms and the allocation of Spanish subsidies, as well as continuing a long-
running clash over priorities, with Maximilian seeking a concentration upon
South Germany and Ferdinand upon Bohemia. Earlier, in the late 1620s, the
expansion of the Imperial army under Wallenstein had hindered the logistics
of its supposed ally, the army of the Catholic League under Tilly.

More generally, supply difficulties, in particular, and their consequences in
the shape of desertion, led generals to campaign in areas whence they could
obtain substantial enforced contributions, which scarcely accords with the
thesis of a military revolution as a major accomplishment of, and tool for, state
policy. The protection of these areas became a leading feature of military
activity. Troops were dispersed to forage and protect, and many, mostly small-
scale, encounters arose from raids and from attempts to define contribution
zones. In these engagements, the writings of battlefield theorists were of no
value. Far from actions being characterised by linear formations and interspersed shot and pike, they were commonly dominated by considerations of
surprise, energy and topography, in which training for battle was less important than morale and leadership. As a parallel argument, soldiers had to be 'far
more skilled in small unit tactics than is often recognised', a perception that
leads to the observation that their tactical ability should not be underestimated.[31]

Similar small-scale encounters marked most of the sieges of the period.
Complete lines of circumvallation designed to cut off relief required many

troops and were generally found only in the case of major sieges. Similarly, only a minority of towns were comprehensively fortified in accordance with contemporary ideals of bastions and flanking fire, for such fortifications were extremely expensive. Alongside set-piece major sieges, such as the Spanish capture of Breda from the Dutch in 1625, there were numerous minor engagements, as towns were stormed or relieving parties attacked.

Thus, the idea of battlefield or siege techniques as causing and, in part, constituting a military revolution pays insufficient attention to the inchoate nature of much fighting and military organisation. The strains of prolonged warfare led rulers to desire effective military instruments, but they also made them difficult to provide. *Leviathan* (1651) was the title of a work of speculative thought, the theoretical creation of Thomas Hobbes, not a description of early modern European government.

## Force, culture and science

Cultural issues are all important. Rather than thinking of the obvious development of a European military system, it is more appropriate to focus on the potential of technology and the potentiality of innovation, and thus to consider complex issues of adoption, dissemination and adaptation. There were varied understandings of the potential of the European military system and different abilities in utilising this potential. Both understanding and utilisation entailed processes of choice. Commentators in the early sixteenth century could debate the value of mercenaries or militia, pikemen or swordsmen, musketeers or heavy cavalry, and how best to use and to combine them.

Debate owed much to the culture of print. In addition, printed manuals on gunnery, tactics, drill, fortification and siegecraft spread techniques far more rapidly than word of mouth or manuscript. Printing made earlier manuscript works more accessible. Leon Battista Alberti's *De Re Aedificatoria*, with its call for sloped and lower fortress walls and for projecting salients, was written in the 1440s but first printed in 1485. Xenophon's *Hippike*, a guide to horsemanship useful for cavalry, was spread by printing. In addition, new texts were produced. Federigo Grison's *Gli Ordinin di Cavalcare* (The Rules of Horsemanship), published in Naples in 1550, had an impact across Europe as a result of printing.[32] Popular works, such as Diego Ufano's *Tratado dela artilleria* (1613), served as the basis for other treatises. Educational ideas could be disseminated in print. Thus, Johann Jacob von Wallhausen, who established the earliest cavalry school in Europe, wrote *Art militaire à cheval* (1616).

Manuals also permitted and made possible a degree of standardisation that both helped to increase military effectiveness and was important for cohesion and the utilisation of military resources. Following Swedish practice, Alexander Leslie, the commander of the Scottish Covenanter forces from 1639, issued his army with printed copies of *The Articles and Ordinances of War*, which laid out correct standards of behaviour for the troops.[33] The first

Russian book on military matters, *Uchenie I Khitrost' ratnogo stroeniya pekhot-nykh lyudei*, was published in 1647. An infantry manual, it emphasised training and included a large number of sketches and plans to teach drill. Casimir Siemienowciz, commander of the Polish artillery, disseminated his ideas with his *Ars Magna Artilleriae* (Amsterdam, 1650). Like drill manuals, works about fortification benefited from the ability of print to convey illustrations as well as prose.[34]

More generally, literacy and printing fostered discussion of military organi-sation and methods, and encouraged a sense of system.[35] The prestige of ancient Rome revived and its military vocabulary was in part employed anew, while Roman military texts such as Flavius Vegetius's fourth-century *De Re Militari* were printed and referred to. Batista della Valle's *Vallo Libro Continente Appertinentie à Capitanij, Retenere e Fortificare una Città con bastioni...*, a very popular work that went through eleven editions from 1524 to 1558, drew heavily on Classical sources. It also indicated the importance of Italian models in the period of the high Renaissance, even though foreign armies were the dominant force there. The first French edition appeared in 1554, with a Classical title page depicting soldiers fighting without the benefit of firearms. The impact of such texts and of the Classical models are, however, controversial.[36]

Adoption of weaponry and tactics required changes within the military, most obviously drill and discipline, and in society as a whole. Yet these changes could be actively resisted. Drill and discipline have generally been discussed in terms of improving firepower, but their real point was a tradi-tional defensive one: to prepare a unit to remain in position while in the face of death, regardless of casualties. This took precedence over tactical matters. The issue of shock versus firepower – of offensive efficacy or effectiveness in causing casualties – was not as important as a unit remaining able to act and tractable to its commander while receiving casualties.

Cultural factors have certainly been linked to enhanced tactical skill and organisational cohesion. This focuses on the ability to keep cohesion and control in battle, and to make effective use of units. This disciplined unitisa-tion of armies and navies may be generally discussed in terms of the Renaissance. More specifically, developments in ballistics can be linked to the Scientific Revolution and seen as an aspect of an understanding of cause and effect, and a determination to take predictable advantage of this relationship. In the 1530s, there was great interest in the possibilities of measuring cannon fire. Cannon became more accurate, not least because of the addition of trun-nions, just forward of the point of balance, which made it possible to elevate barrels. The development of movable carriages increased the mobility of cannon. These developments, and the increased use of quantification in European society for the understanding of space and time, encouraged the prediction and calculation of range, and thus the instrumentation of an important aspect of war.[37] More generally, Europeans showed an unusual interest in innovations, experiments and changes around military technology, organisation and tactics. This was a search process under great uncertainty and there were many failures, but it was important that several policy makers were looking for alternatives and tried to implement them.

The publication of works such as Tartaglia's geometrical models of artillery trajectories in the 1530s and Galileo's kinematics of ballistic motion in a vacuum spread their impact. Niccolò Tartaglia was himself a victim of war. In 1512, during the sack of Brescia by the French, he received a facial wound, although only a boy, that left him with a speech defect leading to his nickname Tartaglia (stammerer). His *Nova Scientia* (1537) was an examination of the fall of heavy bodies that was directly applied to artillery shot. He also demonstrated the measurement of the elevation of cannon and discussed range-finding. In his *Quesiti e Inventioni Diverse* (1546), Tartaglia again addressed the trajectory of projectiles. Galileo's *Discorsi* (1638) demonstrated the parabolic trajectory of projectiles, and also provided a complete table of ranges. Although Galileo's understanding of the issue represented a marked advance over Tartaglia's use of the concepts of Aristotelian physics, earlier developments were important not only in problem setting but also in 'setting the terms of a solution…as a geometrical trajectory with universal reference yielding predictable consequences'.[38]

However, the extent to which these and other developments could be applied effectively has to be questioned. Indeed, it has been argued that the term 'technology' is inappropriate before the nineteenth century. Instead, from the sixteenth to the eighteenth century there were significant changes in the invention and uses of machines in the West, extending to the application of technology, but that technology, in the sense of the full integration of the invention, development and use of machines into society and the economy, was conditional upon a prior social revolution in which earlier social divisions had been blurred, rapid social ascent was possible, financial capital was readily available and mobility of labour was established; in short that technology was effective as part of an entire socio-economic system.[39]

At the same time, there were important developments, although whether they deserve any description as revolutionary is open to question. Thus, the contested crossing of the river Lech by the Swedes in 1632, the Battle of Rain, can be contrasted to battlefield uses of artillery to support attacks (as opposed to its more static employment in defensive operations) during the Italian Wars (1494–1559). In 1632, eighty Swedish field cannon that required only two horses to draw them were moved forward to the riverbank, providing covering fire for the Swedish cavalry, and the cannon then followed the cavalry across the river.

Such discussion has to be set in the wider context of the problems of political and military organisation and support created by professionalisation and the rise of permanent forces on land and sea. Structures had to be created and co-operative practices devised within the context of the societies of the period. It is unclear how far this was a planned process, how far there was a self-sustaining dynamic for change, in an action–reaction cycle or synergy, and how far there was a limit of effectiveness that inhibited the creation of a serious capability gap with forces, both European and non-European, that lacked such development.

At the same time, it is important to be wary of models that assume some mechanistic search for efficiency and a maximisation of force. Instead, military activity has to be placed within a culture in which interests in new methods interacted with powerful elements of continuity. A stress on the value of morale and the importance of honour came naturally to the aristocratic society that dominated war-making, and traditional assumptions about appropriate conduct were important in tactics, although these are generally presented today in functional terms. Thus, it has recently been argued that 'despite new artillery, a revolution in military architecture, and increasing tactical sophistication, the Renaissance art of "modern" war embodied survivals from the medieval chivalric tradition and civic heritage that continued to inform the conduct of sieges, as well as the ways in which society regarded fortifications…In war, as in the tourney, one acquired honour by one's conduct as much as by one's success'.[40] This approach may be of great applicability, not least because the very notion of effectiveness was framed and applied in terms of dominant cultural and social patterns.

## Conclusion

One of the strongest arguments against the general concept of the Military Revolution is that it encourages a uniform perception both of Europe and of the global context of European power, an approach that invites a presentation in systemic terms. This underrates the variety of developments in Europe. Robert Frost, a supporter of the concept of Military Revolution, in light of the fundamental changes he discerns in 'the relationship between governments, armed forces and society', nevertheless suggests it is more helpful to see 'a series of individual military revolutions, not one Military Revolution'. Furthermore, he dates 'the critical point which can be seen as the definitive breakthrough of a new military system' to the seventeenth century: 'in Sweden in the 1620s; in Brandenburg-Prussia in the 1650s; in Denmark in the 1660s and in Russia in the 1700s'.

This valuable regional perspective, which is accompanied by a stress on the continued value of cavalry, and the extent to which Western European ideas and methods were adapted rather than adopted,[41] invites the further observation that there was no one set of Western European ideas, methods and circumstances. Indeed, the following narrative chapters indicate the variety of tasking and contingency that helped to ensure that any attempt to explain military proficiency in terms of an ability to win battles and mount successful sieges is far too narrow. Even when battle is considered, the often-difficult study of 'its face', i.e. of the individual and collective realities of conflict, suggests that cohesion, morale, impact and persistence in hand-to-hand fighting could be much more important than tactical sophistication in the shape of deployment, unit size and firepower drill. This emerges from the most recent detailed study of a battle in this period, that of the White Mountain (1620).[42]

Furthermore, the political and military situation varied greatly outside Europe. European perceptions of the world distinguished between overseas expansion in the Old and New Worlds. European warfare in Africa and South Asia was largely private and conducted under the supervision of chartered trading companies. This helped ensure a different deployment for European regular forces than was the case in the New World. Issues of cost were much more important in Africa and Asia. In short, we may have been overly focused on the quality (and quantity) of the means applied in European expansion, specifically the enabler of technology and technique, and insufficiently focused on motives.

Nevertheless, Parker's willingness to give due weight to European expansion outside Europe in his discussion of the Military Revolution offered an important advance on Roberts's formulation of the concept. It is appropriate to continue the discussion of the significance of European military development in this period by looking beyond Europe.

# 4

# EUROPEAN EXPANSION AND THE GLOBAL CONTEXT 1490–1578

## Introduction

The choice of 1578 as the date to divide the treatment of this topic (with 1578–1660 following in Chapter 9) is deliberately provocative. 1578 saw the most significant defeat for European power outside Europe during this period, the battle of Alcazarquivir. In this decisive clash, Abd al-Malik of Morocco crushingly defeated the Portuguese, in part by making effective use of arquebusiers trained to fire from horseback;[1] in contrast, the arquebusiers used by the Spaniards against the French in northern Italy along the river Sesia on 29–30 April 1524 were carried on horseback, like later dragoons, and dismounted to fire. In both cases, as more generally with horse archers, fire-power and mobility were combined. The Portuguese defeat cost the lives of King Sebastian and his army and led to the end of Portuguese plans for conquering Morocco and also, in 1580, of Portuguese independence from rule by the king of Spain, Philip II, who became Philip I of Portugal. It there-fore serves as a reminder of the danger of treating this period simply in terms of the expansion of European empires.

This chapter and Chapter 9 seek to tackle two related topics, this expansion and the global context of European military power. The latter topic, which will be returned to in Chapter 9, provides an opportunity for judging European military developments and capability.

The early modern period saw both greater interaction between different parts of the world and the rise of European influence and power. The two were linked. It was through the projection of European power that the 'Old World' and the 'New World' were connected, and indeed that the 'New World' was created as an idea as first, Spain and Portugal, and later, England, France and the Dutch conquered and settled important portions of North and South America. It was through the projection of Portuguese naval power from the 1490s that the 'Old' World was reshaped as European trade and mili-tary strength began to make their impact in the Indian Ocean. From an economic point of view, this was part of Europe's attempt to get in contact with the most advanced parts of the world. The cutting edge was European progress in military and, even more, naval technology. It took centuries before

Europe could balance its trade with Asia and export goods from Europe, rather than silver.

European power projection eventually led to a major shift in global power. For much of the fifteenth century, however, the Europeans had been relatively inconsequential on the world stage. Indeed, they were unable to prevent the advance of the Ottomans into the Balkans, a process that led in 1453 to the dramatic fall of Constantinople, the capital of the Byzantine empire, to Mehmed II (r. 1451–81). Ottoman expansion in the Balkans entailed a loss of (Christian) European political control that also led to a movement in religious, ethnic, linguistic and economic frontiers, the consequences of which greatly affect modern Balkan politics.

The fall of Constantinople was symbolic as well as significant. A centre of power that had resisted non-Christian attack for nearly a millennium had finally fallen. No Christian state matched Mehmed's power, and the Ottoman empire became the most important state in Europe. At the same time, it was the Chinese, not the Europeans, who were the leading power in Asian waters; indeed, in the first half of the century, the Chinese sent fleets into the Indian Ocean that were far larger than any European fleet.

By the late sixteenth century, the situation was very different. The Ottomans had made significant advances in Europe and the Mediterranean, capturing Belgrade in 1521, defeating Hungary in 1526, and conquering Cyprus in 1570–1; although their invasion of southern Italy in 1480 had been repelled in 1481, and their attacks had been held at Vienna (1529), Corfu (1537) and Malta (1565).

Further afield, the shift was dramatic. When Spanish forces began to take control of parts of the Philippines in the 1560s, Philip II of Spain, after whom the islands were renamed, became the first ruler with an empire on which the sun never set. Spanish forces had already overthrown the Aztecs of Mexico and the Incas of Peru, a process greatly aided by divisions among other peoples, including Spain's opponents, and by the impact of European diseases. Portuguese warships in the Indian Ocean had destroyed the leading Indian fleets of Calicut (1503) and Gujarat (1558), and also that sent by Egypt (1509).

However, over most of Asia, the European impact was far more limited. In India, the decisive political change was the destruction of Lodi power by that of the Mughals in the 1520s, and the subsequent defence, consolidation and expansion of Mughal power in northern and central India. In Persia, another dynasty relying on cavalry, the Safavids, successfully invaded and established control in the 1500s. Although they were affected by the Portuguese presence in the Persian Gulf, their foreign policy and methods of warfare were dominated by repeated wars with their neighbours, the Ottomans and the Uzbeks.

## The Ottoman challenge

In their conflicts with the Europeans, the Ottomans made effective use of gunpowder weaponry, although their numerical superiority and the diversity of potential manpower sources (centrally barracked, provincial and tribal) from which they were able to recruit were also important.[2] The Ottomans had initially relied on mounted archers, but, in the second half of the fourteenth century, they developed an infantry that became a centrally paid standing army eventually armed with field cannon and handguns. The artillery that drove off the Byzantine navy and breached the walls of Constantinople[3] served notice on military attitudes and practices that had seemed to protect Christian Europe. Relying on fortifications to thwart 'barbarians', to offset their numbers, dynamism, mobility and aggression, no longer seemed a credible policy; and indeed within Christian Europe, artillery had a similar impact on fortifications, and thus on the possibility of holding off attacks without risking battle. Already, the Ottomans had used their artillery successfully at the siege of Salonica (1430) and in breaching the walls at the Isthmus of Corinth (1446). At least twelve cannon were used to take Constantinople.

The Ottomans followed up by further attacks, although in 1456 Mehmed and his artillery failed to capture Belgrade, and in 1480 he failed to take Rhodes. There were still important Ottoman gains, including in Albania, Serbia and southern Greece. In the Aegean, Lesbos fell in 1461 after the successful Ottoman siege of Mytilene, while the capture of key islands and bases in the war with Venice of 1463–79, for example Negroponte (1470) in Euboea, won the Ottomans the decisive position in the Aegean.[4] The capture of Kaffa in the Crimea from the Genoese in 1475 and of Akkerman at the mouth of the Dniester in 1484 similarly cemented the Ottoman position in the Black Sea. This gave the Ottomans control or influence over the rivers that flowed into the Black Sea and thus over the lands around it. The Ottomans, not Muscovy, dominated the lands north of the Black Sea, and were thus best placed to recruit local protégés.[5] The Crimean Khanate, which emerged in 1441, was from 1475–6 closely allied to the Ottomans, and a major source of slaves for them. This encouraged the Tatars to raid Muscovy, with whom relations became hostile from the 1470s. The Russians were made to pay an annual tribute, but that did not prevent raiding for slaves. Control over the Black Sea was important to the development of Ottoman naval power and also helped the Ottomans get the maximum benefit from the conquest of Constantinople.

After Mehmed's death, the Ottomans under Bayezid II (r. 1481–1512) fought an indecisive war with the Mameluke rulers of Egypt and Syria in 1485–91, but were more successful against Venice (1499–1503). Ottoman expansion revived under Mehmed's grandson, Selim I, 'the Grim' (r. 1512–20), although the focus was on Asia, not Europe. The dynamic Safavids, who had conquered Persia and a part of Iraq in the early 1500s, were his principal rival, and in 1514 Selim marched east. The Safavids were defeated at Chaldiran (23

August 1514), in part by the use of firepower (although the extent is a matter of debate); but the logistical and political task of conquering Persia was too great for the Ottomans. The Ottomans were far more successful against the Mamelukes, conquering Syria (1516) and Egypt (1517), in large part by the successful use of firepower. Egypt was to serve as the base for their resistance to Portuguese expansion in the Indian Ocean and the Red Sea.[6]

The Ottomans under Suleiman the Magnificent (r. 1520–66) then turned back against Europe. Belgrade fell in 1521 and in 1526 Suleiman defeated the Hungarians at Mohács. The heavy Hungarian cavalry drove through the lighter Ottoman cavalry, only to be stopped by infantry and cannon fire. The Hungarians, their dynamism spent, were then attacked in front and rear by the more numerous Ottoman forces. Louis and most of his aristocracy died on the battlefield or in the nearby Danube marshes. Aside from greater numbers and firepower, the Ottomans benefited from having more experienced units. In contrast, the Hungarians relied on a feudal force that lacked the necessary experience and cohesion. Standing forces had been developed by the Hungarian crown in the late fifteenth century, but, due to financial factors, it had proved impossible to sustain these.

Suleiman was less successful when he besieged Vienna in 1529: he did not reach the city until 27 September and Vienna was able to resist assaults until the Ottoman retreat began on 14 October. Heavy rains reduced roads to mud, ensuring that the Ottomans lacked their heavy cannon. Campaigning at such a distance from their base caused major logistical problems, as troops and supplies had to move for months before they could reach the sphere of operations and, in addition, the onset of winter limited the campaigning season. Vienna held out, but it is difficult to decide how best to assess military effectiveness in the case of Christian fortresses holding off Ottoman attack, but without any ability to inflict defeat.

There was no battle during Suleiman's next expedition, that of 1532, when the Ottomans besieged Köszeg (Güns). As with the Persians, when they fought the Ottomans in 1534–5, the Austrians had learned that the best policy was to avoid major battles, although it can also be argued that Suleiman failed to provoke such an engagement.[7] The Austrians, however, could not prevent Ottoman gains in areas within effective Ottoman operational range. Until his death in 1540, John Zapolya, who had been elected king of Hungary after Mohács, held the country against Charles V's brother Ferdinand, the ruler of Austria. When János died, Ferdinand sought to enforce his claim, besieging Buda. This led Suleiman to intervene, conquering central Hungary which became an Ottoman province, while Transylvania was given to János's infant son. The Habsburgs held onto 'Royal Hungary' to the north. The Ottomans captured Buda in 1541, Esztergom (Gran) in 1543, Visegrád in 1544, Temesvár in 1552, and Fülek in 1554. When battles were fought, the Ottomans were successful, as at Szeged in 1552. Thanks to Mohács, Suleiman had secured a major shift in the boundary between Christendom and Islam, although the devastation of much of Hungary had a severe effect on local society.[8] Further west, thanks in part to Ottoman support, the Spanish advance in North Africa was stopped and then reversed, with the Spanish loss of the Peñón dominating Algiers in 1529.[9]

The tightening of the frontiers between Europe and the Ottomans was linked, not only to the emergence of a Spanish interest in the Mediterranean, moving from West to East, as the Ottomans moved from East to West, but also to an increase in religious tensions. The seizure of Otranto in Italy by the Ottomans in 1480–1 with attendant atrocities had galvanised Europe to the threat from the east, making real something that Byzantine refugees had been pleading since the 1430s. This was not the limit of Ottoman ambitions in Italy. In 1497, the Ottomans showed an interest in seizing Taranto, although they lacked the capability to maintain such a gain. In 1499, during the Venetian–Ottoman war, Ottoman raids reached the borders of Friuli in north-eastern Italy, and there were rumours of the Ottomans using mastiffs to hunt down Christian peasants.

In response, there was a revival in interest in crusading. The ostensible purpose of Charles VIII of France's invasion of Italy in 1494 was to launch a great crusade. Crusades were proclaimed in 1500, 1517 and 1530. The various Holy Leagues saw their eventual project as an assault on the Ottomans, and they indeed acted to that end in 1538 and 1571.[10] As with the Italian Wars (1494–1559), the Papacy assumed that it should play a major role in creating alliances.

## Portuguese expansion

Thanks to Portuguese transoceanic expansion, a vast new sphere of conflict between Islam and Christendom had been opened in the Indian Ocean, the Red Sea and the Persian Gulf. From the early fifteenth century, the Iberians were increasingly important as maritime powers along, and off, the north-western coast of Africa. Portuguese settlement of Madeira began in 1424 and of the Azores in the 1430s. In the 1440s, the Portuguese explored the African coast as far as modern Guinea. Castilian interest in the Canaries increased.

Rounding Africa, Portuguese naval forces made a major impact in the Indian Ocean from the 1490s. Their chain of fortresses there included Socotra at the approach to the Red Sea (1507), which was rapidly abandoned because there was little water, Ormuz at the mouth of the Persian Gulf (1507, and, having then lost it, 1515), Cochin (1503), Cannanore (1505), Goa (1510), Diu (1534) and Bassein (1534) on the west coast of India, and Malacca in the straits of that name (1511). Whereas for the Ottomans, state policy meant aggressive territorial expansion, Portugal had a different model, that of the Venetian *Empire da Mar* in the Mediterranean: a chain of islands and fortresses protecting entrepôts and enforcing a monopoly or near-monopolistic trading terms. It was important that the monopoly excluded other Europeans.[11]

Not all the Portuguese targets were taken. Affonso de Albuquerque, the expansionist Viceroy from 1509 to 1515, failed at Aden in 1513, an important setback given the role of the Red Sea as the primary route for Islamic naval counter-attack. Rather than the attack demonstrating European technological advantage, the Portuguese sought to assault the walls using scaling ladders, not to breach them with preliminary cannon fire. Instead, cannon were used by the defenders. A second attempt, made in 1517, also failed. Fortifications along the Red Sea, not least at Jeddah, where the Portuguese were checked in 1517, were greatly improved by Mameluke forces sent from Egypt to provide assistance against the Portuguese.[12]

The expansion of the Ottomans into Egypt (1517) and Iraq (1534) lay the basis for Ottoman intervention in the Indian Ocean, although, as a reminder of the role of choice, in the 1520s and early 1530s Suleiman devoted scant attention; and in 1532 cannon were transferred from Suez to the Mediterranean. The 72-strong Ottoman fleet sent to Diu in 1538, the largest fleet the Ottomans ever dispatched to the Indian Ocean, failed to win Gujarati support and retreated before any battle with the Portuguese fleet. En route, however, the Ottomans seized Aden, pre-empting a Portuguese expedition, creating the basis for the Ottoman province of Yemen, and strengthening the Ottoman ability to defend the Red Sea and to intervene in the Horn of Africa. From bases at Aden, Basra and Suez, Ottoman squadrons under Piri Reis and Seydi Ali Reis exerted considerable pressure, sacking Muscat in 1552, although failing at Ormuz then and in 1554.[13]

From the 1560s, Ottoman naval activity in the Indian Ocean declined, although, in 1568, artillerymen and gunsmiths were sent to help the Sumatran Sultan of Aceh against the Portuguese in Malacca. As with Spain and the Ottomans in the Mediterranean (see Chapter 8), a rough division developed. Although the Portuguese had sent an expedition into the Red Sea in 1541, which unsuccessfully tried to destroy the Ottoman fleet at Suez, their hopes of influence there had to be abandoned. However, with the support of Persia, the Portuguese were able to limit the Ottoman presence in the Persian Gulf. Ottoman maritime power was essentially restricted to the Gulf and the Red, Black and Mediterranean Seas. This was appropriate given the nature of their warships: Ottoman galleys were less suited to the Indian Ocean than Portuguese vessels. The Ottomans preferred to attack Cyprus in 1570, rather than send aid to distant Aceh. Frontier, or at least frontier zones, stabilised.

Further east, the Portuguese also encountered resistance, but it would be mistaken to see their expansion primarily in military terms. The Portuguese lacked the manpower to become a major Asian territory. The population of Portugal in the sixteenth century – about one million – was not large, and there were other emigration opportunities, especially to the less remote new colony of Brazil. Especially beyond Malacca, Portuguese bases were generally commercial bases, not major fortified positions. The Portuguese gained wealth from the trade routes they developed from Malacca to the Far East, with bases established at Macao in China (1557) and Nagasaki in Japan (1570), but did not acquire any significant military capability in the region, and were unable to thwart the establishment of Spanish power in the Philippines, despite attempts in 1568 and 1570. In the East Indies, the Sultanate of Aceh limited the Portuguese presence in Sumatra and attacked Malacca, albeit unsuccessfully, in 1553, 1568, 1570, 1573 and 1595. To the east, in what became known as the East Indies (now Indonesia), the Portuguese established fortified posts at Ternate (1522), Solor (1562) and Tidore (1578). However, as Islamic identity in the Moluccas increased, Portuguese relations with the Sultans of Ternate deteriorated. After a five-month siege, the Portuguese were driven from Ternate, and their attempt to create a monopoly over the Moluccan spice trade was lost with it.

The gap in land warfare capability in South Asia was less than in the New World. Unlike the Incas of South America and the Aztecs of Central America, Portugal's Indian opponents had gunpowder weaponry, steel armour and swords, and war horses, and this was also true of some of their other Asian opponents. The Portuguese found 3,000 firearms in the magazine when they captured Goa in 1510. Malacca had numerous bronze cannon, although the decisive clash was between the Sultan's war elephants and a well-co-ordinated and determined Portuguese force relying on pikes as much as firepower. Portuguese cannon, however, were superior to those of their opponents. Nevertheless, the Asians they encountered were able to respond effectively to the Portuguese in both commercial and military terms in the sixteenth century, so that the degree of control enjoyed by the Portuguese in the Indian Ocean should not be exaggerated.[14]

## The New World

The Spanish conquest of the two leading American states, the Aztec and Inca empires, is often presented as the impact of a military new world, Europe, on an old world, for neither Incas nor Aztecs had firearms or horses. Their societies were reliant on wood and stone, not iron and steel. Slings, wooden clubs and obsidian knives were no match for the Spaniards' arms. Their cannon, arquebuses and crossbows all had a greater range and killing power than their rivals' weapons. In addition, the Aztecs probably could not use captured firearms, because they had no gunpowder and also lacked the necessary training, although it is not known whether the Aztecs did or did not use captured guns, or, indeed, when native units which were trained to fire guns began to be used by the Spaniards. In hand-to-hand combat, the Spaniards also benefited from the power and flexibility of their single-handed steel swords and from their steel helmets. In close combat, even without horses, these gave the Spaniards superiority over Aztecs and Incas: metal weapons were more effective than stone; metal armour offered more protection than cotton-quilted.

Technological superiority is widely held to explain the victories of tiny European forces. Hernán Cortés had only about 500 Spanish soldiers, fourteen small cannon, and sixteen horses when he landed at Vera Cruz in 1519. Francisco Pizarro had only 168 Europeans, four cannon and sixty-seven horses; yet in 1531 he overran the Incas, who referred to the shot fired by arquebuses as *yllapas* (thunderbolts). Spanish cavalry crushed an Inca rebellion in 1536: the Incas were very vulnerable in the open. Hernando De Soto, who had served under Pizarro, and who between 1539 and 1543 brutally pillaged local peoples in what is now the southern USA, in 1541 won a battle with the Choctaws at Mabila (Selma) in which his cavalry was able to dominate the open ground without competition. When Magellan arrived at Cebu in the Philippines in 1521 he showed off his firearms and armour in order to convince the population of his potency.

At the same time, the Spaniards encountered difficulties from the outset. They came to the West Indies via the Canary Islands where the native Guanches had mounted a vigorous resistance. Grand Canary did not fall until 1483 and Tenerife until 1493.

In what to Europeans was the New World, although the conquest of some areas, such as Hispaniola, where a concentration of numbers in the initial zone of contact has been held as important to Spanish success,[15] Cuba (1511–13) and New Granada (Colombia, 1536–9), was relatively swift, other conquests took far longer. The reasons varied, but were typically a combination of local resistance, difficult environmental conditions, insufficient interest in expansion and limited manpower. As the Spaniards were most successful in the New World in regions where there was much for them to gain, their failures to expand elsewhere were not necessarily due to military factors. The Spaniards never devoted military resources to the New World that in any way compared with their efforts in European struggles. After their initial successes, the Spaniards faced numerous problems. Northward expansion in Mexico was impeded by the Chichimecas in 1550–90 and, further north, by the discovery that there was no gold-rich civilisation to loot.[16] The Spaniards also encountered problems in Central America. As in Africa in the late nineteenth century, the Europeans found it easier to conquer developed polities, in this case the Aztecs, than acephalous peoples. Spanish control of jungle regions south-east of Mexico was limited, and the absence of major imperial states that could be overthrown complicated the Spanish task. Cortés led a costly campaign in Honduras in 1524. Guatemala was conquered by 1542, but the Itzás of the Yucatán were not defeated until 1697.[17]

In South America, central Chile was conquered in 1540–58, Santiago being founded in 1541. However, further south, the Araucanians, who relied on guerrilla warfare rather than pitched battles, were formidable opponents. They also benefited from a measure of diffusion, learning to ride horses and to use Spanish weapons which they captured.[18]

In Florida, where the Spaniards first arrived in 1513, they were obliged to withdraw by Timucua and Calusa archers. Pánfilo de Narváez's expedition of 1528 was repelled by Apalachees and Autes, whose accurate archers used flint-tipped arrows capable of penetrating Spanish armour. The first fort at St Augustine, built in 1565, was burned down by the Timucua the following spring.[19] Thereafter, although the Spaniards had a number of coastal bases, their control of Florida was limited.

In the Caribbean, the Kulinago of the Lesser Antilles and the Caribs and Arawaks of the Guianas thwarted Spanish attacks and mounted counter-raids with fast, manoeuvrable shallow-draft boats carved from tropical trees.[20] Helped by the difficulty of the terrain, the Caribs of St Vincent kept the Spaniards out.[21]

Similarly in Brazil, which they reached in 1500, the Portuguese made only slow progress at the expense of the Tupinambá and Tapuya, although they were helped by rivalries between tribes and by the alliance of some. Portuguese muskets were of little value against the nomadic Aimoré, mobile warriors who were expert archers and well adapted to forest warfare.[22]

Throughout the New World, however, resistance was greatly lessened by enslavement and disease. The first disrupted social structures, and household and communal economies, leading to famine and population decline. The herding together of enslaved peoples, such as Arawaks brought from the Bahamas to work the gold mines of Hispaniola in the 1510s, exacerbated the impact of disease, both new and old. Smallpox decimated the population of Hispaniola in 1519.[23] Even without enslavement, disease imported by Europeans, particularly smallpox, led to a major fall in indigenous populations.[24]

Spanish conquest was not solely a matter of initial military success. Intended to be more than raiding, conquest was followed by the arrival of colonists and their livestock, by Christian proselytisation and the destruction of rival religious rituals, by the introduction of administrative and tenurial structures, and by a degree of Spanish acceptance of local elites and local material cultures, as well as of local adaptation to the Spaniards. Thus, in the Philippines, where Spaniards from Mexico established a base on Cebu in 1565, cultural assimilation was aided by the animist nature of local religion and the absence of an ecclesiastical structure, and by the willingness of Spain to encourage effective Christian missionary activity.[25]

Any emphasis on these wider contexts of military activity offers an instructive comparison with the situation in Europe where warfare is overly abstracted from these contexts. Although the conquest of much of the New World might seem a clear instance of the triumph of military-technological factors, there were also important other factors, especially the weakness of Aztec and Inca leadership and of their socio-political structures, and the Spanish ability to find local allies. Even if the focus is on technology, it is important not to exaggerate the capability gap. Spanish firearms were few and slow, and much of their impact was psychological. Aztec wooden clubs, studded with flint or obsidian, proved effective against Spanish horsemen thanks to the skill of the warriors. The Spaniards also found it helpful to adopt native quilted cotton armour – it was more appropriate for the climate than metal armour and offered protection against spears and bows – although they retained their metal helmets which were useful against slingshots.

To turn to other factors, leadership weaknesses and mutual incomprehension played an important role in Aztec defeat. Montezuma, the panicky Aztec leader, was fascinated by Cortés, worried that he might be a god or an envoy from a powerful potentate, and unwilling to act decisively against him. Cortéz reached the Aztec capital, Tenochtitlán, without having to fight his way there. Montezuma was killed in 1520, and his energetic brother, Cuitlahuac, who replaced him, died that year from smallpox. Brought by the Spaniards, the disease killed at least half the Aztecs, and weakened the morale of the survivors. Divisions also helped the Spaniards gain allies. Aztec and Inca expansion in the fifteenth century left conquered peoples ready to ally with Spain. The Totonacs and the Tlaxcalans welcomed Cortés, and he encouraged the rebellion of the ruler of Cempoala in 1519. Having been driven from Tenochtitlán in 1520, Cortés recouped his strength with the help of the Tlaxcalans, and his eventual victory in 1521 owed much to the role played by about 200,000 Indian allies. Native support was essential in order to match the massive numerical superiority of the Aztecs, who learned to alter their tactics to counter European arms, especially firepower.[26]

Both of these factors were also important in the conquest of the Incas. Their ruler, Huyana Capac (r.1493–1525), left a disputed succession between the northern and southern sections of the empire, which were led respectively by his son Atahuallpa and his half-brother Huescar. Once captured by the Spaniards, Atahuallpa was used against Huescar, before being strangled in 1533. Reaction to the Spaniards was greatly affected by allegiance to one or other of the factions and, in its early stages, Pizarro's seizure of power was in part a coup. He also received help from the Canari Indians.[27] Local divisions and allies also helped the conquerors elsewhere. In Guatemala, the Spaniards benefited from disputes between Maya groups, while the expedition sent to Pensacola Bay in 1559 helped the Coosa subjugate the formerly subordinate Napochies.[28] Similarly, having taken Malacca, the Portuguese launched an expedition later in 1511 against Muar where the Sultan had taken refuge. Of the 1,300 soldiers on the expedition, 1,000 were Asian auxiliaries.[29]

## Politics and conquest

The local political environment was also crucial in the Philippines, where, by 1573, the Spaniards were in control in Cebu, Leyte, Panaym, Mindoro and the central plain of Luzon. The island nature of the Philippines facilitated Spanish action: this was a territory wide open to maritime attack. The limited nature of local fortifications was also important. When de Legaspi arrived in Manila

Bay in 1572, the local communities were only defended by a bamboo stockade at the entrance to the Pasig River, and only one stone fort is known to have existed in the Philippines before the Spaniards arrived. Yet, political circumstances were more important. The conquest involved relatively little warfare. There was no powerful political entity able to mobilise resistance. The *barangay*, a comparatively small kinship group, was the sole significant political unit, and this limited the organisation of resistance.

More generally, it is difficult to assess political as opposed to more narrowly 'military' factors. Both clearly played a role in most conquests. Thus, the fall of the kingdom of Granada to the Spaniards, which culminated with the surrender of Granada itself in 1492, owed much to divisions within the kingdom, but the Spanish use of largely German-manned artillery was also important. The Moors were outgunned and the Spaniards developed their gunnery, adopting offensive artillery tactics and shifting firepower 'to operational centre stage'. They also benefited from the ability to field a large army. Nevertheless, the conquest took a decade of campaigning. The resourceful Moorish resistance obliged the Spaniards to adapt and adjust their tactics, providing them with crucial training that was to serve them in good stead against the French in Italy in the early 1500s.[30]

## The conquest of Kazan: a case study of expansion

Both factors can also be seen in play in the Russian conquest of Kazan, an event that permanently altered the shape of Europe by permitting a major expansion of Russia. The expansion of Russian power to the east and southeast benefited greatly from divisions among potential opponents, although there was an important defensive dimension to Russian policy, specifically concern about links between Kazan and the Crimea: 'Muscovy simply took over the frontier area to protect itself'.[31] Ivan III (r.1462–1505) began to take the initiative in the long-standing struggle between Russia and the Tatars. He conducted a series of campaigns against Kazan in 1467–9, and then took advantage of dynastic strife within the Khanate, so that in 1487 his forces were able to make a sympathetic claimant Khan.

Ivan's successor, Vasilii III (r.1505–33), initially maintained good relations with Kazan, but the Crimean Tatars organised a pan-Tatar league which ousted the pro-Russian Khan of Kazan in 1521, replacing him with Sahib, the Crimean Khan's brother. The same year, the Crimean and Kazan Tatars advanced on Moscow from the south and east, and the city was only saved by an attack on the Crimea by the Tatars of Astrakhan, a reminder not only of the value of divisions between non-European powers, but also of the extent to which European expansion did not set the political agenda for other states. In 1524, the Khan of Kazan acknowledged the suzerainty of Suleiman the Magnificent, a sign of the spreading reach, or at least pretensions, of the major empires, but in 1532 Vasilii succeeded in installing another pro-Russian Khan, only for him to be murdered in 1535 and replaced by Sahib's nephew. Relations deteriorated with frequent Tatar raids of Russia.

In 1545, Ivan IV (r.1533–84) took the initiative, helped by divisions among the Tatars. He attempted two winter campaigns against Kazan in 1547–8 and 1549–50, but these failed because the Russian army had no fortified base in the region, had to leave its artillery behind because of heavy rains, and ended up campaigning with an exclusively cavalry army that was of no use in investing the fortress of Kazan. At this stage, Russian force structure was similar to that of its opponents.

For the third campaign, a base was secured in what was an impressive demonstration of organisational capability. In the winter and spring of 1551, the Russians prefabricated fortress towers and wall sections near Uglich and then floated them down the Volga on barges with artillery and troops to its confluence with the Sviiaga, only twenty-five kilometres from Kazan, where the fortress of Sviiazhsk was built in just four weeks. This protected the upper Volga towns from raids and also provided a base for operations against Kazan. That summer, siege guns and stores were shipped down the Oka and Volga to Sviiazhsk and, after a Crimean invasion of southern Russia was repulsed near Tula in mid-June, the Russians advanced on Kazan, which they reached on 20 August. They constructed siege lines from which the cannon opened fire and also used a wooden siege tower carrying cannon and moved on rollers. The supporting Kazan cavalry were routed, the ditch surrounding the city was filled with fascines, and sappers tunnelled beneath the walls, preparing a mine. When it was blown up, the Russians attacked all the city gates simultaneously and rapidly stormed the city.

Russian success owed much to their first large-scale use of artillery and mining. They had 150 cannon, compared to the seventy in the city. The campaign also demonstrated the effectiveness of Ivan's new infantry units, but there were other important factors, each of which undercuts any attempt to present a single explanation of success. The demographic balance favoured Russia, and there was also a clear difference in consistency and quality of leadership. Although during Ivan's minority, the Russian government was weak and divided, there was scant comparison with the situation in Kazan, where the throne changed hands six times between 1546 and 1552, providing numerous opportunities for Russian intervention. Once Kazan had fallen, there were serious rebellions in 1553, 1554 and 1556, which were suppressed with great brutality. Organised resistance only ceased in 1556. The Russians were helped by the support of many of the Khanate's former subjects.[32]

More generally, the Russians benefited from divisions among the steppe peoples, and from the support of the Nogais, who lived north of the Caucasus. In the late 1520s, the centre for the Nogai trade in horses was moved from Constantinople to Moscow, helping to cement political links. In turn, the Russians provided goods, including firearms. In 1563, the head of the Great Nogai Horde became Ivan IV's brother-in-law. The Nogai alliance was useful for a number of reasons. The Nogais made possible the Russian conquests of Astrakhan in 1556 and Sibir in 1582. Their supply of horses helped the Russians operate outside the forest belt of northern Russia.

The capture of Kazan contrasted greatly with the failure to keep the Ottomans out of Hungary, and with the defensive character of the subsequent Habsburg response to their advance. Instead, Kazan opened the way for Russian expansion towards the Caucasus, and also across the Urals into West Russia. Much of the Tatar military pressure on the south-eastern frontier was reduced and Muscovy was given greater access to the trade routes of the Transcaucasus and Central Asia. The Russian occupation of the southern Volga ensured that the Ottomans were cut off from Sunni co-religionists and trade partners in Transoxiana. Rivalry between Russia and the Ottomans became more intense and Russia was to become the dominant power in the region.[33]

## Conclusions

More generally, in European expansion, the political context played a major role in guiding commitment, affecting the dynamics of obtaining and sustaining alliances, and determining success. Military capability and resources alone did not guarantee success. This can be seen in the Horn of Africa and the Red Sea. There, the Portuguese attempt to challenge Ottoman power, and the associated Portuguese support for Christian Abyssinia, did not entail a policy of extensive territorial conquest. Instead, the Portuguese relied on warships, bases and the dispatch of a small force to assist Abyssinia against the Islamic Sultanate of Adal. However, Aden's incorporation into the Ottoman (1538), not the Portuguese, system ensured that the Portuguese lacked a base able to challenge Ottoman naval moves from the Red Sea. There is little reason to believe that the result would have been very different had the Portuguese made more of a military effort in the region. They would still have been greatly outnumbered by the Ottomans once the latter had conquered Egypt in 1517, and it is unclear how far Ottoman strength would have been countered by Portuguese military capability. The Portuguese benefited from alternative Ottoman commitments, particularly from their bitter rivalry with the Safavids.

As so often, it is necessary to think not in terms of the West versus the Rest, but of specific Western initiatives and their interaction with the complex rivalries and relationships of local states, a point also true of the expansion of non-Western powers.[34] In addition, non-Western powers benefited from rivalries between the Western powers, although the overseas projection of Western power was such that this benefit was mostly a case of helping resistance to Western expansion. The Ottomans were able to win support against the Habsburgs. In 1543–4, the Ottoman fleet under Khair-ed-Din (Barbarossa) wintered at the French base of Toulon, after co-operating in the capture of Nice. Such strategic and operational co-ordination was, however, unusual.

Nevertheless, opponents of Western powers benefited from divisions within the West. Whereas, Isabella I of Castile (r. 1474–1504) and Archbishop Cisneros of Toledo pressed hard for Spanish crusading in North Africa, where Melilla was indeed captured in 1497 and Oran in 1509, her husband, Ferdinand of Aragon, was far more concerned about thwarting the French in Italy. Instead of reifying the polities into coherent states with clear-cut geopolitical drives, it is necessary to remember the complex nature of identities and interests and the extent of debate over policy.

A reminder of the difficulties facing any simple explanation of European successes can be accompanied by one of the extent and character of European failure alongside those of success. Indeed, it is possible to regard the triumph of the *conquistadores* as unique.[35] This is important for any comparative assessment of European military proficiency, and thus of any attempt to use it to create an explanation of relative global capability.

# 5

# EUROPEAN WARFARE
# 1494–1559

The background to European warfare in this period included not only the response to Ottoman strength, but also the continuing process of change in late medieval Europe. This owed something to new technology, but was also a consequence of political developments, specifically the growing strength of a number of states in the fifteenth century. As populations recovered from the fourteenth-century plague epidemic known as the Black Death, there was economic growth and an important measure of administrative development and political consolidation. This was seen in particular in France. The Valois kings, especially Louis XI (r. 1461–83), strengthened royal government and extended their territorial control within France, particularly through the defeat of England in 1450–3 and through benefiting from the Swiss defeat of Charles the Bold, Duke of Burgundy in 1476–7. The French had a standing (permanent) army, the first in Western Europe for a dynasty ruling a 'national' state.

## The spread of gunpowder technology

To begin with military technology, but without suggesting that it was necessarily crucial to success, these fifteenth-century conflicts saw an increased use of gunpowder weaponry, although that was not the only important shift in weaponry and tactical development of the period. Knowledge of gunpowder was brought from China to Europe in the thirteenth century, although the path of diffusion is unclear. In the following century, it was used in cannon, and in the fifteenth century in hand-held firearms. Between 1380 and 1525, gunpowder led to the supplanting of earlier missile weapons, the crossbow and the longbow, which had challenged the importance of cavalry.

Gunpowder brought major changes in battlefield tactics, fortification techniques, and siegecraft, and, more generally, in training, logistics and military finance. Handguns had greater penetrative power than bows, although they had a limited range, a low rate of fire, were affected by bad weather and were harder to make. Handguns were also not easy to use from horseback. Furthermore, they needed a supply of powder and shot, which was not easy to obtain, and, unlike arrows, not recyclable. Rather than assuming a shift from bows to arquebuses because of their specifications as weapons, it may be the case that it was their lower cost, compared to the crossbow, that led to their adoption.[1]

There was no comparable displacement of a well-established type of weaponry in the case of cannon. Although primarily of interest for their ability to destroy stone walls, and thus for their role in sieges, cannon came to play a greater operational role in campaigns. Outgunned powers were overcome. Cannon played a role in the French defeats of the English at Formigny (1450) and Castillon (1453), the closing battles of the Hundred Years' War, and they also did in the rapid capture of English fortresses in 1449–50.[2] The ability of Charles VII of France (r. 1422–61) to recover from the terrible weakness of his early years was a clear demonstration of the ability through war to secure military and political outcomes, although this recovery has to be linked to political as well as military factors.

Once introduced, there were also important developments in handguns. The arquebus, a handgun in which the powder was ignited by a length of slow-burning match, was developed in the 1420s and 1430s. As a consequence, it was possible to separate aiming the handgun from igniting the gunpowder charge, and this improved the value of handguns. By 1450, the Burgundians and French had them in large numbers. They were effective, as in the Burgundian wars against the Liégeois, and the Swiss and Burgundian wars of 1475–7. At the same time, the size of some armies rose considerably, not least those of France and Burgundy.

The Italian Wars (1494–1529) saw the working through of these themes. The search for the most effective means of employing gunpowder weapons contributed to a remarkable period of tactical experimentation, but, rather than arguing that firearms revolutionised warfare, it is important to focus on the way in which they slotted into existing tactical systems. The emphasis then is on adaptation and the combination of arms. This also leads to a new chronology: 'The effective tactical synthesis of infantry, cavalry and artillery achieved in the Italian Wars of 1494–1529 was contingent on the organisation and sophistication of the combined arms approach of fifteenth-century armies, most strikingly the Burgundians'.[3] Indeed, the Burgundians in the 1470s developed a deployment intended to combine cavalry, pikemen, crossbows, firearms and artillery on the battlefield. The cavalry was seen as the decisive arm, but Charles the Bold intended to use his missile fire, especially his archers, to counteract the Swiss pikemen.

More generally, whether or not this chronology is accepted, for many centuries, battles in Europe had usually involved a mixture of cavalry and infantry, and of firepower and hand-to-hand combat. This remained the case throughout the early modern period, and was to continue until rapid fire reduced the role of hand-to-hand combat while mechanisation led to the fusion of cavalry and artillery in tank warfare. The nature of these mixtures, especially the weaponry and tactics employed, varied and it is difficult to know on what criteria any variation or number of changes can be termed revolutionary. Cases have been made for the revolutionary consequences both of the adoption of the stirrup in the eighth century, which made it possible to use horsemen as shock troops, and of the use of gunpowder in artillery and hand-held firearms. These challenge any focus on the revolutionary character of change in 1500–1660 (see Chapter 3).

## The Italian Wars

The Italian Wars arose from the instability of the Italian peninsula, which was divided among a number of vulnerable powers, but also from a new willingness of outside rulers to intervene. Initially, the most important was Charles VIII of France (r. 1483–98), who had a standing army and an impressive train of artillery on wheeled carriages. Charles's cannon used iron shot, allowing smaller projectiles to achieve the same destructive impact as larger stone shot. This permitted smaller, lighter, more manoeuvrable cannon which were mounted permanently on wheeled carriages. With these, Charles invaded Italy in 1494 and captured Naples the following March. His artillery impressed contemporaries, leading the Aragonese in 1495 to begin to cast iron balls in the Naples arsenal, the Venetians to order the new cannon (100 wheeled 6- to 12-pounders) in 1496, and the Duke of Ferrara to begin the construction of new fortifications the same year.[4] Henry VII of England began stockpiling cannon almost immediately. The Venetians had already begun to replace their crossbows in 1490.

Charles VIII was unable to sustain his initial advantage. His success aroused opposition both within Italy, where there was growing suspicion that he aimed to seize the entire peninsula, and from two powerful rulers who had their own ambitions to pursue: Maximilian I, the Holy Roman Emperor, who ruled Austria and the other Habsburg territories, and Ferdinand of Aragon, ruler of Sicily and Sardinia, half-brother of Ferrante of Naples and husband of Isabella of Castille. Ferdinand combined Italian interests with Spanish resources. Ferdinand joined Venice, Milan and Pope Alexander VI in the League of St Mark (Venice).

Charles was forced to withdraw, although an attempt to cut off his retreat failed at Fornovo (6 July 1495): the Italian forces of the League of St Mark had numerical superiority but were poorly co-ordinated, and their cavalry was affected by the muddy nature of the terrain. The battle was largely a cavalry struggle, and suggested that French heavy cavalry still had a major role to play in achieving battlefield success. In southern Italy, heavy cavalry and Swiss pikemen also brought the French victory in April 1495 at Seminara over a Spanish force sent by Ferdinand of Aragon. However, the Neapolitans largely deserted Charles, French forces left behind in southern Italy were defeated at Atella (1496) and their surviving positions were successfully besieged.

Charles's successor, Louis XII (r. 1498–1515), who had taken part in the 1494 invasion, invaded the Duchy of Milan in 1499, claiming the Duchy on the grounds that his grandmother had been a Visconti. The Venetians also invaded the Duchy. The major positions fell to the French in August–September, while Genoa accepted a French governor. French troops were also sent to help Alexander VI's son, Cesar Borgia, in the Romagna. However, disaffection with French rule led to a rallying of support to Ludovico Sforza who regained Milan in February 1500. In turn, the strength of the French response and the evaporation of Swiss support led to the collapse of Sforza's army. Ludovico was sent a prisoner to France, where he died. Louis's power was reimposed in Milan.

Naples was to prove a more intractable task. Louis and Ferdinand partitioned Naples by the Treaty of Granada (11 November 1500). French troops easily stormed Capua and readily captured Naples in 1501. However, disputes with Ferdinand in 1502 led the French to try to take the entire kingdom.

The resulting battle of Cerignola (28 April 1503) offered a striking demonstration of the value of new weapons. The Spaniards were commanded by Gonzalo de Córdoba, the 'Great Captain', a veteran of the conquest of Granada, where firearms had already played an important role.[5] Córdoba encouraged tactical flexibility and had greatly increased the number of arquebusiers in his army after Seminara. He held his men in defence behind a trench and earth parapet, which stopped the attacking French cavalry, exposing them and their infantry first to Spanish fire, and then to a successful counter-attack. As the French attacked and were held by the trench, which they were unaware of, they were exposed to firepower at the short range at which it was effective. It was not so much the arquebuses that were effective, but rather missile weapons against a stalled assailant. Stalled attacking forces faced serious tactical problems.

This was one of a number of battles in which firearms provided the missile force, but did nothing that longbows and crossbows could not have done. The French were also affected by the fate of their leader, Louis, Duke of Nemours, who was shot from his horse by an arquebusier. Córdoba's revival of the art of field fortification had been used to devastating effect, although this was possible because the French attacked rapidly and without due care. They failed to bring up their artillery against the Spanish fieldworks. Having checked the French, the Spaniards then charged them with infantry and then cavalry, completing the victory.

After Cerignola, most of the French-held positions, including Naples, surrendered, although Gaeta held out. Córdoba defeated the French again at the Garigliano river (28 December 1503), breaking through their positions at the weakest point. Spanish victory led to the surrender of Gaeta on 1 January 1504. Louis XII renounced his claims to the kingdom by the Treaty of Blois of 12 October 1505, and it became part of the Spanish empire.[6]

Cerignola was the first in a series of battles in which a variety of weapons, weapon systems and tactics were tested in the search for a clear margin of military superiority. Italy was increasingly dominated by France and/or Spain, the only powers with the resources to support a major military effort. In contrast, other powers, especially Venice, defeated by Louis XII at Agnadello on 14 May 1509, Milan, the Swiss, and the Papacy, took less important and independent roles. Pope Julius II had formed the League of Cambrai in 1508 to attack Venice, but it was France's role that was decisive. At Agnadello, where the Venetian rearguard took on the much larger French army, the Venetian cavalry broke and fled, while the infantry was crushed, although the arquebusiers in Venetian service inflicted heavy casualties on the French cavalry before being defeated. After the battle, much of the Venetian *terraferma* rebelled, indicating the consequences of defeats in battle, but the impact of the French victory was lessened by Padua's success at resisting a siege in August and September 1509. It was strongly protected by recently-built outlying bastions.

The weakness of the Italian powers did not indicate any inability to respond to the changing nature of battle. Indeed, the Italians adapted to developments in the use of cannon and infantry firearms, and in other weaponry. Thus, they built up artillery parks, used cannon in conjunction with field entrenchments, and adopted both arquebuses and pikes.[7] However, they lacked the resources to match French or Spanish armies readily in battle. As with other periods of military history, however, this in part reflected both strategic culture and the political situation. In the case of the first, the leading independent Italian state, Venice, also had a major maritime role, as well as extensive military commitments in its overseas possessions. Indeed, it was at war with the Turks in 1499–1502. Genoa also focused on naval power. The political situation was also important. Italian rulers adapted to foreign invaders and sought to employ them to serve their own ends. Thus, there was no inherent conflict between these rulers and foreign powers. Instead, the Habsburgs and the Valois were able to find local allies.

## Ravenna, 1512

At the same time, weaker powers could help affect the relationship between France and Spain. Thus, in 1511, Pope Julius II's role in the formation of the Holy League with Spain, Venice and Henry VII of England to drive the French from Italy led to a resumption of Franco-Spanish hostilities. This led initially to the French storming of Brescia (18 February 1512), and then to a major battle at Ravenna on 11 April 1512. The French, under Gaston de Foix (1489–1512), a nephew of Louis XII, besieged Ravenna, and a Spanish relieving force under Ramon de Cardona and, under him, Pedro Navarro, who had commanded the arquebusiers and artillery at Cerignola, advanced and took up a nearby defensive position. This reflected Navarro's conviction that the advantage lay with the defence. The unprecedented length of the artillery exchange at the start of the battle (two hours) testified to the growing battlefield importance of cannon. To force them to attack, the French artillery bombarded the Spaniards, finally prompting an unplanned Spanish cavalry charge. This was repelled by a charge by the French heavy cavalry, but Spanish arquebusiers, sheltered by a trench and parapet, defeated an advance by French crossbowmen. German pikemen (*Landsknechte*)[8] in French service were more successful, but were forced back by Spanish swordsmen. Finally, the French cavalry, now returned from the pursuit, exploited gaps in the Spanish defensive system to turn the flank of their infantry. Encouraged, the French infantry resumed their assault on the Spanish positions. The Spaniards retreated, although they were able to maintain their cohesion. Casualties were very heavy: about 4,000 in the French army and 9,000 in the Spanish.

The French had won, largely thanks to their heavy cavalry and to superior co-ordination of the various arms of their forces. The battle represented a remarkable competition of different weapons systems. This reflected the state of flux in weaponry, and the process of improvisation in adoption and adaptation of weapons and tactics that this entailed. In addition, perceived 'national' differences were linked to fighting methods. The French put their emphasis on heavy cavalry and preferred to hire foreign pikemen, a course that drove up the price of providing pikemen. The French were also not noted for having many arquebusiers. The key element of their peacetime army was the *gendarmerie* (heavy cavalry), organised in *compagnies d'ordonnance* and armed with lances. Mounted archers provided support that was supplemented from the 1550s by mounted pistoleers. The Swiss and Germans were noted as pikemen, equally formidable in offence and defence, but vulnerable to firearms and tactically less flexible than the Spanish swordsmen (or sword-and-buckler men). The latter had a considerable advantage in close-quarter fighting: they could get under the pikes by pushing them up with their shields, but were vulnerable to pikemen at greater distances. The Spaniards also had effective light cavalry.

Ravenna demonstrated the importance of firepower: French cannon fire provoked the Spaniards to charge, but the course of the battle was determined by the greater tactical flexibility of the French cavalry, which were able not only to win the cavalry battle but also, eventually, to determine the fate of the infantry struggle. Foix's death in the closing stages of the battle followed by Swiss intervention against France and opposition to the French in Genoa and Milan helped the Spaniards to regain the initiative. The French retreated across the Alps, while the Spaniards overran Tuscany and Massimiliano Sforza was installed in Milan. Meanwhile, Ferdinand of Aragon had conquered the kingdom of Navarre, which was to be a permanent gain. The French attempt to reconquer the kingdom failed when an unsuccessful siege of Pamploma late in the year was followed by an arduous winter retreat across the Pyrenees. In 1513, the French invaded across the Alps anew, supported by the Venetians.

Sforza and his Swiss mercenaries retreated to Novara where they were besieged by the French, only for the Swiss to send a relief army that moved too swiftly for the French. At Novara (6 June 1513), advancing Swiss pikemen competed with artillery, which inflicted heavy casualties until overrun by the experienced pikemen, thanks to the weakness of the French position – taken by surprise, they had not had time to entrench – and the inferior quality of the *Landsknechte* in their army. Left without protection, the French arquebusiers were also routed: their cavalry was not ready for combat in time. After Novara, Cardona turned against the Venetians, ravaging the *terraferma* to the shores of the Venetian lagoon and defeating Bartolomeo d'Alviano at La Motta (7 October 1513). The following year, Padua fell to the Spaniards.

Soon after coming to the French throne, Francis I (r. 1515–47) invaded the Milanese anew. He was victorious at Marignano (13–14 September) 1515: however, the two days of the battle suggested that different conclusions could be drawn about the effectiveness of particular arms. On the first day, the French cavalry played a major role in resisting the Swiss, and they were held by Francis I's *Landsknechte*. The next day, the attacking Swiss suffered badly from the French cannon, because, on this occasion, the French fought from an entrenched position. The pikemen also suffered fire from crossbows and arquebuses and were attacked in the flank by French cavalry.

Victory led to a new territorial and political order. Having occupied Milan in 1499–1500, and 1500–12, the French occupied it anew from 1515 until 1521. There was also a dynastic settlement. Under the Peace of Noyon of 1516, Maximilian's grandson Charles, later the Emperor Charles V, was to marry a French princess, and the French rights to the kingdom of Naples were to go with her. However, the election of Charles (already Duke of Burgundy, Archduke of Austria and ruler, through his Spanish grandparents, Ferdinand and Isabella, of Spain, Naples, Sicily, Sardinia and the Spanish conquests in the Indies) as the Holy Roman Emperor Charles V in 1519 seemed to confirm the worst French fears of Habsburg hegemony.[9]

## Bicocca, 1522

Successive kings of France were unwilling to accept Habsburg primacy. It challenged both their interests and their prestige. Francis I declared war on Charles in 1521, and the main theatre of conflict was again northern Italy, although there was also fighting in the Low Countries and the Pyrenees. The French lost Milan in November 1521 and suffered a major defeat at nearby Bicocca on 27 April 1522. This was a battle in which the limited control of commanders over their forces played an important role. The French commander Odet de Foix, Marquis de Lautrec, was in a powerful position, besieging Pavia with a larger army, and thus obliging the Habsburgs to attempt a hazardous relief operation. But he was short of funds, and his core troops, Swiss mercenaries, were under only limited control. The Habsburg relief army, under Prospero Colonna, an experienced Italian commander, was entrenched close to Pavia, and Lautrec hoped to cut its supply routes, thus forcing Colonna into the open. The Swiss, however, demanded an immediate attack on Colonna's position in order to gain booty.

The increased emphasis on field fortification that had become a feature of the Italian Wars can be seen clearly in Colonna's position. Behind a sunken road was a parapet manned by four lines of arquebusiers backed by pikemen. Cannon were well-sited in a series of bastions. Lautrec appreciated that this would be a difficult position to take, and proposed to bring up artillery to prepare for his attack.

Unpaid and threatening to return home, the Swiss refused to wait and their 8,000 pikemen advanced in two squares. They took heavy losses from cannon and arquebus fire, losses that mounted as they struggled to scale the parapet. Those who did so were driven back by *Landsknechte*. Thus, the strengths of the Spanish position compensated for one of the major problems with firearms, their slow rate of fire which led to a vulnerability in the face of a rapidly-advancing opponent. Firearms were again proved effective in defence, where the latter could rely on field entrenchments. Having lost 3,000 men, including, crucially, many veterans, the Swiss, still unpaid, returned home; their caution at the battle of Pavia in 1525 was attributed to the losses at Bicocca. These losses fuelled the propaganda campaign against mercenary service launched by Ulrich Zwingli, the leading Swiss Protestant: he had served as an army chaplain.

After Bicocca, Lautrec was left without an effective army and the French position in northern Italy collapsed. In 1523, Venice felt that it had to ally with Charles V. That year, however, invasion attempts on France from Spain, Germany and England all failed to make an impact. In turn, Francis I sent an army into northern Italy, which unsuccessfully besieged Milan, before being driven out in early 1524 by the Habsburg forces reinforced from Germany and supported from Venice.

In 1524, Charles V again attempted to mount a concerted invasion of France with Henry VIII of England and Charles, Duke of Bourbon, a rebel against Francis. These concerted invasions reflect the ambitious scope of strategic planning in the period, although such schemes were not new, while their failure and lack of co-ordination in 1523 and 1524 testified to the limitations of strategic execution. The Spaniards and Bourbon invaded France on 1 July and easily overran Provence, but, in light of the delay of the other planned attacks, the invasion force turned on Marseilles, rather than advancing into central France via Lyons. However, the city was ably defended. Breaches made by cannon fire were filled by earthworks, the Spaniards were unwilling to storm the position, the Spanish navy was unable to drive off its French/Genoese rival, and, in the face of a French relief army, the invasion force retreated.

## Pavia, 1525

In pursuit, Francis invaded Italy again in October 1524. Battered by their unsuccessful invasion, the Spaniards were in no shape to resist in the field. Instead, as in 1523, they concentrated on holding fortified positions. Francis captured Milan and turned to besiege Pavia. Allied from December 1524 with the Pope, Clement VII, and with Venice, Francis detached an army under John, Duke of Albany to invade Naples, but this failed to lead the Spaniards to abandon northern Italy. Instead, they moved to the relief of Pavia, leading to the battle of Pavia on 24 February 1525.

Under pressure from dwindling funds, the Spaniards attacked quickly, achieving surprise by breaching the French lines in the dark. Having placed themselves across the French communication routes, the Spaniards adopted a defensive position, with arquebusiers on the flanks and pikemen and cavalry in the centre, in order to await French counter-attacks. The French cavalry attack defeated the Spanish cavalry, but was held by the pikemen and pummelled by arquebus fire. A subsequent advance by the Swiss pikemen in French service was thrown back by the arquebusiers, without need for much reliance on the Imperialist pikemen (i.e. pikemen in the service of Charles V). Finally, a combination of Spanish pikemen and arquebusiers, particularly the former, defeated the renegade 'Black Band' *Landsknechte*, whose service in the cause of France was illegal under the Imperial constitution. French casualties were far higher and Francis himself was captured.

It is not easy to use Pavia in order to make definitive statements about the effectiveness of particular arms because, even more than most battles, it was confused, thanks to the effects of heavy early morning fog, and also the extent to which many of the advances were both small-unit and unco-ordinated; while the surviving sources contain discrepancies. Alongside arguments about the superiority of a particular weapon in a given confrontation, in this case the arquebus against cavalry, it is also necessary to make due allowance for Spanish effectiveness in the small-unit engagements they sought: 'the Spanish were scattered in small units all over the field without a definite battle line'. These formations were employed in an effective way (although, as in most battles, it would be misleading to emphasise the possibilities for, and extent of, central direction), responding to the French advances by moving out of danger *and* bringing firepower to bear, in particular to enfilade Francis and his cavalry. It is also necessary to give due emphasis to the terrain. Part of the battlefield was poor cavalry country, not least in the early morning fog. Marshy and brush-covered terrain delayed the French cavalry, making them targets for Spanish fire. This emphasises the role of generalship. Francis played to the Marquis of Pescara's advantage by advancing in a way that enabled the Spaniards to use their army to maximum advantage. The French advance also masked their artillery. This was the very opposite of cavalry–artillery co-ordination.

Pavia was a battle decided by the combination of pikemen and arquebus-iers fighting in the open, rather than depending on field fortifications.

Repeated attacks by the French cavalry were defeated. Artillery had played little part. On the Spanish side, the novel skirmishing tactics of Pescara's light infantry were effective.[10] However much advantage in Pavia and other battles is attributed to firepower, as armies developed tactics that did not pitch vulnerable forces against shot, so the edge gained simply by using it diminished.

## 1525–30

Pavia was decisive in the short-term. Albany's army disintegrated, while the captured Francis signed the Treaty of Madrid (14 January 1526) on Charles V's terms, enabling Charles to invest his ally Francesco Sforza with the Duchy of Milan. Nevertheless, once released, Francis repudiated the terms, claimed that his agreement had been extorted, and agreed with Pope Clement VII, Sforza, Venice and Florence to establish the League of Cognac (22 May 1526). This renewed the challenge to Charles in Italy.

War resumed in 1526, with a successful Spanish siege of the citadel of Milan. The Venetian-papal relief army under Duke Francesco of Urbino moved too slowly and cautiously, and those were not the qualities required when mounting a successful relief. Urbino subsequently besieged Cremona successfully, and then turned against Milan, only to be forced to abandon the siege in the face of the arrival of German troops.

In March 1527, a truce between Pope Clement and Charles V left the latter's army unoccupied. Charles was short of money to pay the *Landsknechte*. Angry, the latter marched on Rome under Bourbon and stormed the city on 6 May. The subsequent Sack of Rome inflicted very heavy damage and was a brutal display of the extent to which troops were willing to turn on civil society. Clement was forced to surrender. Francis sought to exploit the situation. An army of 21,000 men under Lautrec sent across the Alps overran the bulk of the Milanese and stormed Pavia, while the imperialist faction lost control of Genoa. Lautrec then invaded the kingdom of Naples and the city of Naples was blockaded by land and sea. However, Francis's mishandling of Andrea Doria, the dominant figure in Genoa, led the Genoese fleet to turn to Charles, while the French outside Naples were hit by plague and forced in August, when Lautrec died of it, to abandon the siege. In northern Italy, the Imperialists had made gains when Lautrec marched south, but were challenged by a new French army under Saint Pol in late 1528. This, however, was defeated on the march at Landriano on 20 June 1529. That month, Clement VII and Charles concluded the Treaty of Barcelona.

Repeated defeats led Francis to accept the Treaty of Cambrai (3 August 1529), abandoning his Italian pretensions. Francesco Sforza was restored to Milan, but with the right to garrison the citadel reserved to Charles, an indication of the importance of the fortifications there. Venice, which had gained control of a number of ports in Apulia in 1495–1509 and 1528–9, finally returned them to the kingdom of Naples; while Ravenna and Cérvia were restored to Clement VII. Imperial power was brutally displayed by the successful siege of Florence in 1529–30, after which Charles V restored the Medici to power. Charles's power was also shown at Bologna on 24 February 1530, when Pope Clement crowned him Emperor.[11] The removal of Artois and Flanders from the suzerainty of the French crown in the treaties of 1525 and 1529 with Charles was the first major retreat of the crown from the frontier of 843. The frontier between the territories of Francis and Charles became that between France and the Empire.

The high rate of battles in this period in part reflected the effectiveness of siege artillery. As fortified positions could not be relied on to hold out it was necessary to risk pitched battle in order to resist invaders. In contrast, the latter stages of the Italian Wars were to see fewer battles, probably because a growing ability to resist sieges, thanks to better fortifications and more cannon in defensive positions, made it possible to rely on garrisons in order to hold territory, and ensured that there was less call to resist invasion by battle unless circumstances appeared propitious.

## The 1530s

War resumed after the death of Sforza in November 1535 led to a disputed succession in Milan. Francis invaded Italy in March 1536, conquering Savoy and Piedmont in order to clear the route into northern Italy. In response, the Spaniards invaded Provence in July 1536, only to find the French army unwilling to fight, and the countryside devastated in order to remove supplies. Unable to force a verdict, the Spaniards withdrew in September. Then also the siege of Peronne by an Imperial force from the Low Countries was abandoned. In turn, the French attacked Artois in 1537, capturing Hesdin, but the local Estates were willing to provide funds for their defence and Francis abandoned the invasion. The inability of either side to secure particular advantage led to an armistice in November 1537, which became a ten-year truce the following June. As this was on the basis of *uti possidetis* (retaining what was held), Francis was left in control of Savoy, while, in 1540, Charles invested his son Philip (later Philip II) with the Duchy of Milan.

Charles had reorganised his Spanish troops into *tercios* (thirds) in 1534, taking further the formation created by Córdoba in 1504. This grouped together companies of pikemen and arquebusiers in order to produce an effective battlefield formation that displayed its tactical flexibility into the following century. The initial ratio was towards pikemen and this indicated the ancillary role of firepower at that stage.

As with the Thirty Years' War (1618–48), the latter stages of the Italian Wars have received insufficient attention. This poses several serious problems for the analysis of the development of warfare in the period. There is an emphasis on the early stages of each sequence of wars and a failure to consider how far conclusions drawn from their analysis are more widely applicable. The war of 1536–8 is largely neglected because there were no large-scale pitched battles. There is a similar problem with the conflicts of the period 1560–1617, in that the emphasis is on the early stages of the Dutch Revolution, especially in the early 1570s, while the warfare of the 1600s and 1610s receives insufficient attention.

## The 1540s

The rivalry between Francis and Charles continued and was encouraged by the latter's suspicion of links between Francis and the Ottomans. Francis was encouraged by the failure of Charles's expedition against Algiers in late 1541. The following summer, the French attacked. Francis invaded Roussillon, but his siege of Perpignan was unsuccessful and the French fell back. Initially successful, the Duke of Orléans's invasion of Luxembourg was not sustained. In addition, the Duke of Vendôme's invasion of Artois did not lead to hoped for risings in Ghent or Antwerp. The allied forces of Duke William of Cleves inflicted considerable damage in the Low Countries, but did not sway the struggle. The 1542 campaign showed the difficulty of mounting concerted operations and, also, demonstrated, what was again to be shown in the 1630s and 1640s, that it was very difficult for France to wage successful operations on several fronts.

In 1543, Francis moved into Hainault, but Charles invaded the lands of the Duke of Cleves, stormed Duren, and forced the Duke to terms which included the cession of Guelders and Zutphen (7 September). This showed the potential tempo and effectiveness of campaigning in this period. Francis's inability to support his ally transformed the strategic situation. Charles then advanced into Hainault, besieged Landrecies and marched out to try to force the nearby Francis into battle. Francis preferred to retreat, which boosted Charles's prestige.

In 1544, the French invaded northern Italy again, leading to a battle as the Spaniards tried to relieve a besieged position. On 11 April, the French under François de Bourbon won the battle of Ceresole in Piedmont. Although the infantry were well-matched, the superior and more numerous French cavalry, operating on good cavalry terrain, defeated their opponents, and the *Landsknechte* withdrew, their casualties over twenty-five per cent. The relatively immobile artillery played little role in the battle. Each side revealed innovation in deployment in the form of interspersed arquebusiers and pikemen, the resulting square formations designed to be both self-sustaining and mutually supporting, although it is probable that, as yet, this system had not attained the chequer-board regularity seen later in the century. Bringing arquebusiers into the pike formations drove up the casualties when they clashed, and contemporaries agreed that they were particularly heavy at

Ceresole. As at Pavia, any summary of the battle underplays its confused variety. As a result of both the hilly topography and the distinct formations involved, the battle was a number of struggles. The French cavalry was successful at the ends of both lines, while, in the centre, the French cavalry swung the devastating battle between the infantry by attacking the flank of the *Landsknechte*. In contrast, on the left, the Spanish infantry defeated its French counterpart and then successfully resisted unsupported French cavalry attacks causing heavy casualties, before retreating when the centre collapsed, only to suffer heavy casualties on the retreat.

Victory at Ceresole did not transform the situation in Italy, in part because a lack of pay made Swiss mercenaries unwilling to fight for Milan. Indeed, the Spaniards retained their fortified positions in Lombardy. Instead, the decisive campaigning, although without a battle, took place north of the Alps where the Imperialists recovered Luxembourg, successfully besieged St Dizier, and advanced via Châlons and Château-Thierry to Soissons. Francis I had to recruit 16,000 Swiss to strengthen his position. Henry VIII had also invaded, although the English sieges of Montreuil and Boulogne did not contribute to Charles V's position. Under pressure, Francis was willing to accept the Peace of Crépy (18 September 1544).

This success, and a truce with the Ottoman's in October 1545, enabled Charles to turn to Germany where the opposition of the Protestant princes compromised his power. After an attempt at religious reconciliation had failed at the Diet of Augsburg in 1530, the Protestant princes had created the Schmalkalden League (1531). Charles, however, continued to hope that a Church council could reunite Christendom. Negotiations at the Diet of Regensburg (1541) failed, and, at the Diet of Worms (1545), the Protestants rejected the suggestion that a General Council of the Church be held.

The Schmalkaldic War began in 1546. Insisting that he was acting against disobedient vassals, rather than Protestants, Charles used Spanish troops under the Duke of Alba to defeat the leading German Protestant, Elector John Frederick of Saxony, at Mühlberg on 24 April 1547. The Elector was captured, and, two months later, the other Protestant leader in opposition, Philip of Hesse, who had been defeated first, surrendered. Victory in Germany helped Charles strengthen Habsburg authority in Bohemia where some of the nobility had looked to the Schmalkaldic powers who had prepared to invade the kingdom. Charles had been helped by the neutrality of France (a consequence of the secret terms of the Peace of Crépy) and by the support of Protestant princes who hoped to benefit personally: Duke Maurice of Saxony (a different branch of the dynasty) and Margrave Albert Alcibiades of Brandenburg-Kulmbach. The victory reflected the combination of military and political factors characteristic of the conflict in the period, not only of the Wars of Religion, but also of the Italian Wars. Charles exploited his victory to dictate peace terms at the 'Armed Diet' of Augsburg. The Electorate of Saxony was transferred to Maurice in 1550.

## 1550s

Had Charles been able to sustain and further this result, then the Reformation would have been more clearly seen in a pattern of medieval politico-religious disorders, and Western Europe might well, even if only temporarily, have had a hegemonic power. Bullion from the New World could have been used to sustain the traditional universalist aspirations of the Holy Roman Emperors.

However, the failure to produce a lasting religious settlement, divisions between Charles and his brother Ferdinand, and the opportunism of Maurice of Saxony and Albert of Brandenburg-Kulmbach, led to a French-supported rising in 1552 which drove Charles from Germany at a time when he was also weakened by renewed conflict with the Ottomans and by opposition in Italy. The burden of pressures and commitments proved too great for Charles's *imperium*, in large part because of rivalry among the Catholic powers. In March, Francis I's successor, Henry II (r. 1547–59), overran Lorraine and seized the bishoprics of Metz, Toul and Verdun, although an attempt to press on to gain Strasbourg failed. Charles had to flee from Germany to distant Carinthia. However, he gathered his forces together and tried to rectify the situation, although his attempt, at the head of 55,000–59,000 men, to regain Metz failed. It was foolish to mount a major siege late in the year.

Both sides were fielding far larger forces than their predecessors had done, although it is difficult to be precise about figures, and the rulers were to be unable to sustain troop numbers. Charles had a total of about 148,000 men under arms around Metz, in Germany, the Low Countries, Italy, Spain and facing the Ottomans. Henry had armies in Eastern France and Italy, and was able to force Charles to abandon the siege of Metz by seizing Hesdin in Artois. Albert switched sides to back Charles, only to be defeated at Sievershausen (9 July 1553) and to be driven into exile the following year.

The compromise Peace of Augsburg was negotiated in Germany in 1555, and a truce between Charles and Henry in 1556. The Augsburg settlement accepted the position of Lutheranism, at least to the extent of allowing Lutheran territorial rulers within the Empire to make Lutheranism the religion of their territories. There was no universal right to religious choice. Charles also divided his empire between his brother, the Emperor Ferdinand I, who received the German part of the inheritance, and his son, Philip II of Spain, who got the rest: Spain, the Italian territories, the Low Countries and the Spanish territories in the New World. This was a division Charles chose, rather than one forced upon him by opponents.

In 1557, war resumed with a French invasion of Italy and a Spanish advance into France from the Low Countries. The latter led to an important victory for the invaders at St Quentin (10 August 1557), when a relieving army for the besieged fortress was heavily defeated. In the battle, the Spaniards made effective use of their cavalry, especially of pistoleers in which they outnumbered the French. Philip II organised the campaign that led to this victory. He followed this up by leading the successful storming of Arras.

The French were defeated again at Gravelines on 13 July 1558, when they tried to take Dunkirk by surprise attack, although, that January, French forces bombarded Calais, England's last foothold on mainland France, into surrender in a campaign characterised by bold French generalship: Mary Tudor, Queen of England (r. 1553–8) was the wife of Philip II, and she had declared war on France in June 1557. Gravelines can be compared to the English victory over the Scots at Pinkie in 1547 and the French over the Spaniards at the battle of the Dunes in 1658: the defeated force suffered from the heavy fire its opponents were able to bring to bear from land and sea; at Gravelines, from English ships under Captain John Malen. The pistoleers in the Spanish army outnumbered their French counterparts, and both won the cavalry fight and hit the French pike, who were also affected by Spanish arquebus fire.

Bankrupt, alarmed by the spread of French Protestantism, and without support from the German Protestants, on 2 April 1559, Henry accepted the Treaty of Cateau-Cambrésis, by which Spain was left in control of Milan, Naples, Sicily and Sardinia. Savoy and Piedmont, which France had seized in 1536, were returned to Duke Emanuel Philibert of Savoy, a Habsburg client. The French also had to yield their positions in Tuscany. The Habsburgs had won the Italian Wars, and this triumph was not to be seriously challenged until the 1640s.

As in earlier periods, the wars of the 1550s in Italy not only saw a clash between major powers, but also related struggles involving others. Thus, Spain fought Pope Paul IV, and also supported Florence in attacking the republic of Siena in 1554: after a ten-month siege, Siena surrendered to be annexed by Florence. This was an example of the extent to which divisions within Italy had interacted with those between the major powers: in 1552, Siena had rebelled against Spanish control and, in co-operation with France, seized the citadel from the Spaniards. Florence under the Medici was, from the late 1520s, an ally of the Habsburgs.

## Reformation warfare

The Schmalkaldic War marked the transition from the Italian Wars to the Wars of Religion that were to characterise the last four decades of the sixteenth century. More generally, from the beginning of the Reformation, religion came to play a major role in conflicts. This was particularly so in Germany, where Martin Luther launched what became the Reformation in 1517. The extensive territories of the numerous ecclesiastical principalities offered many tempting targets for Protestant takeover and secularisation. In addition, religion played a major role in rivalry between princely rulers, as with the seizure in 1542 of the Duchy of Brunswick-Wolfenbüttel by the leading Protestant rulers, the Elector of Saxony and the Landgrave of Hesse.

Religion also played a major role in the outbreak of war among the Swiss Confederation. The Reformation split this already divided body. Zurich, initially the leading centre of the Reformation, argued that religion was a cantonal matter, but in 1524 most of the other cantons tried to cajole it into maintaining Catholicism. However, that summer, Protestants from Zurich sought to spread the faith in the Thurgau where Zurich had jurisdictional rights. Religious activism rapidly led to violence, in this case to an attack on a monastery at Illingen and the destruction of images. At the end of the year, Zwingli tried to make Zurich a centre for Protestant activity. Far from this being restricted to the Swiss cantons, his proposals including raising the Tyrol against Habsburg rule. At the end of 1527, a (Protestant) Christian Civic League was created, but the Catholics responded with a Christian Union and the Habsburgs tried to intervene on the Catholic side. Disputes over the Common Lands of the Confederation and over St Gallen, which Zurich sought to secularise, led to war in June 1528, but the unwillingness of the soldiers of both armies to fight led to a compromise peace later that month. Conflict resumed in October 1531, but the Zurich army was defeated at Kappel on 11 October, Zwingli being among the dead. Another defeat followed near Zug on 24 October, and Zurich had to accept terms. In 1536, however, the Swiss Protestants relieved Geneva from siege by the Duke of Savoy and conquered Lausanne and the Pays de Vaud.

Wars were rarely fought for exclusively religious reasons, but religion was important in transforming local conflicts into either general European ones, or, at least, into 'national' conflicts. In the late fifteenth century, politics and warfare in, for example, northern Germany were only loosely connected to events in southern Germany. With growing confessional antagonism, at least from the 1530s, every local or regional conflict in which opponents were involved who subscribed to different confessional options, which was nearly always the case, assumed a far greater nation-wide importance. Alliances were formed comprising many, if not all, members of a confessional group nation-wide. Confessional antagonism created a national, as opposed to regional, framework for conflict in Germany and Scotland, and, also, in France after 1560. In addition, French willingness to support the German Protestants and to ally with the Ottomans set a pattern in which warring blocs did not equate with religious divisions.

## Fortresses and weapons

A bald recital of campaigns does not help to locate the period in terms of military developments, although it does make it clear that there was a frequency of conflict that encouraged the dissemination of what appeared to be the most effective techniques and also adaptation to their challenge. The frequency of conflict in part reflected the extent to which the ability of European states to finance military activity increased in the late fifteenth and early sixteenth centuries, with their greater political consolidation, administrative development and economic growth, as populations recovered from the fourteenth-century Black Death. Although this process of consolidation was to be challenged from the 1520s, as the impact of the Protestant Reformation increased domestic divisions, the demographic growth of the sixteenth century helped ensure that more resources could be tapped, both manpower and finances. Growing governmental strength and sophistication was most apparent at sea, where fleets far larger and more powerful than those of the fifteenth century were created and maintained.

It was also obvious in the ambitious fortification programmes of the period. Fortifications designed to cope with artillery and, more particularly, fifteenth-century improvements in artillery, were first constructed in large numbers in Italy. The use of earthworks preceded the full *trace italienne*. They were a relatively inexpensive way to strengthen the defences, not least by making it harder to storm them. Free-standing interior earth ramparts helped protect Pisa in 1500 and Padua in 1509 from storming. The polygonal bastion, a more expensive undertaking, developed from the 1450s with important work by Francesco di Giorgio Martini (1439–1501) and the Sangallo family. The techniques of bastioned works were then spread across Europe by Italian architects. Cannon were most effective against the stationary target of high stone walls, so fortifications were redesigned to provide lower, denser and more complex targets, the new system known as the *trace italienne*. Bastions, generally quadrilateral, angled, and at regular intervals along all walls, were introduced to provide gun platforms able to provide effective flanking fire, while defences were lowered and strengthened with earth. New-style fortifications were particularly important in Italy, being built, for example, at Civitavecchia in 1515, Florence in 1534, Ancona in 1536 and Genoa in 1536–8. Alongside the geometrical focus on perfect shapes, it is necessary to underline the extent to which fortification techniques were adapted to terrain and topography and the degree to which many fortresses, for example Berwick-upon-Tweed and Limerick, were amalgams of works from different periods.

The *trace italienne* was not the sole response to the challenge of gunpowder. In Russia, fortresses were adapted to the threat of artillery with a strengthening of stone walls and an increase in the number of firing positions. In 1527, the German artist Albrecht Dürer published a treatise on fortification, *Etlich Underrich zur Befestigung der Stelt Schloss und Flecken*, that proposed walls dominated by massive squat roundrels: towers that would also provide gunplatforms. Strengthened by earth and timber, such squat towers were better able to take bombardment then high walls. In England, Henry VIII built forts that did not employ the *trace italienne* along the south coast. Their chief role was to deny landing points to an enemy fleet, and as the ships of the period did not carry very heavy artillery, it was not necessary to use the *trace*. More generally, for every new fort, there were older positions that had to be adapted. In addition, an important consequence of the bastion system was that its sprawling, multi-lined and comparatively low-lying conformation demanded much larger garrisons than the defence of the old-bastioned castles or walled towns, which on occasion could be held by astonishingly small garrisons.

Stronger defences, which also provided secure artillery platforms, obliged attacking forces to mount sieges with more extensive lines of blockade, and therefore to employ larger numbers of troops, although it has been argued that this was more true of the seventeenth than of the sixteenth century.[12] Improvements in fortification technique lessened the decisiveness of artillery in siege warfare. This was further lessened by the availability of artillery on both sides. To be effective in breaching walls, siege cannon had to fire from close range, but this exposed them to fire from the fortress (as well as to raids by sortying parties). As a result of the former, the attacker dug zig-zag trenches, generally by night, in order to provide cover for the cannon, a time-consuming process. Mining under the walls, and then destroying them by means of an explosion of gunpowder, was an important ancillary technique, but its possibilities depended on the nature of the site, particularly of the underlying rock and the extent of waterlogging. The difficulty of mounting a successful siege ensured that the window of opportunity that had been created by the development of artillery was largely closed.

Fortresses and sieges featured importantly in the Italian Wars, and elsewhere. A series of unsuccessful sieges marked the limits of Ottoman advance. Charles V's failure to take Metz in 1552 led to his loss of strategic impetus. Fortresses were significant as a concrete manifestation of control over an area and many battles, for example that of the Spurs between England and France (16 August 1513), were related to attempts to relieve sieges, in this case the English siege of Thérouanne. However, the expense of constructing, maintaining and garrisoning such positions was a major burden, one of the many ways in which war pressed heavily on state budgets.

Although the limited mobility and slow rate of fire of cannon did not prevent them from playing a crucial role in sieges and at sea (where the mobility of ships compensated for the immobility of cannon), they were less important in battle. The crucial firearms there were hand-held, but, although important, they were not yet sufficiently developed to drive cutting, stabbing and slashing weapons from the field. The accuracy of smoothbore guns was limited. Spherical bullets were less aerodynamically effective than their nineteenth-century replacements. Accuracy would have been increased by rifling the barrel, which helps give a controlled spin to the projectile fire, but this was not practical because of the difficulty of muzzle loading if the shot had to be pushed down rifled grooves. Reloading rifled barrels took longer than smoothbores. Furthermore, the large windage (gap between projectile and inside of barrel) made necessary by the difficulty of casting accurate shot, would have lessened the value of rifling. Too tight a fit might lead to an explosion in the barrel. Recharging and reloading from the muzzle (rather than, as later, the breech) increased the time taken to use the guns. The slow rate of fire ensured a long reloading cycle which led to acute vulnerability.

There were improvements to firearms in this period although they did not overcome their deficiencies. The musket, a heavier version of the arquebus, capable of firing a heavier shot further and thus of penetrating armour, was used from the 1520s. Heavier shot is less affected by deviations than lighter shot, and this made it more accurate. However, even with muskets, accuracy was still low at long range and the ability of spherical shot to inflict lethal wounds at other than short range was limited. This increased the vulnerability of infantry armed with firearms to attack by cavalry or pikemen and thus the need for pikemen to provide defence. The limited ability of shot to inflict dangerous wounds helped account for the continued popularity of body armour as it could provide protection against most gunshot wounds. In terms of 'modernity', this helped ensure that the battlefield did not have the look of the nineteenth- or twentieth-century battlefield on which soldiers did not wear body armour. The musket was a cumbersome weapon which required a portable rest to support the barrel. To complicate the situation, the words 'musket' and 'musketeer' came in part to replace other descriptions of firearms.

From the 1520s, the wheel-lock mechanism also spread. Unlike the arquebus, which required a lighted fuse, and was therefore a match-lock, the wheel-lock relied on a trigger-operated spring which brought together a piece of iron pyrites or flint and a turning steel wheel. The contact produced sparks which ignited the gunpowder. Thus, the glowing (and easily extinguished) match of the arquebus could be dispensed with.

The wheel-lock mechanism was more expensive and delicate than the match-lock, but better suited to the needs of the cavalry, as it required only one hand to operate. Similarly, the stabbing weapons of cavalry were lighter than those of the infantry. Wheel-lock mechanisms worked the pistol used by cavalry. It was possible to fire the pistol while moving, and, as three pistols could be carried, to fire several shots before reloading. Furthermore, the muzzle velocities of pistols were sufficient to cause nasty wounds if targets were hit. Pistols were used by the Imperial troops in their campaigns in Italy in 1544 and Germany in 1546. They were used in the tactic of the *caracole*, in which ranks of cavalry advanced in order and fired their pistols before wheeling away from the enemy. This manoeuvre was criticised by commentators, not least because they claimed that pistoleers fired from too far away and that it discouraged cavalry from closing with opposing infantry. It was understandable that they fired from too far, because pistols were outranged by infantry firearms.

The effectiveness of cavalry firepower depended on the opposing response. Although infantry could offer more formidable firepower, if stationary and unsupported they left the initiative with the cavalry. In 1552, German cavalry armed with pistols defeated the French at Saint Vincent. Such horsemen also pressed the Swiss square at the battle of Dreux (19 December 1562), but were eventually driven back. These horsemen did not tend to wear full suits of armour, and, although such suits continued to be produced, their functional value declined. Pistoleers were a challenge to heavy cavalry, not least if they did not employ the *caracole*, but, instead, fired and then rode into the opposing ranks using swords. The lance still used by French heavy cavalry was insufficiently flexible as a weapon for such a struggle.

Too close a focus on gunpowder weapons makes it easy to overlook the importance of the pike, which transformed infantry tactics. Useless as an individual weapon, because it was heavy and inflexible and could not provide all-round protection, the pike was devastating *en masse* in disciplined formations. This led to a need for trained, professional infantry, far superior to most medieval levies. The Swiss had gained great prestige as pikemen by their defeat of the combined arms forces, especially strong in cavalry, of Charles the Bold of Burgundy at Grandson (2 March 1476), Murten (22 June 1476) and Nancy (5 January 1477), although the sweeping quality of the last two victories owed much to the presence of cavalry able to harry the retreating Burgundians. These victories led other powers to hire (France) or emulate (several German rulers) the Swiss. At Guinegate (7 August 1479), Maximilian used pikemen to beat a French army strong in firepower.

However, as so often with military innovations that created a capability gap, it is necessary to be cautious in assessing the causes, extent and nature of the gap. The Swiss benefited in their victories over Charles the Bold from their pikemen, but also from his poor leadership and from cavalry they were provided with by allies. Far from conferring a long-term advantage, the Italian Wars revealed the Swiss formation of large and dense blocs of pikemen to be vulnerable and their tactics to be rigid. To maintain their mobility, the Swiss pikemen did not generally wear armour, but this increased their vulnerability. Unless pikemen were complemented with firepower, they could not be used to attack cavalry that retained its mobility. In short, combined arms formations and tactics were necessary, a course that the independence of the Swiss pikemen made difficult. Across Christian Europe, handguns were used in conjunction with pikes until the spread of the socket bayonet around 1700, although the ratio in which they were normally employed during the period changed significantly in favour of the former.

## England and Scotland

Warfare elsewhere in Europe was frequently independent of the Italian Wars, but the struggle between the Tudor dynasty of England and the Stuart dynasty of Scotland was related as the Stuarts were allies of France. Their alliance, renewed in 1512, brought war with England in 1513, when Henry VIII (r. 1509–47) invaded France in person, winning the Battle of the Spurs, so-named because of the speed with which the French fled from Henry's cavalry. They were exposed to archery when their advance was checked, and this led them to fall back, eventually in disorder.[13]

James IV of Scotland, irritated with his brother-in-law Henry for a number of reasons, including disputes over cross-border raids, fulfilled his commitment to France by invading England with about 26,000 troops, the largest force that had hitherto marched south. This included a French contingent intended to encourage the use of new military methods. Wark, Norham and Ford castles fell rapidly, the strong Norham to James's artillery. The English under the Earl of Surrey advanced with about 20,000 men. In comparison with the troops then fighting in Italy, this was a militarily 'conservative' force, although that was not to make it less effective. There were archers and billmen, not arquebusiers and pikemen, and the English had few cannon.

In response to Surrey's approach, the Scots took up a strong defensive position on Brandon Hill. In the battle of Flodden (9 September 1513), the English opened fire with their cannon, which led the Highlanders and Borderers in the Scots army to advance, but, after a bitter struggle, the English line held. The Scottish centre was then ordered to advance, but their pikemen were unable to develop momentum in attack, and the more mobile English billmen defeated them, rather as Spanish swordsmen had been effective at Cerignola. The Scottish centre was further pressed as other English troops, victorious over the Scottish right, attacked it in the rear. James IV, much of the nobility and at least 5,000 – and possibly as many as 10,000 – of his subjects were killed. English casualties were far fewer, although still substantial.[14]

After Flodden, negotiations in 1514 secured peace between England and Scotland until 1542, although there was a simmering low-intensity conflict and the scale of fighting in 1523–4 might be legitimately described as a war. In 1542, Henry VIII attacked Scotland in order to cover his rear before a projected invasion of France. A Scottish counter-invasion was crushed at the battle of Solway Moss in 1542. English pressure on Scotland increased under the Duke of Somerset, who acted as Lord Protector of Henry VIII's infant successor, Edward VI (r. 1547–1553). Somerset sought to establish both Protestantism and English influence in Scotland, and to break traditional Scottish ties with France. Invading in 1547 at the head of 16,000 men, he fought the Scots at the battle of Pinkie. The Scottish army, at least 25,000 strong, principally pikemen, was badly battered by English cannon and archers, with over 6,000 killed: English losses were 800. Somerset exploited the victory by taking a large number of positions where he established garrisons, but this policy did not make English rule popular, proved ruinously expensive and, in 1550, had to be abandoned in the face of French intervention.[15] As with the French success in Italy at Ceresole in 1544, victory in battle could not determine events.

Flodden and Pinkie suggest that the Scots were not in a position to challenge the English field army; although after Flodden the Scottish military establishment developed in a similar fashion to other Western European armies, and Highland tactics were influenced by Continental precedents.[16] Their diverse forces lacked the ability to act as a coherent unit, and some individual sections, especially the Highlanders, were disinclined to accept the discipline of remaining on the defensive under fire. The Scots also had less firepower than the English: in addition to their long-standing inability to match English archery, the Scots lacked the resources, expertise and experience to match them in gunpowder weaponry.

Yet these disadvantages did not mean that Scotland was ripe for conquest. The English faced serious problems in locating and sustaining suitable allies in the complex mix of Scottish politics, and there were also significant military difficulties. England was far stronger than Scotland in population and financial resources, and had the English been able to maintain and support a permanent military presence in lowland Scotland, then the Scottish kingdom would have been gravely weakened. However, as Scotland did not yield the funds for its occupation, the impossibly high cost of maintaining enough garrisons would have fallen upon England. The centre of English power was far to the south, and in sixteenth-century Scotland (although not in 1638–40) it was challenged by French intervention. Scotland was not to be conquered by England until 1650–2, when France was distracted by civil conflict and another foreign war.

## Baltic warfare

Conflict in the Baltic was only indirectly linked with struggles in Western Europe. The break-up of stable political units around the Baltic at the end of the fifteenth century, and the emergence of Russia and Sweden as significant regional powers, led to a series of wars characterised by sieges, tactical flexibility and systematic devastation.

The expansion of Muscovite power towards the Baltic threatened the stability of its eastern shores: Novgorod fell to the Muscovites in 1478 and Pskov in 1510. In 1492, the fortress of Ivangorod was built opposite the town of Narva, bringing Russian power to the borders of the Livonian Order of the Knights of the Sword, a crusading order which, like the Teutonic Knights, owned extensive territories on the eastern shores of the Baltic. In 1500, Ivan III (r. 1462–1505) went to war with Lithuania, threatening Smolensk and defeating the Lithuanians on the river Vedrosha. The Livonian Order came to their aid, and defeated the Muscovites at Seritsa (1501) and Lake Smolino (1502). In 1502, Ivan besieged Smolensk without success, but he advanced the Russian frontier to the Dnieper before peace was negotiated that year. War resumed in 1507–8 and 1512–15, and Vasilii III of Russia (r. 1505–33) captured Smolensk in 1514. Russia's advancing pretensions were indicated by a frontier war with Sweden in 1554–7. The 1550s saw a marked development in Russian military capability, not least with the emergence of the central chancelleries and the appearance of military governors on Russia's frontiers.

Further west, there was conflict between Denmark and Sweden, including a long period of war from 1501 to 1520, when the Oldenburg kings, who ruled in Denmark and Norway, tried to gain control over Sweden: King Hans (r. 1481–1513) had done so in 1497, using politics and force, but, from 1501, he faced a rebellion. From 1517, Christian II (r. 1513–23) made a series of attempts to gain control over Sweden. Defeated in 1517 and 1518, he was victorious at Bogesund in 1520 and was recognised as king of Sweden that year, but his harshness provoked a rebellion in 1521 led by Gustavus Vasa. In 1523, Gustavus was proclaimed king and the Union of Kalmar, which had bound Denmark, Norway, Sweden and Finland together under one crown since 1397, finally collapsed. In 1523, Christian was deposed by his uncle, the Protestant Duke Frederick of Schleswig-Holstein, who became Frederick I. In 1524, the Danes recognised Gustavus as King of Sweden. Gustavus joined Frederick I of Denmark in defeating Christian when he invaded Norway with a Habsburg-supported army in 1531. After Frederick died in 1533, Gustavus also supported Frederick's Lutheran son, Christian III, against his Catholic-backed brother Hans in the civil war that began in Denmark in 1534. Christian III finally captured Copenhagen in 1536. He then took control over Norway from a Catholic faction that had looked for Habsburg support. The two states, Denmark-Norway and Sweden-Finland, increasingly came to compete for hegemony in the north. The trade of the Baltic was a rich prize as the region was the major source of European ship-building materials, and an exporter of copper, iron and grain.

## Rebellions

European warfare is generally thought of in terms of struggles between states, but it is necessary to recognise the protean quality of states and the difficulty they faced in monopolising authority. It is also important to stress the extent of 'popular' warfare. The best-known instance, which drew on a long and strong practice of rural disaffection, was the German Peasants' War of 1524–5. This was a major conflict motivated by social tension and economic discontent, encouraged by the volatile atmosphere in Reformation Europe.[17] In the end, the forces of princely power and seigneurial authority restored control, although this involved large-scale clashes, especially Landgrave Philip of Hesse's victory at the battle of Frankenhausen (15 May 1525), which ended the rising in Thuringia. The peasants used a *wagenburg* ('fortress' made up of wagons strengthened to create a defensive position) in the fashion developed by the Hussites in the early fifteenth century, but it could not resist the attack that followed a cannonade. Further south, the Swabian League under Truchsess defeated the insurgents at Wurzach (13 April 1525). At Böblingen (12 May 1525), he used cannon and cavalry to achieve the same result. Truchsess followed up with another victory at Königshofen (2 June 1525). The princely forces benefited from their military experience and confidence, and from their possession of cannon. Thus, in Alsace, Duke Anthony of Lorraine used mercenaries to suppress the rising with heavy casualties. However, in the early stages, the princes were often forced to rely on fortified positions, such as the castles at Salzburg and Würzburg. The peasants' attempt to storm the latter was a costly failure. Peasant risings in the same period in Denmark were defeated, that in Skåne being suppressed in 1525 and another in Jutland in 1534. There was also a major peasant revolt in Friuli in 1511. Udine was sacked and many aristocrats were murdered, with their castles stormed.[18]

Opposition to authority elsewhere was also suppressed. A popular rebellion in Genoa led to the overthrow of the nobility in 1506 and the end of French control in 1507, but Louis XII forced the Genoese to yield later that year. Spanish troops restored order in Palermo in 1516. Risings that followed the accession of Charles V (Charles I of Spain) in Spain, the rising of the *Comuneros* in Castile (1520–1) and the socially more radical *Germanías* (brotherhoods) in Valencia (1519–22) and Majorca, were suppressed, crucially with the victory of Villalar (23 April 1521) over the *Comuneros* and with another that October outside the city of Valencia over the *Germanías*. The revolution in Majorca that began in 1522 was suppressed in 1523. The failure of the *Comuneros* to retain aristocratic support was crucial to its suppression. At Villalar, their army was largely bereft of the valuable leadership and fighting force of the Castilian nobility, which had been alienated by the growing social radicalism of the movement.

Opposition to Charles in the Low Countries was also suppressed, including a major rising in Ghent in 1539. The approach of Charles V and an army led Ghent to submit without resistance in February 1540. One of the terms of the pardon was the construction of a fortress. Other signs of urban independence were also unsuccessful, including the brutally suppressed attempt to establish a communistic regime in Münster in 1535. The city, whose fortifications had not yet been modernised, was successfully besieged by an army deploying numerous cannon, but it is noteworthy that it held out from early 1534 until it was betrayed and captured on 24 July 1535. Furthermore, the disease and starvation that came from blockade did more damage than cannon fire.[19]

The Tudor regime in England faced a number of serious rebellions. The dissolution of the monasteries by Henry VIII was very unpopular and led to a major rising in the North, the unsuccessful Pilgrimage of Grace (1536–7).[20] Hostility to the spread of Protestant practices played a major role in the widespread uprisings in southern England in 1549. The Catholic revolt in the South-west in 1549 was primarily directed against Protestantism, and the local gentry failed to suppress it. Professional troops from outside the region had to be used at the battles of Fenny Bridge (28 July) and Clyst Heath (4 August). Opposition to landlords, especially to their enclosure of common land and to their high rents, resulted in Kett's Rebellion in East Anglia in 1549.[21]

The rebellions of the period faced important political and military disadvantages. Political ambiguity about the notion of rebellion ensured that there was often a fatal confusion of purpose. Militarily, the untrained amateur forces raised in the English rebellions were no match for the professional troops that the government could deploy, as was demonstrated on 27 August 1549 when John Dudley, Earl of Warwick, cut Kett's Rebellion to pieces at Dussindale. The rebels tended to lack cavalry, firearms and cannon. At the same time, it would be misleading to exaggerate the automatic effectiveness of regulars. Thus, in the Dackefejden rebellion in Sweden in 1542–3, the pikes of Gustavus Vasa's German mercenaries were of limited effectiveness, and instead the king came to rely on Swedish troops equipped with crossbows and firearms.

Most rebellions could not challenge the government effectively if it had firm leadership and the support of an important portion of the social elite. Yet, in some cases, divisions among the latter could extend to conflict. Thus, after the death of Louis II of Hungary at Mohács in 1526, the Hungarian estates divided over his successor, leading to conflict between John Zapolya, Voivode of Transylvania, and the Habsburg candidate, Ferdinand I of Austria. This conflict interacted with that between Habsburg and Ottoman, a reminder of the danger of trying to segregate international from civil conflict. Furthermore, there could be a popular dimension to conflict between rulers. In July 1495, the French lost control of the city of Naples to a popular uprising in favour of Ferrante II that involved street-fighting. Like the French-backed rising in Siena in 1552, this reflected the strength of urban traditions of political action.

## Military Revolution?

The division of the warfare in the Europe section of this book (Chapters 5, 6 and 7), and also of the section on European warfare elsewhere (Chapters 4 and 9), risks introducing inappropriate discontinuities, but it also permits a scrutiny of general theses, such as that of the Military Revolution, that is more specific because of the use of a smaller range of time. This lessens the possibility of running together several examples from across the entire period 1494–1660 in order to prove a thesis, and then arguing from thesis back to examples (in labelling those which do not fit in as exceptions). Any periodisation does not imply that the dates at either end (in this case 1494, 1559–60, 1617–18, 1660) marked major turning points or that the periods themselves had causal power, but rather that they provide the basis for comparison.

In the case of the first sub-period within this book, there is the obvious difficulty of the need to look back. In so far as military developments or the growth of state forms are concerned, there was no major shift in the early 1490s. Instead, those years most effectively mark a turning point in terms of Europe's relations with the outside world. Even that should not be exaggerated. The Portuguese had been moving south along the Atlantic coast of Africa for decades. Furthermore, if Columbus had not 'discovered' the West Indies in the 1490s then someone else would very likely have done so shortly afterwards.

The outbreak of the Italian Wars were once held to be a decisive step in the onset of a modern state system, but, like the voyages of discovery, they can primarily be seen as a consequence of earlier developments. As far as warfare was concerned, the spread of gunpowder technology in Europe was long-established, although the incremental improvements in firearms in the late fifteenth century were important, not least in terms of the diffusion of these firearms. At the same time, it is important not to exaggerate what could be achieved by new weaponry and methods, not least because of the ability of other powers to match or counter developments.

Thanks to political changes in the fifteenth century, a number of dynasties were able to take particular advantage of military developments and the possibilities created by war, and thus to pose a challenge to rivals. Terms such as 'new monarchies' and 'Renaissance monarchies' are over-used, but there was a distinct shift between the politics of the first half of the century and that of the 1490s. In France, England, Spain and Muscovy, stronger polities had been created. The term state can be employed as long as it does not imply an anachronistic comparison with the situation in 1900. The Valois rulers of France had seen off the challenge of England and Burgundy, and France had emerged as a strong monarchy. In England, the Wars of the Roses ended with the Tudors under Henry VII (r. 1485–1509) enjoying considerable power and authority. In Spain, Castille and Aragon were linked in 1479 by dynastic union and Granada, the capital of the last Moorish kingdom, surrendered in 1492. These states were better able to wage warfare, and it is this, as much as the technology they employed, that contributed to military capability.

It had seemed possible that one or other of these states would serve as the basis for a hegemonic power, and this appeared close when Francis I pursued election as Emperor and also after he was defeated by Charles V in 1525. The warfare of the period was a record of the failure of such hopes and fears. This failure attracted the attention of later commentators who saw an international balance of power as characteristic of European political society, progress and strength. The balance was seen as a particular characteristic of a post-medieval world defined by the successful challenge to papal authority and the pretensions of the Emperor from the early-sixteenth century. In his influential *History of the Reign of the Emperor Charles V. With a View of the Progress of Society in Europe, from the Subversion of the Roman Empire, to the Beginning of the Sixteenth Century* (1769), William Robertson focused on the Italian Wars:

> that great secret in modern policy, the preservation of a proper distri-
> bution of power among all the members of the system into which
> the states are formed...From this aera we can trace the progress of

that intercourse between nations, which had linked the powers of Europe so closely together; and can discern the operations of that provident policy, which, during peace, guards against remote and contingent dangers; which, in war, hath prevented rapid and destructive conquests.[22]

It is important to consider how far the changing nature of warfare, as well as the contingent circumstances of war and politics, led to this result. This has certainly been argued in the literature: 'Charles V's legacy, Spanish hegemony in Italy, eroded at the same time and for the same reason that the Habsburg position in the Netherlands collapsed: angle-bastion fortifications.'[23]

Such an observation is arresting, but faces a number of limitations. Modern fortifications without a field army in support that could threaten besieging forces were not of much use against a major enemy. Dutch cities fell one after another to the Duke of Parma and the Army of Flanders in the 1580s until the Dutch created an effective field army. As a consequence, victory in battle helped to determine the fate of fortified positions throughout the period. Thus, the crushing French victory over the Bretons at St Aubin-du-Cormier on 29 July 1488 was followed by the fall of St Malo and by Duke Francis of Brittany accepting harsh terms.

Furthermore, conflict was not simply a matter of establishing territorial control. There was also the more serious political–military challenge of forcing opponents, both domestic and external, to accept one's will. That was a central challenge for the Habsburgs, and, in some respects, the very resort to warfare on their part, as in Germany in 1546, or to a large-scale military intervention, as in the Low Countries in the late 1560s, was indicative of failure. It represented an unwillingness to accept the existing nature of hegemony within Habsburg-ruled entities. These can be compared with the loose hegemonies enjoyed by, for example, the Mughals across much of India, and also with the Habsburg position in Mexico and the Philippines, where monarchical strength and 'state formation' rested on political and cultural incorporation, rather than on the need to conquer and occupy everywhere. The failure of this model to work in Europe was the consequence of the Reformation, which was far more deadly for both traditional and novel methods of state creation than angle-bastion fortifications, or any other development in weaponry. There is an analogy with the impact of communism and, more specifically, liberation ideas on the maintenance of European colonial empires in the twentieth century.[24] It was no accident that Spain was able to re-create its power and authority in Italy after they were challenged in the 1640s, but, earlier, had no comparable impact on the Protestant-ruled United Provinces.

The effectiveness of the armies of the period, and (a separate issue) the extent to which they encapsulated revolutionary military changes, is open to different interpretations. It is possible to focus on Habsburg success in the

1550s and to argue that the Spanish success against France in the Low Countries testified to an inherently strong and effective military system, whatever the drawbacks revealed by failure in 1552. At the same time, the emphasis that can be placed on Spanish success is in part compromised by the deficiencies of her opponent. The weakness of the French army in 1558 has drawn comment. Although, on 8 August, Henry II was able to inspect 40,000 men at Pierrepont, the crown's inability to create a powerful native infantry was reflected in the fact that 28,000 of the men were German or Swiss mercenaries. Furthermore, the army was a medley of units that had scant experience of operating together, an important constraint on the combined-arms tactics required for success in battle. This was accentuated by the financial problems that made it difficult to maintain troop numbers or to prevent the disbanding of much of the army at the close of a campaign.[25]

More generally, combined arms tactics are far easier to outline in theory than to execute under the strain of battle. The contrasting fighting characteristics of the individual arms operated very differently in particular circumstances, and this posed added problems for co-ordination. So also did the limited extent to which many generals and officers understood these characteristics and problems. Consideration of the warfare of the period suggests that 'military adaptation' is a more appropriate term than revolution.

# 6

# EUROPEAN WARFARE
# 1560–1617

The Protestant Reformation helped to change the political environment of much of Europe, and provoked much warfare both domestic and international. Religious divisions lent new intensity to conflicts between and within Christian powers. Religion, hitherto the prime focus for social and ideological cohesion, came to play a major role in a culture of violence within Christian Europe. With opposition to the Reformation playing a leading role in the Catholic Counter-Reformation, strife became a major part of religious sensibility. Inhibitions affecting waging war against and killing fellow Christians, especially of civilians, became weaker. Savagery and high casualty rates were more the results of religion and political crisis than of military technology.

In the British Isles, France, the Low Countries, the Empire, the Austrian Habsburg territories, Sweden and Poland, states and societies were riven by conspiracy, the search for assistance from foreign co-religionists, and regional, social and factional differences exacerbated by religious antagonism. It was a political world in which everything was seen to be at stake because of the prospect of state-directed religious change. Peasants revolted against their lords, as in Austria in 1594–7, and rulers were assassinated or removed by revolt. Two successive kings of France, Henry III and IV, were killed in 1589 and 1610, Mary, Queen of Scots and Sigismund Vasa of Sweden were stripped of their power in 1567 and 1598, and Philip II of Spain was deposed as ruler of the Netherlands by the rebellious Dutch provinces in 1581.

## French Wars of Religion

France witnessed a protracted crisis of order and civil society. The French Wars of Religion led to a collapse of royal authority, social strife and foreign intervention, especially by Spain, England and Savoy. The Wars lasted until the Edict of Nantes in 1598, resuming during the reign of Louis XIII (r. 1610–43), and ending in royal victory in 1629. Their origins lay in the fragility of the monarchy after the death of Henry II following a jousting accident in 1559, but it is important to note the crucial role of religious differences in causing division and providing much of the agenda of the wars.[1] Henry II's weak successors, his sons Francis II (r. 1559–60), Charles IX (r. 1560–74), and Henry III (r. 1574–89), were unable to control the factionalism of the leading nobility, a factionalism exacerbated by the struggle between Catholics and Huguenots (Calvinists).

Open conflict broke out in 1562, leading not to a continuous period of conflict, let alone high-tempo campaigning, but to a series of distinct wars, separated by agreements and periods of peace that reflected a widespread desire for settlement, but against the background of persistent differences and a high level of civil violence. As a result, years of peace were in reality uneasy armed truces. On 1 March 1562, at Vassy, the most prominent Catholic aristocrat, Francis, Duke of Guise, with his affinity was involved in a dispute with a Huguenot congregation that led to the massacre of the latter. The Huguenots saw this as a sign of war. What it showed was that a prominent aristocrat travelled through France in peacetime with numbers of supporters sufficient to start a conflict. The military strength of the aristocracy was further demonstrated when Guise and some other leading nobles rode to the royal palace at Fontainebleau with 1,000 horsemen and intimidated Charles IX into returning to Paris. On 2 April, the Huguenot leader, the Prince of Condé seized Orléans, a major step in the beginning of hostilities, as it was a clear attack on royal authority. The First War saw the Huguenots capture a large number of cities, including Lyons and Rouen. As it took time to raise a large army, the royal response was slow, but in the summer the main royal army recaptured Blois and Bourges, while Guise's brother besieged Rouen, which fell, after the main body of the royal army arrived, at the end of seven bloody assaults. Condé's advance on Paris was thwarted when Guise reinforced the city, and on 19 December 1562 the two armies fought at Dreux.

Dreux was a confused battle, which was neither planned nor anticipated by the Huguenots, who were inferior in numbers. It was triggered by the need for money to pay the Protestant troops, especially the Germans. The royal army was still the splendid organisation that Henry II had built up, and the success of the royalist arquebusiers against the Huguenot cavalry should not be underestimated (the comparison with Pavia springs to mind), whereas the Huguenot infantry were generally of poor quality. The initial reports of the battle all focus on the fate of the senior commanders on both sides. The Constable, the Duke of Montmorency was wounded and captured: Marshall Saint-André and the Duke of Nevers were both killed; and the Prince of Condé was captured. The deaths and captures had more significance than the overall battlefield losses, which at 6,000 were heavy, and played an important part in bringing about an accommodation between the two sides

Dreux was a lengthy engagement in which the tide of success changed several times. It is also instructive as it indicates what helped to ensure victory at the start of what Michael Roberts presented as the Military Revolution. As in the Italian Wars, the two sides contained a mix of units that to a considerable extent operated independently. Success required not only their success in fighting on their own, but also their co-operation or co-ordination with other units on their own side. In particular, cavalry-infantry co-ordination was an issue, as was the ability of the cavalry to retain coherence, rather than dispersing in order to loot baggage. The Huguenot cavalry wrecked the left of the royal army, including the Swiss infantry, but then pursued their fortune in looting the royal baggage, giving the royal army, especially the *gendarmes* (heavy cavalry) the opportunity to inflict heavy casualties on the Huguenot infantry. In the closing stages of the battle the Huguenot cavalry reappeared, only to be stopped by royalist arquebusiers. Casualties were very heavy on both sides. The battle demonstrated the continued battlefield success of heavy cavalry, not only at the expense of other cavalry but also at that of infantry. Although the battle was more fluid, in some respects a direct line can be drawn from Dreux to Rocroi (1643) and Naseby (1645) in order to indicate the continued decisive battlefield role of cavalry in the period covered by this book.

The French crown was able to make a major effort to confront the Huguenots, deploying a substantial army that was the dominant campaigning force in northern France. By the end of 1562, the royal army was possibly 48,000 strong, although this put a very heavy financial burden on the crown, helping to lead it towards peace. The same happened in 1568 at the close of the Second War. Aside from the cost of the army, the cumulative impact of debts and the disruption of revenue collection by civil war made it difficult to sustain the struggle. The need to recruit costly mercenaries, sometimes at very short notice, and the inability of the crown to raise enough money to meet these obligations and to sustain a long military campaign, helped make it difficult for the crown to win.

The First War ended in 1563, with the Pacification of Amboise (19 March) seeking to settle religious differences. This was followed by the successful siege of Le Havre, which the English had occupied during the war. A French army that included forty cannon captured the poorly-fortified port in July 1563. Its defence had been weakened by plague among the garrison. The expulsion of the English proved a means of temporarily reconciling the warring French factions.

Although France was now largely peaceful, tensions remained, and the Protestant leaders feared fresh attack, especially as a result of an agreement allegedly made at a meeting at Bayonne in 1565 between the French court, the Queen of Spain and the Duke of Alba. This led to alarmist concerns about a Catholic conspiracy and a Europe-wide religious struggle, concerns exacerbated in 1566 by the outbreak of serious disorder in the Low Countries, followed in 1567 by the march of a Spanish army under Alba thither. Charles IX began recruiting Swiss mercenary pikemen in response to the news of the movement of the Spanish field army along France's eastern border. The Huguenots mobilised in response to the King's mobilisation, which led inexorably to clashes and the second outbreak of 'war'. The Huguenots were able to assemble their essentially cavalry army more rapidly than the royal army, but the latter had superior organisation, experience and leadership once they were mobilised. In September 1567, the Huguenots sought to intimidate Charles IX into changing his policy. Having failed, the Huguenot forces blockaded Paris in October while violence swept France. The indecisive Second War (1567–8) was rapidly followed by the Third (1568–70), after persistent attacks on Huguenots and the gathering of royal troops led the Huguenots to mobilise anew. The one-sided nature of the Peace of Longjumeau at the close of the Second War, requiring only the Huguenots to disarm, led directly to the pre-emptive strike which unleashed the next war. More generally, the inadequate enforcement of the various peace settlements was itself a cause of renewed conflicts.

The Wars involved full-scale battles and sieges. Huguenot defeats in the 1560s at Dreux (19 December 1562), Jarnac (13 March 1569), and Moncontour (3 October 1569), especially the last, stopped the Protestant advance. The royal army proved better at co-ordinating infantry and cavalry on the battlefield. It is also, however, important to remember Huguenot successes, such as La Roche-l'Abeille (1569), as well as indecisive battles, such as Arnay-le-Duc (1570). Foreign intervention on the Huguenot side had only limited impact, although in 1576 an English-financed 20,000-strong German army under John Casimir, son of Frederick III of the Palatinate, joined Huguenot forces in France, despite a check at Dormans (10 October 1575). Their deployment in central France helped lead Henry III, whose unpaid and weak army was unable to offer battle, to bring an end to the Fifth War of Religion in May 1576. An army of 9,500 under John Casimir had earlier strengthened the Huguenots in the Second War, and another, under Duke Wolfgang of Zweibrücken in 1569, in the Third War. The English provided considerable financial support to the Huguenots, while in 1572–3 their maritime help was crucial to the successful defence of La Rochelle.

Given the character of the conflicts as civil wars, it was not surprising that one of the most important features of battles was whether they led to the death of leaders, and this certainly attracted the attention of contemporaries. Thus, the battle of Saint-Denis (10 November 1567), the first clash of the Second War, was noted for the death of the Constable Montmorency, the commander of the royal army. He had stationed himself in the centre, with the elite units, the heavy cavalry and the 6,000 Swiss pikemen hired earlier that year, but the Huguenot cavalry under Condé broke through. Similarly, at the battle of Jarnac, the first major clash of the Third War, Condé was killed after a rash cavalry charge exposed his force to more numerous royal cavalry.

The Wars involved a large number of sieges, and they became more important to the course of the conflict than at the outset. Artillery was effectively used against fortified positions. Thus, in 1569, the fortress of Lassy, which had been very extensively rebuilt in 1458 after being heavily damaged in 1417 and 1422, fell after the walls had been breached. However, bombardment could only do so much. In March 1568, the Huguenots stormed Chartres, the wall of which had been breached by their nine cannon, but the attack was defeated and the breach sealed. Even when positions were captured, their defence could have an important operational and strategic impact by taking time to overcome and by weakening the attacking army through the disease, desertion and casualties that sieges entailed. This was the fate of the royal army under the Duke of Anjou (later Henry III) when it successfully besieged Saint-Jean d'Angély in late 1569, and also of a royal force under Matignon that took four months to capture Lusignan in the winter of 1574–5.

Alongside the campaigning history of the principal armies, it is necessary to remember that, as in other civil wars, there was fighting elsewhere. Thus, in the Third War, the main sphere of operations in Poitou was matched by conflict in Languedoc and Béarn. The lesser battles have received insufficient attention. They showed the importance of successfully exploiting topographical features and of experience, morale and leadership in clashes that did not readily conform to text-book descriptions of sixteenth-century warfare.

The end of the Third War, with the Peace of Saint-Germain of 8 August 1570, was followed in September 1571 by the admission of Coligny, now the Huguenot leader, into the royal council. He sought to unite France behind a plan for intervening against the Spaniards in the Netherlands and was instrumental in sending Huguenot forces to Mons and Flushing in support of the Dutch Revolt. Concern about Coligny's intentions and military preparations, especially from the king's influential mother, Catherine de Medici, interacted with popular anti-Protestantism to create a volatile atmosphere in which the attempted murder of Coligny at the behest of the Guises on 22 August 1572 led to fears of an imminent religious war. To pre-empt this, Charles IX and his council seem to have decided to kill the Huguenot leaders. The St Bartholomew's Eve killing of leading Protestants (24 August 1572) was followed by a widespread massacre of Paris's Huguenots by the Catholic populace, and the slaughter was copied in many other cities. This touched off the Fourth War (1572–3), rapidly followed by the Fifth (1574–6). In each of these five conflicts, the royal army was unable to inflict a defeat on the Huguenots sufficient to transform the overall situation. However, whereas in the early wars control of the capital was a central goal, after 1572 the Huguenots were largely concerned to consolidate their position in the South and West.

A lengthy and unsuccessful siege of Huguenot-held La Rochelle was the main event in the Fourth War. The Huguenots now lacked the strength for pitched battles they had been able to field in the 1560s, but they benefited from their defensive positions, particularly in southern France. The failure of the siege reflected the strength of La Rochelle's position, not least as a port, which permitted ready supply, but also the difficulty of managing the operation, not least divisions within the royal army. The royal army mounted eight major attacks on La Rochelle in February–June 1573, supporting its efforts with bombardment and mining, but the strength of the position was accentuated by the construction of interior fortifications and by a resolute defence supported by seaborne English supplies. The royal army was hit by a shortage of powder and balls for the artillery – a problem for any protracted siege – as well as by the impact on numbers and morale of disease and inadequate supplies. There are no precise casualty figures for the royal army, but losses through combat, desertion and disease were possibly 12,000. Alongside serious financial problems, this greatly lessened the ability of the royal army to mount operations on the scale of those of the 1560s. Charles IX felt obliged to abandon the siege and to conclude peace with the Huguenots.

The Fifth War ended in 1576 with the royal army, bereft of funds and Charles's successor, his brother Henry III, unable to set the terms for the peace. Aside from the German force under John Casimir marching through central France, Henry faced opposition from his brother, François d'Alençon, who called himself 'Protector of the liberty and public good of France', as well as widespread Huguenot opposition and the independent role of the 'Malcontents', nobles such as Montmorency-Damville, who called for a dramatic change in royal policy. In the context of a civil war, such nobles were able to play an important independent role; while the importance of dynastic factors in a system of hereditary monarchy was indicated by the role of Alençon, heir to the childless Henry.

An unwilling Henry III had to accept what became known as the Peace of Monsieur (6 May 1576), which gave Huguenots freedom of worship, the right to build churches, and surety towns, while the Malcontents received their governorships back and Henry agreed to call a meeting of the Estates General.

Catholic dissatisfaction undermined the peace settlement. Meeting at Blois, the Estates General wanted religious uniformity, not the concessions offered to the Huguenots, and this wrecked the peace. However, in the Sixth War (1577), Henry found it impossible to secure funds for the royal army, which was small and short of ammunition. La Charité and Issoire were successfully besieged, but the unpaid royal army could not press on to attack other Huguenot positions, and Henry was happy to reach a settlement in September 1577 which accepted Protestant worship but limited the rights granted in 1576.

The brevity of the Sixth War owed much to the weakness of the royal army which lacked the resources to sustain effective operations after some initial successes. The cost of sustaining conflict was too great for the heavily-indebted royal government, and fiscal expedients ran out, a problem that faced France more spectacularly in its war with Spain in the late 1640s. In the French Wars of Religion, financial problems prevented orderly demobilisations and thus ensured that the peacetime royal army was not ready for any resumption of conflict. Financial problems also hit the Huguenots. In the Second War they were hit not only by the cost of their forces, but also by the need to pay German troops. Unpaid, the Huguenot troops deserted over the winter of 1567–8, helping lead their leaders to accept the Peace of Longjumeau (23 March 1568), which did not provide them with the *places de sûreté* they sought.

The years 1577–84 were generally peaceful in France. Huguenot forces were deployed in the Netherlands under the Duke of Anjou and were largely funded by Queen Elizabeth of England. However, a high level of violence continued in the provinces which led to the Seventh War (1579–80). Full-scale conflict resumed after the Protestant Henry of Navarre became heir to the throne on the death of the Duke of Anjou (formerly Alençon) in June 1584. The Guise family formed an association that September to exclude Henry and turned to Philip II of Spain for support. By the Treaty of Joinville of 31 December 1584, Philip II and the Guise agreed to co-operate against Protestantism, and to support Charles, Cardinal Bourbon for the throne, and Philip agreed to subsidise the new Catholic League.

The following year, the League nobles, especially the Guise family, took over much of north and central France and raised a considerable force that intimidated Henry III into granting the Treaty of Nemours (7 July 1585) under which Protestant worship was banned and Henry of Navarre deprived of his rights to the succession. As a characteristic sign of the burden of supporting troops and the efforts made to shift it, Henry III undertook to pay for the Guise forces, an obligation that he was unable to fulfil. Strong in the south, the Huguenots fought on. The first major battle, at Coutras (20 October 1587), was a victory for Henry of Navarre over Henry III's favourite, the Duke of Joyeuse, who was killed when the Huguenots won the cavalry clash that was central to the battle. The size of the armies, only about 5,000–7,000 on each side, indicated the impact not so much of the devastation of many years fighting as the breakdown of the political and governmental system which led to a multiplicity of forces pursuing local struggles, and an absence of the institutional framework necessary to consolidate resources behind a large field army. The customary process of attrition through casualties, disease and desertion hit small armies. Earlier in the year, the royal army under Joyeuse that had overrun Poitou had been officially 8,000 strong, but, although successful, its size was hit by campaigning. Guise defeated another English-financed German army at Vimory (26 October 1587) and Auneau (24 November 1587).

Relations between the king and the Guise deteriorated. On the Day of the Barricades (12 May 1588), Henry III lost control of Paris to a pro-Guise rising, despite his force of 4,000 Swiss guards. Henry's desperate response, the murder of Guise at Blois on 23 December 1588, did not solve the problem. The Catholic League, now under Guise's brother, the Duke of Mayenne, turned completely against the king, whose power was soon substantially restricted to a section of the Loire valley as many towns rallied to the League. In January 1589, the Parlement of Paris declared the Cardinal of Bourbon king as Charles X. Weak and short of funds, Henry III felt it necessary to ally with Henry of Navarre in April. They jointly besieged Paris, but Henry III was assassinated by a Dominican friar on 1 August. Before dying, he recognised Henry of Navarre as his heir, but said he could only succeed if he became a Catholic. The new king found that the commanders of Henry III's army were only willing to serve under him if he agreed that captured positions be placed under Catholic control, but much of the royal army deserted and Henry had to abandon the siege.

Henry of Navarre's eventual victory was a product of military and political factors. His victories over Mayenne at Arques (21 September 1589) and Ivry (14 March 1590) enabled Henry to gain the initiative. At Arques, Henry's outnumbered force was in an entrenched position. The first entrenchment was outflanked, but the second defensive position held firm. At Coutras (20 October 1587) and Ivry, Henry's cavalry used a mix of pistol and shock tactics. At Ivry, the cavalry charged with their swords after firing their pistols. Henry's cavalry broke through the opposing formation under Mayenne, and, once the League cavalry had been defeated, their infantry was crushed with heavy casualties in dead and prisoners. More generally, cavalry played a greater role in the Wars of Religion than they had done in the Italian Wars where their role, though considerable, had been greatly restricted by pikemen, field entrenchments and arquebusiers. In the French Wars, cavalry tended to be well-equipped and experienced, and the role of infantry was less prominent than in the Italian Wars. The cavalry in question carried firearms and were not heavily armoured.

After Arques, Henry marched on Paris, beating the city militia in the suburbs, but, without artillery or funds, was unable to mount a siege. Henry campaigned during the winter months on a regular basis. His winter campaign of 1589–90 was made possible by the availability of English infantry and finance to supplement his forces. The following spring, the two armies manoeuvred in order to block their opponent's sieges. The battle of Ivry arose from Mayenne's advance to relieve Dreux which was besieged by Henry IV. Henry then advanced to besiege Paris, although the urban militia was over twice as large as the royal army. The privations of the siege were harsh, but Paris was relieved by the Duke of Parma, who advanced from the Netherlands with 14,000 Spanish troops and joined Mayenne. Henry tried to engage Parma in battle, but he was outmanoeuvred. Parma, who was strong in infantry, used entrenchments to block Henry's advantage in cavalry. The siege was abandoned.

Short of money, Henry was helped by the death of the League's choice as monarch, Charles X, on 9 May 1591. This left the League divided over who should be king. Keen to win subsidies from Elizabeth of England, who was concerned that League positions on the Channel would serve as invasion bases for another Spanish Armada, Henry besieged Rouen in November 1591, joining an English force under the Earl of Essex. Attacks were repulsed and Parma relieved the city in April 1592. Parma avoided meeting Henry in open battle, and was able to extract his army from Rouen after he had lifted the siege, by building a bridge of boats across the Seine. The pontoons were assembled up river and floated into place at dusk, allowing the army to disengage and withdraw during the night. The bridge had been disassembled and the rearguard withdrawn over it by dawn, before Henry realised what had happened. The strategem demonstrated not only Parma's mastery of set-piece warfare, but also the cohesion of the organisational structure of the Army of Flanders and its high level of training. The experience of campaigning in the difficult environment of the Low Countries had forced the Spanish Army to develop comprehensive support services. Henry failed to engage Parma in battle that May and the Spaniards were able to return to the Netherlands.[2]

Henry was helped by his enemies' political divisions, not least over whether a Spanish succession was acceptable, and by their lack of unified leadership, while his willingness to become a Catholic again (July 1593) was important in winning allies and helped lead to a political solution to the conflict. So also did his willingness to give large sums of money to key players.[3] Henry played on the serious tensions within the League, and made overtures to the League moderates. This worked very well in permitting his entry into Paris on 22 March 1594; he had been crowned as Henry IV at Chartres the previous month. Henry's gain of Paris helped destabilise the League, and was followed by a rapid increase in reconciliations with the King. Henry's leniency ensured that by the end of 1594 the majority of the League towns in northern France, including Amiens, Bourges, Orléans, Rouen and Troyes, had submitted, as had Lyons. The following year, Henry received absolution from Pope Clement VIII, and Mayenne agreed terms in January 1596. Opponents remained within France, especially the Dukes of Mercoeur and Epernon in Brittany and Provence respectively, but Henry's success and his willingness to make concessions discouraged continued opposition, and most nobles followed Mayenne. In January 1596, the League was dissolved. The following month, Henry's opponents in Marseilles were overthrown and the Spanish troops there were forced to leave. A Spanish fleet that sailed in October 1596 to seize Brest was scattered by storm.

Spanish intervention had helped to prolong the conflict, relieving Paris in 1590 and Rouen in 1592, while other Spanish forces operated in Brittany (from late 1590) and east France.[4] Concern about the prospect of a fresh Spanish invasion, and of links between Philip II and the remaining Leaguers, led Henry IV to declare war on Spain on 17 January 1595. Henry defeated a Spanish army invading Burgundy on behalf of Mayenne at Fontaine-Française (5 June 1595). The royal army was greatly outnumbered, but Henry forced the tempo of the battle by leading a powerful cavalry attack that drove the Spaniards back. He was very much a king who led from the front, a risky policy but one that contributed to his position as a charismatic cavalry commander. After the battle, Henry consolidated his position in Burgundy, and the citadel of Dijon surrendered to him. Whereas some battles were not followed by the loss of fortified possessions, this comparatively small-scale battle was. Spanish troops operating from the Low Countries captured Cambrai (1595), Calais and Ardres (1596), and Amiens (March 1597). However, Henry regained Amiens after a long siege (April–September 1597). Mercoeur, the last major League noble to submit, did so in March 1598 after Henry had advanced towards Brittany with an army. Mercoeur had been bolstered in his continuing resistance by the presence of a Spanish naval base at Blavet, on the south coast of Brittany established in 1590 .

Like England in Scotland, Spain had discovered the problems of intervening in the domestic affairs of another state, but its powerful military machine ensured that when peace came, by the Treaty of Vervins (2 May 1598), the terms of Cateau-Cambrésis (1559), which had recognised Spanish predominance in Western Europe, were repeated. The Huguenots were satisfied with the Edict of Nantes (13 April 1598) which granted them liberty of conscience and a measure of public worship. As far as the military dimension was concerned, the Huguenots were not allowed to levy troops or build fortifications, although they were granted the right to retain garrisons in about 200 towns they occupied in 1597, with the crown agreeing to pay the garrisons of about half the towns.

Duke Charles Emanuel of Savoy exploited the crisis in France to seize the Marquisate of Saluzzo in the Piedmontese Alps in 1588 and to invade Provence in 1590. Henry IV demanded the return of Saluzzo in 1598, but the Duke refused. When war broke out, Charles Emanuel was well placed to retain Saluzzo, but his territories near the Rhone were far more vulnerable and were indeed overrun, while the French also moved into Savoy. In October 1600, Charles Emanuel advanced on French units laying siege to Montmélian, yet again a siege proving the focus of operations, but the onset of winter led him to withdraw to the Piedmontese side of the Alps. In the eventual peace, Charles Emanuel retained Saluzzo, but had to surrender Bresse, Bugey and Gex.[5] This cut the Spanish Road west of the Swiss Confederation, forcing the Spaniards to rely on the route to the east via the Valtelline. Charles Emanuel failed when he launched a surprise attack on Geneva in 1603.

The French Wars of Religion have received particular attention because they are seen as important in the development of warfare in this period, rather than as a conflict that revealed a debased form of warfare, as civil war both altered military goals and limited resources. In the later analysis, the French Wars are seen as less important than the Dutch Revolt, an assumption that rests on the participation in the latter of the Spanish Army of Flanders, generally seen as the leading Christian force, and one that is accentuated by the role of the Revolt in discussion of the Military Revolution. Instead, the French Wars serve as a reminder of the continued role of cavalry, of the continued interaction of fortifications/sieges with wide-ranging operations, and of the international dimension alongside local struggles. As a result, the French Wars prefigure the Thirty Years' War (1618–48), and also can be seen in terms of a continuation of the campaigning of the 1550s, albeit with the important addition of the dimension of a lengthy civil war (unlike the short-lived conflict within Germany in the early 1550s).

## The Dutch Revolt

A stress on the French Wars of Religion can also lead to a search for parallels (and contrasts) with the Dutch Revolt, the other leading war in Western Europe in the period. What it does is to question the understanding of Western European warfare largely in terms of the Army of Flanders and the emerging military capability of the Dutch Republic. Instead of the campaigning (and political strategy) of the Spaniards in the 1580s and 1600s and of the Dutch in the 1590s, none of which fulfilled their strategic goals, it is possible to focus on Henry IV's success in achieving his in 1592–1601, although Spain could make interventions in France, while France could do little, directly, for the Dutch. The Army of Flanders had a higher operational capability than any other Western European army until the rise of the Dutch army in the 1590s, but it is important to dispense with the idea of the Army of Flanders, the reforms of Maurice of Nassau and the campaigning of the Dutch Revolt, as constituting the characteristic features of Western European armies and conflict, and instead to appreciate the varied nature of the warfare of the period.

The revolt of the Dutch provinces against imperial rule also revealed the problems of political control, and the strength of the Spanish military machine. Philip II's unpopular religious and fiscal policies and his neglect of the Dutch nobility, as well as Dutch demands to autonomy, led to opposition, culminating with a breakdown of control in 1566–7 that began in August 1566 when Calvinists seized churches and destroyed their Catholic images, a dramatic demonstration of a shift towards force. Concerned about his duty to the Church and about the danger that, if mishandled, the crisis would help Protestantism and French goals throughout Europe, Philip decided to send a large army under the experienced Duke of Alba to restore order, although, in fact, much of this was done earlier by the native nobility. The arrival of Alba in August 1567 (he entered Brussels on 22 August) revived Spanish control, although it helped militarise religious rivalries. Alba imposed new taxes that helped to make his regime unpopular, as did his harsh treatment of opponents, over 1,000 of whom were executed, including prominent nobles: the Counts of Egmont and Horne were beheaded for treason in June 1568. This helped justify rebellion against Philip on the grounds of preserving 'ancient liberties'. Invading Dutch rebel forces under William of Orange's brother, Louis of Nassau, were victorious at Heiligerlee (23 May 1568), only to be defeated at Jemmingen (21 July 1568) when they left their entrenched position to launch a counter-attack, although discontent over pay among Louis's German merce-naries was also a problem. William invaded in October 1568, but was defeated by Alba at Jodoigne (20 October) and retreated. Concerned about the Turkish threat in the Mediterranean, Philip was unable to send help, but in 1568, Alba comprehensively outmanoeuvred the Nassau brothers.

However, in 1572, Alba had to turn south to deal both with a threatened French attack and an actual invasion under Louis of Nassau in May that captured Mons. This allowed the Sea Beggars, a force of opponents of Philip, about 1,100 men strong, that sailed on a fleet of Dutch privateers, to seize the Zeeland towns of Brill and Flushing (April 1572) and to press on in May to make gains in Holland. In June, the Low Countries were also attacked from the east by William of Orange's brother-in-law Count William van den Berg, who seized Zutphen, but Alba focused on besieging Mons, near the – to him – vital French frontier. Orange, the leader of the rebellion, invaded the Maas valley in July, capturing Roermond and advancing towards Mons, near where on 17 July an attempt by a Huguenot force from France to relieve the city had been surprised and defeated. Orange's relief attempt failed in September and he then retreated into Germany, his army unable to resist Alba.

After the threat of French attack was ended by the killing of the Huguenot leaders in the St Bartholomew's Eve Massacre (24 August 1572), Alba was able to re-establish Spanish power over most of the Low Countries, Mons and other cities surrendering. Alba used harshness in the shape of the sacking of Mechelen, Zutphen and Naarden, to encourage surrender. He mistakenly believed that ferocity would work, while his son, who held the tactical field command, failed to anticipate or cope with the difficulties presented by the water defences and canal systems surrounding Haarlem. Alba lost impetus when he was delayed by the seven-month siege of Haarlem (December 1572–July 1573). Once it had surrendered most of the garrison, over 1,000 men, was executed. Short of money and ships, in large part because Philip (who was at least thinking of a peaceful settlement to the Dutch crisis) was concentrating his resources on fighting the Ottomans, Alba was unable successfully to contest coastal waters or to regain Zeeland. The Dutch ability to gain naval superiority gave them a vital advantage in the provinces of Holland and Zeeland. Alkmaar resisted successfully in 1573. As far as fortifica-tions were concerned, Dutch defensive successes were not due to the bastion system, but to improvised earthen barricades behind the breaches. The Spaniards found enormous difficulty in carrying out effective siege operations against Haarlem, Alkmaar and Leiden, as the Dutch had difficulties at Middleburg, due to the extensive nature of the water defences. These prevented the proper concentration of force at a specific point, as it was diffi-cult to build up the sconces for the siege artillery, and all attacks were along very narrow frontages. Mining was also out of the question because of the low water table, which also allowed waterborne re-supply. In the coastal regions, where the Dutch could use the water and their ships to their advantage, they did well. When they tried to confront Alba in the open plains of Flanders or in the eastern areas of the country, they were defeated.

As an instructive contrast to Alba's operations, the successful attempt by Duke Philip of Burgundy to conquer Holland and Zeeland from his cousin Countess Jacqueline of Bavaria in 1425–8 owed much not only to his ability to maintain both initiative and tempo but also, more specifically, to his success in blocking the waterways, in particular by constructing blockhouses, and by using moored ships with troops on board as another form of garrison. Alba's policies were criticised in Spanish government circles. They were expensive in manpower and money and were failing to overawe the Dutch.

Under Alba's replacement as Captain General, Don Luis de Requesens, the Army of Flanders reached its peak strength of 86,000 men in 1574. The Army of Flanders retained its battlefield superiority, destroying Louis of Nassau's army at Mook (Mookerheyde) on 14 April 1574, and killing both him and his brother Henry; but the coastal regions proved far harder to control. The Dutch captured Middleburg in February 1574 and the Spanish siege of Leiden (May–October) ended when the Dutch breached the dykes, flooding the region and forcing the Spaniards to retreat. Dutch ships were able to sail across the flooded polders.

Unable to suppress the rebellion, the Spaniards turned to negotiation; although religious issues proved insuperable in 1575. This course was encouraged by Philip II's bankruptcy (suspension of payments to bankers) in September 1575. The resulting collapse of the credit system of Spanish power led the army, from July 1576, to mutiny, abandon Holland and Zeeland, where their opponents were under great pressure, and, on 4–5 November, sack Antwerp with over 6,000 civilians slaughtered. This fostered political pressure for the expulsion of Spanish troops, leading, on 8 November, to the Pacification of Ghent, an agreement to co-operate to that end. Requesens's successor, Philip's half-brother, Don John of Austria, the victor of Lepanto, agreed to the Perpetual Edict (signed on 12 February 1577) by which Spanish forces were to be withdrawn and Catholic worship restored. Spanish troops began to leave in April 1577, but Holland and Zeeland were unwilling to accept the agreement, as was William of Orange.

In a tense situation, Don John abandoned conciliation and seized Namur in July 1577, leading the Low Countries to rally against him. However, major divisions between Catholic and Protestant and the developing radicalism of the Protestant cities of Brabant, especially Ghent, led to a collapse of the revolt's precarious unity. Furthermore, a truce with the Ottomans in the Mediterranean led Philip to order the return of his troops. The Catholic nobility of the Walloon south were keen to reconcile themselves with Philip II and to restore social discipline. On 31 January 1578, Don John won a victory at Gembloux, again demonstrating Spanish superiority in battle. Having defeated the Dutch cavalry, the Spanish horse were able to catch the Dutch infantry unprepared and to inflict heavy casualties.

Don John's successor after his death on 1 October 1578, his nephew Alessandro Farnese, later Duke of Parma, continued to woo the southern nobles. In May 1579, the southern provinces agreed the Union of Arras in order to obtain a reconciliation with Philip II, and Parma agreed to withdraw the Spanish troops. They were to be used in the overrunning of Portugal and the conquest of the Azores. However, the northern provinces negotiated the Union of Utrecht to continue to resist the authority of Philip. The Spanish troops returned and conflict resumed. The States General deposed Philip II in July 1581 by an Act of Abjuration; Francis, Duke of Anjou was accepted as a ruler, but rapidly squandered his limited goodwill and died in 1584.

Parma was an able general, and he captured many rebel towns in the south: Maastricht and 's-Hertogenbosch (1579); Courtrai (1580); Breda and Tournai (1581); Oudenaarde (1582), by when Parma commanded about 60,000 men; Dunkirk, Nieuwpoort and Eindhoven (1583); Bruges, Ghent and Ypres (1584). William of Orange was assassinated on 10 July 1584. The pace of Spanish advance continued, helped by the extent to which the superiority of the Army of Flanders prevented any real chance of the relief of fortified positions, and thus encouraged them to take the better terms that a swift surrender ensured. In some cases, as at Lier, Parma was helped by treason on the part of some of the defenders. In 1585, Antwerp fell after a fourteen-month siege that had won the attention of Europe. Brussels, Mechelen and Geertruidenberg fell the same year. Parma also pushed north across the river line of the Rhine and Maas, taking Zutphen (1583) and Deventer (1587). From late 1585, the English, under Elizabeth's favourite, Robert, Earl of Leicester, intervened on behalf of the rebels with about 8,000 troops, but this proved no bar to Parma, whose opponents had become disunited and war-weary. Parma's operations revealed the potential of the Army of Flanders and helped ensure the high reputation of the Spanish military. They also, however, indicated the difficulty of translating military into political success. In military terms, the Spanish reliance on garrisons in order to control a distrusted population, used up large numbers of troops, as did the sieges required to take Dutch positions. This led to what has been presented as a war of attrition, although it is also possible to see the run of success from 1579 as evidence of the ability to achieve predictable results with an effective army. Parma was a capable diplomat as well as a superb strategist. He consolidated his base in the south of the Netherlands by a combination of political and military means. He consolidated the political allegiance of the Walloon nobility by establishing a zone of military control. He secured his border with France, his lines of communication along the Rhine, the coastal ports, and the Flanders towns along the south bank of the River Scheldt. This provided the base area and the room to manoeuvre his army to allow him to mount the siege of Antwerp. Following the prolonged siege, a number of other towns surrendered after only a token resistance. His steady, remorseless, systematic advance had the potential to 'strangle' the centre of Protestant resistance in Holland

and Zeeland. He was using military methods to achieve realisable political ends. The fall of Antwerp finally persuaded Elizabeth to sanction overt intervention, and provided the Dutch with a field army under Leicester that could be used in mobile operations to disrupt Parma's strategy. The operations in 1586 against Doesberg and Zutphen showed what the eager English 'gentlemen volunteers', and the veteran English infantry who supported them could achieve. The English allowed their forces to become bogged down in garrisons at Flushing, Brill and Ostend, the so-called 'cautionary' towns, and in the towns they captured, such as Deventer. Leicester became entangled in political wrangles that distracted him from his military tasks, and lost him political support. He failed to use his fleet effectively in 1587 to relieve Sluys, and was discomforted by the desertion of two of his veteran commanders, Stanley and Yorke, who handed over their charges to the Spaniards in 1587. His failures allowed Parma to continue his strategy of consolidation, although the seige of Sluys also provided Parma with an embarkation port for Philip's projected invasion of England. Even the failure of the intended invasion did not distract Parma. His army was moving against Bergen-op-Zoom, guarding the north bank of the Scheldt and the northern entrance to Antwerp, almost as soon as the unfortunate Armada had been dispersed in the action off Gravelines. The resolute defence of the town by its largely English garrison, thwarted his plan, but not his design. Philip II and the events in France, not the military situation in Holland, dictated the change in his strategic direction in 1590.

The Army of Flanders was hampered in its efforts to overcome the Dutch, from 1590, by the need to intervene in France to prevent the collapse of the Catholic League. Parma took his strike force into France in 1590 and 1592. Subsequent advances led to the capture of Cambrai (1595) and Calais (1596), and Archduke Albert led the Spanish army into Artois in 1597. Spanish losses to the Dutch in this period showed the importance of a field army for the retention of fortified positions.[6] Spanish strategy in the Netherlands was 'distorted' not just by the war against the French, but also by the need to support the loyal Catholic population of the north-east. This indicated the primacy of 'political' considerations, although these cannot be separated from military issues.

The Dutch benefited from going onto the offensive from 1590. Their commander was Maurice of Nassau, second son of William of Orange, who was elected President of the Council of State (1584). He accumulated offices, including the statholderships of Holland (1585), Zeeland (1585), Utrecht (1590), Overijssel (1590) and Gelderland (1591), and this helped advance and consolidate his position. Maurice adopted the same tactics as Parma, by trying to create a zone of control, with defensible borders and room for manoeuvre. The great river barriers that the Dutch had in any case been forced back to, and the removal of the Spanish mobile field army for operations in France aided him.

Maurice took Breda by surprise in 1590, before capturing Deventer, Hulst, Zutphen and Nijmegen the following year in very short sieges. The Dutch made good use of the rivers in order to move their cannon. They were also helped by the impact of mutinies on the Spanish war effort. In 1592, Maurice made major gains at the expense of the Spaniards in the north-east, capturing Coevorden and Steenwijk. Geertruidenberg fell in 1593 and Groningen in 1594. In 1597, Maurice, with English support, defeated a Spanish force that was caught on the move at Turnhout (24 January). The Dutch made good use of pistoleers at the battle. Maurice then advanced in the Lower Rhineland, capturing a number of fortresses, including Moers, west of Duisberg. His objective was to give the Dutch room for manoeuvre, create a buffer zone of fortified positions, and cut Spanish supply and communication links, especially along the Rhine and with the northern-eastern Low Countries. Dutch siege warfare, directed by Simon Stevin, the Quartermaster-General, was well organised and successful.

This was a war of sieges, not battles, but on 2 July 1600 Maurice was victorious at Nieuport. Maurice did not wish to carry out the operation that resulted in the battle. He was directed to do so by the States General, who believed it was important commercially and politically to capture the port of Dunkirk, which housed a 'nest of audacious pirates'. Maurice was reluctant to denude the United Provinces of their field army, and felt the amphibious insertion of a large force into Ostend, followed by a march on Dunkirk, past the enemy occupied fortress at Nieuport was unnecessarily risky. Like Parma before him, he had to bow to political rather than military imperatives, but he did insist on a number of members of the States General sailing to Ostend to to share responsibility. His misgivings were to prove well founded. His landing at Ostend was prevented by adverse winds, and instead his 12,000 strong force came ashore at Sas Van Ghent, west of Ostend, and took five days to march to Nieuport. The Spanish commander, the Archduke Albert, used the time to good effect and reacted with remarkable speed. By making extravagant promises, he persuaded his mutinous army of 11,500 veterans to return to duty. The mutinous condition of the Spanish field army had been one of the main reasons for attempting the risky enterprise. It was not anticipated that they could be brought back to the colours so quickly, and it says a lot for Albert's leadership. The rapid advance caught the State's army divided by the tidal creek of Nieuport harbour, and their advance guard clashed with the Dutch covering force, which consisted of the Scottish brigade and some Zeeland units. The Scots tried to hold the Spaniards long enough to enable Maurice to form up his troops, and they were virtually annihilated. The vanguard of the Dutch force consisted of Sir Francis Vere's foot bands and the Frisian brigade, and these bore the brunt of the fighting for over three hours, and suffered heavy casualties. They were assisted by naval gunfire from Dutch ships. These emulated the example of Admiral John Malen, who had contributed to the Duke of Egmont's victory at Gravelines in 1558, by sailing close inshore to fire his broadsides into the massed ranks of French pikemen. Vere slowed the Spanish advance but his troops had begun to give ground when Maurice threw in his last reserves, and the English and Dutch cavalry broke the exhausted and disorganised Spanish and Italian infantry who fled. Their withdrawal was covered by his Irish brigade, the remnants of Stanley's deserters from Deventer in 1587. The largest majority of the States' casualties were from England and Scotland, and the Irish figured prominently amongst the 5,000 Spanish casualties. The battle demonstrated the fact that the Spanish *Tercios* could be defeated in the open field, and showed how international the nature of the conflict had become, presaging the military situation that developed during the Thirty Years' War. Dutch losses lessened the value of victory, not least because it was difficult to replace veterans. In the specific case of Nieuport, Maurice was also discouraged by the approach of Spanish reinforcements and withdrew.

In 1602, Maurice marched south again, this time with over 25,000 men. Advancing via Maastricht into Brabant, he found the outnumbered Spaniards under Francisco de Mendoza entrenched near Tirlemont and unwilling to engage him in open battle. As with Gustavus Adolphus in 1632 (see p. 135), this removed the operational advantage from Maurice. He felt that Mendoza was too strong to attack, but too powerful to leave in his rear. As a result, Maurice withdrew in order to besiege Grave. Mendoza's attempt to threaten the siege was pre-empted by Maurice's skill in preparing his defences, while the Spanish army was affected by a lack of experienced troops, as well as of drivers for the artillery, and by a shortage of pay and food that led to mutiny. Grave fell.

The following year Maurice besieged 's-Hertogenbosch, but the Spaniards were able to reinforce the city, and Maurice abandoned the siege. The campaigning of the year focused on sieges, including the Spanish siege of Ostend, and that of mutineers in Hoogstraeten who were relieved by Maurice. These moves did not involve any large-scale clashes. Instead, generals were cautious about attacking nearby entrenched forces. In 1604, the States-General decided to relieve Ostend by sending Maurice to feint towards Sluys, in order to draw the Spanish army besieging Ostend into battle. Maurice was averse to the risk of battle, and preferred to besiege Sluys. The Spaniards eventually tried to break through the Dutch lines to relieve Sluys, but they were fought off on 17 August, and the garrison surrendered next day. Ostend, in turn, fell to the Spaniards. As so often, operations in the field (either a battle or the decision not to engage) helped determine the fate of a fort, as the garrison now had no hope of relief.

## The Spanish Road

Rivalry between Spain under Philip II and Philip III (r.1598–1621) and their opponents ensured that political disputes elsewhere in Western Europe (and, to a limited extent, in Eastern Europe also) were complicated by the intervention of both sides. They sought to recruit support and also to deny it to each other; support taking the form of troops and also of strategic positions. They also tried to foster diversionary conflicts. This could be seen clearly in the Swiss cantons. These were important as a source of troops, although less so than in the Italian Wars. Spain signed a treaty with the Catholic cantons in 1587 to enable her to recruit.

The Swiss cantons were also important because of their strategic position across and near the major military axis of the Spanish empire, from the Duchy of Milan to the Army of Flanders. Along this 'Spanish Road' moved the important contingents of Italian troops in that Army, as well as other resources. Furthermore, troops from Spain to the Low Countries moved via Milan, in large part because of the limitations and hazards of the direct sea route through the Bay of Biscay and the English Channel. The route via Milan involved sea transport from Barcelona to Genoa and movement north from the Milanese beyond the eastern frontier of France. In detail, there were a number of routes via Savoy, Franche-Comté and Lorraine, and, further east, via Tyrol, south-west Germany, and Alsace into Lorraine.[7] The 'Road' was not a permanent structure, and teams of pioneers under the direction of military engineers prepared the route and constructed temporary bridges ahead of the marching columns.

The importance of the 'Spanish Road' also ensured that attempts were made to interdict it. These included efforts by France and Venice to persuade the Swiss to close the routes. In particular, attention focused on the Valtelline passes which belonged to the Grisons League, a Protestant body whose firm rule over the Catholic inhabitants led to tension. Thus, local tension in the valley was registered on the international scene, while the pressures of the latter affected relations in the valley. In 1600, the Viceroy of Milan negotiated an alliance with the Grisons which greatly raised tensions in the Valtelline and with Venice.

Less directly, Spain's concern about her strategic position encouraged intervention in Germany. Thus, in 1581, Parma sent troops to overawe Aachen, where Protestants had seized control. The contest over the Archbishop-Electorate of Cologne was strategically more important. A dispute over whether Archbishop Gebhard could marry and retain his see, the prelude to Protestantism, led both sides to turn to outside aid in 1583. In January 1584, Gebhard defeated his opponents, under Duke Frederick of Saxe-Lauenburg, at Alost, but lost his capital, Bonn, when the mutinous garrison surrendered. Duke Ferdinand of Bavaria drove Gebhard from his territories that spring. Spanish troops had also been deployed and they were needed in 1587–9 when supporters of Gebhard challenged the position of the new Archbishop, Ernst of Bavaria. Parma's troops captured Neuss (1587), Bonn, (1588, which the Archbishop had lost in 1587) and Rheinberg (1589). In pursuit of its interests in the strategic Jülich–Cleves area in the Rhineland, the Spaniards seized

Wesel in 1598. Contests over control of dioceses also occurred elsewhere. In 1592, a double election of bishops in Strasbourg led to conflict, the Brandenburg candidate being supported by Huguenot troops in Dutch pay.

## The last stages of the Dutch Revolt

The end of the war in France in 1598 strengthened the Spaniards in the Low Countries, and suggests that Dutch success in the 1590s owed more to Spanish commitments in France than to the impact of Dutch military reforms, a reminder of the need to put military improvements in their political contexts. From 1604, the Spaniards also benefited from peace with England. However, it is important not to exaggerate the increase in Spain's offensive power in 1598 and 1604. Comparing 1603–7 with 1580–5, in both of which periods Spain was fighting the Dutch alone, there was a very clear improvement in Dutch military performance.

The new Spanish commander, Ambrogio Spínola, captured Ostend in 1604 after a siege that had lasted three years and seventy-seven days. Artillery bombardment was important, but so also was the willingness to storm positions, such as the outworks on the west side on 14 April 1603 and on Sand Hill on 13 September 1604, the last the decisive episode of the siege. The Dutch had kept Ostend re-supplied from the sea, but the Spaniards forced its surrender by gaining control of the coastal sand dunes, which enabled them to mount batteries to dominate the harbour entrance. Spínola forced the pace of the siege by his willingness to sacrifice troops in determined assaults.

The Dutch tried to regain the initiative, but their surprise attack on Antwerp in 1605 was no surprise and was repelled. Once Spínola, with a larger army, was in the field, Maurice established a camp at Biervliet, only to find himself faced with a new higher tempo of Spanish campaigning, as Spínola moved to take Oldenzaal and Lingen in the Dutch rear. Forced into action, Maurice advanced to protect Dutch positions on the German frontier, only to be defeated by Spínola on 8 October, in another surprise attack that lost surprise, and then losing two more forts.

In 1606, Spínola moved the campaigning north after a surprise attack on Sluys had failed. Spanish forces crossed the Maas and Rhine in July, invaded Overijssel, and then turned west. Using defensive lines and taking advantage of fortifications constructed the previous year and of the atrocious weather, Maurice stopped Spínola on the Ijssel, but the Spaniards successfully besieged Lochem and Grol before moving south to capture Rheinberg. However, financial problems led to desertion and mutiny, giving Maurice the opportunity to recapture Lochem, although failing at Grol when Spínola advanced to relieve the fort. A cease fire was concluded the following April, and a twelve-year truce in April 1609.[8]

The conflict in the Low Countries indicated the dual importance of battles and sieges. If an army could not be faced in the field, it could attack fortresses as it chose, as Parma demonstrated in the 1580s and Spínola, in the face of Maurice's caution, in 1606; as well as Istvan Bocskai in Transylvania in 1605. Equally, a lengthy siege could so delay operations that the strategic initiative was lost or the campaigning season consumed.

Military techniques were far from static. Changes introduced in the Dutch army in the late sixteenth century included broader and shallower troop formations which permitted more soldiers to fire at once, and, from the 1590s, the use of a volley technique to maintain continuous fire. Impressed by Aelian's account of the drill of Roman javelinmen and slingers, Maurice proposed six rotating ranks of musketeers. He also adopted paper cartridges containing a pre-prepared amount of powder, thus increasing each muske-teer's rate of fire. The process of retraining was assisted in 1599 by the availability of funds to equip the entire field army with weapons of the same size and calibre, while its reorganisation into smaller units improved the mobility of the Dutch infantry.

General histories of war discuss Maurice's military 'reforms', but not the campaigning history of the last years of the conflict. Were they to do so, they might find any emphasis on the reforms inappropriate. Instead, the continued vitality of the Army of Flanders emerges. Spínola's 1605 and 1606 campaigns revealed a willingness to rethink the conflict and to seize the initiative to considerable effect. If Spínola failed to break the Ijssel line, he had neverthe-less demonstrated his ability to campaign north of the Maas and Rhine, and to take the war to the enemy. Yet, the situation was similar to the War of the Bavarian Succession (1778–9), when Frederick the Great of Prussia's invasion of Bohemia was also blocked by an opponent (Austria) entrenched behind a river, because the political and financial context did not permit a lengthy conflict at this point. Under great financial pressure, Philip III needed peace.

There is another way in which the stress on the 'reforms' appears inap-propriate. Accounts of the operations indicate the multiple deficiencies of both armies, which, for the Spaniards sent against Zwolk in 1606, included shot that was too large for their cannon. These deficiencies can be presented in a number of ways. They can be extenuated by referring to the length of the struggle, the range of commitments, the friction of war and, specifically, the weather. Both sides were heavily indebted. Against that background, the efforts made by both sides were impressive. Yet if military capability is to be seen as involving, as it must, government finances as well as battlefield capa-bility, then it is apparent that both sides were under extraordinary pressure. If each fought the war on credit, there was an obvious comparison with twentieth-century wars, but generals in the latter did not confront the situa-tion facing Spínola. He had to pledge his own credit, and in 1606 faced mutiny by nearly 2,500 troops.

The failure of the Spaniards to suppress the Dutch revolt raises both specific questions about Spain and more general issues of comparative tasking and capability. Why, for example, were the weaker English able to conquer Ireland

and the French crown to check and, eventually, destroy the Huguenots, when the far stronger Spanish empire could not succeed in the Low Countries? The most common response is that of imperial overreach – the combination of the range of Spanish commitments with the problems of operating the Spanish empire, specifically deficiencies in resources and communications. This interpretation, termed by Geoffrey Parker the 'materialistic model', has a number of deficiencies not least the extent of Spanish success (which included the reconquest on a number of occasions of much of the Low Countries), the role of other factors in creating problems for Spain, principally policy mistakes, the possibility of counterfactuals operating to allow more success, and the extent to which Philip's strategic and political assumptions led to a set of priorities in which the Dutch Revolt was not foremost.[9]

The last returns us to the debate about agency versus structure, a debate that is of importance not only for political history, but also for its military counterpart. In recent decades, structure has dominated non-operational (i.e. non-campaign) accounts of war, particularly with the emphasis on technological analyses of development, that present an almost automatic corollary in military effectiveness, and also with the interest, in the 'new military history', in social contexts. This structural emphasis has a number of weaknesses, not least its proneness to determinism and the extent to which it does not match the emphasis on agency seen in operational military history and in the studies of the international relations that helped determine military tasking. In the case of the Dutch Revolt, the range of Philip's options included different political strategies in the Low Countries, the choice of subordinates and the allocation of resources between different spheres. It is difficult to see how structural interpretations can be sustained.

## British Isles

There were also wars of religion in Scotland, with English support for the Protestants in 1560. The French troops that had played an important role from 1554 during the regency of Mary of Guise, were expelled. Mary, Queen of Scots, a weak and discredited monarch who returned to Scotland in 1561 after her husband Francis II of France, died, faced opposition from a group of powerful Protestant aristocrats, the Lords of the Congregation. She was forced to abdicate in favour of her infant son, James VI, in 1567 after she married James, Earl of Bothwell, who had been responsible for the death of her second husband. Mary escaped in 1568, but was defeated at Langside and fled to England, where she was imprisoned by the Protestant Elizabeth I (r.1559–1603).

Elizabeth herself was able to defeat the unsuccessful Northern Rebellion of 1569 that owed much to Catholic opposition. The threat from the rebel Earls of Northumberland and Westmorland was diminished by the absence of foreign military support, and from their inability to reach and release the imprisoned Mary. The Earls also failed to recruit a broader base of similarly disaffected lords, and were affected by a lack of adequate weapons and money. They subsequently disbanded their forces and fled when a strong royal army advanced.

The most sustained fighting in the British Isles was in Ireland. In 1490, the English Crown had wielded only limited power there. As Lord of Ireland, the monarch had important claims of overlordship, but control was restricted to the Pale, the area around Dublin. The Reformation transformed the situation. Henry VIII was concerned about the risk of Papal or Spanish intervention, and in 1541 had himself proclaimed King of Ireland. Under his successor, Edward VI, the 'plantation' of areas outside the Pale with English settlers began. This increased the security of the Crown's position, although the expropriation of Gaelic landowners was unpopular. The pace of plantation increased from the late 1560s, and English rule became more military in character and intent, leading to fresh attempts to extend and enforce control.

These in turn provoked rebellions, culminating in a major Gaelic uprising in Ulster in 1595. This was ably led by Hugh O'Neill, Earl of Tyrone, who also sought support from the 'Old English': English settlers who were Catholics. He raised a substantial army of 10,000 and spread the rebellion across Ireland.

The character of the fighting is a useful reminder of the variety of types of European warfare. From mid-century, firearms, in the form of the arquebus, had been introduced into Ireland, but, in the 1560s, Shane O'Neill's forces still relied principally on traditional weapons, especially axes, bows, javelins and swords. These were used alongside firearms in his victory over the MacDonnells of Antrim at Glentaisie in 1565.

By contrast, his nephew, Hugh O'Neill's men used modern firearms, the musket and the caliver, and were as well-armed as the English. Many had served in the Spanish army, and O'Neill trained his entire force in the use of pikes and firearms. However, there was more emphasis on irregular warfare than elsewhere in Western Europe. Employing firearms, this warfare was combined with infantry shock tactics that used sword and target (shield).[10] The wooded and boggy terrain of Ulster was well-suited to guerrilla conflict, and at Clontibret in 1595 O'Neill successfully ambushed an English army. Three years later, at Yellow Ford, another English force was even more effectively attacked while on the march. Musket fire combined with charges led to 1,600 English casualties.

These defeats only encouraged the English to persist. The Earl of Essex was sent with a major force in 1599, and marched over much of southern Ireland, but the Irish avoided battle. The following year, a more effective leader, Charles, Lord Mountjoy, was appointed as the new Lord Deputy. He decided to campaign in the winter in order to disrupt Irish logistics, trying to immobilise the migrant herds of cattle which fed the Irish army. Mountjoy brought a new determination to the conflict, and also enjoyed numerical superiority.

However, his attempt to invade Ulster was defeated at the battle of Moyry Pass (1600) by O'Neill's use of musketeers protected by field fortifications.

English fears of Spanish intervention were realised in September 1601 when Philip III sent 3,500 troops under Juan del Aguila to Kinsale to support O'Neill. Mountjoy responded by blockading the port, but his force was rapidly weakened by sickness. However, instead of blockading Mountjoy, O'Neill's relieving force decided to attack. The night march on Mountjoy's camp was mishandled, and, on 24 December, O'Neill unusually lost the tactical initiative, allowing Mountjoy to move first. O'Neill also deployed his men in the unfamiliar defensive formation of the Spanish *tercio* (square), which proved cumbersome. The English cavalry drove their Irish counterparts from the field, and the Irish infantry retreated, those who stood being routed. The Irish lost 1,200 men but, more seriously, the pattern of victory was broken. The Spanish force at Kinsale, which had had little positive impact on the campaign and had failed to co-operate with the Irish, surrendered, O'Neill following in 1603.

The Nine Years' War in Ireland provides evidence of the strength of the Irish combination of traditional Celtic tactical methods with modern firearms. It also reveals the risk of seeking to transform such a force into the standard Western European pattern and, specifically, of requiring them to maintain the tactical defensive. Until 1601, O'Neill combined a strategic defensive – protecting Ulster – and a tactical offensive. The switch in strategy proved fatal. Yet, although the Irish could live off the land and use the terrain, and benefited from 'modernity' in the form of muskets, O'Neill was also pitted against a powerful state, with a more sophisticated military and logistical organisation, and naval support.[11]

## The conquest of Portugal

Religious rivalry did not play a role in the Spanish conquest of Portugal in 1580. Philip II was able to enforce his claim to the succession, employing both widespread bribery and troops. Supported by a fleet from Cadiz, Alba and about 47,000 troops, half of them German and Italian mercenaries, invaded in late June. The frontier fortress of Elvas fell without resistance on 18 June and the bulk of the army advanced into Portugal on 27 June. Sétubal fell on 18 July, Lisbon in late August, after street-by-street fighting, and Coimbra on 8 September.[12] The Portuguese were defeated at Alcantara, in one of the most rapid and decisive campaigns of the century.

The limited attention paid to this campaign is worthy of note. Had it lasted longer, and, even more, had the Portuguese succeeded, the campaign would probably receive more attention and be cited to demonstrate the truth of maxims about sixteenth-century warfare. Although circumstances were very different, Portugal fell more rapidly than the Aztec and Inca states. Longer Portuguese resistance under the claimant Dom Antonio was limited to the

Azores, which had a strategic position thwart maritime routes. A Spanish attempt to take the islands failed in 1581. In 1582, Dom Antonio was provided with French support, including about 6–7,000 troops, the largest French expedition sent overseas during the century. On 26 July 1582, the French fleet was defeated by a Spanish-Portuguese fleet off St Miguel and, the following year, the Azores were conquered.

Portugal, one of the two leading transoceanic empires, had been taken over by its rival, Spain, with relatively little fighting, a marked contrast to the contest between Portugal and Islam. This reflected the primacy of the dynastic theme in Europe: the death of the childless King Sebastian in 1578 (see p. 55) and the absence of effective claimants entailed the end of an independent Portugal. The process of dynastic takeover was eased by the willingness to maintain distinct institutions and separate practices and privileges, as with Scotland and England when James VI of Scotland became James I of England in 1603. Philip II became Philip I of Portugal. No new state was created.

## Baltic warfare

The Wars of Religion also extended to the Baltic. The Reformation accentuated the question of the fate of the extensive lands of the crusading orders, the Teutonic Knights and the Livonian Order, although both had already suffered from political developments in the region. The Reformation also separated Catholic Poland from Protestant Sweden and Orthodox Russia. In response to intervention by Sigismund Augustus of Poland-Lithuania, Ivan IV of Russia, Ivan the Terrible (r.1533–84), sought to gain the lands of the Livonian Order, capturing Narva (1558) and Polotsk (1563), but being defeated by the Lithuanians at Czasniki and on the Ula river (1564). The Russians benefited from the military changes introduced by Ivan early in his reign, including the creation in 1550 of a permanent palace infantry guard of 3,000 musketeers, the *streltsy*, that owed much to the Ottoman janissaries for its inspiration. At Polotsk, the Russians deployed 12,000 musketeers. Like the Ottomans, there was no emphasis on pikemen, but there was an attempt to develop field artillery. A regular force structure was developed as were administrative support agencies including, in 1577, a Musketeers' Chancellery.

In place of the weaker states that had formerly opposed Russian advances, Ivan now had to face both Denmark and Sweden in the eastern Baltic and the powerful Poland-Lithuania and Ukraine which formed a permanent union in 1569. The major Estonian port of Reval put itself under Swedish protection in 1561 and successfully resisted Russian sieges in 1570–1 and 1576–7. Ivan's focus on the Baltic gave Devlet Girei, the Khan of the Crimean Tatars, the opportunity to sack Moscow in 1571. Ivan conquered most of Livonia in 1575–6, but his army was crushed by the Poles and Swedes at Wenden (1578), the Swedes fording a deep stream under cover of their field artillery. The Swedes then drove the Russians from Kexholm, to the east of

Finland (1580), and in 1581, under the able French mercenary Pontus de la Gardie, stormed Narva, slaughtering the entire population. By the end of the year, the whole of Estonia had been regained. In the winter of 1581, the Swedes marched over the frozen Gulf of Finland from Viborg in Finland to Ingria, a particularly bold step.

The Russians were also under pressure from Stefan Bátory, King of Poland, who had been able in 1578 to persuade the *Sejm* to vote a significant level of taxation for two years. Bátory wished to regain Livonia, but did so by attacking Muscovy itself. He retook Polotsk (1579), and captured Velikie Luki and Kholm (1580), but his long siege of Pskov (1581) failed. In 1582, Ivan was forced to make peace with Poland, and in 1583, giving up his gains, signed a three-year truce with Sweden, later extended to 1590. Sieges played a major role in the conflicts in the eastern Baltic, although blockade rather than bombardment seems to have been decisive in gaining success. Raiding was also important. There is scant sign that the Russians lost because of their slowness to adopt new firearm line tactics.[13]

Further west, political and economic rivalry between Denmark and Sweden led to war in 1563. The Danes captured Älvsborg (Gothenburg), Sweden's sole outlet to the North Sea, that year, prompting Erik XIV of Sweden (r.1560–8) to seek a new route through southern Norway. Trondheim fell to the Swedes in 1564 (it was swiftly recaptured), much of southern Norway was overrun in 1567, and Oslo was taken, but the Swedes were held at Akershus. From 1565 until 1569, the Swedes also held Varberg to the south of Älvsborg.

Erik relied on native troops, but he transformed their fighting methods by training them in the combined use of pikes and firearms in linear formations. He made the pike the basis of offensive infantry tactics, leading Roberts to refer to him as 'the first of the revolutionaries', although the novelty and effectiveness of his innovations have been challenged. Frederick II of Denmark (r.1559–96) used German mercenaries who were usually more successful, severely defeating the Swedes at the sole major battle of the war, Axtorna (20 October 1565), where Erik's troops fought well but were poorly commanded. The Danish army managed to advance as far as Norrköping in late 1567 before being forced to retreat by the weather. Both sides were exhausted by 1568, and peace was agreed at Stettin in 1570 without any territorial gains to either side. Älvsborg was returned in exchange for a ransom.

This enabled Sweden to fight the Russians in the 1570s and early 1580s. In 1590, the Russians again attacked Sweden. Fighting extended to the White Sea coast, where the Swedes failed to take Kola in 1590 and 1591. A Swedish attempt to besiege Novgorod in 1591 failed. By the Treaty of Teusino (1595), Russia abandoned claims to Estonia and Narva, while Sweden gave back Ingria, which had been occupied since the truce of 1583.

The Swedes then turned to a brief civil war. The Catholic Sigismund Vasa (Sigismund III of Poland, r.1587–1632) became king of Sweden in 1592, but his Catholicism helped his uncle, Duke Charles of Södermanland, to organise opposition to him. In 1597, civil war began, and the following year Sigismund arrived in Sweden with a force of German and Hungarian mercenaries, making a practically unopposed landing at Stegeborg, at a time when Charles's larger army was elsewhere. The subsequent conflict showed both the potential decisiveness of warfare in the period and its close relationship with political factors. Technically, Sigismund's force was superior and at the battle of Stångebro his mercenaries fought well. However, the conflict was not settled by technical military superiority. Instead, adroit generalship – Charles's surprise attack at Stångebro under cover of mist – was important, but so, even more, was the degree of determination of the two sides: the Swedes in Sigismund's army were unwilling to fight at Stångebro while, in general, Sigismund failed to show the willingness to fight and manoeuvre to the death necessary in such circumstances. He returned to Poland in 1598, abandoning his supporters, and was deposed by the *Riksdag* in 1599 at the behest of Charles, who became Charles IX in 1604.[14]

Conflict in Eastern Europe broke out anew in the 1600s, as a disputed succession in Russia accentuated by foreign intervention led to the Time of Troubles (1604–13). Sigismund III of Poland sought to exploit the situation in order to gain control of Russia. Smolensk, on the route to Moscow, withstood a siege from 19 September 1609 until it was stormed on the night of 2–3 June 1611. The fortifications, strengthened in 1595–1602, comprised a four-mile circuit of walls, thirty-eight towers, deep foundations and a system of revetted listening galleries that thwarted Polish attempts to dig mines under the Russian defences. Russian counter-mines blocked Polish mines in early 1610, and the Poles only succeeded after the garrison's strength had been reduced by the long siege. After victory at Klushino in 1610, the Poles entered Moscow and Sigismund's eldest son, Wladyslaw, was acclaimed Tsar, but anti-Polish attitudes thwarted this attempt and, in 1612, the Polish force in the Kremlin was starved into submission. The only way the Russians would have accepted Wladyslaw in the longer term would have been if he had converted to Orthodoxy and 'gone native'. This was unlikely, as he would have ruled himself out of the succession in Poland. Sigismund was unable to prevent the new Romanov dynasty from consolidating their control of Russia, but, by the Truce of Deulino (1619), he gained Smolensk from the war.

The invasion of Russia had been driven by private enterprise, with Sigismund III and the Polish Commonwealth getting involved only at a later stage. Many of the troops involved were Cossack freebooters. The Polish nobility was not prepared to tolerate the prospect of financing a large standing army over a prolonged period. Instead, they were happy to settle for Smolensk once it became clear that retaining Moscow was not going to be an easy option. There was always doubt about the feasibility of the whole business. The nobility's real concern was the preservation of their rights and liberties, and the strengthening of the monarchy, which permanent success in Moscow would have involved, was not an appealing prospect. In addition, there was an intermittent state of civil war in Poland in 1607–9, the *rokosz* of Sandomierz, which was essentially an armed response by a large part of the nobility to the perceived threat posed by Sigismund to their liberties. Even Sigismund's supporters, militarily the victors, were opposed to any significant strengthening of royal powers.

A Swedish attempt to conquer Livonia had led to conflict with Poland from 1600. When that failed, Charles IX in 1608–9 eagerly involved Sweden in the Russian troubles, partly to gain territories and partly to block Polish ambitions in Russia.

The Swedes were bought off by Russia in 1617 at the cost of Ingria and Kexholm. Poland also clashed with Sweden which, in turn, fought with Denmark in 1611–13: the Danes captured Kalmar (1611) and Älvsborg (1612), and Gustavus Adolphus, the new king of Sweden, had to make concessions to obtain peace by the Treaty of Knäred. These conflicts in Eastern Europe were far more than a footnote to the history of European warfare, and are an important reminder of the growing prominence of Russia and Sweden.[15] Sieges, for example of Reval and Smolensk, played a major role in the fighting, while devastation was used to reduce the logistical capability of opponents. The tactics employed were less formalistic than those developed in Western Europe, and the troops sometimes less specialised in weaponry, but their warfare was well-suited to campaigning in Eastern Europe with its great distances and small populations.

Cavalry played an important role in battle and campaigning. The Poles won cavalry victories over the Swedes at Kokenhausen (23 June 1601), Reval (June 1602), Kirchholm (27 September 1605) and, over a much larger Russo-Swedish army, at Klushino (4 July 1610), although at Klushino the firepower of the Polish infantry and artillery also played a major role. At Kirchholm and Klushino, the mobility and power of the Polish cavalry, which attacked in waves and relied on shock charges, nullified its opponent's numerical superiority and the Poles were able to destroy the Swedish cavalry before turning on their infantry. Exposed once the cavalry had been driven off, the Swedish infantry suffered heavily. At Kircholm, they lost over 70 per cent of their strength. This was a powerful reminder of the need to avoid an account of European military development solely in terms of improvements in infantry firepower. Similarly, on 8 July 1659 at Konotop, Russian cavalry were heavily defeated by steppe cavalry: the Crimean Tatars allied with Hetman Vyhovsky of the Ukraine and the Cossacks. The Russians lost largely due to poor reconnaissance and generalship: they let their main corps get lured into a swamp.

Polish cavalry tactics influenced those further west, not least thanks to commanders such as Pappenheim who had served in Poland. Aside from providing a warning about the customary emphasis on infantry, these battles also suggested that the novel military techniques that are held up for particular praise, were of only limited value. At Klushino, the Swedish force was largely composed of mercenaries familiar with conflict in Western Europe, while one of the commanders, Jakob de la Gardie, had served under Maurice of Nassau.

## Rebellions

As in the earlier period, there was an important series of rebellions. In addition to those already mentioned, these included the revolts of the Moriscos (1568–70) and Aragonese (1591) against Philip II. Such rebellions were important because they interacted with the international conflicts of the period. Thus the Moriscos unsuccessfully sought Ottoman support, while Philip II was concerned about a possible relationship between the Aragonese revolt and the French Wars of Religion. Don John of Austria commanded the forces that brutally repressed the Morisco rising. Large numbers of Moriscos were slaughtered, while the Spaniards benefited from importing large quantities of firearms from Italy to equip the troops raised by their nobles. The dispatch of a force of about 15,500 men rapidly suppressed the limited opposition in Aragon. This army, largely recruited by the Castilian nobility from their estates,[16] indicated the continued importance of that military resource, as did the force raised by nobles in 1580 to provide supplementary support to the army sent to invade Portugal.

The Corsican rebellion against Genoese rule in 1564 was also located in an international context. The leader, Sampiero Croso, received French and Ottoman support, while the Genoese were backed by Spanish troops. The war was waged by skirmishes rather than battles and the rebels used the difficult terrain to advantage in their guerrilla tactics. However, aside from the professionalism of the Spanish troops, the Corsicans were divided, a product of the long hold of factional feuds; and by 1569 Genoese control had been re-established.

Also in the 1560s, a local rebellion in Finale on the Ligurian coast of Italy drove out the harsh ruler, Alfonso del Carretto, but when in 1571 Philip II intervened on behalf of the Empire, he took over the principality for himself rather than restoring the ruler. The ability of the Spaniards to intervene in northern Italy was also displayed in Casale Monferrato, where Spanish troops helped the ruler, Duke Guglielmo of Mantua (r.1560–87), suppress resistance to his attempts to limit tax and judicial exemptions. Spanish troops also helped the Papacy against the substantial bandit forces that dominated large areas of the Papal States. Not all revolts in Italy provided opportunities for the display of Spanish power. Thus, in 1573, Guidobaldo II, Duke of Urbino harshly repressed a revolt against new taxes without Spanish assistance.

Force also played a major role in internal politics within Russia. In Ivan IV's later years, when his paranoid tendencies became very pronounced, he created a separate government, the *Oprichnina*, with its own army which was responsible for a high level of internal violence, including the sacking of Novgorod in 1570. The Russian Time of Troubles escalated from peasant revolts (1603) and the appearance of the first pretend Tsar (1604) to full-scale foreign intervention by Poland and Sweden. The first False Dmitry was backed by Jesuits and Poles. The situation did not stabilise until Michael Romanov became Tsar in 1613.[17]

The interrelationship of rebellions and international competition serves as a reminder of the 'multiple tasking' facing contemporary states and their forces. It was far from clear which challenge would take precedence or what was the most effective way of responding. The high-cost scenarios of large, professional armies, substantial artillery trains, state-of-the-art fortifications and dedicated navies with new vessels confronted political, military and financial contexts and constraints that suggested that they were not necessarily the wisest solution. It was also clear that the presence, let alone cost, of such forces was unwelcome to many political elites. Thus, the Spanish troops left the Low Countries in 1561 because otherwise the local Estates were unwilling to vote taxes.

## The Military Revolution revisited

As with the previous chapter, it is appropriate to consider the warfare of the period in terms of the general theses discussed in Chapters 2 and 3. If military development is seen in terms of effectiveness, then the inability of large military establishments to bring conflict to a close despite protracted efforts is readily apparent, while it is also clear that rulers and ministers found it difficult to organise and sustain effective levels of mobilisation and supply. This was readily apparent with the English military and their expeditions in the 1590s. It is of course possible to explain the lengthy nature of the Livonian War by reference to the number of participants and the difficulty each experienced of dominating the combat zone, combined with the possibility of them deploying forces from their distant bases. In this respect, the war prefigured the Thirty Years' War. Similarly, the length of the Dutch War can in part be explained by reference to the problems of Spanish force projection combined with other calls on Spanish power. In the case of the French Wars of Religion, the problems of civil conflict combined with poor kingship hindered the chances of a speedy resolution:

> Military innovations of some magnitude were needed before solutions to the problems of the inadequate nature of existing standing armies, large-scale, long-term warfare, and fiscal and organizational inefficiency were to be found. In France internal war had the effect of postponing rather than abetting the most significant changes, which were eventually to solve the problems the Military Revolution posed. The Military Revolution required internal peace.[18]

Other uses of force did not lead to lengthy conflicts. Thus, the contested succession to Alfonso II, the last Duke of Ferrara (r.1559-97), which hinged on differences between imperial and papal authority, led Cesare d'Este and the Pope to raise armies, only for the former to back down when he did not receive French support. As so often, the international context proved crucial.

Alongside the discussion of effectiveness, it is relevant to point to important tactical innovations. These have generally been attributed to Maurice of Nassau, but it is possible to adopt a different focus and to stress the role of pistoleers in lessening the value of heavy cavalry in the third quarter of the century. This altered the force requirements of infantry. As the risk from heavy cavalry declined, so it became less necessary to have a high pike-to-shot ratio. Indeed, an increase in the ratio of shot lessened the threat from pistoleers to infantry. The fact that pistoleers only required one hand to fire their pistols, and could ride smaller and thus less expensive horses than heavy cavalry was of only limited value in any confrontation with infantry.

This provided the background for a period of experimentation in infantry formations that included, but was not defined, by the Nassau reforms. At the same time, the revival of cavalry shock tactics under Henry IV (and later Gustavus Adolphus and others), but now using sabre and pistol not lance, forced the infantry to retain pikes for protection against cavalry, irrespective of their value against other infantry.[19] This revival also serves as a reminder of the adaptability and flexibility of the cavalry arm. This was not simply a matter of tactical practice, but also of developments in horse breeding and equestrianism that led to a faster and more agile war horse. Rather, however, than seeing shifts in cavalry warfare in terms of a single model of effectiveness and a uniform direction of change, the mistake too often made in infantry warfare, it is more appropriate to note a variety of fighting techniques. Furthermore, it is important not to focus on cavalry attacks on infantry to the detriment of cavalry–cavalry conflict. The combination of the two ensured the need for a continuing capacity to fight from the saddle: it was not enough to be a mounted infantryman.[20]

## The 1610s

Warfare involving Russia, Poland, Sweden and Denmark in the 1600s and 1610s serves as a reminder that there can be no ready compartmentalisation based on a break between the warfare of the late sixteenth century and the Thirty Years' War that began in 1618. Such a notion can only arise from a misleading focus on the major struggles in Western Europe, where indeed 1598–1609 witnessed a series of agreements and treaties that brought an end, or at least truce, to the French Wars of Religion, the Dutch Revolt, the Nine Years' War in Ireland, and conflict between England, France and Spain. The Ottomans and Austrians ended their war (see pp. 198–9) in 1606.

Yet there was also an important series of crises in the 1610s that look towards the greater level of conflict that began in 1618. A major war had nearly broken out in 1610 between France and Spain. Although this has been traced to French fears of Spanish encirclement and to the specific issue of the Jülich-Cleves succession dispute in the Rhineland, research, based in part on the medical records of Henry IV, has resulted in the suggestion that his personal, especially sexual, problems and perceived inadequacies led him to take an aggressive stance.[21] War was only pre-empted by Henry's assassination in Paris on 14 May. This would have been a widespread struggle, not least because Duke Charles Emanuel I of Savoy assembled an army to support French schemes in Italy. As it was, the death in 1609 of the childless Duke John William of Jülich-Cleves had been followed by the occupation of the inheritance by the Protestant claimants, in defiance of Imperial jurisdiction and mandates, with the exception of the fortress of Jülich into which the Emperor Rudolf II sent a garrison. Henry IV and the Protestant Union of German princes agreed to co-operate against Jülich, and, after Henry IV died, a French force was sent to aid the siege, which also included Dutch troops under Maurice of Nassau. On 1 September 1610, Jülich surrendered. The Union had also sent troops into Alsace in order to overawe Archduke Leopold, Bishop of Strasbourg and Passau, although in August the two sides agreed to end hostilities there.

The Rhenish duchies continued to be the cause of controversy, especially when one of the claimants converted to Catholicism in 1613 and won the backing of Philip III. His rival, the Elector of Brandenburg, in turn sought the help of Maurice of Nassau and in 1614 Maurice advanced to confront Spínola, who occupied Wesel. However, the issue was settled that year with a partition of the Jülich-Cleves inheritance by the Treaty of Xanten.

France faced serious political problems during the minority of Henry IV's infant son, Louis XIII (r. 1610–43), but that did not prevent a testing of Habsburg, both Austrian and Spanish, strength and intentions over the following decade. The determination of Venice to maintain its independence and interests was the particular point of tension, although in part that arose from the aggressive policies of Habsburg agents, especially Osuna, the Viceroy of Naples.

Tension between Venice and Spain in northern Italy was matched by rivalry on Venice's frontier with the Austrian Habsburgs. The latter led to conflict in 1613–16. Although there were no dramatic advances in the war by either side, it helped to keep tension high and also provided employment and training for a large number of soldiers: Venice turned to German, Swiss and other mercenaries. In 1617, Venice recruited 4,000 Dutch troops to help against Austria, and the following year made efforts to obtain the support of a Dutch naval squadron against Spain, which was interfering with Venice's Adriatic shipping. The Venetian government alleged that Spain was plotting to overthrow the republic, a useful reminder to contemporaries that there was no compartmentalisation of military conflict from domestic subversion. To distract Spanish forces in Lombardy, Venice financed Charles Emanuel I of Savoy-Piedmont's schemes in Monferrato, which he invaded in 1613, 1615 and 1617 in pursuit of a succession claim. Spain and its Italian allies defeated him on three occasions. As another aspect of its defensive strategy, Venice pressed on with its fortification policies. It hired Francesco Tensini, who carried out works at Bergamo, Crema, Peschiera and Verona, and in 1624 dedicated his *La Fortificatione* to the Doge and Senate.

These conflicts were, again, important because of the employment and experience they provided for troops from across much of Europe: Charles Emanuel used many French, German and Swiss troops. Furthermore, the warfare helped keep international tension high. Charles Emanuel sought to maintain and exploit differences between France and Spain, and also tried to develop links with the German Protestant Union. This had been formed in 1608 in response to the seizure by the Catholic Duke Maximilian of Bavaria the previous December of Donauwörth where Catholic–Protestant relations had seriously deteriorated. The Union was a defensive league headed by the Elector Palatine. Also in 1608, disputes between the Austrian Habsburgs, specifically between the Emperor Rudolf II and his brother Matthias, led to the invasion of Bohemia by the latter in a successful attempt to seize control of Austria, Moravia and Habsburg Hungary. The militarisation of politics in the region was further displayed in the early 1610s with a high level of armed preparedness by the Estates. In 1611, the Estates of Bohemia clashed with Archduke Leopold (who Rudolf wanted as his successor), who had raised an army in his nearby diocese of Passau and advanced on Prague. The determination of the Estates led Rudolf and Leopold to back down. Leopold's force left, inflicting much damage as it did so, and, in concert with the Estates, Matthias entered the city with an army. Rudolf was intimidated into abdicating and Matthias was crowned as King of Bohemia.

Although there was no large-scale conflict in the region, the use of intimidation and force in order to ensure the succession prepared the way for events in Prague later in the decade. Well before the outbreak of the Thirty Years' War, with fighting in Bohemia in 1618, there was a sense that a major war would break out. It was widely assumed that such a war would follow the expiry of the twelve years truce between Spain and the Dutch, due in 1621, and the expectation of this helped condition Spanish policy.[22] Thus, war seemed normative and the outbreak of war likely.

# 7

# EUROPEAN WARFARE 1618–60

## The Thirty Years' War

The Thirty Years' War (1618–48) acted as the focus and culmination of the struggles between Catholic and Protestant, Holy Roman Emperor and German princes, Spain and France.[1] Seen by many German contemporaries as parts of an essentially continuous war dating back to 1618,[2] it brought together several different conflicts, including those between Spain and the Dutch, and the dynastic struggle within the Vasa family between the kings of Poland and Sweden. The war has played a major role in discussion of military history. This is particularly so because of the role of the campaigns of Gustavus Adolphus in the original formulation of the Military Revolution (see Chapter 3). The revision of the thesis to take note of the Spanish army further directed attention to the conflict, specifically to the major Austro-Spanish victory over the Swedes at Nördlingen in 1634.[3]

Irrespective of the debate over the Military Revolution, the Thirty Years' War has played a major role in military history. This reflects its inherent interest, and its importance for the course of German history and European international history, as well as the prominent part of German scholars in military history. The Thirty Years' War, and the conflicts closely related to it, especially the war between France and Spain that became full-scale in 1635 and lasted until 1659, will take a major part in this chapter, but it is also necessary to give due weight to other conflicts in this period. This is due not only to their inherent importance for the development of other countries, but also to their role in military history. In particular, it is appropriate to consider how far analyses of military development focused on the Thirty Years' War are more generally appropriate.

The war initially began as a rising against the Habsburg position in Bohemia, that stemmed from recent crises in its political and religious situation. The Bohemians rejected the authority of the Habsburgs who had held the elective crown for nearly a century. Instead, Frederick V, Elector Palatine (r. 1610–23), a Calvinist and the leader of Protestant activism in the Empire, was elected king. The Habsburg Duke Ferdinand of Styria, who had already been elected King of Bohemia and Hungary (1617), and was to become the

Emperor Ferdinand II (r. 1619–37), was unwilling to accept being deposed as King of Bohemia. A Catholic stalwart, Ferdinand was unprepared to accept this challenge to the Habsburg position in the Empire and the Habsburg hereditary lands. The election of Frederick threatened the Habsburg grasp on the Imperial crown as it altered the balance among the Electors to four Protestants versus three Catholics.

Bohemia was invaded after Upper and Lower Austria had been overrun by Austrian and Bavarian forces and after Bohemian and Transylvanian attempts to besiege Vienna in 1619 had failed. The rising was crushed by larger forces at the hard-fought battle of the White Mountain outside Prague (8 November 1620). The densely-packed attacking forces broke through the defending lines of infantry. Frederick fled, and Prague fell the following day. Habsburg authority was then reimposed and Bohemia was Catholicised.[4] The Habsburgs had been supported by the Catholic Duke Maximilian of Bavaria (r. 1598–1651) and the Lutheran John George I, Elector of Saxony (r. 1611–56). As a reminder of the danger of regarding the struggle in terms of a conflict of Protestant with Catholic, John George was prepared to take a role, not only because Ferdinand offered him the territory of Lusatia, but also because, like most Lutherans, he was hostile to Calvinists and, like most German princes, worried about any violent disruption of the Empire and loyal to both Emperor and Imperial constitution. John George overran Lusatia and Silesia, meeting little resistance. His major contribution was to destroy Frederick's hopes of Protestant solidarity.

The war spread as the dominions of the Elector Palatine were attacked. In 1620, Spanish troops from the Army of Flanders under Spínola overran much of the Lower Palatinate, helped by units from Bavaria, which also annexed the Upper Palatinate.[5] However, Spínola moved slowly and it was not until late 1622, that both Heidelberg and Mannheim, the two leading cities in the Lower Palatinate, had fallen. Ferdinand deposed Frederick and transferred his Electoral title to Maximilian. The competition of the Bavarian branch of the Wittelsbach family with the Palatine branch was a prominent instance of the divisions between German ruling houses that helped ensure divisiveness within the Empire. The rise of Bavarian power hit the influence and interests of John George of Saxony, but he remained on the Imperial side. Re-Catholicisation was pushed in both the Lower and the Upper Palatinate.

War resumed between the Dutch and the Spanish in 1621, and the Dutch then encouraged opposition to the Habsburgs in Germany. However, the pace of operations and success was set by the army of the Catholic League under Count Johan Tilly, a Fleming who had served for long under Parma before fighting the Ottomans for the Austrian Habsburgs in the 1600s. On 6 May 1622, at Wimpfen, the army of the League under Tilly and a Spanish force under Don Gonzalo Fernández de Córdoba heavily defeated an army under George of Baden-Durlach. Tilly then defeated Christian of Brunswick at Höchst (20 June 1622) and Stadtlohn (6 August 1623).

The war had moved north, with Ernst von Mansfeld playing a bigger role in organising resistance to the Catholic forces. However, he was defeated at Dessau on 25 April 1626 by Albrecht Wallenstein (1583–1634), a Bohemian military entrepreneur to whom Ferdinand II had entrusted his troops.[6] Using Bohemian resources and benefiting from his ability to seize resources from the areas in which he campaigned, Wallenstein built up a large Imperial army. Christian IV of Denmark intervened on the Protestant side in order to pursue his plans for expansion in north-west Germany where there were a number of prince-bishoprics, which he wished to have his sons elected to rule, and also because he was concerned about princely liberties in the face of what he saw as an inexorable Habsburg advance. At Lutter (26 August 1626), he was heavily defeated by Tilly, with thousands of casualties. Lutter was a battle in which cavalry played a major role.[7]

As a reminder of the wide-ranging nature of the struggle, Wallenstein had then to march south-east to stop Gábor Bethlan, Prince of Transylvania, from advancing on Vienna. He and Tilly then drove the Danes from northern Germany, capturing Wismar (1627), defeating an amphibious invasion of Pomerania under Christian IV at Wolgast (2 September 1628) and forcing Christian out of the war (1629). This completed the process by which the armies of Tilly and Wallenstein had demonstrated a clear superiority in fighting quality over their opponents. Their run of victories, and the attendant political consequences, demonstrated how campaigning could produce apparently decisive results.

Christian's supporters, the two Dukes of Mecklenburg, were deposed for rebellion against the Empire and their duchies given to Wallenstein. The latter's army remained in north Germany, supporting itself by 'contributions' (war taxation) and seizing supplies in a way that brought great damage to territories like Brandenburg. 'Contributions' were a more systematic way of raising supplies than plunder. They also ensured control of the troops, as the contributions were distributed by the army staff. Wallenstein's freedom of action as a commander contrasted markedly with greater state control of military affairs a century later, but it is important not to read backwards from the situation in the 1720s and 1730s in order to make Wallenstein and the military system he represented and ruthlessly developed appear anachronistic. To the west, the Spaniards captured Breda in 1625, but were unable to inflict any major defeat on the Dutch, although the latter launched no offensives until 1629 when they captured 's-Hertogenbosch.

Further east, Gustavus Adolphus of Sweden (r.1611–32) attacked Poland in 1617–18, 1621–2 and 1625–9, capturing Riga (25 September 1621), a major Baltic port and the principal city in Livonia, after a siege in which he benefited from the small size of the garrison and the absence of an effective relief army. Gustavus also allegedly employed creeping barrages (systematically advancing artillery bombardment), although given the nature of early-seventeenth-century artillery, which needed to be realigned after recoil following every shot, this degree of accuracy seems impossible. Gustavus overran Livonia in 1625, and attacked Royal (Polish or West) Prussia in 1626. There were close connections between the wars in Germany and Poland, partly because Sigismund and the Spanish Habsburgs had ambitious naval plans in the Baltic. Gustavus launched his offensive against Royal Prussia (the base area for a Polish navy, and a most important area for Polish grain exports) in 1626 at a time when Denmark had started a major Protestant counter-offensive supported by the Dutch and England. Gustavus hoped that Russia and, possibly, Brandenburg would soon join Sweden against Poland and that the Protestants would be able to roll back the Catholic and Imperial forces. The total effect of this might force Sigismund III of Poland (who placed high hope on his Habsburg dynastic connections) to negotiate about Livonia and the Swedish throne on Gustavus's terms and eliminate the potential Habsburg-Polish naval threat. This was feared as something which might take the war to Sweden.

These calculations almost totally failed. A series of extreme and rapid disasters struck the Danes and the Protestant Germans, the Dutch and the English did not join the Protestant war efforts in Germany, and Russia, while sympathetic towards Sweden and markedly anti-Habsburg, did not join the war against Poland. Gustavus was unable to defeat the Polish general Stanislaw Koniecpolski in his campaigns in Royal Prussia of 1626-9, where the two armies were roughly equal in quality. In view of the strength of the Polish cavalry, Gustavus was unwilling to meet the Poles in the open without the protection of fieldworks, while Polish cavalry attacks on supply lines and small units impeded Swedish operations. In turn, the Swedes benefited from superior firepower. Their army suffered heavily from disease each year in Prussia from 1626, but was recreated again and again.

After victory at Wolgast in September 1628, Ferdinand II sent 12,000 troops to the aid of Sigismund III, his brother-in-law, and the joint army advanced down the Vistula in 1629, pressing Gustavus hard at Stühm/Honigfelde on 27 June: the Swedish cavalry was driven from the field with heavy casualties and Gustavus retreated to a fortified position at Marienburg. The combined Polish-Habsburg forces were unable to force the Swedish army out of this fortified position, just as Wallenstein's main forces had been unable to take Swedish-supported Stralsund in 1628.

The Polish nobility was tired of the war, and the resulting taxes, and blamed it on Sigismund, who was also suspected of conspiring with the Habsburgs. The Poles understood that the leading French minister, Cardinal Richelieu, an opponent of the Habsburgs, and the Dutch wished to bring Sweden out of its Polish war, and that made these mediators useful for the Poles. The mediators could not rescue Gustavus or the Poles from anything. The French had no political leverage on their own in the Baltic in 1629. By then, only the Swedish forces in Prussia and Stralsund remained of what, three years earlier, had looked like a powerful, if informal, Protestant alliance. The

Habsburg victory in Germany helped wreck Gustavus's war plans, as he had to divert forces to Stralsund, did not gain any allies against Poland, and finally had to meet an Imperial army in Prussia. Had Christian IV defeated Tilly at Lutter, Gustavus might have been an obscure figure in European history, but he might have inflicted serious defeats on Poland in alliance with Russia. That was the war he had planned in 1626. Instead, in September 1629, French mediation helped lead to the Truce of Altmark. Gustavus was left with Livonia and also with control of two ports in the Polish fief of East Prussia.[8]

## Sweden enters the Thirty Years' War 1630–2

The Polish war ensured that the Swedes were battle-hardened when Gustavus invaded Germany in 1630. He was concerned about the position of Protestantism, but also about Habsburg interests in the Baltic, specifically the extension of Habsburg power to its southern shores, co-operation with the Poles, and naval plans against the Dutch that might challenge Sweden's commercial position in the Baltic. The latter encouraged him to try to control the key ports on the southern shores of the Baltic.[9]

Gustavus was not the first ruler who sought to resist the Habsburgs, and it was possible that he would have been no more successful than Christian IV of Denmark. However, the Swedish army was an experienced and well-honed war machine, and Gustavus a general of great ability and flexibility. He strengthened conscription, developed field artillery and emulated Polish cavalry tactics, although with less of a commitment to the shock value of an attack at full gallop than was at first claimed by scholars. Instead, there was a transition from the *caracole*, with Gustavus at times ordering his first line to fire only one pistol, so that they could more rapidly move to the use of their swords, with the lines behind maintaining momentum by only using their swords.[10]

In addition, Gustavus benefited from the confusion affecting his likely opponents. Concern about Wallenstein's power and intentions, and anger at his ruthless pursuit of resources for his troops and privileges for himself, had led the Catholic League, particularly Maximilian, to insist on his dismissal. However, although Tilly became commander of the Imperial army, it was not merged with the League army. Aside from the problems of managing these forces, financial problems exacerbated growing war weariness, leading the League to decide in November 1630 to cut its army even though Gustavus had already invaded.

Landing at Peenemünde on 26 June 1630 with 14,000 troops (the total invasion force mustered 38,000 men, including the Swedish garrison in Stralsund), Gustavus rapidly overran Pomerania and Mecklenburg, and then advanced south into Brandenburg in April 1631, capturing Frankfurt-on-Oder. His army grew in size as it provided employment for the large number of soldiers in Protestant Germany. By September 1631, the total Swedish army in Germany contained 48,600 troops, with another 33,100 allied German troops under Gustavus's command.

The Imperial army under Tilly responded to Gustavus's advance and besieged Magdeburg, which had declared for him. On 20 May 1631, Magdeburg was stormed and brutally sacked by Tilly, which helped lead Brandenburg into Gustavus's camp. Saxony followed.

The Swedes followed Tilly into Saxony and crushed him at Breitenfeld just north of Leipzig (17 September 1631), a battle which established Gustavus as the leading general of the Thirty Years' War, and the single engagement that dominates discussion of battle in the century, beginning, for Russell Weigley, a new period of warfare characterised by a search for decisive victory on the battlefield.[11] The Imperialists were outnumbered, and were also outgunned by the more mobile and numerous Swedish artillery. Tilly had also put all his strength in one line, failing to leave himself sufficient reserves to permit a response to developments. The less experienced infantry of John George, Elector of Saxony, on the Swedish left quickly broke when attacked, but the flexible and well-disciplined Swedish infantry in the centre of Gustavus's line remained firm and were able to halt Tilly's attack with musketry and artillery fire. The Swedish cavalry on the other flank overcame their Imperialist opponents and drove them from the field, before turning on Tilly's centre. Exposed to artillery, infantry and cavalry attack, Tilly's infantry took a heavy battering before retreating. Imperialist casualties were 7,600 killed, compared to 1,500 Swedes and 3,000 Saxons; over 7,000 Imperialist soldiers were also taken prisoner during their retreat from the battlefield, and all of Tilly's artillery was lost. So also was the prestige of the Imperial army.

Tilly retreated west over the Weser, leaving Bohemia and the Main valley exposed to Saxon and Swedish advances. The battle led many German Protestant princes, through preference or fear, to rally to Gustavus, who advanced into central Germany, taking Würzburg and Mainz, while the Saxons captured Prague. The absence of a competing field army encouraged the rapid surrender of fortified positions to Gustavus.

Had Gustavus's forces been crushed at Breitenfeld, his army would have collapsed and been pushed back to the Baltic. Ferdinand would have dominated northern Germany and would have established a degree of practical control in the Empire that would have been unassailable. It is unlikely that Richelieu would have been able to bring the French into the war to prevent a pro-Imperial peace, and he would not have been assisted, as he was in 1634–5, by the obvious belligerent intentions of the Habsburg powers towards France.

In 1632, Gustavus planned to overrun Bavaria and then conquer Austria. Maximilian had allied with Louis XIII in 1630, but the French were not able to deter Gustavus from invading Bavaria. Pressing south from Nuremberg, he crossed the Danube at Donauwörth. Tilly was mortally wounded at the river Lech in the battle of Rain (15 April 1632) in an unsuccessful attempt to prevent the invasion of Bavaria, the Swedes crossing under powerful artillery cover, and Munich fell to the Swedes on 17 May. In response to the crisis, Ferdinand II had reappointed Wallenstein as overall commander in December 1631, and his threat to Saxony led Gustavus to return northwards. The Swedes, however, were unable to drive Wallenstein's forces from a heavily-fortified position at the Alte Veste near Nuremberg, where Gustavus could not employ his cavalry or artillery effectively. This was a major success for the combination of terrain, field entrenchments and a well-directed defence. Gustavus's army lost heavily from desertion that owed much to supply problems in the devastated countryside. The great number of Germans in the ranks encouraged desertion; the Swedes in the army showing more cohesion and resolution. Gustavus then withdrew to the north-west, while Wallenstein overran Saxony.

Convinced that the campaign was over, Wallenstein began to disperse his troops for the winter, only to be attacked by Gustavus at Lützen (17 November). This was a fog-shrouded and bitterly-fought battle. Wallenstein remained on the defensive, taking advantage of a ditch dug to the front of his position. Unlike Tilly at Breitenfeld, he deployed in a series of lines, which provided him with reserves. A mist delayed the Swedish attack, giving the Austrian cavalry commander, Pappenheim, time to add his 3,000 cavalry to Wallenstein's army, so that it matched Gustavus's strength of about 19,000 men: Pappenheim rushed his cavalry back to support the main army and charged them straight into the Swedish flank, at which point he was killed by a wire-mesh missile fired from a Swedish cannon. The Swedes eventually won the cavalry battle on their right but the return of Pappenheim's cavalry may well have saved the day for Wallenstein. In the centre, the Swedish infantry, led by Gustavus, who was shot in the arm but pressed on, pushed back the opposing musketeers holding the ditch at the front of Wallenstein's position, but was unable to drive back the main Austrian line. Gustavus died in the mêlée, shot three times. Wallenstein stabilised the situation on his left by sending cavalry reinforcements under Piccolomini who mounted furious assaults on the Swedes, but, at the close of the battle, the Swedes on their left captured the village of Lützen and the nearby Austrian artillery that had commanded the battlefield from a rise, and Wallenstein retreated under cover of darkness. Both sides lost about one-third of their strength, and Wallenstein retreated to Bohemia, leaving the Swedes in control of Saxony.

## 1633–5

In 1633, more foreign troops moved into the Empire, with an army of about 20,000 Spanish troops under the Duke of Feria advancing via the Valtelline into south-west Germany where Constance and Breisach were relieved and Bregenz and Rheinfelden recaptured. Meanwhile, the French overran Lorraine. With Gustavus dead, the Swedish army lost impetus. The Swedes sought to share the burden of the war by creating an allied league, the League of Heilbronn, which was established in April 1633 under the Directorship of the Swedish Chancellor Axel Oxenstierna. The League was to maintain an army, but the crisis and eventual mutiny caused by arrears in military pay came to drive the pace of Swedish and allied policy in 1633 with units given the right to levy contributions and officers to buy land cheaply. The combination of mutiny and the quest for contributions put paid to Swedish chances that campaigning season in south Germany. In addition, there were growing political tensions, with George William of Brandenburg justifiably concerned about Swedish territorial ambitions in neighbouring Pomerania, which, given the imminent extinction of the ducal line and an inheritance agreement, he stood to inherit. Furthermore, tension between Sweden and Saxony affected their joint campaign in Silesia, where Wallenstein forced a Swedish force to surrender at Steinau in October. He sought to exploit these tensions by negotiations with Saxony and Brandenburg, but was unsuccessful.

Ferdinand II meanwhile had come to distrust Wallenstein, particularly for his tendency to pursue negotiations with minimal reference to Vienna. The sense that he had created an expensive army that was not under control was accentuated when Wallenstein made the colonels swear to owe him their first loyalty. Ferdinand ordered Wallenstein's seizure and, failing that, killing, which happened on 25 February 1634 as he fled towards Saxony. Wallenstein was replaced by Ferdinand's son, the future Ferdinand III, in a determined attempt to secure Habsburg control of the army. Ferdinand became titular head of the Imperial army, but the acting generalissimo was Matthias Gallas, a general of considerable mediocrity, who had joined the conspiracy to have Wallenstein assassinated and gained the reward of the command, whereas Piccolomini, had he been more disloyal to Wallenstein in 1634 and been chosen for the overall command, would have made an outstanding overall commander of the Imperial forces and might well have decisively tilted the balance of power in central Europe.

The killing of Wallenstein helped the Protestants take the initiative in 1634, with the Saxons under Hans Georg von Arnim successfully invading Bohemia, while the Swedes advanced into Bavaria, capturing Landshut. However, the Austrians under Ferdinand advanced in southern Germany, capturing Regensburg and Donauwörth and besieging Nördlingen. They were joined by a Spanish force under the son of Philip IV, the Cardinal Infante Ferdinand. His command required that the Imperial troops should be commanded by a figure of comparable social rank; which was why the future Ferdinand III was given active command of the Austrian forces that united with the Spaniards. On 6 September, the joint forces heavily defeated the outnumbered Swedes outside Nördlingen.

This led to the Swedish loss of southern Germany and, in 1635, the settlement of German problems when most German princes were reconciled to the Emperor (Saxony by the Peace of Prague), and also France's entry into the war to resist Habsburg hegemony, an entry that Spain had sought to provoke in order to win the backing of Ferdinand II against France. Richelieu deliberately only declared war on Spain in 1635. He was still hoping to separate the two Habsburg powers and to avoid an open conflict with the Emperor. This approach failed. Austrian forces were only too prepared to engage with the French in the Rhineland and Alsace, and in 1636 Richelieu conceded the inevitable and declared war on the Emperor as well.

The Empire rallied to the Emperor. In 1636, Austria, Saxony and Brandenburg formed an alliance against Sweden. The houses of Brunswick made peace with Emperor Ferdinand III (r.1637–57) in 1642, leaving only Hesse-Cassel among the major German states at war with Austria. But for France's entry into the war, it is probable that the Peace of Prague would have served as the basis of a general peace and one that would have left the Emperor in a powerful position. Sweden would probably have had to accept the settlement. In 1635, Sweden had been recently defeated and there were long-standing tensions with Denmark and Poland that Ferdinand II could have sought to exploit in order to encourage her acceptance.

## The War of Smolensk

Sweden's commitment in Germany lessened her ability to intervene further east. There, encounters with the Swedes had led both Poland and Russia to experiment with new military ideas. In 1632–3, the Poles created musketeer units, replacing the earlier arquebusiers, and attempted to standardise their expanding artillery. Imitating the Swedes, the Poles introduced 3- to 6-pounder regimental guns between 1623 and 1650. The Russian government, conscious of Swedish developments and dissatisfied with the *streltsy*, the permanent infantry units equipped with handguns founded in 1550, decided in 1630 to form 'new order' military units, officered mainly by foreigners and trained in Western European methods. Eight such regiments, totalling about 17,000 men, amounted to half the Russian army in the War of Smolensk with Poland (1632–4). This conflict met Swedish hopes for a second front against the Poles. However, the Russian siege of Smolensk, fortified even more strongly by the Poles using Italian-style bastions, was unsuccessful, and the Polish relief army under Wladyslaw IV (r. 1632–48) inflicted a heavy defeat on the Russians. The siege was broken in September 1633 and in October the Poles fought their way round the Russians, so that their position was enveloped. Without relief, the Russian army surrendered on 1 March 1634. The 'new order' troops proved less experienced that Poland's mercenaries, although the principal reasons for the failure to capture Smolensk was the delayed arrival of Russian artillery, due to poor weather and primitive roads, and the operational flexibility the Poles enjoyed thanks to their superiority in cavalry. This enabled them to win the battle for territory, supplies and mobility once the siege was raised. The Russian infantry lost its ability to operate offensively. Crimean Tatar invasions of central Moscovy during the

Smolensk campaign helped force Tsar Mikhail's government to negotiate peace at Polianovk and to turn its attention to the securing of Muscovy's southern steppe frontier.[12]

## Thirty Years' War 1636–48

The struggle between France and Spain in 1635–59 has dominated historical attention to the detriment of the latter stages of the Thirty Years' War in Germany. However, these saw wide-ranging campaigns in which control over much of Germany, especially Saxony, was bitterly contested. Despite her commitment against Spain, France also sent a number of armies across the Rhine and, although they were not always successful, they contributed to the heavy military pressure on the Austrian Habsburgs, which greatly helped the Swedes.

Victories by Johan Banér at Domitz (22 October 1635) and Kyritz (17 December 1635) helped stabilise the situation for the Swedes after their defeat at Nördlingen and the Peace of Prague. Victorious under Banér over the Austrians and Saxons at Wittstock on 4 October 1636, the Swedes overran Brandenburg, only to be pushed back from Saxony to Pomerania in 1637, but in 1638 they drove the Austrians into Silesia. In 1639, the Swedes defeated the Saxons and Austrians at Chemnitz (14 April) and advanced as far as Prague, but were unable to capture the city. In 1640, the juncture of French and Swedish troops at Erfurt, their first combined operation, had no strategic consequences.

The following year, Frederick William (r.1640–88), the new Elector of Brandenburg, felt it necessary to abandon his alliance with Ferdinand III, and in July 1641 he signed a truce with the Swedes. The terms demonstrated the inability of Ferdinand III to bring peace to the Empire and also the strength of Sweden around the Baltic. More generally, the impact of military operations on the policies of Brandenburg, Saxony and other German princes was a reminder of the potential value of victory in battle, as well as of the ability to extort contributions. The Swedes were left in control of forts across Brandenburg, and treated it as a part of their war-system, raising 'contributions' and troops as they chose. Swedish control of the region served as a basis for operations further south and west. In 1641, their forces advanced to Regensburg. Banér's death led to the appointment of Lennart Torstensson, who had commanded the Swedish artillery at Breitenfeld. In 1642, Torstensson invaded Silesia and Moravia, before defeating the Austrians at the Second battle of Breitenfeld (2 November), a sweeping victory that receives so much less attention than First Breitenfeld because the strategic consequences were less profound. As with so many battles, Second Breitenfeld arose from a siege. Torstensson had advanced into Saxony and besieged Leipzig, a target that forced the Austrians to respond if they wanted to show any ability to protect their ally. The arrival of the Austrians led Torstensson to withdraw and then to attack them. In the battle, the Austrian cavalry was successful, but the battle was decided by the triumph of the Swedish infantry. Similarly, Prague acted as a lodestar of besieging and relieving battles, leading to confrontations or battles such as at Jankov.

War with Denmark (then negotiating with Austria) was very tempting after the victory over the Imperial army, and reflected the extent to which an advance on Vienna was lower on the Swedish list of priorities than conquests of Danish territory. War broke out in 1643.

French attempts to advance east of the Rhine were bitterly resisted, especially by the Emperor's ally, Maximilian of Bavaria. The French army in Germany was surprised in its winter quarters and defeated by the Bavarians under Franz von Mercy at Tuttlingen (24 November 1643). This forced the French army into a winter retreat to the Rhine, abandoning its baggage and losing most of its men. The following year, French forces in Germany suffered heavily at the hands of the Bavarians at Freiburg (3–5 August 1644), although the Bavarians failed to capture Breisach, while the French took Mainz and Philippsburg. The effectiveness of the Bavarians showed that it is misleading to think of the latter stages of the conflict as being controlled by non-German powers. More specifically, it challenged the French position in Alsace. The French commitment in Swabia in the 1640s was similar to that of the Swedes in 1633–4: it was seen as a rich area able to support troops. This led to interest in controlling the region. In contrast, the French were happy to try to ravage Bavaria, but they knew that they could not overwinter there. As a result, it played a different role in their strategy.[13]

In 1644, Torstensson overran Jutland and also outmanoeuvred the Austrians under Matthias Gallas, forcing them back into Bohemia. Another Swedish force conquered the secularised bishoprics of Bremen and Verden which had been occupied by Denmark. After lengthy peace talks, the Peace of Brömsbro (23 August 1645) led to the Swedish gain of Gotland and Ösel in the Baltic and the provinces of Jämtland and Harjedalen from Norway.

In 1645, the French, Swedes and Transylvanians planned a joint attack on Vienna. Torstensson invaded Bohemia, and was victorious at Jankov (6 March). The battle showed the growing sophistication of the Swedish army. Torstensson was able to move his artillery during the battle. His understanding of what it could achieve stemmed from his background as an artillery commander, which was unusual for the period. As a consequence, he moved the cannon while the battle was in progress (as he had also done at First Breitenfeld and Lützen, although more so) and this helped to decide the course of the hard-fought conflict. The Swedes repositioned their artillery so as to be able to fire down on the exposed flank of the Austrian positions and, finally, break their resistance. However, this move took many hours, which underlined the relatively static nature of artillery throughout this period Jankov had the significant result of finally persuading the Imperial Privy Council to begin peace negotiations in earnest.

After their victory, the Swedes were delayed by the siege of Brno, but advanced to reach the Danube at Krems. The French were victorious at Allerheim near Nördlingen (3 August), but neither could maintain their advances. The fortresses captured by the French were recaptured by the Bavarians when they drove the French back. In 1646, the French and Swedes advanced again to invade Bavaria and capture Landsberg.

Again, it is interesting to note that the wide-ranging Swedish advances of the later stages of the war have not had the attention devoted to Gustavus Adolphus's campaigns in Germany. This reflects a number of factors that are important in setting the agenda of military history, not least the focus on apparently great commanders and great battles and the repetitive character of the agenda. In the case of the Thirty Years' War, there is also the language factor. Michael Roberts, the scholar who wrote in English about the Swedes in the war, concentrated on Gustavus. More specifically, there is a sense that Gustavus campaigned to a purpose, while his successors simply advanced to gain control of areas from which to seize supplies and fought on for the ignoble goal of territorial gains and other compensation for the Swedish war effort. This is a travesty of the situation, but it is still implicit or explicit in many of the judgements made and, more particularly, in the lack of attention devoted to the campaigns. That is unfortunate, as they were considerable achievements. In particular, much of the available resource base had been exhausted or degraded by repeated campaigning. Furthermore, Sweden's opponents were now accustomed to fighting her armies.

The Swedish commanders showed an ability to overcome difficulties that in some respects were more serious than those confronting Gustavus. Banér restored the cohesion and morale of the army in Germany after the Nördlingen disaster and the subsequent collapse of the Swedish position. Torstensson showed himself an effective battlefield commander and a vigorous campaigner. His ill-health led in 1645 to the appointment of Karl Gustav von Wrangel, another impressive campaigner. One important difference that affected strategic, operational and tactical options, is that after 1635 the size of armies operating in Germany was considerably lower than in the first half of the war, as well as having a different force structure with a greater percentage of cavalry. This lower size reflected the difficulty of maintaining armies. The Austrian and Swedish armies in the mid-1640s were considerably smaller than they had been, although all numbers are necessarily tentative.[14]

As a reminder of the extent to which the war was an umbrella conflict, involving a number of related but different struggles, in 1645 Hesse-Cassel attacked Hesse-Darmstadt in pursuit of a territorial dispute over Marburg, which Hesse-Cassel forces seized. In 1647, the Swedes campaigned as far south as Bregenz at the eastern end of Lake Constance, which they captured, and in 1648 the Swedes and French defeated the Austrians and Bavarians under Peter Melander south of the Danube at Zusmarshausen (17 May), which permitted them to ravage Bavaria for the remainder of the war. As the war ended, the Swedes were besieging Prague.

The ability of French and Swedish forces to advance far into the Empire and both support their armies, after a fashion, by the contributions they exacted and to deny resources to their opponents, helped lead Ferdinand III to terms. At the same time, military strategy was heavily influenced by the search for supplies; although that did not so pre-empt other military and political factors that it could be termed controlled; 'influenced' is the more accurate description.[15] Another aspect of the role of supply considerations was the timing of the campaign seasons. Campaigning could be conducted in mid-winter, but it was not usual to start campaigns prior to May, as grass in the fields and roadsides was necessary for the horses that pulled the cannon and supplies as well as providing cavalry mounts.

To stress logistical factors is not, however, to suggest that the warfare of the period was unduly limited: logistics have always been a factor in war. The interplay of strategy and supply was similar to that of the English in the Hundred Years War.[16] Furthermore, as armies remained comparatively small (certainly compared to the 1690s) and used relatively simple equipment, it was easier to supply them from the campaign zone as long as they did not fix their position by conducting a siege.

The treaties that ended the war in 1648 were signed at Münster and Osnabrück, and are collectively known as the Peace of Westphalia. The Austrian Habsburgs were left in secure control of their hereditary lands, and they were not to lose Bohemia until their empire collapsed in 1918. The Swedes gained much of Pomerania (whose last Duke had died in 1637), as well as the ecclesiastical principalities of Bremen and Verden, and Wismar; these gains brought control over the estuaries of the Elbe, Oder and Weser, and consolidated Sweden's position as the leading Baltic power. Brandenburg-Prussia also gained much territory, including the prince bishoprics of Halberstadt and Minden, eastern Pomerania and the reversion to the prime-archbishopric of Magdeburg, and emerged ahead of Saxony as the leading north German Protestant state. France gained control over much of Alsace. The Upper Palatinate became part of Bavaria, but the Lower Palatinate was restored to the Palatine branch of the Wittelsbach family; both had the Electoral dignity from 1648. Calvinism was accepted as a permitted religion in the Empire. Rulers in the Empire were allowed to ally amongst themselves, and with foreign powers, to ensure their preservation and security, in other words, not for offensive purposes, and only on condition that the alliances were not directed against the Emperor, the Empire or the terms of the treaty. France and Sweden were made guarantors of the peace, and thus given important opportunities to intervene in German politics.[17]

The Thirty Years' War caused terrible devastation in Germany, although its impact on German demography and society has long been controversial. It is necessary to distinguish between the actual devastation wrought by military action and the attendant pressures of the conflict. For many, the first stage of the war was most damaging due to the *kipperzeit*, a widespread and disruptive currency inflation. The financial pressures that stemmed from the conflict included not only the contributions system but also a more general extension of, and rise in, taxation. This culminated with the money raised after the war to pay off the various armies, especially that of Sweden which maintained garrisons in Germany until 1654 to ensure repayment. Alongside the disruption of the war, including that of commercial and credit networks, this taxation hit purchasing power and thus depressed demand. As a result, urban and rural manufacturing areas lost markets.[18]

It is difficult to disentangle the impact of the war from that of the more widespread economic and demographic downturn that affected Europe in the early seventeenth century.[19] Furthermore, it has been argued that structural characteristics of local societies and economies were crucial to their very different demographic response to frequently similar experiences of war.[20] The religious and political compromises the war brought helped to lessen conflict in Germany for nearly a century. Furthermore, the major efforts made by German rulers to fight France and the Ottomans in this period suggest that it is wrong to claim that the war had exhausted the Empire.

## France suppresses the Huguenots

By 1648, both France and Spain had been severely battered by their war, but they were to fight on until 1659. Full-scale French intervention in the Thirty Years' War had been delayed by divisions among French policy makers and by a major struggle between the Crown and the Huguenots (French Protestants). In the 1620s, although the French army, 15,000 strong outside La Rochelle in 1627, was relatively weak by the standards of Spain, it was able to bring an effective end to the major challenge to the military, political and religious authority of the Crown. In 1620, Louis XIII led the army to distant Béarn in south-west France in order to coerce the local Huguenots into accepting royal authority and Catholicism. He succeeded without fighting, but in 1621 the royal forces encountered resistance. The fortified town of St. Jean-d'Angély fell after a month-long siege, but Montauban successfully resisted a siege that decimated the besiegers through disease and desertion. On 15 April 1622, however, a Huguenot army under the Duke of Soubise was destroyed on the Île de Réz, north of La Rochelle, wrecking Huguenot operational independence, while Louis marched through west and south France, capturing numerous positions before the Huguenots accepted the Peace of Montpellier on 19 October which removed their rights to have garrisons.

When war resumed in 1625–6 and 1627–9, royal forces very much took the initiative. La Rochelle, the major Huguenot stronghold, was besieged in 1627–8 and a mismanaged English relief attempt was defeated in 1627. La Rochelle was starved into surrender on 28 October 1628, with nearly half the population dying. In 1629, French forces overran Huguenot centres in southern France, such as Privas and Montauban, and the Huguenots accepted royal terms by the Grace of Alès (28 June). The fall of La Rochelle had demoralised the Huguenots, and served as the equivalent of a major battlefield victory in affecting the subsequent campaign. Furthermore, the slaughter of the garrison of Privas and the sack of the town in May 1629 discouraged other towns from mounting a strong resistance.[21] Louis XIII's command of the army in person also helped maintain the momentum of the campaign.

## The War of the Mantuan Succession

The French were also active in Italy. In combination with Savoy, they tried to seize Spain's ally Genoa in 1625, only to be driven back by the Spaniards. Two years later, the end of the direct male line of the Gonzaga family produced a contested succession for the Duchies of Mantua and Monferrato. Spanish intervention in the dispute led to a joint Savoyard and Spanish invasion of Monferrato in March 1628 in pursuit of a partition. A Spanish army besieged Casale, the capital as well as a major fortress in Monferrato and a crucial point on the western approaches on the Milanese. The French initially tried to stop this consolidation of Spanish power in northern Italy by backing the leading claimant, Charles, Duke of Nevers. He was permitted to raise troops from his French duchies and his governorships of Champagne and Brie on his own sovereign authority as *Prince Souverain* of Arches. The French army itself was engaged in the struggle against the Huguenots.

Nevers was able to raise 6,600 troops, in part thanks to the effort of his nephew, the Duke of Longueville. This was a pointed reminder of the extent to which what are generally understood as the 'states' of the period did not monopolise military power. At the same time, Richelieu was unimpressed by Nevers's plan, thinking it lacking in support and preparation. As French power was at stake, the crown provided some support, although, as an opponent of Nevers, the Governor of Dauphiné in fact hindered the expedition. Advancing into Savoy, Nevers's force was beaten in a skirmish in August 1628 and then dissolved.

Concerned about the situation in northern Italy, and in particular that Nevers might turn to Spain, Louis XIII and Richelieu decided to act after La Rochelle surrendered in October 1628. The Alpine pass at Susa was forced on 6 March 1629, a reminder that campaigning did not cease in the winter. This led Savoy to terms and the Spaniards to abandon the siege of Casale. However, the Spanish government was determined to fight on. It was unintentionally assisted by the maladroit Nevers who had mounted an attack on Lombardy from Mantua. Although he was able to raise only 2,500 men, this led to his being placed under the Imperial ban. Helped by his success against the Danes, Ferdinand II was able to send about 30,000 Imperial troops into northern Italy and in late 1629 they besieged Mantua. After a winter break, the siege was renewed in May 1630 and Mantua surrendered on 18 July. Meanwhile, the French decision to garrison Casale, rather than entrust it to Nevers, had encouraged the Spaniards to send fresh forces into the Monferrato in the autumn of 1629. Even after the war with the Huguenots had ended, the French lacked the forces necessary to defeat their opponents in northern Italy. Richelieu argued in November 1629 that 39,000 troops would be required, but the French were handicapped by the need to prepare a strong army to prevent the danger of an Austrian or Spanish attack on France from Germany.[22]

Under Richelieu, France lacked the resources or organisation to field more than one large and effective campaign army. This is a reminder of the danger of reading from the notional total army sizes sometimes quoted and from the wide-ranging nature of hostilities and confrontation in order to assume that several effective armies could be deployed at the same time. In the case of France, as David Parrott has pointed out, 'a military system that was geared to the fighting of short campaigns in a single theatre was finally confronted in 1630 with the reality of a very different type of war', and found wanting.[23] The same was true for other states. This indeed helps to account for the character of much of the campaigning in the Thirty Years' War, in particular what might appear a disjointed series of marches in which rival forces sometimes confronted each other. There was insufficient manpower for a war of fronts in Germany or Italy, and maps in historical atlases that suggest otherwise are misleading. Indeed, the absence of fronts helped confer additional importance on fortresses.

In addition, the political–military nature of the war itself was in part set by the problem dissected by Parrott. The availability of only one really effective field army ensured that it was necessary for powers to fight one opponent at a time, or to accept that successful offensive operations could only be mounted against one opponent. This encouraged a military diplomacy in which peace, truce, or stasis with one rival was sought so that another could be attacked. The 1629 agreement between Sweden and Poland was a good instance of this. Similarly, Spanish involvement in the War of the Mantuan Succession left the Army of Flanders short of funds and therefore with its operational effectiveness compromised, and the army downright mutinous.

The need to focus on one opponent established an important constraint on military capability and effectiveness. In so far as the categories are helpful, it had both a political and a military dimension, as the range of factors summarised under the term resources can be seen in both these lights. For example, there was the issue not only of the availability of money but also of experienced troops.

As a reminder of the interlocking nature of military struggles, and thus of the role of politics, the Habsburgs were militarily successful in northern Italy in 1630, taking Mantua and, under Spínola, pressing Casale hard, while the French relief operation languished. However, Ferdinand II withdrew from the conflict in response to the Swedish invasion of northern Germany and the problems for Imperial preparedness in the Empire created by the dismissal of Wallenstein in response to pressure from the Imperial Diet. This weakened Spanish resolve, as did the death of Spínola, leading to talks with France. As a consequence, the French were able to relieve Casale in October 1630, forcing a negotiation which finally hardened into the two treaties of Cherasco in the spring of 1631 that brought the war in northern Italy to a close.

## Franco-Spanish conflict 1635–42

War resumed in 1635, as Louis XIII and Richelieu responded to the deterioration in the anti-Habsburg position in Germany.[24] They sought a single decisive campaign and launched a number of attacks, but were unsuccessful. An invasion of the Spanish Netherlands linked up with Dutch forces but collapsed, with supply failures leading to large-scale desertion. Another French army advanced into the Moselle valley, while the Duke of Rohan took the Valtelline Pass, the strategic route between Austria and Lombardy that was crucial to a branch of the Spanish Road, but swiftly found himself without sufficient food, fodder or pay for his troops. He discovered that his troops were no better supplied than when he had taken part in the Huguenot rebellion of 1625–9. In 1636 Rohan invaded Lombardy itself, but his officers were unwilling to abandon their booty from the Valtelline, and his troops were sick and mutinous. Without cannon, munitions or money, Rohan dared not move into the Lombard plain. Rohan was also unable to move onto the plain because the main French 'Army of Italy' that was intended to support him by pressing on Lombardy from the west through Piedmont did not move beyond Provence for most of 1636, where the bulk of the troops were engaged in trying to drive the Spaniards off the Isles des Lérins just off the coast near Marseilles. The whole of Rohan's position and army collapsed in the winter of 1636 when his unpaid troops mutinied and the local units went over to the Spaniards. In 1637, Rohan had to abandon the Valtelline fortresses he had captured. The French lost control of the Valtelline for the remainder of the war, and Rohan decided not to return to France, taking up service as an ordinary officer in the army of Saxe-Weimar.

A Spanish counter-invasion of France in 1636 caused great anxiety in Paris, with Spanish forces advancing as far as Corbie and Roye, both of which fell. Exploding shells fired by Spanish siege mortars led the unprepared French to surrender the fortresses of La Capelle and Le Câtelet rapidly. The French feared that they would lose Paris, although no advance that far was planned by the Spaniards. This campaign emphasised the vulnerability of France to attack from the Spanish Netherlands: the centre of French power was nearby, and there were no major natural obstacles. Furthermore, there was a danger that the Spaniards would maintain a position within France and subsist their forces there, denying resources to those of France. In fact, the Spaniards withdrew, while the French abandoned the siege of Dôle in the Spanish-ruled

Franche-Comté and concentrated on recapturing their lost positions. Thereafter, the French launched offensives into the Spanish Netherlands, unsuccessfully besieging Saint-Omer (1638), and capturing Landrecies (1637), Le Câtelet (1638), Hesdin (1639), and Arras (1640).

Elsewhere, French success was more mixed. The Spanish force invading Languedoc from Catalonia in 1637 was defeated before it could reach Narbonne at Leucate (28 September), by an army containing a high proportion of militia under Charles de Schomberg, Duke of Hallwin and Governor of Languedoc. Richelieu hoped that Schomberg might carry the war back into Spanish territory with an invasion of Roussillon, but he had neither the resources nor the will, particularly as he suspected that it would have to be supported from his own and from provincial funds. The French invasion of Franche-Comté in 1636 was unsuccessful, and in 1638 an invasion of the Basque country was stopped at Fuenterrabia when a besieging army under Henry II, Prince of Condé, was defeated by the Spaniards. French forces in Italy failed to achieve success in 1637 and their position deteriorated in 1638 and, even more, 1639. On the German frontier, the experienced forces of Duke Bernard of Saxe-Weimar, now in the service of Louis XIII, consolidated the French position in Alsace, crossed the Rhine, defeated the Austrians at Rheinfelden (2 March) and starved Breisach into surrender (12 December 1638), cutting Spanish routes between northern Italy and the Netherlands and opening the way into Germany. However, exploitation was limited: the following year, the greatly outnumbered French were defeated at Thionville (7 June), when the besieging army was attacked by the Spaniards under Piccolomini. In the Spanish Netherlands, another French force was defeated by the Army of Flanders at Honnecourt (29 May 1642). Only in Roussillon, where the French profited from a rebellion against Habsburg control in Catalonia in 1640 and, by dint of concentrating their efforts, captured Perpignan in September 1642, was French success significant. In Catalonia itself, a Franco-Catalan force checked an advancing Spanish army at Montjuich outside Barcelona on 26 January 1641, which gave the rebels an opportunity to consolidate their position.

Although France was the most populous state in Western Europe, had a well-developed agricultural base and was allied to the Dutch and the Swedes, it was unable to crush the Habsburgs. The French lacked a system of effective military administration and sound finances, and the strains of the war revealed the inadequacies of their reliance on expedients. Logistical failures led to massive desertion, and also to campaigns in which the search for supplies played a major role, undermining the attempt to execute bold strategies.

## Franco–Spanish conflict 1643–59

Seen as a crucial step towards French success over Spain, the battle of Rocroi, fought on 19 May 1643, has dominated attention. Like many battles, it resulted from an attempt to end a siege. The Army of Flanders under Francisco de Melo, besieging the fortress of Rocroi in the Ardennes while advancing into France, was challenged by a larger army (23,000 to 17,000 men) under the 22-year-old Louis II de Bourbon, Duke of Enghien. The cavalry under his personal command on the French right defeated the opposing cavalry, but on the other flank the Spaniards under Isembourg won the cavalry battle. Isembourg turned on the French centre, and was held off only by the commitment of every available French reserve. Enghien took the dramatic option of leading his cavalry behind the Spanish centre to rout Isembourg. He then attacked the Spanish infantry, which held off the French cavalry until weakened by French cannon and infantry fire. The battle had a great impact on contemporary observers and subsequent historians because of the high reputation of the Army of Flanders. It also established Enghien, with his resilience and rapid responsiveness in action, as one of the leading generals of the age. The French lost 4,000 dead and wounded out of an army of 23,000, but most of the Spanish infantry was wiped out.

The consequences of Rocroi have, however, been exaggerated, for the Spaniards rapidly regrouped. They could do so because a substantial part of the army under the command of Beck had not been engaged at Rocroi at all, failing to get to the engagement in time to adjust the numerical disadvantage. After Rocroi, Beck's soldiers could hold the frontier and stabilise the Spanish position.[25] Despite major efforts in the mid-1640s, decisive victory continued to elude the French, although they did succeed in making progress on multiple fronts several times: in 1645, they won the battle of Llorens in Catalonia and Allerheim in the Empire, and made advances in the Low Countries; in 1646, they took Dunkirk, pillaged Bavaria, and captured Porto Longone; in 1648, they took Tortosa and won the battle of Zusmarshausen in preparation for another invasion of Bavaria. Operations in Italy played an important role under Richelieu's successor as leading minister, the Italian-born Cardinal Mazarin. In 1646, the French captured Piombino and Porto Longone on the island of Elba, important bases that controlled naval movements, but attempts to take Genoa, Finale and Orbitello, and thus cut links between Spain and Italy, failed. So also did attempts to exploit anti-Spanish rebellions in Palermo and Naples in 1647–8. The French sent troops to the support of the Catalan rebels, but lost Lérida to Spanish forces in 1644 and unsuccessfully besieged Tarragona in 1644 and Lérida in 1647, although they captured Tortosa in 1648.

After the mid-1640s, it was less a question of French defeats than of a failure to make much progress, certainly progress commensurate with the need to defeat Spain before debt overwhelmed France's finances. Enghien captured Dunkirk, Spain's North Sea naval base, in 1646 after a short siege, but it and other French gains, such as Gravelines and Ypres, were lost when the Spaniards took advantage of the crisis in French power caused by the *Frondes*, the French civil wars of 1648–53. This led to a revival within France of the types of operations seen in the Wars of Religion, although without the element of religious hostility. There were a series of *Frondes*, the first, the *Fronde parlementaire*, focusing on Paris, followed by the princely *Fronde* in 1650–1, and then the 'Spanish' *Fronde* from late 1651 led by Condé. The royal army besieged Paris in 1649, and also clashed with aristocratic forces, leading to battles, for example du Plessis- Praslin's defeat of Turenne at Champ Blanc (15 December 1650), and Condé's victory over Turenne (now a royal general) at Gien (6–7 April 1652), and his defeat in turn by Turenne at Saint-Antoine in the suburbs of Paris (7 July 1652). This victory was crucial in greatly weakening the *Frondeurs*. Condé's abandonment of Paris and move with his army to join the Spaniards in the Spanish Netherlands that October marked the effective end of the *Fronde* as a civil war within France, and its pursuit by different methods. Condé was able to continue to wage a protracted war against Mazarin's government, fought across the north-east of France and drawing on his Spanish allies.[26] As with the Wars of Religion, especially during the late 1580s and early 1590s, control of Paris was the leading objective, vying with the defeat of the opposing field army. Both Condé and Turenne translated the eagerness for battle they had shown in the Thirty Years' War to conflict within France, and in France there were far fewer fortified positions to lessen the impact of victory.

During this period, the Spaniards also regained Porto Longone and Piombino (1650), captured Casale (1652) and regained Catalonia. The Catalans were weakened by plague, while their French allies were engrossed with the *Frondes*. In 1651, the Spanish forces advanced on Barcelona. The city surrendered on 13 October 1652, after a fourteen-month blockade had reduced the population to starvation. The Spaniards also benefited from the Peace of Westphalia of 1648, which ended the war in Germany as well as the struggle between Spain and the Dutch. The Spaniards had to accept Dutch independence, but the French had lost their valuable allies, the Dutch and the Swedes. The Spanish recapture of Dunkirk in 1652 stabilised the frontier with France and prevented the French from using the well-defended harbour of Dunkirk as a base for privateering.

The end of the *Frondes* brought little improvement in French prospects, although a Spanish attempt to regain Arras in 1654 was unsuccessful. In 1657–9, Spain failed to reconquer Portugal, which had successfully rebelled in 1640, and had benefited from the Spanish focus on the Catalans in 1640–52. Furthermore, Portugal benefited from its defeat of Dutch schemes in Brazil, and from its consequent profits from its control of the colony. The failure of the French siege of Pavia (1655) and defeat at Valenciennes (16 July 1656) led France to offer Spain reasonable peace terms, only for Philip IV to reject them. His precondition that Condé be restored to his status and position in France was unacceptable to Mazarin, while Philip was unwilling to abandon Charles IV of Lorraine. Pavia was followed by the overrunning of the pro-French Duchy of Modena and by further Spanish victories in Lombardy.

Valenciennes was a spectacular victory, in which the French baggage train and supplies were captured. It seems premature to refer to the Decline of Spain at this juncture.

Spanish defeat came only after the intervention of fresh English forces on the side of France tipped the balance in Flanders, although relations between the two powers were far from cordial. Oliver Cromwell's Ironsides helped Turenne to defeat the Army of Flanders under Don John of Austria at the battle of the Dunes (14 June 1658), as the Spaniards tried to relieve the siege of Dunkirk. The Spanish army was outnumbered, its artillery had not arrived, the terrain prevented use of its superiority in cavalry, and its flank was bombarded by English warships. Victory transformed the strategic situation. Having captured Dunkirk, Gravelines, Menin and Ypres, Turenne could threaten an advance on Brussels. The Peace of the Pyrenees (1659), which brought the long war to an end, was a compromise, not the last rites of the Spanish empire, but Spain lost Artois and Roussillon to France and Dunkirk to England.

A re-evaluation of the Spanish military effort in the 1650s contributes to a more positive account of Spain than that of unremitting decline. Spain was still the largest empire in the world in 1660, while domestically she had borne tremendous strains without collapse. There was no crisis comparable to the *Frondes* until after the crown came into dispute in the War of the Spanish Succession (1701–14). Possibly if a work comparable to J.H. Elliott's influential treatment of the Catalan revolt of 1640 as a product of Spanish imperial failure (and, more specifically, the pressures of sustaining the war)[27] was written on the reconquest of Catalonia, then we might have a more rounded picture of Spanish strength. José Sanabre's *La acción de Francia en Cataluna, 1640–1659* (Barcelona, 1956) has not been translated and has never received wide attention.

The alliance between France and England showed the extent to which, although religious differences helped to cause and exacerbate disputes, they did not dictate them. Just as the French had supported the Protestant Dutch against the Spanish Habsburgs and the Protestant Swedes against the Austrian Habsburgs, so they allied with the Protestant, republican, usurpatory regime of Cromwell against Catholic, monarchical and legitimist Spain.

## Military Revolution reviewed

The relationship between the battles in these wars and the idea of an early modern military revolution advanced by Michael Roberts (see also Chapter 3) is complex. Roberts cited the Swedish victories as evidence of a revolution in which the rise of larger, permanent, professional state forces was related to tactical innovations. The importance of mercenaries and the hiring of foreign officers helped spread these innovations. Greatly influenced by the Nassau tactical reforms, Gustavus was able through constant drill and practice to improve Swedish reloading speeds. Whereas the Dutch had used the rotation of ranks of musketeers defensively (having fired, they retired to reload while colleagues took their place), Gustavus used rotation offensively, the other ranks moving forward through stationary reloaders. He also equipped his infantry units with mobile small cannon and encouraged his cavalry to press home in a shock charge.

However, tactical differences were not the crucial factor in battlefield success. Mansfeld adopted Dutch tactics without conspicuous success. The Saxons at Breitenfeld adopted Dutch-style formations, but they broke when the Austrians attacked. In contrast, Saxe-Weimar rejected Dutch formations and tactics and, in the late 1630s, used his heavily cavalry-based army, which was essentially self-sustaining, to fight in an aggressive fashion, winning a number of battles by manoeuvre. More generally, there were fewer differences between armies in weaponry and tactics than there had been in the Italian Wars, but, alongside this greater degree of tactical symmetry, there was more flexibility in formations and tactics than is frequently appreciated.

It is a mistake to assume that, while the Dutch and Swedes adopted new tactics, other armies stood still and continued to fight in large and relatively undifferentiated formations. Indeed, infantry formations generally became less deep, the exact relationship between pike and shot depending in large part on the size and nature of particular units and the lie of the land.[28] In the Army of Flanders there was a definite trend towards firepower, with a new establishment in 1634 in which three-quarters of the infantry were armed with muskets and only a quarter with pikes.

Battles were usually won by experienced and motivated troops whose dispositions had been well-arranged and, if forces were evenly matched, they were either inconclusive encounters or were determined by other factors, such as terrain, the availability and employment of reserves, and the results of cavalry clashes on the flanks, which owed much to which side attacked first. These could lead to the victorious cavalry attacking the enemy infantry where they were very vulnerable: in flank or rear, as at Rocroi or Naseby. Experienced and well-deployed infantry were usually safe against frontal attack by cavalry, but not necessarily by other infantry. The French attacked entrenched Bavarian forces at Allerheim, with roughly equal odds, and were successful, a result which indicated that the defence was not always superior. Nevertheless, the strength of the defence threatened a tactical impasse in infantry warfare that led to a particular need for skills in generalship and for flexible and effective cavalry.

Innovative ideas were not necessarily superior. The more innovative linear formations, only five or six ranks deep, were far more vulnerable to flank and rear attack than the long-established squares or columns. Instead, flexibility and an ability to create and respond to possibilities were more significant. At Jankov, the Swedes, supported by Hessians, were initially unable to defeat roughly equal Austrian forces (about 15,000 troops on each side), but succeeded by outmanoeuvring and attacking them from the rear, as well as by an adept and energetic use of field artillery. The Austrian army was destroyed, and the Swedes benefited from the tactical flexibility of their more experienced force.

Victory tended to go to larger and more experienced armies, like the Spaniards, Swedes, and some of the Austrian and Bavarian units, rather than simply to those which adopted new, Dutch-style tactics. Although numbers are not precise, at the White Mountain, there were 25,000 men in the army of the Catholic League and 22,000 opponents; at First Breitenfeld, Gustavus outnumbered his opponents by 42,000 to 35,000 and at Rain by 37,000 to 22,000; at Nördlingen, the Swedes were outnumbered by 33,000 to 25,000; and at Rocroi there were 24,000 French troops and 17,000 Spaniards. In manpower terms, First Breitenfeld was the largest battle of the war, and exceptionally so for a conflict in which field armies were rarely more than 30,000 strong. At Lützen, the numbers were more equal, and, partly for that reason, the battle was essentially inconclusive. Wallenstein had also ordered his cavalry to copy the Swedes. Other battles in which heavy outnumbering was important to the outcome included the Austrian victory over the French at Thionville.

However, numbers alone were only of value if they were handled ably. At Allerheim, the French army was large, but the cavalry on the Bavarian left under Werth successfully defeated the French right, giving the Bavarians the chance of victory. It was thrown away when their left attacked the French baggage, allowing the French under Turenne to break the Bavarian right and to turn on their infantry before Werth returned from the baggage. It is easy to criticise the loss of control over the cavalry but once formations had been disrupted by a charge followed by fighting, it was difficult to reform them. Aside from good command, the extent of discipline, morale and perseverance among the troops was also important. This was true not only of the Thirty Years' War but also of conflict elsewhere, for example in the British Isles.

An emphasis on battlefield numbers draws attention to the organisational and other means by which such numbers were achieved: 'In early modern war, success came more from higher combatant densities than greater firepower. Inside Europe these densities were achieved by marching, animal traction, and rowing',[29] although it is more pertinent to mention money and supplies.

Fortifications were more important in the Low Countries than across much of Germany, where the economic value and political importance of towns was lower. The struggle between the Dutch and the Army of Flanders was largely waged by means of sieges, although at Fleurus (26 August 1622) German forces in Dutch service defeated Córdoba. The Spaniards took the initiative in the 1620s, unsuccessfully besieging Bergen-op-Zoom in 1622, but capturing Breda in 1625. After 1629, when they took 's-Hertogenbosch, the Dutch advanced. Thus Venlo, Roermond, Straelen, Sittard and Maastricht fell in 1632, Breda in 1637, Sas Van Ghent in 1644 and Hulst in 1645. A Spanish attempt to retake Maastricht failed in 1634, although a surprise assault won them Schenkenschans that year and in 1637 the Spaniards captured Venlo and Roermond. The following year they defeated the Dutch at Kallo.

It has been argued that the Dutch benefited from Spain concentrating on France, although this interpretation has been challenged by Jonathan Israel. He has advanced a powerful case for Spain focusing on the Dutch until 1640. Thereafter, the Catalan revolt led the Spaniards to press on the French frontier in order to prevent the French from sending more troops to help the Catalans. The war ended for the Dutch in 1648 with modest territorial gains and no series of clashes to test the respective battlefield merit of the two armies.[30]

Major fortifications and their sieges took up large numbers of men. This could be seen as an example of the limitations of military advances. It was impossible to provide adequate garrisons for some major fortifications, without lessening the numbers available for field forces. The fortifications of Mainz were so extensive that they needed a garrison about 7,000 strong. Such fortifications served a number of purposes, including the affirmation of power, but in military terms, their construction did not necessarily serve the defensive purpose that might have been intended, as the resultant lessening of the field army confirmed the operational advantage of the attacker. Furthermore, a very large garrison created insuperable problems of supply during any protracted siege, as well as huge expense on a day-to-day basis. The 'new' fortifications were often larger and more complex than any existing garrison of normal size would be able to defend.

The uncertain outcome of most of the campaigns in the Thirty Years' War was due largely to difficulties in the supply of men, money and provisions; to the strength of fortifications; to the size of the disputed areas; and to the security of the key centres of Vienna, Paris, The Hague and Stockholm. In considering the reasons for the length of the struggle, it is instructive to compare it both with the Italian Wars and then, more specifically, with that touched off by the outbreak of the Schmalkaldic War in 1546. The position of the Italian states in the Italian Wars was similar to that of their German counterparts in the Thirty Years' War in that they could not control the course of a conflict increasingly set by outside powers whose home bases were little threatened by external attack. Furthermore, these outside powers increased and decreased their intervention as they saw fit and in response to an international competitiveness that was not set by the local powers. In contrast to the conflict of 1546–56 (renewed 1557–9), whereas the initial Habsburg response in both wars was effective, in 1552 Charles V was more successfully challenged than Ferdinand II was to be in the 1620s by external intervention. However, this intervention was more limited in extent than that in the 1620s and 1630s, and thus Charles was able to negotiate a settlement in Germany (1555) and to focus on the war with France, whereas Ferdinand, having effectively settled the German (and Danish) question, was challenged by Sweden (1630) and France (1635). The intervention of the Dutch, Denmark and Sweden in the Thirty Years' War reflected developments after 1559, not only the creation of an independent Dutch state, but also the growing ability and willingness of Baltic powers to intervene in Germany, and the greater sense of Europe as one international system.

Alongside an emphasis on battle and siege in 'functional' terms, as stages in the defeat of opposing forces, it is necessary to adopt a broader approach to victory and to underline the extent to which success had a symbolic value. From this perspective, decisiveness had to be reconceptualised, away from an emphasis on total victory, understood in modern terms as the destruction of opposing armies and the capture of their territory, and towards a notion that may have more meaning in terms of the values of the period. This would present conflict as a struggle of will and for prestige, the end sought being, first, a retention of domestic and international backing that rested on the gaining of *gloire* and, second, persuading other rulers to accept a new configuration of relative *gloire*. To argue that this led to 'non-rational' strategies, such as the concentration of forces on sieges made important only by the presence of the king as commander, is to misunderstand the rationality of the states of the period.

## War in the British Isles

Different types of war were waged in the British Isles and in Poland. In the former, there was a variety of struggles, including war between England and Scotland (the Bishops' Wars of 1639 and 1640, the Scottish invasion of England in 1648, and the English conquest of Scotland in 1650–2), civil war in England (1642–6, 1648), Scotland (1644–6), and Ireland (1641–9), and the English conquest of Ireland (1649–52). Far from being separate, these struggles overlapped and interacted,[31] and commanders and troops found themselves called upon to fulfil a variety of military tasks which were, in large part, shaped by the particular political circumstances. Experience and discipline proved crucial to fighting quality. They helped the Scots win the Bishops' Wars. Many of their commanders had served in the Swedish or Dutch forces, such as Alexander Leslie under Gustavus at Lützen. Similarly, in 1642 Irish veterans returned from the Spanish Army of Flanders brought new energy to the rebel cause in Ireland.

The First Bishops' War was essentially a matter of inconsequential border manoeuvres. The supporters of the National Covenant (an agreement to resist ecclesiastical innovations), or Covenanters, under Leslie, captured Aberdeen and Edinburgh Castle without loss in 1639, and went on to deploy a large army to block an invading force under Charles I, which encamped near Berwick. The English army was poorly prepared, with its logistics wrecked by inadequate finance. When fighting resumed in 1640, the Scots successfully invaded Northumberland and Durham, capturing Newcastle.[32]

Far from war strengthening government and expanding the state, it forced Charles to turn to Parliament which he had avoided doing during his 'Personal

Rule' that began in 1629. The subsequent political crisis gathered pace when the need to raise an army to deal with a major Catholic rising in Ireland in November 1641 polarised the situation. Who was to control this army?

Fighting in England started in Manchester in July 1642, and Charles raised his standard at Nottingham on 22 August. The subsequent civil war is worth considering at some length, not simply because of its importance for British political development, but also because it redirects attention from the Thirty Years' War and the related struggle between France and Spain. They were very important, but were not the definition of military history in this period. Instead, as with the sixteenth century, it is necessary to note the variety of military circumstances and, more specifically, the extent and importance of civil conflict.

In England, as with other civil conflicts, there was a widespread desire to remain neutral, for example in Cheshire, Lancashire, Leicester and East Yorkshire, but the pressure of war wrecked such hopes, and the conflict spread. Both sides tried to raise the Trained Bands (militia). As in other civil wars, initial moves by the combatants rapidly defined zones of control. Thus, William Cavendish, First Earl of Newcastle, speedily established the royal cause throughout Durham and Northumberland, including Newcastle, before moving into Yorkshire. On 11 January 1642, Charles appointed the Earl of Newcastle Governor of Hull, but, at the same time, Parliament appointed a wealthy East Riding landowner, Sir John Hotham, as Governor. Hotham secured Hull, but in March 1642 Charles stationed a garrison in nearby York. Hotham was forced to show his hand on 23 April when he refused Charles entry to Hull on the grounds it would be compromising the town's security. Charles declared him a traitor. William, Marquess of Hereford tried to rally Somerset for Charles, but found Wellington, Taunton and Dunster held for Parliament, and was driven from Wells.

As with the early French Wars of Religion and the Catalan rising, control of the capital was a central goal. In the first major battle of the war, Charles narrowly defeated the main Parliamentary army under Robert, Third Earl of Essex at Edgehill (23 October), but he failed to destroy Essex's army or follow up by driving decisively on London. The Royalist impetus was not maintained. Blocked by larger Parliamentary forces at Turnham Green on 13 November, Charles failed to press home the attack, and retreated to establish his headquarters at Oxford. His best chance of winning the war was past.

In 1643, in what was a very fluid campaign, the Royalists overran most of western England, crushing the Parliamentarians at Stratton (16 May) and Roundway Down (13 July). Bristol fell to Royalist assault after a brief siege. However, the Royalist sieges of Gloucester and Hull were both unsuccessful, and the principal battle in the vital Thames region – the first battle of Newbury (20 September) – was inconclusive: the Royalist cavalry outfought its opponents, but the infantry was less successful, and the infantry battle was not determined by that between the cavalry as it had been at Rocroi.

Although the Royalists had many triumphs in 1643, they did not challenge the Parliamentary heartland. The eleven-mile long defence system rapidly constructed for London – an earthen bank and ditch with a series of forts and batteries – was never tested in action, but was a testimony to the resources available to the Parliamentary cause.

It is understandable why general works of this type focus on major engagements, and derive accounts of capability and progress from them. However, as well as the major battles, there were also many small-scale actions that were important locally, for, like other civil wars, this was both a national conflict and a series of local struggles.[33] Indeed, it has been calculated that 47 per cent of the soldiers who died in conflict in England died in skirmishes in which fewer than 250 died, while only 15 per cent died in major battles.[34] Military units had a sense of locality, and many were reluctant to travel far from home. In 1645, the Royalist Northern Horse was allowed to return from Oxford to Yorkshire after threatening mutiny. But, in 1643, the Royalist Yorkshire Trained Bands had moved into the Midlands and James, Seventh Earl of Derby had sent his best regiments from Lancashire to the main Royalist field army at Oxford.

At the local level, conflict was largely organised around garrison positions, and at the national level these were also crucial. It has recently been argued that 'the characteristic military action of the British and Irish Civil Wars was an attack upon a fortified position'.[35] In towns, like Parliamentary Northampton and Royalist Worcester, surviving medieval walls were supplemented by new fortifications. In addition, castles provided good bases for garrisons, and many were brought back into habitation and use. Their supposed redundancy in face of a siege train was of limited importance to the course of local struggles. The Parliamentary garrison in Warwick Castle dominated the county, while Hartlebury Castle and Dudley Castle were major Royalist sites in Worcestershire, and Dunster Castle, after its capture in 1643, in Somerset. From Northampton, the Parliamentarians competed for control of the south-west of the country with Royalists from Banbury Castle, which had been refortified and established as a garrison to protect Oxford. The Royalist position in Worcestershire was challenged from Gloucester, leading to advances as far as Worcester in 1643. The garrisons, their struggles and their search for supplies led to great pressure on civilian society. In this respect, the Civil War was very similar to the Thirty Years' War. The Parliamentary garrison in Leicester and its Royalist counterparts in the stately homes of Ashby de la Zouch and Belvoir Castle brought much devastation to Leicestershire.

Control over bridges, such as those at Upton-upon-Severn, Pershore and Tadcaster, was also very important in local campaigning; as they also were in the movements of field armies, although pontoon bridges or bridges of boats could be employed. The bridge over the Avon at Stratford was broken by the Parliamentarians in December 1645 in order to cut communications between Oxford and the West Country. Bridging points, such as Liège, Mainz,

Philippsburg and Strasbourg, were also very important in Continental warfare, and their strategic value was enhanced by fortifications. Because there were no bridges over the Meuse north of Maastricht, it was of particular strategic interest for operations in the region.

Control over the crossings over the River Trent was important to the course of the English Civil War in the East Midlands: Derbyshire was a linchpin of the Parliamentary cause there, and, therefore, the goal of Royalist attacks from Yorkshire and the Midlands. Control of Derbyshire and the Trent crossings would have linked these areas and helped the Royalists to apply greater pressure on the East Anglian-based Parliamentarian Eastern Association. Royalist failure in Derbyshire lessened the co-ordination of their field armies, and led to longer lines of communications. Thus local struggles interacted with the national, and the latter could transform the former, although, as in the French Wars of Religion and the Thirty Years' War, the relationship was often indirect. Thus, the war in south-west Wales swayed to and fro with only a limited relationship with the struggle elsewhere.

The arrival of field armies could lead to the capture of positions that had conferred local control. Thus, on 30 May 1645, a Royalist force of over 10,000 stormed and took Leicester. Ably-defended positions, however, could resist such pressure, as Gloucester demonstrated in 1643. The varied fate of fortified positions was shown by Taunton: captured by the Royalists in 1643 and regained in 1644, it resisted a Royalist siege in 1645 until relieved after the defeat of the Royalist field army.

As with both civil and international conflicts elsewhere, the Civil War saw growing demands on the localities from both sides, as the cost of the conflict rose, and resources available in the early stages were used up. In order to try to achieve central control, reliable and experienced commanders replaced local gentlemen in positions of local power. Sir William Russell was succeeded as Royalist Governor of Worcester in December 1643 by Sir Gilbert Gerrard. Localism was eroded, just as neutralism had been ended.

In 1644, the balance of advantage shifted against Charles I. In January, the Scottish Covenanters entered northern England on the side of Parliament. Advancing south they joined a Parliamentary army and crushed the Royalists under Prince Rupert, Charles's nephew and the son of Frederick V, Elector Palatine, at Marston Moor on 2 July. The battle was followed by the surrender of York and by the fall of other Royalist positions in the north: Newcastle was stormed on 20 October. Earlier, on 29 March, the Parliamentary position in southern England had been stabilised when Sir William Waller defeated the Royalists under Sir Ralph Hopton at Cheriton in Hampshire. The possibility of a Royalist advance on London from that direction was now at an end. In the Midlands, the Royalists were beaten at Nantwich (25 January), but held off Parliamentary attack near Oxford at Cropredy Bridge (29 June). The Royalist cause was showing serious signs of strain in several counties, including Gloucestershire and Wiltshire. Morale was suffering, as were finances: tax receipts declined from late 1643. Royalist divisions were also growing more acute. Nevertheless, the war was not over. The Earl of Essex advanced into Cornwall, only to be cut off by Charles I and defeated at Lostwithiel (2 September). Returning to Oxford, Charles fought off a larger Parliamentary army at the inconclusive second battle of Newbury (27 October); both battles revealed the incompetence of the Parliamentary commanders. Charles felt able to reject advice that he negotiate with Parliament, advice that he again rejected in January 1645.

That year the Royalists were heavily defeated, and with decisive results, at Naseby (14 June 1645, see p. 159). In the words of Clarendon, the Royalist historian of the war, Naseby was where 'king and kingdom were lost'. Carlisle had successfully resisted a Scottish siege since the previous October, but it asked for terms when news of Naseby arrived.

Thereafter, with the main field army heavily defeated, the Royalist situation was one of inexorable collapse, although, hopeful of success in Scotland and naturally stubborn, Charles still refused to negotiate. Thanks to superior Parliamentary firepower, the principal Royalist army in the west was defeated at Langport (10 July 1645). Two months later, Bristol was successfully stormed. By the end of 1645 the Royalists were reduced to isolated strongholds and, on 5 May 1646, Charles gave himself up to the Scots army in London. The remaining Royalist strongholds surrendered.

Experience and discipline were important in the development of the war-winning Parliamentarian force in England, the New Model Army, which was eventually commanded by Oliver Cromwell. This army defeated the Royalists in England and Wales, and subsequently the Scots, both in England and in Scotland, and the Irish. Aside from the fighting quality seen in victories such as Naseby over the Royalists, and Preston (17 August 1648), Dunbar (3 September 1650) and Worcester (3 September 1651) over the Scots, the New Model benefited from a strong infrastructure. In the Civil War, Parliament was backed by the wealthiest parts of the country, London, the major ports and the navy, and this helped finance and sustain the war effort. When they invaded Ireland in 1649, Cromwell's forces were well-supplied, enabling them to operate most of the year round. Well-equipped with carts, wagons and draft-horses, they retained the initiative, and were also supported by the navy.[36]

It is also necessary to emphasise the diversity of fighting forces and military environments in the British Isles. Thus, the Irish rebels who rose in 1641 were poorly armed and disciplined and had a weak supply system which made mounting lengthy sieges difficult. Instead, the rebels relied on avoiding battle, and on ambushes and raids. The rebels created the Confederation of Kilkenny, which sought to establish a Catholic Ireland loyal to Charles I. However, it failed to conquer Dublin or the Protestant settlements in Ulster.[37]

In Scotland, James Graham, Marquess of Montrose, the commander of Royalist forces in 1644–6, employed different tactics to those that dominated fighting in England. Thus, at Inverlochy (2 February 1645), his men delayed firing until the last moment and then followed up their devastating volley with a successful charge. A brilliant tactician, Montrose was a master of flank victory: putting his best troops on his flanks in order to defeat the enemy flanks before his weaker centre engaged; Montrose subsequently destroyed the opponent's centre.[38]

The social practice of war also varied. The Royalists under Charles I essentially relied on traditional notions of honour, obligation and loyalty to raise troops. Charles headed the social hierarchy, and his armies reflected this. Leadership for the Royalists was in large part a function of social position, although an increasing number of Royalist officers came from outside the social elite. Aristocrats played a major role in the Parliamentary leadership in the early stages, but less so subsequently. The contrast between Prince Rupert and Oliver Cromwell, or between the Marquess of Newcastle and Sir Thomas Fairfax, was one of different attitudes towards responsibility, position, quality and merit. In this respect, the New Model Army prefigured the Continental Army of the American War of Independence, the Republican Army of the French Revolution and the Red Army in the Russian Civil War. In each case, the army served as the expression of the political thrust of the revolution, as well as providing its force.

The New Model's equipment and tactics were essentially similar to those of their opponents; the major difference was that they were better disciplined and supported by a more effective infrastructure and supply system. Promotion was by merit, and Cromwell favoured officers and men imbued with equal religious fervour to his own.[39] Furthermore, the social and ideological politics of the New Model ensured that it was impossible to demobilise, and the military dominance of politics was only ended by the implosion of the revolutionary regime in 1659–60, an implosion followed by the restoration of Stuarts in the person of Charles II[40] and leading to a marked rundown in the size of the army. That is a salutary point. The creation of a 'modern' military, in the shape of the New Model, did not lead to a lasting governmental (or military) development. Furthermore, it is striking how far the New Model was exceptional in European terms.

As in the Thirty Years' War, victory in the wars in the British Isles tended to go to larger armies, although other factors were also important, not least an ability to keep control of the tempo of the battle and, crucially, to achieve infantry–cavalry co-ordination during its course. Like many battles over the previous century and a half, Marston Moor (2 July 1644) arose from an attempt to relieve a siege, in this case York by Parliamentary and Scottish forces. The Royalists mounted a relief effort under Prince Rupert. Outnumbered by about 18,000 to 27,000, he suffered a surprise attack at about 7 p.m. The Royalist cavalry under Rupert was successful on the allied right but, on their left, Cromwell and Leslie drove their opponents' cavalry from the field. The infantry struggle in the centre ended when Cromwell's cavalry joined the assault on the Royalist infantry. The allies lost about 1,500 men, the Royalists about 3,000 and their artillery, but more seriously, their cohesion was broken and their cause in the north fatally defeated. At Naseby (14 June 1645), the Royalists were outnumbered by about 7,600 to 14,000, but the battle was decided by the superior discipline of the Parliamentary cavalry. Rupert swept the cavalry on the Parliamentary left from the field, but was unable to prevent his troops from dispersing to attack the Parliamentary baggage train. Cromwell, on the right, defeated the Royalist cavalry opposite, and then retained sufficient control to turn on the veteran, but heavily outnumbered, Royalist infantry in the centre, which succumbed to an over-whelming attack. The leading Royalist field army had been destroyed.

Yet, before a pattern to explain victory is built up on this basis, it is neces-sary to emphasise the tactical variety seen in battles in the period. The ability to grasp and exploit the initiative and to make good use of topography were both important. Cromwell's victories over the Scots at Preston and Dunbar were particularly good examples of the former. Surprise also played a major role in David Leslie's victory over Montrose at Philiphaugh (13 September 1645), a battle that shattered his prestige, which was a decisive factor in gener-alship. Although Cromwell outnumbered Charles II at Worcester, 27,000 to 15,000, he was himself outnumbered two to one at Dunbar, but still won the battle.

Marston Moor, Naseby, Dunbar and Montrose's victory at Kilsyth (15 August 1645) demonstrated the importance of cavalry for success. Montrose, in particular, specialised in attack victories, using both infantry and cavalry with great aggression. This helped him take and keep control of the battle. More generally, although firepower played a role in this process, both for infantry and cavalry, the nature of attack victories ensures that battles should not be seen primarily in terms of firefights, with the accompanying tempta-tion to view military progress in terms of technological and tactical innovations designed to increase firepower. A stress on cavalry also underlines the issue of command skills, as some commanders, such as Cromwell and Lambert, were far better at retaining control over their cavalry than others.

## War in Eastern Europe

In Poland, there was a revival of conflict in the 1650s, involving Russia, Sweden, Brandenburg and Transylvania. The expanding crisis began when the Cossacks rebelled under Bohdan Khmelnytsky in 1648. The Cossacks won support in their rejection of Catholic and Polish control. Instead, they pressed a distinct sense of identity that had not been incorporated into the Polish Commonwealth. This drew in part on the Orthodox Church, but also on support from those worried about political and social changes. In May the rebellious Cossacks, supported by Tatars, defeated the Poles at Zhovti Vody (16 May) and Korsun (26 May), defeats that reflected the extent to which the Polish army had been run down after the war with Russia had ended in 1634, as well as the reliance of the Poles on Cossack support and the consequences of poor and divided Polish leadership. In 1648, the Cossacks were able to advance as far as the gates of Lwów, where they were bought off.

The new king, John Casimir (r.1648–68), an effective military leader, heavily defeated the Cossacks at Berestechko on 29 June 1651. As with many battles, this was a coalition struggle and the Cossacks suffered when their Tatar allies withdrew at a critical moment. John Casimir had benefited from the support of German mercenaries. The following year, however, a Polish army was successfully ambushed at Batih (23 June). As an indication of the bitterness of the struggle, the Cossacks killed all their Polish prisoners. Both sides were divided, and unable to ensure a military or political verdict to the struggle. In 1654, at Perejaslaw, Tsar Alexis (r.1645–76) took the Dnieper Cossacks under his protection and moved his troops into the Ukraine. He also set out to conquer Belarus as he wanted to recover Smolensk, Chernigov and Seversk for Russia, but victory led him to expand his objectives. The Lithuanian army was heavily defeated at Shepeleviche (24 August 1654) and this left Smolensk clear for Russian attack. The failure to repair the damage done in 1633 and the small size of the garrison helped ensure its surrender on 3 October. Alexis overran Lithuania in 1655: Vilna (8 August) and Grodno fell and Alexis offered protection to Danzig (Gdansk). Another Russian army invaded Galicia and threatened Lwów. There was a strong religious element. Russian troops were sprinkled with holy water and fought under holy banners, officers were ordered to take communion and Orthodox churches were built in captured towns. The armies Alexis sent into Belarus and Ukraine in 1654 were very large and of unprecedented size for Russia.

In 1655, Charles X of Sweden (r.1654–60) attacked Poland in order to make gains, particularly on her Baltic coast, from a state that appeared to be collapsing before the advancing Russian armies. Despite improvements to the Polish army, it was too weak to prevent Charles X from defeating the Poles at Zarnów (16 September) and Wojinicz (3 October), and seizing Warsaw (8 September) and Cracow (19 October). This led the Poles to avoid battle with large Swedish formations, relying instead upon surprise attacks and raids. In 1656, these tactics obliged the Swedes, unable to maintain their supplies, to withdraw. Charles X discovered the difficulty of any invader imposing his will on Polish politics. Anger at Swedish exactions, not least the 'contributions' necessary to pay for the occupying army, compounded with fury at the treatment of the Catholic Church by the Protestant invaders, had led to a massive increase in resistance from the autumn of 1655, and this greatly affected the campaign of 1656. Charles found himself outnumbered and no longer able to determine the tempo of the war. To avoid encirclement, he had to abandon his planned siege of Lwów in early 1656. A Swedish force was destroyed by Polish cavalry at Warka (7 April), and Charles was forced to abandon Warsaw and fall back on Polish Prussia. In addition, he was under pressure from Alexis, who attacked Sweden in May 1656 and that November allied with Poland in return for the promise of the crown after John Casimir died. The Russians overran most of (Swedish-ruled) Livonia, which was poorly protected, but well-fortified Riga successfully resisted Russian siege.

However, with his resources exhausted by several years campaigning, Alexis could not sustain a war on so many fronts, while, in operational terms, the need to assemble an army each campaigning season delayed the start of the season sufficiently to make a major siege unlikely to succeed. In 1658, faced with Polish and Tatar attacks and trouble in the Ukraine, where the Cossack elite, concerned about Russian policy, sought closer links with Poland, Alexis abandoned his hopes of a Baltic seaport and signed a truce with Sweden. It also became clear that the Polish throne would elude him. Cossack opposition was a major problem. Cossack forces defeated invading Russians at Konotop on 8 July 1659. Unprepared for a major battle, the poorly led Russian cavalry was lured into a swamp.

In June 1656, Charles X allied with Frederick William of Brandenburg. Their joint forces defeated the Poles at the three-day battle of Warsaw (28–30 July 1656). Both sides had largely cavalry armies, and the Polish cavalry was outfought. Charles was unable to exploit his victory, however, as Frederick William cut short his commitment. The main Swedish army fell back to Prussia in late 1656, but mounted a new offensive into Poland the following year, this time in co-operation with the Transylvanians. The two captured Brest Litovsk and Warsaw (17 June 1657), but were unable to force the Poles to battle. Furthermore, as with the Thirty Years' War, the international context proved crucial. Concerned under Transylvanian ambitions, the Austrians sent troops against the Swedes, and this encouraged Frederick III of Denmark to declare war and invade Sweden and the Swedish territory of Bremen. Charles turned against the Danes, leaving the Transylvanians to be defeated by the Poles and Cracow to be captured by a Polish–Austrian army. Charles overran Jutland in late 1657.

He was even more successful against the Danes in 1658, and demonstrated then the extent to which campaigning could be decisive. The main Danish army in Jutland had been decisively defeated in late 1657 when the Swedes captured the fortress of Frederiksodde. This enabled a rather small army to advance on Copenhagen the following February without meeting much resistance. Charles led his troops across the frozen Little Belt and then the more hazardous Great Belt, arriving outside Copenhagen and leading his unprepared opponent to accept harsh terms. Swedish victory led, under the Treaty of Roskilde of 8 March 1658, to the permanent gain of the Danish territories on the eastern side of the Sound in what is now southern Sweden. The Swedes also gained Bornholm and Trondheim, the latter splitting Norway. Relations remained tense, and in July 1658 Charles resumed the war and besieged Copenhagen. However, the Dutch were not only allied to Denmark but also unwilling to see one power dominate the Baltic. Well-fortified and defended, Copenhagen successfully resisted the Swedish siege, while the Dutch fleet broke the blockade that November. Austria and Prussia joined in on the Danish side, besieging Stettin, the major Swedish position in Pomerania.

Under pressure in an unexpectedly wide-ranging struggle, the Swedes agreed to the Peace of Oliva (3 May 1660) with Poland, Austria and Prussia and the Peace of Copenhagen (6 June) with Denmark. Sweden lost Bornholm and Trondheim back to Denmark, as part of a peace settlement that left no single power in a hegemonic position in Northern Europe.

Although the infantry techniques of counter-marching and volley fire were not without relevance in Eastern Europe, the small number of battles fought between linear formations and settled by firepower is a reminder that these innovations were not all-powerful. Cavalry strength and tactics remained especially important, not least because the strategy of raiding could be employed to undermine an opponent's logistics. Sieges also played a relatively small role, although control of bases such as Riga, Stettin and Danzig (Gdansk) was of great importance, and the failure of the Russian siege of Riga and the Swedish siege of Copenhagen were important to the course of events. Under the pressure of war with Sweden and Poland, the percentage of the Russian army consisting of 'new order' troops trained in Western European methods dramatically increased.[41]

## Smaller-scale conflict

Alongside major international conflicts, it is again appropriate to note the importance of smaller-scale wars and of domestic conflicts. As an example of the first, in 1642–4, Tuscany, Modena, Venice and Parma joined against Pope Urban VIII in the Castro War over the fate of Italian fiefs and the extent of papal pretensions. The war was over possession of the Duchy of Castro, a Farnese territory but claimed by the Barberini papacy in lieu of unpaid Farnese debts; and envisaged as a potential Barberini duchy, giving the family the same permanent dynastic status in the peninsula as had been obtained by the Farnese in the 1540s thanks to the acquisition of Parma-Piacenza. A Parmesan army, strong in cavalry, gained the initiative in September 1642, advancing deep into the Papal States. The following year, the Papal field army was crushed at Nonantola (19 July) by the Modenese under Raimondo Montecùccoli (1609–80), one of the leading generals of the 1660s and 1670s. Papal forces were routed by the Tuscans at Mongiovino (4 September 1643), another reminder of the frequency of battles in the period. The following March peace was negotiated, with Urban VIII restoring the contested town of Castro, which he had had successfully besieged in October 1641.[42]

Some domestic conflicts, such as the rising of the Catholics in the Valtelline against rule by the Grisons League in 1618, the Huguenot rising of 1625–9, and the struggle between the Duchess of Savoy and her brother-in-law in 1637–41, were closely involved with the international arena. The Neapolitan rising of 1647 was in large part a response to the fiscal demands of a Spanish government desperately short of funds for the war, and the French sought to exploit the disaffection. However, divisions within Naples helped the Spaniards recapture the city in February 1648. The pressures of supporting the war also played a major role in the uprisings in Evora (1637), the Alentejo and Algarve (1637–8) and Lisbon (1640) in Portugal, and in Catalonia in 1640. The Cossack rebellions in the Ukraine from the 1590s to 1654 did more to change the international balance of power than any other rebellions. Consideration of them can also serve to integrate narratives of Ottoman, Muscovite and Central European military development.

Other conflicts were less directly related to the international arena, although the pressures of war finance were a constant theme. The financial demands of the French crown led to major peasant revolts, particularly in Gascony in 1636–7 – the *croquants* – and in Normandy in 1639 – the *nu-pieds*. The *croquants* appeared a threat because they had muskets and gunpowder, were led by some local gentry and included in their ranks veterans of the siege of La Rochelle.[43] These risings had to be suppressed by large organised forces. Thus 3,000 troops under the Duke of La Valette defeated the *croquants* at La Sauvetat in 1637, while 10,000 royal troops were deployed against the *nu-pieds*. The diversion of these troops affected operations against the Spaniards. There was also a rising in Sologne in 1658.

As peasant, like urban, risings were local or regional rather than national in scope, and directed against the local or regional agents of authority, especially the central government, rather than seeking the overthrow of the state itself, it was possible for governments to temper their response. However, the prevalent elite emphasis on order and social subordination encouraged a forceful suppression of disorder.[44] In addition, in some cases there was a marked political and/or religious character to the disorder, and this certainly encouraged a violent response. Regular Austrian and Bavarian troops were used to suppress the major peasant rising in Upper Austria around Linz in 1626, while the New Model Army suppressed the far more small-scale radical Leveller movement in 1649.

## War and state-building

Yet again, this period offers an ambivalent response to the question whether war and the military led to 'state-building'. It is clear that they could lead to a more assertive and powerful monarchy. Thus, in Brandenburg in the late 1630s, war with Sweden and the existence of a largely mercenary army under the control of the Elector were used by the leading minister, Count Schwarzenberg, in order to overawe opposition by the Estates and to raise taxes without consent. Frederick William, who became Elector in 1640, felt it expedient to restore control of taxation and of the raising of troops to the Estates.

Conventionally, France under Richelieu has been seen as a state with a synergy of war, military expansion, and the development of state power, but that approach has been dismantled by David Parrott[45] in a fashion that emphasises the need for comparable scholarly accounts for other countries. Rather than war and military acting as enablers for state growth, they were both heavy burdens that encouraged a government of expedients to match the politics of opportunism. At the same time as Schwarzenberg was over-awing the Estates of Brandenburg, Duke Bernard of Saxe-Weimar, angered by the failure of the French to provide promised support, was unwilling to allow French troops to take control of Breisach. The disagreement was only resolved by Saxe-Weimar's death in July 1639. The French then had to negotiate new terms of service with the leaders of Saxe-Weimar's army.

The French military were not alone in facing serious strategic constraints as a consequence of resource problems. A recent study of the Catholic Confederacy in Ireland in the 1640s has revealed a similar situation, as well as demonstrating the difficulty of creating a new war state, not least because 'the insurgent war effort was too regional'.[46] More generally, the failure of the Confederacy, as of the Catalans, indicates the limitations of Charles Tilly's aphorism: 'The state made war and war made the state'.[47] Instead, a range of bodies made war, the making of war did not necessarily lead to state forma-tion, and engaging in war undermined the state.

More specifically, the contributions system can only be reconciled with statebuilding by an approach that underrates the inefficiencies it created and the expediency it represented. It is true that, if it was a damaging way to pay for war and tap resources, so also were the responses of later societies, particu-larly inflation and penal taxation in the twentieth century; and, moreover, contributions accorded with the limitations of early modern government and the opportunities created by campaigning. However, the problems created by this system helped ensure serious post-war pressures on military finances, and thus army size, as contributions were not a system that could be employed in peacetime, although, after the Thirty Years' War, a certain amount of such occupation continued, particularly by the Swedes but also by the combatants in the continuing Franco-Spanish war, for example in the Prince-Bishopric of Liège. Most German rulers, however, had to try to pay their remaining forces after 1648 by increasing taxes. Introducing excises was the most common means, a policy that, by depressing consumption, hit economic growth but avoided the political problems of confronting the landed elite. Thus, the Thirty Years' War can be seen as an important stage in the development of German states, not least because raising taxes was a concrete demonstration of authority and a means to further power. However, the relationship is more complex, as the war can also be seen as a period of expedients, not to say confusion even chaos, that precluded such a clear-cut process of development. Furthermore, the armies of the German states that were at peace in the 1650s were not as large as their successors were to be towards the close of the century, which again suggests that much of the focus in accounting for developments in army size should be on the second half of the century, rather than on the Thirty Years' War.

Irrespective of the governmental consequences, the warfare of the period 1618–60 was important to European political development. The origins of late-seventeenth-century absolutism can be found both in the long-term search for a restatement of order in reaction to the turmoil of the sixteenth century, a period of acute disorder that had political, social and religious dimensions, and in a series of political crises in the first half of the seventeenth. The most important were not only the troubles of the mid-seventeenth-century crisis, but also the reimposition of an effective Catholic hegemony in France and the dominions of the Austrian Habsburgs in the 1620s. This did not automatically lead to civil order and good crown–elite relations, as the *Frondes* demonstrated, but it created the necessary coherent ideological and political context within which such relations could develop and be encouraged, particularly by traditional patronage methods.[48]

## War and decisiveness

Alongside the political conclusion, it is appropriate to underline the potential decisiveness of war in this period. It is frequently claimed that the armies were unable to achieve major strategic or political goals, and that operations were frequently inconsequential, although also destructive.[49] Such a discussion risks present-mindedness: modern concepts of decisiveness owe much to the achievement of unconditional victory in World War Two, but that is misleading even as a description of twentieth-century warfare. It is also necessary to distinguish between different understandings of decisiveness, whether in terms of tactical or strategic considerations and whether defensive or offensive. A decisive battle or campaign can achieve a defensive goal. In addition, it is far from clear that discussion of decisiveness should centre on victory in battle. If the objective of a war was to win territory that could be retained at a subsequent peace, then successful sieges can be seen as 'decisive' to that end. Ultimately the problem is cultural. It is difficult for many to accept that warfare was 'for real' in a world in which artifice, convention and style played such a major role; and this is particularly the case because it has been contrasted with the apparently more vital, clear-cut and successful warfare of the Age of Revolution, more particularly the forces and ideologies of the American and French Revolutions. There is also a tendency to underrate the determination and ability of aristocratic societies.

Such views are rarely expressed explicitly, but they are no less influential for that. However, they adopt a misleading teleological approach and mistake style for substance. In fact, there was nothing inherently indecisive about tactics and strategy. Indecision was, if anything, a product of political rather than military factors, especially the inability of states to exploit fully and effectively the potential resources of their societies. An account of warfare in 1618–60 reveals a series of decisive outcomes, including Dutch success in retaining independence (and territory), the conquest of the British Isles by Parliamentary forces, and the capacity of the Swedes to crush the Danes in both the 1640s and 1650s in extremely rapid and overwhelming campaigns, such that without the intervention of the Dutch and other powers it seems unlikely that the Danes would have maintained their position. Battles and sieges could be decisive instruments of policy, while the threat of battle and siege shaped campaigns and policies even when no battle or siege occurred.[50] War was neither inconsequential nor predictable. It played a major role in determining European history.

# 8

# NAVAL DEVELOPMENTS

It is useful to treat navies on their own terms – the usual approach – and with reference to the lessons learned from an analysis of armies. In the case of navies, it is possible to present a model of change driven by military technology and operational considerations. In this model, the prime means of, and reason for, change would be the rise in the sixteenth century of the large specialised warship, built and maintained just for war, rather than also acting as a peacetime trader. These ships, able to take part in sustained artillery duels at close range, were expensive to build, administer, and maintain. As a consequence, the number of potential maritime powers was restricted and, by the end of the period, the powerful naval state was no longer coterminous, as it had earlier been, with the commercial territory or port, although particular ports and related entrepreneurial groups were very important to its operation.[1]

This approach helpfully links technological changes with those in the wider political context, but it possibly suggests a more automatic process of development than was in fact the case. The lesson from shifts on land was that there was no such process and that it was far from clear what was the most effective at any particular stage. As with land warfare, this was further complicated by the range of factors involved in effectiveness and the need for trade-offs between mobility, armament and firepower. However, the range of factors in effectiveness was more extensive than those appertaining to land warfare and was more complex than the mobility–armour–firepower combination that applied to cavalry. Balancing cargo capacity, even for warships, sea-keeping quality, speed, armament types and numbers, optimum size of crew and draught all depended on the role of the ship. European purpose built warships were typically 500–600 tonnes in the second half of the sixteenth century, while armed merchant vessels were in the 200–300 tonnes range. Portuguese East Indiamen relied on their vast size for defence, while Spanish *fregates* relied on speed for their safety.

As another instance of the role of choice or agency, it is also necessary to consider why particular states chose to develop their naval power. Issues of identification and image played a major role, although, alongside any stress on political cultures that placed an emphasis on commercial interests, it is also necessary to underline the importance of particular geopolitical strategies and the choices of individual rulers and ministers. This was especially apparent in the case of powers that had to prioritise between Mediterranean and Atlantic commitments, particularly Spain under Philip II.[2]

## Ships

Naval strength entailed a commitment of resources which was often greater than that required for warfare on land. The wooden warship equipped with cannon, whether driven by sails, muscle power (for galleys) or both, was the single most costly, powerful and technologically advanced weapons system of the period. The introduction of large numbers of cannon on individual ships made maritime technology more complex and increased the operational and fighting demands on crews. The construction, equipment, manning, supply and maintenance of a fleet required considerable financial and logistical efforts.[3] The construction of large warships using largely unmechanised processes was an immense task and required large quantities of wood. The capital investment required was formidable, but ships generally had a life of only twenty to thirty years. Maintenance was also expensive, as wood and canvas rotted and iron corroded. Warships therefore demanded not only, by the standards of the day, technologically advanced yards for their construction, but also permanent institutions to manage them. The construction and logistical infrastructure of a fleet constituted the major 'industrial' activity of the sixteenth century, with a requirement for a commensurate administrative effort to support it. This applied to all countries involved in the creation and support of fleets, and the remains of arsenals, for example, in Copenhagen, and also at Venice are still visible, and are well recorded in contemporary drawings.

Warships provided effective mobile artillery platforms that lacked an equivalent on land, and an individual vessel might carry heavy firepower capacity comparable to that of an entire army. The cannon carried on some European warships from the middle of the fifteenth century were made with a particular concern for their use at sea in a fashion distinct from that of land-based weaponry: an important aspect of specialisation; although it is important not to exaggerate the differences between guns for siege warfare, fortifications and naval warfare. To a large extent, they were interchangeable, although the mountings had to be changed. Field artillery was different as it had to be as light as possible.

The demands upon naval power also changed. The trading wealth unlocked by the 'Age of Discoveries' encouraged the development of naval strength to both protect and attack long-distance trade routes.[4] Warships were also the most effective means of attacking distant hostile bases. In European waters, the strategic commitments of many powers involved maritime links, for example between Spain and both Italy and the Low Countries, or Sweden and the eastern Baltic.

From *c*.900, the Europeans had been able to apply force across the Mediterranean, but, from the later fifteenth century, it was a case of force applied across the oceans. There had been no earlier examples by Europeans, as the Viking presence in North America was very limited and did not represent a military effort. Modernity has been seen as arriving in the shape of a heavily armed warship capable of sailing long distances. The sixteenth century saw the establishment and growth of state navies and the greatly increased use of heavy guns in galleys and sailing warships. The increase in cannon size mounted in sailing ships in the first two decades of the sixteenth century was impressive, although they did not compare in size to the fortress artillery that the Knights of St John employed in their unsuccessful defence of Rhodes against the Ottomans in 1522. Sailing warships had important advantages over galleys, the most important ship in the Mediterranean, the sea that had dominated the trade of medieval Europe, although even English Atlantic sailors held the sea-fighting capability of galleys in some respect well into the sixteenth century. English warships of the 1560s–1570s were built with forward and rear firing cannon to meet the threat posed by cannon-armed galleys. Large sailing ships with three masts required fewer bases than galleys, which relied on human power: thanks to a reliance on wind, their crews were smaller than galleys and their larger hull capacity allowed them to carry more food and water. With their shallow draught, galleys were also particularly vulnerable to storms.[5] Able, as a result of their relatively small crews, to transport a large cargo over a long distance at an acceptable cost, sailing ships, thanks to their cannon, could also defend themselves against attack. Whereas galleys had been *primarily* designed to board other vessels and to carry troops, rigged warships were built and used far more in order to fight one another.

There were, however, different forms of fighting. In the medieval period, it had been common to board rival warships. Boarding was not suddenly replaced by firepower. The capture of prizes, by boarding, was a fundamental of maritime war in the sixteenth century. Very few naval battles were concerned to sink the enemy, as there was little gain to be had in it. Even during the Armada engagements there was a determination by the English to capture vessels, and the rich booty from the *Rosario* demonstrated why. Equally, the Spaniards tried hard to capture the *Revenge* off the Azores in 1591 by boarding her. The naval battle off Terceria and some of the clashes in the Baltic war were the exceptions to the rule. There was a long transition in which boarding followed a missile exchange, now conducted by gunpowder weaponry. However, there were different fighting requirements for boarding and bombardment, such as there were between bows and arrows, and firearms for the missile exchange. An emphasis on cannon had obvious implications in terms of ship-killing requirements: for armament, supply and tactics.

Furthermore, the force projection of warships increased with advances in gunpowder technology.

Heavy guns were carried in the Baltic and by English and French warships from the early 1510s. Carvel building (the edge-joining of hull planks over frames), which spread from the Mediterranean to the Atlantic and Baltic from the late fifteenth century, replaced the clinker system of shipbuilding using overlapping planks. This contributed significantly to the development of hulls, which were stronger and better able to carry heavy guns.[6] Also, their sizes grew. The English *Henry Grace à Dieu* (also known as *Great Harry*) had a 1514 specification of 186 guns. The Danish, French, Lübeck, Maltese, Portuguese, Scottish, Spanish and Swedish navies all included ships of comparable size during the course of the century.

## Portuguese naval power

Initially, the most impressive naval power was Portugal. Her naval strength was based on sailing ships which were strong enough to carry cannon capable of sinking the lightly-built vessels of the Indian Ocean. Their heavier armament was crucial in the face of the numerical advantage of their opponents. Drawing on late fourteenth and fifteenth-century developments in ship construction and navigation, specifically the fusion of Atlantic and Mediterranean techniques of hull construction and lateen and square-rigging, and advances in location-finding at sea, the Portuguese enjoyed advantages over other vessels, whether they carried cannon or not. Developments in rigging permitted greater speed, improved manoeuvrability and a better ability to sail close to the wind. Information played a major role. Thanks to the use of the compass and other developments in navigation, such as the solution in 1484 to the problem of measuring latitude south of the Equator, it was possible to chart the sea and to assemble knowledge about it, and there-fore to have greater control over the relationship between the enormity of the ocean and the transience of man than ever before.

Portuguese naval strength was based on full-rigged sailing ships which were strong enough to carry heavy wrought-iron guns capable of sinking lightly-built vessels. The Portuguese fleet was a state-owned and controlled body. The ships were built in the royal dockyards at Lisbon and Oporto, but, as with the Spaniards at Havana, the Portuguese also discovered the value of developing colonial dockyard facilities. This was useful both for constructing vessels from durable tropical hardwoods, like western Indian teak, and for repairing warships locally. The Portuguese built a large 800-tonne ship at Cochin in 1511–12, established a major dockyard at Goa in 1515, and devel-oped ship-building facilities at Damao and Macao. A key element in the Portuguese expansion along the coast of Africa and into the Indian Ocean was its string of fortified naval bases. They replicated the role of the ports that were so indispensable to Mediterranean galley operations, but over a vastly greater distance. Portuguese sailors knew that they could replenish in safety at a series of 'way stations' on their long voyages to and from Asia. Their 'sea lines of communication' rested on their bases, a policy that the Dutch and English copied in the seventeenth and eighteenth centuries. Cape Town was developed by the Dutch as an area to grow green vegetables to replenish their ships sailing to and from Asia.

The Portuguese initially relied on the caravel, a swift and seaworthy but relatively small ship, ideal for coastal exploration and navigation, and the *nau* or 'great ship', a very large carrack-type vessel, but they then developed the galleon as a vessel able to sail great distances. It was longer and narrower than earlier carracks, with a reduced hull width-to-length ratio, and was faster, more manoeuvrable, and capable of carrying a heavier armament. The cannon were fired from the side of the vessel, a change that owed much to the development of the gunports just above the waterline and of waterproof covers for them. This ensured that guns could be carried near the waterline as well as higher up, thus reducing top-heaviness and increasing firepower. Such cannon could inflict serious damage near the waterline and thus hole opposing warships. The Portuguese continued to rely on the great ship as their primary trading vessel throughout the sixteenth century. Its size and speed made it extremely difficult to capture, and the battle to board the *Madre de Dios* in 1592 involved six English vessels, one of which had to attach itself to the bowsprit of the vessel to slow it down.

The Portuguese navigator Vasco da Gama arrived in Indian waters in 1498, dropping anchor near Calicut on 20 May, with vessels carrying cannon that Asian warships could not resist successfully in battle. This technological gap gave the Portuguese victory over the Calicut fleet in 1503, although the latter was supported by Arab vessels. Portuguese gunfire saw off boarding attempts. The Portuguese were also successful over the fleets of Japara and Gujarat in 1513 and 1528 respectively. An Egyptian fleet, partly of galleys, sent from Suez in 1507, and supported by Gujarati vessels, initially defeated a greatly outnumbered Portuguese squadron at Chaul in 1508, but was largely destroyed off Diu on 9 February 1509 by Francisco de Almeida, the first Viceroy of Portuguese India.[7]

The Egyptian, and later Ottoman, vessels that sailed to the west coast of India or between the Red Sea and the Persian Gulf were different in their long-distance capability and were also less heavily gunned. Whereas there was considerable diffusion of new weapons and techniques to non-Western powers in land warfare in the sixteenth century, there was no comparable diffusion of naval weaponry and techniques. The European combination of ships with hull-mounted cannon, fortresses and garrisons remained particularly effective.[8]

This did not mean that European warships were invulnerable. In African, Indian and Indonesian waters, heavily gunned Portuguese vessels, with their deep draught and reliance on sails, were vulnerable to shallower draught oared boats. This was true for example of the Straits of Malacca, where the Sultan continued to resist after the loss of Malacca. More generally, Portuguese warships, like those of other European powers, had only limited value in the important inshore, estuarine, deltaic and riverine waters of the world, a situation that was not to change until the introduction of shallow-draught steamships carrying steel artillery in the nineteenth century. However, the Dutch used shallow craft effectively in their riverine war with the Army of Flanders, especially in its early phases, and without the specialised nature of their vessels they could not have had an effective navy. The Russians had a capability for river operations. Flotilla expeditions were sent down the Don against Azov and the Khanate of the Crimea from 1646.

The problems faced by deep-draught European warships outside European waters could be matched in the latter, and this serves as a reminder of the diversity of naval warfare within Europe. Thus, the long-established Viking tradition of longship-building continued in the islands off west Scotland until the late sixteenth century. In an analogue of the cavalry forces of the Cossacks, the Hebrideans had a military system that relied on mobility and was able to support itself by raiding. In 1533, the English attempt to impose their power by using the new technology failed when the *Mary Willoughby* was captured by longships off the Shetlands.[9] The use of Viking style long ships by the Western Islemen, notably the MacDonalds, enabled them to transport mercenary *redshanks* from the Isles into Ulster, using Lough Foyle as their landing area, throughout the sixteenth century. Attempts to intercept the fleets with English sailing ships were unsuccessful, as were attempts to penetrate into the lochs of the Mull of Kintyre to attack the vessels at source. Only the occupation of Lough Foyle by the English finally solved the problem. In the Baltic and the Mediterranean, the continued need for galleys reflected the extent of inshore waters.

South-East Asian rulers responded to the threat posed by European warships not only by copying them but by building bigger armed galleys whose oars gave them inshore manoeuvrability. A fleet of about fifty Cochin Chinese galleys destroyed three Dutch warships in 1643. The Portuguese developed coastal fleets composed of local oared vessels or small sailing ships at Goa, Diu and in the Persian Gulf. These were of great value when the Portuguese resisted Dutch and English attack in the seventeenth century, as they could be used to harass English and Dutch big ships and could circumvent blockades by them.[10] Francis Drake and other English privateers took small oared pre-fabricated raiding vessels with them to assist with operations in the inshore waters of the Caribbean. Such small ships do not appear in lists of naval strength as the latter focus on what became ships of the line, but this is a reminder of the need to be cautious in assuming any one measure of naval power. The ability successfully to transport amphibious and expeditionary forces over long distances was another important measure of naval power, or perhaps maritime power, for Spain, Portugal, the Ottomans and Venetians, the English and the Dutch.

Nevertheless, European vessels in deep waters were difficult to attack successfully, and, on the oceans of the world, there was little challenge to European military technology. In part, this reflected the lack of interest shown by China, Japan and Korea in developing a long-distance naval capability to match their powerful short-range effectiveness. A Chinese fleet employing cannon defeated a Portuguese squadron off Tunmen (Tou-men) in 1522, but Tunmen is near Macao: the Portuguese were fortunate they did not reach the Indian Ocean when the Chinese deployed fleets there, as Chinese ships were sturdier than Indian ones, but by the sixteenth century, although the Chinese had an inshore naval capability, they no longer deployed distant fleets as they had done in the fifteenth century.[11] The Portuguese were to have a fleet defeated off Johor in 1603 but by the Dutch, not by an Asian power.

At one level, the very ability to project power over a long distance is of greater consequence than its effectiveness in a given sphere. For example, a Portuguese presence was an issue for both China and Japan, but not vice versa. This argument has to be handled with care: Viking power extended to Newfoundland but to scant effect. More generally, the definition of naval power is an issue. It was a function of ships, manpower, bases and logistical support, each of which was intimately related to the others, and it is important not to adopt a single definition of naval power. In addition, the temptation to think in terms of violence as a form of seizure of resources, of the gains to be made through the use of power, has to be related to the symbiotic nature of trade and the need for maritime powers which had developed a monopoly of regular long-range ocean transport to accommodate themselves to the demands and opportunities of land-based economic systems if they were to be much more than transient plunderers. After technology had given them an initial advantage, the Portuguese sought this accommodation.

## Naval warfare

Medieval naval warfare had been dominated by coming alongside and boarding, and this continued to play a role. The rising importance of firepower, however, led to a shift towards stand-off tactics in which ships did not come into direct contact and boarding became impossible. The Portuguese were the first systematically to exploit heavy cannon to fight stand-off actions against superior enemies, a development often incorrectly claimed for the English at the time of the Spanish Armada (1588). In northern Europe, the shift towards stand-off tactics can be seen by contrasting the Anglo-French war of 1512–14, in which the fleets fought in the Channel in the traditional fashion, with the gunnery duel in which they engaged off Portsmouth in 1545. This shift had important implications for naval battle tactics (although truly effective ways of deploying naval firepower were not found until the next century), and it further encouraged the development of warships primarily as artillery platforms.

The term 'ship of the line' is possibly more applicable to the seventeenth than the sixteenth century. Certainly the French, English and Scottish kings built 'large specialised warships' in the first decades of the century, but these were as much statements of royal power, even fashion, rather than functional warships. The English constructed purpose-built warships along new techno-logical lines in the 1570s, the 'race built galleons', but they were essentially for the defensive task of dominating the English Channel, although they were hired out by Queen Elizabeth for commerce raiding on an *ad hoc* basis. The Portuguese, who constructed vessels of similar size and capability, built them for Atlantic convoy escorts, and the Spanish only began to build royal warships in the same class, such as the 'twelve apostles', during the last decade of the century. The considerable force of French and Spanish ships that engaged in what was essentially an artillery duel off Terceria in 1581 were a mixture of types, but with armed merchantmen and privateer vessels from a mixture of sources predominating. The Danes, Swedes and Hanse merchants of Lübeck built large specialised warships that fought artillery duels during the naval war in the Baltic in the 1560s, but they also sought to board each other's vessels. The Dutch used their fleet to great effect in the second half of the century, but they were predominantly armed merchantmen.

At the same time, it is important to avoid any teleological assumption that it is only if ships were able to use gunfire to sink others that they were effec-tive, and that therefore there was a revolution in naval warfare with the development of the more powerful 'ship-killing' warships.[12] Instead, it has been argued that fifteenth-century developments were important, and that it is necessary to focus on a 'process of technological and tactical evolution which began with the advent of gunpowder weapons on land, and then progressed through the placement of these guns on board ships, their use in naval engagements as anti-personnel weapons, their increase in size and numbers, and finally their changes in technology, separate from similar weapons used on land', in order to produce weaponry that was effective by contemporary criteria.[13] It is also unclear, if naval revolution(s) are being sought, whether the focus should be on shipping or weaponry. If the former, changes in ship construction and design in the fourteenth and fifteenth century, particularly the increase in the number of masts, the number of sails per mast and the variety of sail shapes, and the spread of the sternpost rudder,[14] may be seen as more important than those in the sixteenth century.

Wrought-iron cannon were dangerously unreliable. They were not much in use after the third quarter of the sixteenth century and, judging by evidence from the Danish, English and Swedish navies, they were probably scrapped by the end of the century, as navies converted to copper guns. The manufacture of large cast-iron weapons was initially beyond the technological scope of the period, but, from the mid-fifteenth century, firepower was increased by the development of large cannon cast instead from lighter, more durable and workable 'brass' (actually bronze, an alloy of copper and tin). They were thick enough to withstand the high pressure from large powder charges and able to fire iron shot with a high muzzle velocity and great penetrative force. The stone shot used in early cannon was phased out. In most European languages, the word for cannon made from bronze was normally 'copper', possibly because the tin was a much smaller part of the alloy than in other types of bronze and the gun metal probably looked very similar to copper.

From the 1540s, cast-iron cannon were produced in England. They were relatively cheap. Cast iron guns imported from England were in use in Denmark from the 1560s. The Dutch were able to produce cast-iron cannon by the 1600s, but such cannon were preferred for merchantmen not for warships, as they could burst when overheated through rapid firing. Successful cast-iron guns began to be mass-produced in Sweden in the 1610s with the help of Dutch technicians. There had been small-scale production in Sweden for several decades, but it had not been very successful. Even in England and Sweden, which had domestic cast-iron gun production, 'copper' guns dominated in the navies until the third quarter of the seventeenth century. After that, more determined efforts were made to replace even the heavier types of copper guns (18–36 pounders) with cast-iron guns. Cast-iron cannon did not become the leading naval cannon until after 1650: a list of the cannon on English warships at sea in 1595 revealed that 80 per cent were brass and only 20 per cent cast iron. The early cast-iron guns were usually of small or medium calibres, and they were to a large extent used on armed merchantmen. The rapid development of successful Dutch and English armed merchantmen for trade in dangerous areas, especially the Mediterranean and the East Indies, was closely connected with the spread of cheap, small and medium cast-iron guns, while the growth of the big battle fleets after 1560 would have been more expensive if cheap large-calibre cast-iron guns had not been available. Demand from buyers interacted with the development of cast-iron technology. In addition, the process of modification and improvement in naval ordnance helped to give the Europeans a major comparative advantage. Simultaneously, improvements in gunpowder increased the range of cannon.[15]

It is important not to assume that the development of rigging, muzzle-loaded cast-metal cannon and heavy cannon on the broadside all occurred at once, and were mutually dependent. Indeed, by the mid-fifteenth century, galleys were being built to carry cannon, and in 1513 these showed their ship-killing capability at the expense of the English fleet off Brest.[16] In the sixteenth century, the emphasis on firepower in galley warfare increased.[17]

## Mediterranean warfare

For long, the imaginative character of naval conflict was dominated by galley warfare in the Mediterranean, not only because of the issues at stake but also because it involved Europe's two leading naval powers, Spain and the Ottomans. The frequency of their conflict in the first three-quarters of the sixteenth century was also important. The Ottomans had created a fleet to help prevent Constantinople from being relieved when they attacked it in 1453; an earlier fleet had been destroyed by the Venetians in the Dardanelles in 1416. The move to a port capital whose support depended on maritime links led to an increased role for naval concerns. The Ottoman fleet was swiftly a major force in the Aegean, employed to support amphibious attacks on Mitylene (1462) and Negroponte (1470).[18] The Ottomans subsequently developed their fleet for more distant operations beyond the Aegean and to carry cannon, which they used with effect against the Venetians at the battles of Zonchio in 1499 and 1500. On galleys, cannon were carried forward and supplemented the focus on forward axial attack already expressed by the presence of a metal spur in their bow. This might damage enemy oars and might be pressed into the hull of an enemy galley if a boarding was attempted. The strengthened and lengthened prow provided the access/boarding ramp onto an enemy ship. These spurs could not sink ships as (underwater) rams were intended to do, but the latter was a weapon of the Classical period that had disappeared. Like spurs, cannon were intended to disable the opposing ship as a preparation for boarding.

In their war with Venice of 1499–1502, the Ottomans successfully combined a strong fleet, which was more powerful than that of Venice, and intended to support amphibious operations rather than to seek battle, with heavy siege cannon moved by sea in order to drive the Venetians from their bases in the Peloponnese. Lepanto fell in 1499, Modon and Coron, 'the eyes of Venice', in 1500.[19]

More generally, the effects of prevailing wind patterns, currents and climate in the Mediterranean ensured that voyages were easiest if they began near the northern shore. As a result, shipping was generally restricted to a certain number of routes, affecting strategic options and leading to pressure to control nodal points on these routes.[20] Carrying soldiers increased galleys' consumption of food and water, and therefore affected their range. Few harbours and anchorages were able to support and shelter large fleets carrying substantial numbers of troops, a measure that affected operational methods and strategic goals. Galley conflict was not unchanging. Aside from the introduction of cannon, galleys became easier to row in the mid-sixteenth century, as one-man oars (with the typical galley having three men on a bench with one oar each) gave way to larger three-man oars.

The conquest of Egypt and the vital port of Alexandria in 1517 facilitated and encouraged a major growth in Ottoman naval power. Links between Constantinople and Alexandria were only really viable by sea, and this encouraged a determination to dominate the Mediterranean.[21] Cyprus became a tributary in 1517, and Rhodes was captured in 1522 after a lengthy siege. The Ottomans also extended their control along the North African coast, allying with Khair-ed-Din, who dominated Algiers and was appointed admiral by Suleiman the Magnificent. Concerned about the Ottoman threat, the Venetian government reconstructed a Roman quinquereme in 1529, only to find its sea trials unsatisfactory. The Ottomans benefited from the decline of Genoese and Venetian power, neither of which were able any more on their own to mount a powerful resistance. This enabled the Ottomans to dominate the Aegean. Karpathos and the northern Sporades (1538) and Naxos (1566) were captured from Venice and Samos (1550) and Chios (1566) from the Genoese. Neither Venice nor Genoa had the capability to protect such exposed positions, a far cry from the naval reach enjoyed by both powers during the Middle Ages.

In 1537, the Venetian-ruled island of Corfu was invaded and ravaged. The Ottomans, however, retreated without attempting a major siege of the powerful Venetian fortress. They had attacked Corfu as a stepping stone towards Italy. In response, in 1538, Venice, Charles V and the Papacy deployed a combined fleet against the Ottomans in the Adriatic. The Ottomans however were able to check the combined fleet at the battle of Prevesa on 27 September. The Ottomans had withdrawn their galleys onto the beach under cover of their fortress guns, with their forward galley guns facing out to sea. This immediately robbed the Genoese admiral, Andrea Doria, of the initiative, as his crews were consuming their food and water as they tried to hold their station outside the port on the open sea. He had the choice of attacking the Ottomans in their fixed position, firing from stable gun platforms with a secure retreat, or landing troops and attempting to storm the fort and its outer defence works with inadequate siege equipment. As neither option offered much prospect of success, his only realistic option was retreat. The moment he began to withdraw, he exposed his sailing vessels to the Ottoman galleys, whose fresh crews were able to overhaul and board them. Accounts of the battle vary. In one view, the wind fell, causing Doria to hold back the Habsburg fleet for fear of separating his galleys from the sailing vessels. The Ottoman fleet also held back, hoping for just such a separation. Another explanation blamed Doria for leaving the bulk of the action to his Papal and Venetian allies, who lost several vessels in what turned out to be a minor defeat as retiring Allied warships were attacked by the Ottomans.[22]

After 1540, the focus shifted from Greek waters and the Adriatic to the waters between Italy and North Africa. In 1541, Charles V led a crusade against Algiers, a major amphibious expedition that was a considerable logistical achievement. However, attacking late in the year, his fleet was badly damaged by an autumnal storm and the expedition failed. In 1542–4, Khair-ed-Din with 110 galleys co-operated with the French against Charles V, raiding Catalonia (1542), capturing Nice (1543) and harrying the Italian coast (1544), although a disagreement over objectives ensured that there was no combined attack on Genoa. Tripoli fell to the Ottomans in 1551, and in 1552 when Henry II attacked Charles V, the Ottomans sent about 100 galleys to the western Mediterranean. Each year until 1556 and again in 1558, the Ottomans sent large fleets, although for logistical reasons they returned each winter to Constantinople. This gave their opponents opportunities to 'share' the sea, so that in 1553 the Ottomans invaded Corsica, only for Genoese control to be re-established when the fleet left. The Ottomans did not use their expeditions to accumulate conquests that might establish a permanent position, but they created grave problems for the articulation of the Spanish empire and for the coastal communities in the region. During the period 1540–74, the number and scale of amphibious operations mounted in the Mediterranean by the major combatants was impressive. The size of armies that were transported, the distances they were transported and the speed of transit were all very impressive, and highlighted a degree of competence and capability that was largely due to the experience of the commanders and sailors involved.

In 1560, Philip II launched an expedition to regain Tripoli, but it was surprised at Djerba on 11 May 1560 by the Ottoman fleet with devastating consequences. In contrast, in 1563 a Spanish and Genoese galley fleet succeeded in raising the siege of Oran and Mers-el-kebir.

Malta, the principal Christian privateering base in the Mediterranean, was a threat to Ottoman trade and in 1565 Suleiman the Magnificent sent a powerful expedition of 140 galleys and about 30,000 troops. The defenders, under Jean de la Valette, the Grand Master of the Order of St John, had only 2,500 trained soldiers to defend the three fortresses of St Elmo, Senglea and Birgu. Landing on 18 May, the Ottomans initially focused on St Elmo which they needed to obtain a safe harbour. Repeated attacks were covered by artillery fire and about 60,000 shot were fired. The 1,500 defenders of St. Elmo used their twenty cannon to repel these attacks, but the walls were destroyed and the last of the garrison fought to the death. In July, major attacks were launched on Senglea and Birgu but, hampered by divided leadership, the summer heat and logistical problems, including the supply of drinking water, the Ottomans could not prevail over the determined defence. A number of reasons were responsible for the successful defence of Malta by the Knights of St John, over and above the undoubted courage and tenacity of the individual knights and their mercenaries and local levies. One of the most important reasons for their success was the supply of adequate gunpowder, a gift from the Duke of Tuscany, just prior to the arrival of the Ottomans. The failure of the Ottoman land and sea commanders to agree and implement a co-ordinated and effective command structure and plan was also to have serious repercussions for the Ottomans.

The defenders could only repel the attacks: they were not strong enough to mount a sortie. Unlike the siege of Rhodes, however, a relief army was being prepared. In late August, a Spanish relief force was sent from Sicily. Forced back twice by bad weather, the Spaniards, 11,000 strong, landed on 7 September. The besiegers retreated, unwilling to face the new foe. They had suffered perhaps as many as 24,000 casualties, while the defenders lost about 5,000, including Maltese levies. The Ottomans never again attacked Malta.[23]

Effective resistance combined with relief from a nearby base had saved Malta, not a naval battle. The strength of the Spanish response in 1565 reflected the major effort made by Philip II in the Mediterranean in the early 1560s. Aside from the Djerba expedition, the Spaniards broke the blockade of Oran in 1563 and sent an expedition to gain the Peñón de Vélez in 1564.

Cyprus was an easier target for Ottoman conquest than Malta. It was closer to the centres of Ottoman power and the Venetians appeared less formidable. In 1570, Selim II sent 116 galleys and 50,000 troops who rapidly overran the island, including the newly completed and massive bastioned enciente around Nicosia, but a substantial garrison continued to hold Famagusta. The defences of the port were on a par with those of Malta, and it contained one of the best ports in the eastern Mediterranean, as Richard III of England had been quick to spot during the Third Crusade. Although gunpowder stores ran down, Venetian relief vessels did break through with supplies during the siege, and there was good reason to believe that the city would hold out. Ottoman cannon fire had failed to breach the land walls and they had been forced to commence mining operations. Had the garrison realised that the Ottomans would not honour the terms of their surrender, it is unlikely that they would have surrendered, and the relief vessels that were en route could have changed the outcome of the siege. The real Venetian failure was in failing to keep open lines of communication to the garrison.

In response to the Ottomans, in May 1571, a Holy League of Spain, Venice and the Papacy was organised by Pope Pius V. The Christian fleet under Philip II's illegitimate half-brother, Don John of Austria, found the Ottoman fleet at Lepanto off the west coast of Greece, with both sides determined to fight. The Ottomans, under Müezzinzade Ali Pasha, had more ships, about 282 (although recent Turkish work has reduced that figure to about 230) to about 236, but fewer cannon, 750 to 1,815, and Don John had made modifications to his ships to widen their field of fire. More than 100,000 men took part in the battle on 7 October. Don John relied on battering his way to victory, although he also benefited from having a reserve squadron, which permitted a response to the success of the Ottoman offshore squadron. Superior Christian gunnery, the fighting qualities and firepower of the Spanish infantry who served on both the Spanish and the Venetian ships, and the exhaustion of Ottoman gunpowder, all helped to bring a crushing victory in four hours' fighting.

The cannon of six Venetian galleasses (three-masted lateen-rigged converted merchant galleys which were longer and heavier gunned than ordinary galleys, they carried firing platforms at poop and prow and sometimes along their sides), played a particularly important role in disrupting the Ottoman fleet. Their height also gave them a powerful advantage as they could fire down on opponents. If they were able to crash into the side of, or sweep away the oars of, an enemy galley, the impact of their weight was much larger than that of a normal galley. The deployment of galleasses, to break the force of the Ottoman assault, represented a considerable tactical innovation, especially when it was combined with a reserve squadron.

The willingness of both sides to engage in an open sea battle was important. The Ottomans could have pulled back under the guns of the fortress at Lepanto and forced the Christian forces into a risky amphibious assault. Good morale and determined leadership characterised both sides, and this may have led to a riskier approach being taken by both commanders. The normal caution of the Christian galley commanders was overridden by the charismatic and determined leadership of Don Juan, who brought a land perspective to the battle. Casualty figures vary greatly, and the limited extent of the Ottoman sources is a serious problem, but all agree that the Ottomans lost far more men, possibly 30,000 dead (including the admiral) to maybe 9,000 Christians, while the freeing of maybe 15,000 Christian galley slaves accentuated the disruption to Ottoman naval manpower. The Ottomans lost about 113 galleys sunk and 130 captured as well as their cannon and naval stores, the victors about 12 galleys.[24]

The battle was applauded as a triumph throughout Christian Europe, a decisive victory over a feared foe. However, it was late in the year, and could not be followed by the recapture of Cyprus, let alone, as Don John hoped, by the liberation of Palestine. An attempt to retake Modon failed in 1572. The Ottomans avoided battle in 1572 and 1573, and rapidly constructed a new navy which included *mahones*, their version of galleasses. By April 1572 about 200 galleys and five *mahones* were ready for action. In order to improve firepower, there was a stress on an ability to use handguns among those called on to serve in the fleet. In 1573, Venice agreed peace terms with the Ottomans, recognising the loss of Cyprus. Tunis, which had fallen to the Ottomans in 1570 and been regained by Spain in 1573, fell to the Ottomans the following year: they deployed 280 galleys and 15 *mahones*.[25] Under serious pressure, especially in the Low Countries, the Spaniards were unable to respond. Spain followed with a truce in 1578.

Lepanto was decisive more for what it prevented – a possible resumption of the Ottoman advance in the Mediterranean and Adriatic – than for pushing the balance of military advantage towards the Christians. The loss of skilled Ottoman manpower was also important. The outcome of the battle, although disappointing from the Christian viewpoint, was fatally undermined by the Venetian decision to sue for a unilateral peace with the Ottomans. The end result was the *de facto* establishment of a Spanish and an Ottoman sphere of influence in their respective halves of the Mediterranean.

Large-scale naval warfare between Ottomans and the Mediterranean Christian powers did not revive until the mid-seventeenth century. Although the Ottomans and the Austrians were at war in 1593–1606, they did not fight at sea at any serious level, and Spain crucially did not use the opportunity to join Austria in attacking the Ottomans (although an unsuccessful assault on Algiers was launched in 1601). This can be seen as a sign of a more widespread stagnation of Mediterranean galley warfare,[26] but it is also necessary to give due weight to the other commitments of the combatants and potential combatants. These help explain why the Spanish galley fleet in the Mediterranean declined. Until 1645, the Ottoman fleet was able to concentrate on action against privateers and other defensive tasks. There was no need for major force projection.[27]

In August 1645, the Ottomans invaded the Venetian island of Crete, sending over 100,000 soldiers and a massive fleet of about 400 ships, of which, however, only 106 were warships, the remainder being *karamursel*, ships used only for transport. Canea was rapidly captured, and Rethymnon fell in 1646, but the siege of the capital, Candia, lasted until 1669. The Venetians sent reinforcements, including 33,000 German mercenaries, while political divisions undermined the Ottoman war effort. The Venetians blockaded the Dardanelles in 1648, helping to precipitate the fall of Sultan Ibrahim, and again from 1650. An Ottoman fleet which evaded the blockade was defeated off Naxos in 1651 and in 1656 the Venetians largely destroyed the Ottoman navy off the Dardanelles. However, the vigorous Mehmet Köprülü became Grand Vizier and rebuilt the fleet, and the blockade was broken in 1657.

## Baltic warfare

Meanwhile, 1563–70 saw the first modern naval war between sailing battle fleets in European waters, as Denmark and Sweden fought for control of invasion routes. The Danes were supported by the semi-independent German city of Lübeck, no longer the great sea power it had been, but still able to make an important contribution. Both sides sought to destroy the opposing fleet, and seven battles were fought between 1563 and 1566, a very high tempo of conflict. For example, at the battle of Oland (30–31 May 1564), the Swedes lost their new flagship, the *Mars*, after repeated Danish-Lübeck attacks. The *Mars* was successfully boarded on the second day of the battle, caught fire and blew up. Both fleets then withdrew for repairs. In general, however, the Swedes, under Klas Kristersson Horn, with their modern bronze artillery, systematically used stand-off gunfire to block Danish boarding tactics: sheer weight of metal was decisive. Both navies expanded greatly and, by the late 1560s, the Swedes may have had the largest sailing fleet of the period. At the same time, the conflict indicated the limitations of naval power. It proved difficult to co-ordinate with land operations, and the vulnerability of warships to weather was shown in 1566 when several ships in the Danish-Lübeck fleet were wrecked during a gale when at anchor off Visby; although intense summer gales were very unusual in the Baltic.[28]

## Atlantic warfare

During the same period as the great Mediterranean galley wars, there was a great deal of comparable activity going on in the Atlantic area of operations. These included Anglo-French naval conflict in the 1540s and 1550s, not least the attack on the Isle of Wight by the French in 1545, and the seaborne resupply of Boulogne's defenders by the English, and the English amphibious operations against Scotland during the reign of Edward VI (r. 1547–53). These culminated, under Elizabeth I (r. 1559–1603), in 1560 when an English fleet was decisive in leading to the defeat of the French attempt to suppress the Protestant Lords of Congregation who had rebelled against Mary Queen of Scots, then also, as wife of Francis II, Queen of France. The English under William Winter cut links across the Firth of Forth, leading the French to abandon operations in Fife, before successfully blockading Leith. The English land assault failed, but the naval blockade led the French to negotiate the withdrawal of their force. The English were less successful in 1562–3 when they tried to use their fleet to maintain links with their garrisons in Dieppe and Le Havre and to relieve Huguenot-held Rouen. The scale of operations, in terms of numbers of ships and troops deployed, or cannon balls fired, was considerable, and indicated the importance of combined operations. However, the failure of English seaborne support sealed the fate of Le Havre in 1563. In the 1550s, the Habsburg government of the Low Countries co-operated with Amsterdam and the states of Holland to ensure that fleets were deployed to protect their shipping from French and Scottish privateers.[29]

The potential of naval power in these waters was shown during the Dutch Revolt. Philip II had sold his Dutch navy after peace with France in 1559, and was therefore unable to respond to the privateering attacks of the Sea Beggars that began in 1568. In some respects, this indicated a lack of responsiveness to the potential and threat of maritime power, but Philip had pressing problems in Spain (the Moriscos revolt) and the Mediterranean (from the Ottomans), and the Duke of Alba appeared to have restored order. The crisis that began in April 1572, when the Sea Beggars took over Brill and the Dutch Revolt spread, revealed the deficiencies of a Spanish system that relied on hiring and requisitioning armed merchantmen. Alba had done so, mostly from Amsterdam, but these warships were defeated, particularly in a battle on 13 October 1573. This led to a crucial lack of control in Dutch waters. In turn, Philip II prepared a fleet in northern Spain in 1574, only for the scheme to be shelved when illness hit the fleet. In the absence of Spanish naval power, it required a huge military effort by the Duke of Parma to recapture Antwerp in 1585.

The fleet of 1574 was not the end of plans for Spanish naval action, but other problems and options came to the fore and the major effort the Spaniards mounted in the Atlantic in 1582–3 was the conquest of the Azores. The scale of Spanish operations against Portugal (1580) and the Azores was comparable to some of the largest operations against the Ottomans. However, the outbreak of war with England in 1585, with an English expedition sent to the Low Countries and a fleet to harass the Spaniards in the West Indies, ensured that now Spain had an enemy that could only be decisively attacked by sea. Philip decided to mount an invasion of England, although it had to be postponed because in 1587 the English under Sir Francis Drake successfully attacked Cadiz. The Spaniards were also delayed by the immensity of the necessary preparations.

## The Armada

The Armada of 1588 was of a totally new order of magnitude. It translated earlier hopes into an organised ocean-going force, and replaced the small Spanish force that had landed in Ireland in 1580 (it was swiftly defeated) with a bold plan for large-scale concerted operations. Anglo-Spanish naval hostilities contrasted with the minor role of naval forces in the French Wars of Religion. However in 1588, Philip failed to co-ordinate adequately two disparate plans: one for an amphibious invasion of England from Spain by the Duke of Medina-Sidonia's fleet, and the other for a crossing from the Spanish Netherlands by the Duke of Parma's army. The final plan was for the Armada to proceed up the Channel and then cover Parma's landing, but the details of how the two elements were to co-operate had not been adequately worked out. Philip underestimated the difficulties facing the Duke of Parma. Parma could not keep his troops sitting in their invasion barges for extended periods, and required a significant period of time to load them. He worked on the assumption that the time would be available, once the Armada had destroyed the English fleet guarding the Channel, and also the Dutch ships that were blockading his embarkation ports. The vulnerability of his open barges to attack by Dutch *flybotes* in the shallow waters around Ostend and Sluys was never appreciated by Philip.

On 28 May 1588, the Armada of 130 ships and 19,000 troops left Lisbon. Storm damage necessitated refitting in Corunna, and it was July before the slow-moving fleet appeared off the Cornish coast. The Spanish warships then headed for Calais, maintaining a tight formation to protect their more vulnerable vessels, and harried by long-range English gunnery. This did little damage, and, during nine days of engagements, the Spaniards retained their formation. With the advantage of superior sailing qualities and compact four-wheeled gun-carriages, which allowed a high rate of fire, the English fleet suffered even slighter damage. It was, however, threatened by a shortage of ammunition. In contrast, many of the Spanish guns were on cumbersome carriages designed for use on land.

When Medina-Sidonia anchored off Calais, he found that Parma had been able to assemble the transport vessels necessary to embark his army for England, but that they could not come out until after the English and Dutch blockading squadrons had been defeated. The Spanish fleet, however, was disrupted by an English night attack using fireships, and the English fleet then inflicted considerable damage in a running battle off Gravelines. The brunt of the battle was borne by the galleons of the Portuguese navy, in Spanish service: they were experienced in stand-off gunnery.

A strong south-westerly wind drove the Armada into the North Sea. With no clear tactical objective after Parma's failed embarkation, the disappointed Spanish commanders ordered a return to Spain via the hazardous north-about route around the British Isles. A succession of violent and unseasonal storms lashed the fleet as it passed north of Scotland and down the west coast of Ireland; ship after ship was smashed or driven ashore, and only part of the fleet reached Spain. The loss of so many trained and experienced men was a serious blow for the Spaniards, but, as with the Ottomans after Lepanto, the fleet was rapidly rebuilt, although the renewed Spanish fleet was not as powerful or effective as its Ottoman counterpart which regained Tunis in 1574. Spanish losses in men and material in 1588 were considerable but are sometimes overstated. The primary aim of the English 1589 expedition was to destroy the remainder of the Armada fleet. Spain was able to prepare fleets for British and nearby waters again in 1596 (in large part directed against Brittany) and 1597, although both expeditions were stopped by autumnal storms.[30]

The English themselves found it difficult to win lasting naval victory. In 1589, Elizabeth I authorised a counter-stroke against Spain, but the expenditure on the fleet in 1588 resulted in shortages of money, and the expedition was funded as a joint stock enterprise. This meant that Elizabeth's aims, to destroy the remnants of the Spanish fleet, were at variance with those of the force commanders, Drake and Norris, both in high favour after the success of the campaign in 1588. The presence of the Portuguese pretender, Dom Antonio, offered the prospect of driving the Spanish from Portugal, and gaining commercial access to Lisbon. This aspiration was the motivation behind the substantial funding put up by merchants from the City of London. The result was the worst possible compromise. An attack on Corunna, in deference to Elizabeth's directive, managed to destroy a small number of Armada survivors, but the majority were in ports deeper into the Bay of Biscay. By attacking Corunna, the force gave away the essential element of surprise, while failing to satisfy even the minimum requirement of Elizabeth. The force then made a successful opposed landing at Peniche on the Atlantic coast, some fifty miles from Lisbon. Hopes that the countryside would rise in support of Dom Antonio proved to be unfounded, and the landing gave away the tactical initiative to the Spaniards. As Norris and the army trekked across the broken country towards Lisbon, losing men all the time to heat exhaustion, Drake sailed to the mouth of the Tagus, but failed to force the forts guarding the entrance to Lisbon. There is little doubt that had the expedition sailed directly for Lisbon and seized the forts by an amphibious assault from Cascais, as the Duke of Alba had done in 1580, Lisbon would have fallen and, with it, the whole of Portugal. Elizabeth was not prepared to countenance such a grandiose scheme, however, and refused permission for Norris to take siege artillery with him. Drake could still have retrieved the situation. He had carried out extensive surveys of the forts and the estuary in 1587, even sending barques deep into the estuary and up to the port of Lisbon under cover of darkness. Had he forced his way past the forts guarding the narrow channel into the Tagus estuary, he could have attacked Lisbon from its unde-fended waterfront. His reticence may have been due to his reluctance to risk any of the Queen's ships.

The problem of multiple aims and objectives was that ultimately nothing of substance was achieved. The Armada survivors were refitted and formed the basis of a revived Spanish fleet; the English expeditionary force was totally decimated by disease; the nascent Portuguese resistance was crushed; the oper-ation failed to cover its cost; and Drake and Norris lost their reputations and the favour of the Queen. The expedition probably offered the best strategic opportunity of the entire war with Spain, but lack of vision or conviction on the part of Elizabeth limited its potential for success, and lack of conviction on the part of the commanders squandered the opportunities that a large force with surprise on its side could have achieved. Elizabeth would undoubt-edly have forgiven Drake and Norris for disobeying orders if they had captured Lisbon and reinstated Dom Antonio. Had Lisbon been taken, it might have been possible to derive strategic benefit, in terms of overturning Philip II's position in Portugal, a development that would have been of major naval and political consequence, although Philip might have been able to use the resources of Spain to mount a powerful counter-attack.

The Queen backed a major ship-building programme after the Armada which led to a major increase in the size of the royal fleet, but she continued to try to make the maritime war pay for itself in 1590, 1591 and 1592. However improved Spanish fortress defences and a fleet of purpose-built warships meant that the English failed to intercept the *flota* (the Spanish trea-sure fleet), although they came close to it on several occasions. In the process they did capture the East Indiaman, the *Madre de Dios*, but lost the *Revenge*.

A resurgence of activity by the Spanish and the English occurred in 1596–7. The threat of a Spanish Armada led to a pre-emptive strike being mounted against the coast of Spain in 1596 by a large Anglo-Dutch amphibious force. The English were lucky as the Spanish fleet was dispersed by storms, and their own force achieved the most significant tactical gains of the maritime war. Having gained complete strategic surprise, the fleet fought its way past a combined Spanish force of modern galleons and galleys, supported by the guns of the city of Cadiz, and conducted a successful opposed landing, followed by the successful storming of the city. This was a considerable achievement. However, the concentration on the landing allowed a fleet of merchant vessels, sheltering in the inner harbour, to be burnt by the Spaniards, with the loss of much valuable booty for the expeditionary force. The loot from the city was still immense, though, but the commanders failed to control their troops and the Queen did not get her share of the proceeds. An attempt by Drake and Hawkins to achieve a similar success in the West Indies was thwarted at Puerto Rico by the improved naval and fortress defences. However, the Duke of Cumberland, using an indirect approach, did manage to capture the city a year later when he attacked the landward approaches to the city. Neither Cumberland at Puerto Rico nor Essex at Cadiz could sustain a garrison in the cities they had captured. It was beyond the capability of sixteenth-century logistics, and therefore the overall result was minimal, and degenerated into acrimonious arguments with Elizabeth over the division of the booty. As with Corunna in 1589, such amphibious attacks led to no permanent gain. There was no equivalent (nor was any attempted) to the Portuguese bases in Africa or the Indian Ocean, or to the earlier English position at Calais. However, the role of the English navy in the campaign against Spanish–Irish forces at Kinsale in 1601 did have an impact that was strategic in its consequences.

Both the Armada and Drake's 'Counter-Armada' illustrate the limitations of naval power in this period, not least its vulnerability to storms, the problems of combined operations and the heavy supply demands posed by large fleets. The defeat of the Armada also underlined the growing technical skill of English and Dutch seamanship and naval warfare, and underlined the importance of superior naval gunnery and appropriate related tactics and leadership. The English naval effort was an uneasy co-operation between government and private maritime interests. This worked effectively in 1588, but less so in offensive operations when disparate goals became more apparent. However, the ability to draw on privateers was an important aspect of English naval capability. Privateer operations brought an important synergy to English naval capability. They provided an indispensable pool of highly capable leaders and battle-trained seamen. The Spanish had no equivalent source of manpower to draw on.[31]

## Dutch naval power

In the early seventeenth century, there was a major development in aggregate European naval strength, especially on the part of the United Provinces, which became the leading naval power in Europe.[32] This gave the Dutch a powerful advantage in war with Spain, although the resistance of the Spanish navy should not be underrated and the Spaniards built up their navy in the late 1610s and early 1620s.[33] The extent of Dutch maritime power was such that other states seeking warships tried to hire them from the Dutch. In 1625, the French hired twelve Dutch ships as part of the fleet that drove the Huguenot navy from French waters, a crucial step in exerting pressure on La Rochelle.

Dutch power rested in large part on its maritime strength and dynamism. The United Provinces became an entrepôt for European and global networks of trade, in which comparative advantage brought the Dutch profit. Economic advantage became a source of power.[34] This, in turn, made the Dutch a tempting target for others, and encouraged other powers to try to match the

Dutch in the synergy of commercial expansion and maritime strength. They also challenged Dutch naval power.

Alongside the treatment of naval conflict, and thus capability, in terms of battle, it is necessary to give due weight to the role of commerce raiding, and this was a particularly important tool for the opponents of the Dutch. Battle was easier to avoid at sea than on land but, without trade and fishing, maritime activity would cease and both presented a tempting target for Spanish attack. The ability of the Spaniards to respond, particularly from Flanders, to the opportunities provided by Dutch maritime links, indicated the danger of assuming that they had somehow become redundant at sea. They made heavy inroads on Dutch and French trade, and privateers from the Spanish Biscay coast hit the French especially hard. Near the end of 1621, a new seaward approach to Dunkirk, Spain's North Sea harbour, was discovered by local mariners. The lack of secure deep-water harbourage that had crippled Spain's tactical flexibility in the previous generation was remedied. The harbour was developed to accommodate more and larger vessels. The Spaniards were particularly successful in their attacks on the Dutch fishing fleet, which resulted in the deployment of expensive convoy escorts. Dunkirk was able to serve not only as a major privateering base, but also as the linchpin of an offensive war at sea, a harbour for large battle-fleets.

In the mid-1620s, Philip IV and Olivares came to think of counter-attack, not consolidation, although the Dutch success in capturing a Spanish treasure fleet in the Bay of Matanzas on the coast of Cuba on 8 September 1628 was a major check, not least because it led Philip to see the defence of the Atlantic routes as his major naval priority, while Spain devoted much of its expenditure to its armies. Nevertheless, this was the sole occasion on which the Spaniards lost a treasure fleet, and the painters who worked in 1632 on the celebratory canvases commissioned to adorn the Hall of the Kingdoms in the Buen Retiro Palace depicted Spanish victories, nearly half of which were due to the exercise of naval power. In the early 1630s, the activities of the Flanders armada returned to the levels of the mid-1620s, although privateering triumphs were bought at the cost of heavy losses. Dutch blockade could never seal off the Flemish ports completely, while by 1637, Spain's various ocean-going fleets contained a total of 150 warships.[35]

However, in what was the first global war at sea,[36] the Dutch were not only able to mount a major series of offensives against Spanish and Portuguese interests and possessions around the globe, but also in Europe to protect their coast line and their maritime links, and to cut the naval link between Spain and the Spanish Netherlands. The Dutch campaign against the sea lines of communication culminated in a major naval victory at the battle of the Downs on 16 September 1639. This battle was sought by the Spaniards as a decisive fleet engagement designed to transform the strategic situation between Spain and the Dutch. In the battle, the Dutch kept their distance, preventing the Spaniards from closing and employing boarding tactics. In the ensuing artillery exchange, the Dutch inflicted greater damage, in part thanks to superior command skill, but both sides ran out of ammunition. The Spaniards took refuge in the Downs where they were attacked with heavy losses on 21 October: in the confined waters, the Spaniards were vulnerable to fireships and to the more manoeuvrable Dutch warships. The Battle of the Downs demonstrated that, for all their improvements in ship design, the Spanish had still not adopted a policy of naval combat with artillery, and clung to the tactics of boarding. This may well have reflected the tendency for military commanders to hold authority over their naval counterparts.

Massive losses at the hands of the Dutch in 1638–40 were followed by French advances into the Spanish Netherlands, although, both on land and sea, the Spaniards displayed considerable resilience and had some success. The final loss of Dunkirk in 1658 led, however, to the gradual disappearance of the Armada of Flanders from the records as Spain concentrated her resources further south, using the Flanders ships from 1659 to attack rebellious Portugal.

## French navy

In the 1620s, the French developed a permanent battle fleet for the first time since the 1560s, but their navy did not match Dutch strength, in large part because the French focused on their armies. France's Spanish opponent could be better attacked by land. However, the French did acquire a valuable capability to project their strength in the West Mediterranean and in Atlantic waters. This was due to Richelieu's determined support. In 1626, he created the post of Grand Maître de la Navigation et Commerce for himself, and he used the navy in the operations against La Rochelle that were crucial to the consolidation of royal power. The first ships of the permanent royal fleet created by Richelieu were four warships bought from the Duke of Nevers in 1624. A far larger French fleet destroyed a Spanish squadron at Guetaria on the Basque coast on 22 August 1638, in part by the use of fireships. The French developed a greater ability to project their power in the Mediterranean, and this enabled them to support the Catalan Revolt and to intervene against Spain in Italy in the 1640s, for example in attacks on Finale and the Presidios in the 1640s, and in the dispatch of a fleet to Naples in 1647 and again in 1648. By 1646, there was a standing French fleet of thirty-six ships, including seventeen above 500 tons and with thirty or more cannon.[37]

## English naval power

Further afield, the Dutch and English deployed their heavily armed sailing ships with increasing regularity. Philip II banned Dutch trade with Lisbon in 1594, encouraging the Dutch to seek spices at their Asian sources. The first English ships in the Indian Ocean arrived in 1591. The *Edward Bonaventure*, captained by James Lancaster, captured three Portuguese ships in 1592. He went on to command a fleet that captured the Portuguese base of Pernambuco in Brazil with great booty in 1595, and to command the first fleet of the English East India Company formed in 1600. Thanks to the autonomous structure of their East Indian mercantile enterprises, the Dutch and English were able to use the profits of their East Indies trade to support their forceful stance.

The English remained an important naval power throughout the period, although amphibious expeditions against Spanish (Cadiz, 1625) and French (relief of La Rochelle, 1627) targets in Europe in the 1620s were unsuccessful. The withdrawal of royal support for the navy by James I (r.1603–25) and his antagonism towards piracy and privateering removed the underpinning of naval capacity, and the expeditions of the 1620s showed that, within twenty years, the naval capability of England had been severely diminished, with a dramatic decrease in the competence of its commanders. In the 1630s, disputes over financing the expanding navy accentuated distrust of Charles I,[38] but the republican 'Rump' parliamentary government which replaced him developed a formidable naval power. Between 1649 and 1660, some 216 vessels were added to the fleet, many of which were prizes, but half were the fruits of a ship-building programme. The earlier dependence on large merchantmen ended with the establishment of a substantial state navy which, in 1653, employed almost 20,000 men. The English navy had become the largest in the world by 1650.[39]

In 1652–4, England fought the Dutch in what was to be the First Anglo-Dutch War. Traditionally explained as a mercantilist struggle largely due to commercial and colonial rivals, this conflict has more recently been explained in terms of the hostility of one Protestant, republican regime towards a less rigorous counterpart.[40] This was a war of fleet actions in European waters, fought with heavy guns, as well as of commerce raiding and colonial strikes. Attempts to preserve or cut trade links, crucial to the financial and military viability of the two powers, played a major role in the war. Both sides realised the advantage of having a large permanent navy and greatly increased their naval strength with the construction of new and larger ships.

In 1652, the English won battles off Dover and the Kentish Knock, but were badly defeated by a larger Dutch fleet off Dungeness. In February 1653, the English won a battle fought from Portland to Calais (the Three Days Battle) and another at the Texel in which the Dutch Admiral Tromp was killed. Their victories closed the Channel to Dutch trade and this helped lead the Dutch to peace. But, because the English warships were larger than the Dutch, they were unable to mount a close blockade of the Dutch ports. On the other hand, being larger and having a higher ratio of cannon per ton than the Dutch made the English warships particularly effective. The sole major Dutch victory in 1653 was the destruction of an English squadron off the Mediterranean port of Leghorn (Livorno).[41]

Having replaced the Rump Parliament, Oliver Cromwell was happy to negotiate peace, but he subsequently used English naval power elsewhere. Robert Blake, the leading English admiral of the period, destroyed a Barbary pirate squadron with minimal losses at Porto Farina on the Tunisian coast (April 1655) and captured Tenerife (April 1657). The English also captured Jamaica from Spain. Naval power enabled the English to play a role in the Baltic rivalry of Denmark and Sweden; although Dutch intervention was more important, and broke Swedish blockades of Danzig (1656) and Copenhagen (1658).

The development of line-ahead tactics for warships was an important change at the close of the period. Tromp employed line-ahead tactics at the Downs in 1639. In 1653, the English fleet was ordered in its fighting instructions to provide mutual support. While this was not an instruction to fight in line ahead, it encouraged the line formation that maximised broadside power. The stress on cohesion reflected a move away from battle as a series of struggles between individual ships, although, as William Maltby has suggested, 'the line ahead is probably as old as the shipboard gun'. In part, certainly in the case of the English, it reflected a transfer of military models to sea, as commanders with experience of combat on land sought to apply its lessons and to devise a formation that permitted control and co-operation during the battle. In practice, the nature of conflict at sea made it difficult to maintain cohesion once ships became closely engaged.[42]

The wars between England and the Dutch were fought at sea and in the colonies. There was no land conflict between the two sides in Europe. As a consequence, the conflicts are somewhat atypical of the use of seapower in the period; although it could also be argued that there was no dominant paradigm and instead a variety of uses. It was more generally the case that seapower was supposed to act in direct support of land operations. These took two forms. One was an invasion in which the entire land force was transported by sea, as with the English attacks on Cadiz. The other was the use of shipping to support a land invasion, as with most French operations against Italy. Thus in 1494, Charles VIII invaded Italy by land, but, after the French fleet had repulsed its Neapolitan opponent off Rapallo on 8 September, the French siege train was moved by sea from Marseilles to Genoa and then on to La Spezia.

The presence of English and Dutch squadrons in the Mediterranean in the 1650s was part of a longer term process in which improvements in armaments, rigging and sail patterns helped to ensure that sailing ships, rather than galleys, became more important in Mediterranean warfare, although the French and Spanish sailing ships that clashed off Orbitello on 14 June 1646 were towed by galleys in very light winds. Galleys were also more manoeuvrable in inshore and other shallow waters, for example in the Aegean. Sailing ships freed warships from dependence on a network of local bases, and carried more cannon than galleys. They were also less susceptible to bad weather. The English and Dutch roundship, or *bertone*, that introduced new methods into the Mediterranean was copied by the local powers; first by the North African Barbary states, who adopted Atlantic naval technology from the late sixteenth century through the intermediary of English and Dutch privateers. Venice hired twelve armed Dutch merchantmen in 1618 and both Venice and the Ottomans hired Dutch and English armed merchantmen in their war of 1645–69. Indeed, the Venetian fleet in this war was increasingly a sailing fleet of hired merchantmen. However, the Barbary ships, like those of the Omani Arabs based in Muscat from 1650, were essentially commerce raiders, rather than the more regimented and standardised fleets of the European navies with their heavy, slow ships designed for battering power. By the mid-seventeenth century both Venice and, more slowly, the Ottomans were shifting their force structure towards galleons, the Ottomans being influenced by the advantage gained by the Venetians in the war that broke out in 1645.

## A Naval Revolution?

More generally, European warships were becoming more heavily gunned. Instead of relying on converted merchantmen, the English, French and Dutch used purpose-built warships, heavily gunned and, accordingly, with strong hulls. This led to a professionalisation of naval officership, senior ratings and infrastructure, but also ensured that less heavily gunned vessels, such as those of the Dutch in the First Anglo–Dutch War, were rendered obsolete.

These fleets were the product of state activity, and underlined an important shift across the period as a whole, namely the concentration of naval force in the hands of territorial rulers able to deploy considerable resources. These financial resources were most useful if they could be combined with the already strong naval traditions of major maritime centres, not least because fleets required large numbers of sailors. Thus, at Lepanto about a quarter of the Spanish galleys were rented from Genoese entrepreneurs. However, by 1650 these centres were less able to deploy large quantities of naval strength alone (although the process was less pronounced than on land where cities lost their military independence). Thus in the Baltic, Lübeck had been overshadowed by the strength and competition of Denmark and Sweden, while in the Mediterranean, although Genoa and, particularly, Venice remained a naval presence, they were overshadowed by the fleets of territorial states. In the case of Genoa, the shift was dramatised in 1453 when Mehmed II captured the Genoese Old Arsenal at Pera. By the following century, it had replaced Gallipoli as the leading Ottoman naval dockyard. Pera was expanded in capacity, enabling it to construct or maintain about 250 galleys.[43]

It would be mistaken to exaggerate the novelty of this shift towards territorial rulers. Fleets furthering the interests of these states had been important prior to 1494, but they became more permanent and more clearly under government control in the early modern period. The relationship between maritime interests and states had shifted. Thus, in Spain the crown came to take more control over ship-building from 1598. This provided more government direction for the system in which the crown used private ships, which they had rented, and frequently also requisitioned.

At the same time, it is important not to exaggerate the extent of state direction and control. Although he has emphasised the success of larger political units in mobilising resources to develop effective navies, Jan Glete has argued that navies organised by states were far from universally successful in comparison with private solutions to the problem of protecting trade, as well as pointing out that navies closely controlled by private interests were efficient, and that there were wide differences in quality between different states. Indeed, as he points out, private Dutch and English shipping often proved superior to Spanish and Portuguese naval power in the Mediterranean. Carla Phillips has suggested that a permanent navy was not necessarily better than a private/public system: 'The difficulty with a standing navy came in forcing a nation to bear its cost in peacetime'. Aside from this valuable reminder of the domestic context, which she shares with Glete, Phillips also points out that best practice was not clear: 'everything depended upon how well and how consistently a state could tap into the productive capacity of its land and people, without destabilizing the state'.[44] Repeatedly, it is the weakness of governments in controlling naval resources that emerges; unsurprisingly so given the continued reliance on private interests and the lack of consistent or comprehensive state financial support. Thus, in the United Provinces, where there were five separate Admiralties (three in Holland, one each in Friesland and Zeeland) from 1598, the degree of co-ordination by the States General or by the Admiral General, a member of the Orange family, was frequently less than the impact of local pressures and interests. Furthermore, the deficiencies of the state system, the Admiralties, not least a lack of co-operation between them and of anticipated income, was such that another form of public/private partnership was created that lasted until 1656:

> In 1631 the States General had to accept the creation of private local navies in cities like Amsterdam, Hoorn and Edam for the purpose of escorting shipping to and from the Baltic and Norway. Local boards of directors (burgomasters and merchants) began to fit out a number of heavily armed merchantmen annually. Expenses were covered by special duties placed on the merchantmen involved...The naval administration could fall back on only a small standing fleet.[45]

Such systems and problems were not, however, the same as naval weakness, as the Dutch demonstrated at the expense of Spain in 1639. Furthermore, the Dutch navy demonstrated an impressive level of effectiveness. It was very large, not only in comparison to the population but also compared with much larger states, and the mercantile marine it had to protect dwarfed anything else in Europe. Furthermore, the Dutch navy before mid-century was the sole European navy that even attempted to protect trade around all European coasts. Private solutions to trade protection was normal in Europe, and the Dutch state was ahead of its time when it tried to protect all Dutch trade in Europe. Dutch 'private navies' were only a supplement to the Admiralty-run forces and a useful addition to the national war effort. The Dutch state was certainly deficient compared to an ideal model of state organisation and activity, but, compared to other states of the period, it was a model of efficiency.

The English navy that fought in the First Anglo-Dutch War (1652–4) was an impressive force but, rather than searching for the development of a major state navy prefiguring it and the major Western European navies of the 1660s, and even more, the 1690s, it is more appropriate to note the ability to devise different workable solutions. Alan James's important recent study of the French navy argues that in the 1650s it 'continued to be an effective instrument of royal policy, generally meeting its strategic objectives', and also that 'the persistent dislocation between local and national interests and the perennial challenge in France of constructing a lasting consensus in maritime affairs could, under normal circumstances, be managed successfully'. Instead, 'a new age of naval warfare defined by the Anglo-Dutch conflict' changed the situation.[46] In other words, a workable early seventeenth-century system proved less so from mid-century, yet again an indication of the divide then that testified to the formative period 1660–1760, although, in the case of naval power, this period should be seen as beginning in the 1650s.

Another aspect of the growth of government control was provided by the struggle with piracy.[47] Thus, Spain, Genoa and Tuscany tried to protect the west coast of Italy from corsair raids. At the same time, this can be located in a wider international context of resisting privateers and pirates that served Ottoman or French interests. Opposition to piracy was an aspect of the wider-ranging attempt by rulers to control naval forces, or at least to prevent hostile naval developments from within their own territories. Thus, the organisation of an independent Huguenot admiralty in 1621 was a challenge, not least because it was followed that October by the successful operations of the Huguenot fleet against Breton warships in royal service.

However, the major challenge to the control of naval conflict by the territorial states was from semi-independent naval forces with an international dimension. The Barbary corsairs of North Africa were linked to the Ottomans, while their opponents could call on the Knights of St John, from Rhodes and, later, Malta, and, to a certain extent in the Adriatic, on the piratical Uskoks of Senj in the Croatian–Ottoman border area. Such raiders tended to maintain a high level of violence; indeed, conflict was integral to their economy and *raison d'être*. The economy of Senj was based almost entirely on plunder. To supply the town, the Uskoks needed regular and profitable booty – or regular payments from tributaries. The Uskoks interpreted their circumstances in terms of the imperatives of holy war, the ideal of honour and the right to vengeance.[48] The Uskoks and Knights of St John were both perfectly willing to attack Venetian vessels, despite their Christian crews if they thought they were trading with the Ottomans.

Similarly, from the late sixteenth century, the Dnieper and Don Cossacks began to raid the Ottoman positions on the Black Sea. As an example of the more general point about the limited value of deeper draught vessels, the Cossacks used portable rowing boats with flat bottoms and no keel, which were able to use shallower waters than those of the Ottoman galleys. This had a major effect on Ottoman attempts to pursue the Cossacks in 1614–15. As a consequence, from the 1630s, the Ottomans copied the Cossack boats; while fortifications also played a role, with the Ottomans recapturing Azov and re-fortifying Ochakov.[49] Although attacks by Barbary corsairs, Uskoks and Cossacks lacked the scale of the operations of the Ottoman or Spanish forces, and all three could be seen as more akin to brigands than to competing states, it is important not to adopt overly rigid definitions about early modern warfare. At the same time, on the other side of the continuum, piracy, or robbery at sea, was possibly nearly as common between Christians in the Channel as in the Mediterranean, and was perhaps more an unavoidable hazard of sea-borne trade than evidence of a state of war between nations, states or creeds.[50]

In so far as the term military revolution is helpful, it is more pertinent to apply it to naval than to land capability, which is a reminder of the problem of treating the two as if they conformed to the same pattern. Yet, at the same time, the extent of privateering during the mid-seventeenth-century crisis that has been discerned in the 1640s and 1650s serves as a warning against stressing the extent of any such revolution. Rebellion and civil war across much of Europe ensured that there was a host of authorities able to issue letters of marque to licence privateering. For example, the privateering frigates of Randall, Marquess of Antrim in the 1640s have been described as doubling as the Irish navy. Rebellion and civil war also greatly lessened the ability of states to suppress privateering and to protect trade and therefore revenues. As a result, although there are no comprehensive figures, it is probable that the European stock of seagoing vessels fell considerably. The situation in the Channel in the 1560s was akin to the situation in the 1650s. The Huguenot Prince of Condé, the English Earl of Warwick and the Prince of Orange all granted 'letters of marque' to privateers, and the sailors of the English West Country, La Rochelle, the Breton ports and Zeeland were only too willing to take them up.

The extent to which governments encouraged privateering can be presented both in purposeful and 'progressive' terms, as a response to the weakness of opponents, and, possibly less benignly, as a product of their weakness and the resultant need to tap any military resources that might be available, even at the cost of very limited control. The creation of large fleets using partnership arrangements with commercial and investment interests, and the retention of capability by state sponsored piracy, showed a degree of originality in thinking and organisational flexibility that had parallels with the military entrepreneurs of the period.

To turn to tactical issues, comprehensive fighting instructions existed in the 1590s, and were employed for the Cadiz expedition of 1596. They were steadily developed as line tactics evolved, but a high degree of discipline and organisational cohesion were present as early as the Armada battles in the Channel, although they did not maximise broadside firepower.

Looking ahead from the 1650s, it is possible to see fighting instructions and line tactics as instilling discipline and encouraging a new stage in organisational cohesion that permitted more effective firepower,[51] one that was further enhanced when merchantmen ceased to appear in the line of battle of European fleets in the late seventeenth century. However, it is necessary not to read back from this situation to the more inchoate position earlier as governments struggled to create and maintain effective fleets in a difficult political and organisational context and faced with the particular resource requirements of naval strength.[52]

# 9

# EUROPEAN EXPANSION AND THE GLOBAL CONTEXT 1578–1660

The dynamic of European expansion was maintained throughout the period. Russian power spread across Siberia to the Pacific, ensuring that, for the first time, China acquired a land frontier with a European state. Across the oceans, the Dutch, English and French took over much of the eastern seaboard of North America, while the Dutch gained control of some of the crucial spice-producing regions of the East Indies.

However, over most of Asia, the European impact was far more limited. In East Asia, the major struggles were between Japan and China, a struggle that focused on Korea in the 1590s, and the conflict between the Manchu and China which led to the Manchu conquest of China in the 1640s–1650s. In addition, although European adventurers had an impact in coastal parts of Southeast Asia, particularly Burma and Cambodia, they played little role in the ebb and flow of power in Siam (Thailand) and Vietnam.

## Conflict with the Ottomans

Furthermore, there was no decisive shift on the Islamic–Christian frontier, although, given Christian losses over the previous century, this could be seen as a major success for the Christian powers and one that built on the defensive victory at Malta in 1565 and on the failure of Suleiman the Magnificent's 1566 campaign to make major gains. In the Mediterranean, the active campaigning of the early 1570s was followed by a long period of strategic stasis that, in part, reflected alternative commitments for both Spain and the Ottomans: the Dutch Revolt and war with Persia (1578–90) respectively. The absence of any major gap in military capability was also important. Both sides had effective fleets of cannon-bearing galleys, although their range was affected by prevailing wind directions and the presence of bases. Whereas in southern Russia the abortive 1569 expedition against Astrakhan demonstrated the limitations of Ottoman operational effectiveness set by distance, in the Mediterranean the Ottomans had not exceeded their range. Corfu, southern Italy and Malta still remained possible targets.

The extent to which the Ottomans were affected by improvements in Christian fortifications and by the heavy expenditure made available to that end is unclear, although Geoffrey Parker sees it as important.[1] Christian losses like Modon (1500) and Rhodes (1522) were made before the introduction of the new angle-bastioned military architecture, which the Venetians were very quick to use in their *Empire da Mar:* on Crete, a fort was built at Candia (Iraklion) in the second quarter of the century, and a major fortress at Rethymnon after 1573. Also in the late sixteenth century, the Austrians improved the leading fortresses in the section of Hungary they had retained, using the cutting-edge expertise of the period: Pietro Ferrabosco, Carlo Theti and other Italian military engineers provided the plans and directed the works. This process was helped by Ottoman commitment to war with Venice and then Persia. Fortresses at Eger, Ersekujvar, Kanizsa, Karlovac, Komáron and Gyór were built or rebuilt.[2]

The impact of such fortresses is difficult to assess. In 1570, Nicosia in Cyprus, a town encircled by the Venetians with an extended *enceinte* entirely constructed according to the most modern design,[3] fell to the Ottomans, but only due to brute force and guile (frequently a deadly combination). However, during the Thirteen Years' War (1593–1606), the Ottomans were able to capture many of the fortresses recently modified by the Austrians, including Gyór (Raab, 1594), Eger (1596), Kanizsa (1600) and Esztergom (Gran, 1605). When the Ottomans invaded Crete, Candia mounted a long resistance (1645–69), although Rethymnon fell relatively quickly. Other fortresses built on the coasts of Sicily, Naples and Sardinia deterred pirate raids, but also contributed to the heavy cost of military confrontation.

The sensible conclusion appears to be that the artillery fortress made less of a difference than has been suggested. Rather than providing a paradigm leap forward in the defensiveness of Christendom, it appears necessary to examine the fortress, like other forms of technology, in particular circumstances, and to remember that defences were only as good as their defenders. Fortifications (and their defenders) left without support were of limited value, but, in co-operation with an active field army or a fleet, they might be highly useful for defence. The possibility of resupply by sea could be crucial, as also with conflict between Christian powers, for example in Riga's success in thwarting a Russian siege in 1656. Modern fortifications at carefully selected places might strengthen the defence by delaying the enemy and restricting his operational freedom, but only in combination with a good strategic use of mobile forces. Early modern states sought to create fortresses or even a fortress system near their borders, and these often worked. The Portuguese system of fortified places around the Indian Ocean would have been less effective without naval support. There was little equivalent Ottoman fortification re-evaluation to that of the *trace italienne* and no large-scale equivalent to the new European fortifications to that in Austrian-ruled Hungary; although the Ottomans scarcely required such a development in the sixteenth century: they were not under attack.

1566 saw the last large-scale campaigning between the Austrians and the Ottomans until 1593 and the two concluded a peace in February 1568. The outbreak of the Thirteen Years' War of 1593–1606 followed on from the end of the Ottoman–Safavid (Persian) war in 1590. As so often, the course of Ottoman pressure on Europe can only be understood if seen in the wider context of Ottoman commitments. Large-scale border raids by irregulars on both sides led, in 1592, to the intervention of regulars. In 1593, the Austrians renounced the peace treaty and defeated an Ottoman force besieging Sisek in Croatia. However, that Austrian army soon collapsed due to logistical problems.[4] Ottoman logistics were more effective, although the permanent garrisoning of numerous border fortresses created financial pressures.[5] More generally, the Hungarian frontier required a disproportionately large percentage of Ottoman garrison forces.

In 1594, Prince Michael of Wallachia rebelled against the Ottomans. The following year, the Austrians reversed initial Ottoman gains in northern Croatia, capturing Esztergom (Gran) and threatening Bosnia, while Transylvanian forces captured most of the fortresses along the Maros River and defeated the Turks near Giurgiu (25 October). Ottoman forces overran most of Wallachia, but guerrilla activity and a severe winter forced them out, leading to a revolt in Moldavia. The war saw more effective Austrian infantry firepower, in particular the use of muskets rather than arquebuses; and this disconcerted Ottoman commentators. Ottoman cavalry was affected by the greater strength and aggression of Austrian infantry, and the latter was no longer dependent on entrenched positions for its safety on the battlefield. However, there was no total shift in battlefield capability, in part because the Ottomans recruited more musketeers, although they do not appear to have been able to fire volleys. When, in 1596, Mehmed III took personal charge of the army (the first sultan to do so since Suleiman the Magnificent in 1566), he demonstrated its continued effectiveness. The Austro-Transylvanian forces had to abandon their siege of Temesvár, Erlau was successfully besieged by the Ottomans, and, at the battle of Mezökeresztes (23–6 October), Mehmed, with a significant advantage in artillery and cavalry, outflanked and defeated the Austrian infantry which had used its firepower superiority to good effect to break the Ottoman centre, advancing in mixed pike/arquebus squares.[6]

Thereafter, the Ottomans took the initiative during the war each summer in both Hungary and Wallachia, but found it difficult to sustain their position during the winter. Ottoman political problems, however, corroded army discipline and the Austrians were able to surprise and capture Györ (Raab, 1598), which they had lost in 1594. In 1598, the Austrians used a petard to destroy a gate through which they broke into Györ, although they failed to capture Buda. That year, the Ottomans unsuccessfully besieged Varad in an attempt to exploit tension between Austria and Transylvania. Their logistics failed, they were badly affected by heavy rainfall, and the troops mutinied.[7] In 1599, while the Ottoman army remained immobile due to instability in

Constantinople, Michael of Wallachia overran Transylvania, after victory at Sellenberk on 28 October, and then in 1600 Moldavia as well, but Ottoman–Polish action in 1601–5 helped restore Ottoman suzerainty. An Austrian army invaded Wallachia in September 1600, defeating Michael at Miriszló (18 September). The Estates of Transylvania swore allegiance to the Emperor Rudolph, but Sigismond Bátory at the head of a Polish army intervened in 1601. The Austrian commander Giorgio Basta defeated him at Goroszló (3 August) and then had Michael, who had been co-operating with him against Bátory, murdered. Bátory briefly regained control with Ottoman help, but in 1602 Basta overran Transylvania. With Wallachian help, the Austrians eventually overcame an Ottoman-backed rising in 1603 before withdrawing the following year. The fighting moved back and forward, which was not a sign of indecisiveness but of the military capability of the powers.

Sieges played a major role in the Thirteen Years' War. The Ottomans successfully besieged Kanizsa in 1600, only in turn to be besieged in 1601. In 1601, the Ottomans lost the fortress of Istolni Belgrad (Szekesfehervar), only to regain it the following year. The Austrians took Pest in 1602, but besieged Buda in 1602 and 1603 without success. Under a new commander, Lala Mehmet Pasha, Ottoman forces regained Pest (1604) and took Esztergom (1605). Ottoman siege technique was as good as that of the Austrians. Their sappers were particularly good. The Ottomans also benefited from the support of Hungarians alienated by oppressive Habsburg policies, especially from István Bocskai, who was victorious near Almosd (15 October 1604), captured Kassa (11 November) and was recognised by the Ottomans as Prince of Translyvania. Bocskai and the Ottomans overran much of Royal (Habsburg) Hungary in 1605 and the Diet elected Bocskai Prince of Hungary in April 1605. Furthermore, from 1603 the Ottomans were at war with Persia. Habsburg policies of Catholicisation prompted resistance in Hungary and Transylvania. As in Western Europe, the political context was crucial to the course of the conflict, as was the ability to provide resources. Peace was restored in 1606, on the basis of the status quo, by the Treaty of Zsitvatorok. Neither side had decisively altered the military balance. Under the peace of Vienna, Bocskai was recognised as Prince of Transylvania, but it remained part of the kingdom of Hungary and was to revert to it after his death.

Conflict resumed with the Ottoman-Polish war of 1620–1 and, further west, in the late 1650s when the Ottomans attacked George Rákóczy II, Prince of Transylvania. He defeated them at Lippa (1658), but was eventually forced to yield to Ottoman demands.[8] In the early seventeenth century, the Ottomans were involved in a lengthy conflict with Persia that includes major offensives into Mesopotamia, in an effort to regain Baghdad, in 1624, 1629–30 and 1638, and others against Erivan in 1616 and 1635. Peace was not negotiated until 1639. This lengthy conflict led to a strain on Ottoman resources. This has to be assessed alongside improvements in European weaponry when considering Ottoman relative capability. The role of political factors is also suggested by a comparison between Ottoman resilience in 1593–1606 and failure in 1683–99 when opposed by a more powerful coalition, although other factors were also involved and, in 1716–18, the Austrians were able to defeat the Ottomans without allies.

## European expansion

On the global scale, there is evidence of an at least partial slowing down of European expansion in the period 1578–1660. This can be seen with the Portuguese in Angola, Mozambique and Morocco, especially the last, although their expansion continued in Brazil. Defeat at Alcazarquivir in 1578 was not like the Italian disaster (at the hands of the Ethiopians) at Adua in 1896, a simple exception to the rule of European expansion. The Italians recovered from Adua to conquer Libya and then Ethiopia. There was no comparable Portuguese recovery after Alcazarquivir. As an example of the slowing down of European expansion in another sphere, although no defeat was involved, Ivan IV's conquests of Kazan and Astrakhan in the 1550s were not followed by any overrunning of the Ukraine nor by war with the Crimean Tatars. The Crimea was not conquered by Russia until 1783, although the conquests were followed by attempts to make the Nogais vassals and to co-opt the Don Cossacks, and by a very ambitious programme of construction of new fortress towns on the steppe.

In addition, Spanish expansion slackened in this period in the face of strong resistance in Chile, as well as on Mindanao in the Philippines, and to the north of Mexico. In Chile, the Spaniards were pushed back from the Southern Central Valley in 1598–1604; thereafter, the River Bió Bió was a frontier beyond which the Araucanians enjoyed independence. To the north of Mexico, the pueblos of the upper Rio Grande were conquered in 1598, becoming the isolated colony of New Mexico, and, over the following century, the province of New Vizcaya expanded north to meet it, but there was no expansion to compare with that of the sixteenth century.

In the case of the Dutch, later entrants on the colonial scene, expansion and attempted expansion in 1590–1670 was largely at the expense of other European powers, especially the Portuguese,[9] and initial gains elsewhere, as at Cape Town and on Java, did not lead to widespread expansion.[10] This reflected a limited interest in territorial conquest. Moreover, in South Asia it was easier, more profitable and more necessary to create a European presence short of conquest than was the case in the Americas. There was a major difference between the establishment of a 'plunder and trade' presence, or even empire, and conquering and establishing authority over far-flung but lightly populated territories. The latter was true of Siberia and North America, in both of which European powers made major gains.

## The conquest of Siberia

Siberia was a vast area inhabited by small numbers of nomadic and semi-nomadic peoples who were well attuned to the hunting, fishing and pastoral possibilities of their environment. Siberia was also the world's leading source of fur, a vital form of wealth and prestige. Russian access had long been blocked by the Khanate of Kazan, but its capture by Ivan IV in 1552 made possible an advance to the Urals and then across the accessible southern Urals, through which there were a number of low passes.

In 1581, an 800-strong Cossack force under Yermak Timofeyevich, in the service of the Stroganov merchant family of Novgorod, advanced, conquering the Tatar Khanate of Sibir in 1582 after several battles. Their firearms gave them a major advantage over their opponent's bows and arrows, but the Tatars were superior in numbers and mobility and in 1585 wiped out most of Yermak's force. The Siberian Tatars were not overcome until 1598.

Although, as a result of serious logistical problems, it was difficult to replace stores of powder and shot, and they had to be used with care, the Cossacks in Russian service used firearms effectively in their subsequent advance across Siberia. This advance was anchored by the construction of towns including at Samara, Ufa and Tyumen (1586), Tobolsk, near the site of Sibir (1587), Yeniseysk (1619), Yatuksk (1632) and Okhotsk (1647). The Pacific was first reached in 1639, and a post was then established at the mouth of the Ulya river. Russian towns were typically stockaded, and each contained buildings of control and power: a fort, a barracks, a prison, a church and the governor's residence. Forts maximised the defensive potential of firearms, although Okhotsk was stormed by the Tungus in 1654.

As with the earlier Russian conquest of Kazan, resistance was weakened by local divisions. Several of the mutually hostile Siberian tribes provided the Russians with support. The Russians exploited conflicts on the Yenisey between Kets and Tungus, gaining the support of some of the former against the latter. Prominent Tatars and others who agreed to become vassals of the Tsar were allowed to retain their position in return for military service.

Those who resisted were treated barbarously. In combination with the cruel way in which the Russians extorted *yasak* – forced tribute in furs – the seizure of local women, and the spread of new diseases, particularly, from the 1630s, smallpox, this led to a dramatic fall in the population. This fall hit native capacity for resistance. Eighty per cent of Yakuts perished due to smallpox. However, successful resistance to Russian expansion continued in north-east Siberia and Kamchatka.

In south-west Siberia, where the Russian frontier of settlement advanced southwards, the Russians had to fight warlike horsemen, who were able to acquire firearms technology, possibly by capturing Russian guns or by illegal trade. Yenisey Kirghiz were using guns against the Russians as early as the 1640s. The Russians found it necessary to construct fortified lines in south Siberia, such as the Ishim Line.[11] Further west, in the Ukraine, there was a use of defensive positions in support of cavalry patrols to move Russian power southwards, with the construction in the 1580s and 1590s of garrison towns such as Belgorod and Voronezh. This process continued in the seventeenth century, with successive southward advances.[12] However, the Russian policy of exploiting local divisions had only limited success in the northern Caucasus, where Russian attempts to create anti-Ottoman coalitions failed in the 1580s and 1590s, and Russian expeditions were totally routed in 1594 and 1605. Persia, not the Ottoman Empire or Russia, became the dominant power in the region.

## North America

If in Siberia there was only a limited transfer of military technology, in North America both firearms and horses were acquired by the natives. In the Pequot War of 1637, firearms helped bring the English victory in the Connecticut river valley, although they also benefited from the lack of support for their opponents from other tribes. However, from the 1640s, the spread of firearms made the natives more effective opponents. As experts with bows and arrows, they were already adept in missile warfare.[13] In 1626, the Mohawks attacked Dutch settlers in the Hudson valley, who were trying to expand their trade network, and defeated a force of Dutch and Algonquian Mohicans. In 1645, Mohawk attacks forced the French to abandon Fort Richelieu, established at the mouth of the Richelieu river in 1642. By 1648 the Mohawks had amassed at least 800 muskets. This spread of weaponry owed much to the presence of a number of European powers. Québec was established by the French (1608), Jamestown in Virginia (1607) and Plymouth in New England (1620) by the English, and New Amsterdam, now New York (1614) and Albany (1624) by the Dutch. The Europeans became drawn into conflict between native tribes and abandoned bans on the supply of firearms to natives. The French had initially refused to supply firearms, but the Dutch provided them and, as warfare increased in scope, restrictions on the supply of firearms decreased. In the early 1640s, the French began to sell muskets to baptised native allies to strengthen them against the Mohawks, who themselves traded freely for Dutch muskets after agreements in 1643 and 1648.[14]

The power balance between native and colonist was shifted more by demography than by weaponry. The Europeans came not only to trade but also to colonise, and they came in increasing numbers. In contrast, native numbers did not grow and were hit by disease: smallpox affecting the Iroquois in 1633 and the Hurons in 1634. Native disunity was also important: in 1609 Hurons joined with the French under Samuel de Champlain against the Mohawks.

## Africa

The Europeans were less successful in Africa[15] and South Asia. The major attempts at conquest were made by the Portuguese in Angola. However, disease was as devastating for the Europeans in Africa as for their opponents in the New World. About 60 per cent of the Portuguese soldiers in Angola in 1575–90 died of disease; most of the rest were killed or deserted. In addition, horses could not survive in sub-Saharan Africa. Furthermore, whereas Mexico and Peru were populous and had a well-developed agricultural system that could provide plenty of resources for invaders, Africa lacked comparable store-houses, food for plunder, and roads. The Portuguese also found the Africans well armed with well-worked iron weapons, as good in some ways as Portuguese steel weaponry, and certainly better than the wood and obsidian weapons of the New World.

In Angola, the Portuguese were effective only in combination with African soldiers, and, without them they could be defeated, as by Queen Njinga of the Ndongo at Ngolomenc (1644). The slow rate of fire of muskets and the openness of African fighting formations reduced the effectiveness of Portuguese firearms, while their cannon had little impact on African earth-work fortifications. The Portuguese were unable to deploy anything larger than a small force of cavalry, and could not therefore counter their opponents' open order of fighting. Thus, the experience of fighting in Europe was no guide to the situation abroad.

Firearms were diffused rapidly and Africans possibly had them in equal numbers already in the 1620s, when quantities of them were reported in the first war against Njinga (1626–8). As a reminder of the danger of reading uncritically from particular battles, Portuguese victory over the shield-bearing heavy infantry of the kingdom of Kongo at Mbumbi (1622) was the result of overwhelming numerical superiority, not weapons superiority. The Portuguese army withdrew very quickly and even returned captured slaves when the main Kongolese army reached the region. Central Angola was not to be conquered until the late nineteenth century.[16] Elsewhere in Africa, Portuguese attempts from Mozambique to gain control of the upper Zambezi failed.[17] In addition, Fort Jesus, the Portuguese base at Mombasa, fell to a surprise storming in 1631, although the Portuguese were able to regain it.[18]

## South and East Asia

Hopes of expansion in Asia continued to be pressed by Iberians in the late sixteenth century. The Spaniards tried to expand their power in, and from, the Philippines, although they encountered serious resistance from areas where Islam had made an impact: Sulu and Mindanao. Spanish expeditions failed in 1578 and 1596 respectively. In 1589, Philip II instructed his governor of the Philippines to occupy Formosa (Taiwan) and in 1598 two Spanish warships were sent to seize the harbour of Keelung, only to be thwarted by the weather. Spanish-supported adventurers, led by Diego Veloso, a Portuguese mercenary, attempted to take over Cambodia in the 1590s, and their candidate was proclaimed king in 1597; but in 1599, the greatly outnumbered Spaniards were killed in a rebellion. That year, Philip de Brito, a Portuguese adventurer, was given charge of the port of Syriam in modern Burma by the ruler of Arakan, whom he served, and Portugal sought to benefit by granting him the captaincy of Syriam.

In the early seventeenth century, the Dutch, not the Portuguese, expanded in Asian waters. Jayakerta, where they had a trading base from 1603, became the centre of Dutch power in the East Indies from 1619 after the town was stormed and the forces of the Sultanate of Bantam defeated. In 1628–9, now called Batavia, the town survived two sieges by the Sultan of Mataram.

However, there were also a series of European failures, particularly for the Portuguese, whose empire was gravely weakened by union with Spain and the consequent need to support the war with the Dutch.[19] Syriam fell to Burmese siege in 1613: Goa did not send a fleet speedily enough to relieve the post and it was betrayed when one of the defenders opened the gates. In the Persian Gulf, Ormuz fell to Persian siege in 1622. Two years later, a large Chinese army invaded the Pescadores Islands west of Formosa, where the Dutch had established a base in 1622, and forced them to withdraw to Formosa.[20] In 1630 and 1638, Portuguese armies in Sri Lanka were defeated, in each case with the death of the Captain-General. After a siege in 1632, Selim Shah of Arakan forced Portuguese adventurers to abandon their positions on Sandwip Island at Chittagong and Dianga. The Mughal Governor of Bengal took Hughli. In the 1650s, Sivappa Hayaka of Ikkeri captured the Portuguese possessions on the Kankara coast of India: Honawar, Basrur, Gangolli and Mangalore.[21] In 1636, the Portuguese were expelled from Ethiopia. In 1650, the Sultan of Oman captured Muscat from the Portuguese and then used it as a base for a powerful navy that attacked Portuguese trade and positions.[22]

Thus, alongside European successes, there were failures. Furthermore, some positions that were retained were only held because they survived sieges, Goa, for example, by the Sultan of Bijapur in 1654 and 1659. The fear of Bijapuri attack that 'gripped' Goa in the early 1630s scarcely suggests much confidence in the strength of the European position.[23] Outside Siberia, the European military impact on land in Asia was still limited.

## Conflict between European powers

Much of the European military effort outside Europe in this period was devoted to conflict between European powers. This was particularly the case between the Dutch and the Portuguese, a war that still requires systematic study, although other wars that spread outside Europe included those between England and France, England and Spain, and England and the Dutch.

The Dutch were the world's leading naval power in the first half of the seventeenth century, their naval primacy closely linked to their maritime commercial position as premier trade brokers.[24] In Asian waters, the Dutch

East India Company profitably linked trading zones, thus enhancing economic specialisation and exchange. This encouraged the Dutch to displace competitors and also gave them the resources to do so.[25] The English were driven from Ambon in the Moluccas, as the Dutch destroyed rivals in the spice trade. In 1641, the Dutch failed to overrun the Spanish positions on Formosa, but the following year a Dutch force of eight warships and 690 men were able to drive the Spaniards to surrender. The Dutch also drove the Portuguese from coastal Sri Lanka (1638–42), the Malabar coast of India and Malacca, which fell in 1641. However, despite initial successes and major efforts, the Dutch failed to drive the Portuguese from Angola, Brazil and their positions in West Africa. In 1630, the Dutch captured Recife and established New Holland, which covered much of north-eastern Brazil. However, in 1645 their position was challenged by a widespread rebellion by Portuguese planters, while a major Dutch expedition sent in December 1647 failed to stabilise the situation by capturing Bahia as planned. Attempts to break the Portuguese siege of Recife by sorties led to defeats at Guararapes in April 1648 and February 1649, and the Dutch position in Brazil was weakened by a lack of support for all-out war from within the United Provinces, especially in Holland. Furthermore, the outbreak of the First Anglo-Dutch War (1652–4) forced the Dutch to focus their efforts on a more threatening foe. In 1654, Recife and the other Dutch forts in Brazil surrendered to the Portuguese.[26]

On the other side of the Atlantic, in 1637, a Dutch fleet took Elmina, the leading Portuguese base on the Gold Coast in West Africa. The island of Fernando Po and the ports of Luanda and Benguela in Angola followed in 1641, but, in 1648 they were recaptured.

The English made only limited impact on the Spanish empire during their war of 1585–1604. Attacks on Spanish treasure movements and bases proved far more difficult in execution than imagination. However, in 1629 the French base of Québec was starved into surrender by an English force, although it was returned in 1632 after a peace agreement. When England fought Spain again in 1655–9, hopes of gaining Cuba and Hispaniola – the Western Design – proved wildly over-optimistic, but Jamaica was conquered from 1655, although not without very heavy losses to disease.[27]

It is therefore possible to reconceptualise the global dimension of the putative early modern Military Revolution. In place of an emphasis on the European ability to dominate the globe, a claim that would have looked ludicrous in East and South Asia, where the bulk of the world's population lived, or in Africa, it was the capacity of European powers to fight each other far from Europe that was impressive, and that contrasted with other military systems.

This ability owed much to native assistance, although from the native perspective, it was frequently a case of Europeans playing a role in local struggles. In 1639, the Portuguese and Dutch took opposite sides in the conflict among Vijayanagara grandees in southern India.[28] In addition, European forces could be used by native rulers against other European powers. In 1605, in the Moluccas, Dutch support for the Hituese led the Portuguese to surrender their fort on Ambon, and Sultan Zaide of Ternate received Dutch assistance in driving the Portuguese from Ternate and Tidore.[29] Shah Abbas of Persia used the English desire to trade with Persia and English rivalry with Spain in order to obtain English support against the Portuguese base of Ormuz. Deprived of a friendly hinterland after the Safavids overran the mainland possessions of the indigenous ruler of Ormuz, and of naval support by English action, Ormuz surrendered in 1622 after a siege. The Ottomans, in turn, sought Portuguese help against the Persians in 1624, although this did not amount to much.

European conquests depended in part on local support. Rajasimha II of Kandy allied with the Dutch against the Portuguese in Sri Lanka and, in 1640, joint attacks led to the capture of Galle and Negombo. In 1641, Abdul Jali, Sultan of Johor, helped the Dutch capture Malacca from the Portuguese; he had earlier helped Malacca resist attack by Aceh.

Despite the native roles, the wide-ranging nature of the conflict between the Dutch and Portugal in the 1640s and the Dutch and England in the 1650s, 1660s and 1670s was both impressive and different to the situation at the outset of the period and during the Italian Wars. At the global level, this was striking. There was nothing comparable between Japan and China in the 1590s nor Persia and the Mughals in the 1640s, because no other states possessed this global range.

This increase in capability was not true of the entire European 'system', but only of the Atlantic powers, and this underlines the limitations of thinking in terms of one trajectory of European military development and, indeed, of focusing on the customary narrative of land-based capability and warfare. Furthermore, as with much else, the dramatic developments were to occur not in the 'Roberts' century', 1560–1660, but rather in the following century. The global dimension of the Anglo–Dutch wars was more pronounced in the Second (1665–7) and Third (1672–4) Wars than in the First (1652–4). In the Second, the English captured New York and the Dutch Surinam, and in the Third the Dutch recaptured New York. More seriously, the Seven Years' War between Britain and France (1756–63) revealed a level of capability and had an impact that was totally different to the war between England and France in 1626–9. A similar contrast can be made between Anglo–Spanish hostilities in 1624–30 and the British capture of Havana and Manila in 1762.

This is part of a more general suggestion that, in so far as an early modern Military Revolution existed, it occurred after 1660. Whether or not that is accepted, it is still the case that earlier developments were important, not least in setting goals. Possibly the most striking was the idea that the Atlantic powers should be able to pursue their conflicts with each other across the oceans, and that such a pursuit would directly contribute to their standing and success in Europe.

## The relative effectiveness of European power

Alongside any contrasting of European with non-European forces, it needs to be accepted that the variety of the latter was such that some were closer to European forms than to those of other non-European peoples. The essential divide in both Europe and elsewhere was between standing (permanent) forces, which involved continuous expenditure, and societies and states that relied, in whole or part, on forces that only served during campaigns. These societies and states did not have to adopt the financial and governmental techniques necessary to provide for standing forces.

This divide was more like a continuum. Nevertheless, there were significant sociological and operational consequences. These were revealed where different military systems clashed, as in North America. It has also been argued that there was an important cultural contrast between a European willingness to kill large numbers and suffer high rates of casualties and other societies, such as those in North America, where there were less extensive notions of the acceptable social limits of casualties.[30]

In sociological terms, on the global scale, the societies that lacked standing forces generally relied on pastoral agriculture, were less populous, and had less developed governmental structures. They did not therefore tend to develop comparable military specialisation, especially in fortification and siegecraft. While the agricultural surplus and taxation base of settled agrarian societies permitted the development of logistical mechanisms to support permanent specialised military units, nomadic peoples generally lacked such units and had a far less organised logistical system. In war, they often relied on raiding their opponents.

This organisational divide, which owed much to factors of terrain and climate, was linked to one in methods of warfare. Nomadic and semi-nomadic people exploited mobility and generally relied on cavalry, whereas their opponents placed more stress on numbers, infantry, and fortifications. The Ottoman military combined the strengths of different systems: organisational/bureaucratic and fiscal strengths, alongside tribal forces including allies and tributaries, especially the Crimean Tatars. The diversity of the Ottoman military system was an inherent source of strength; and one that was linked to the breadth and depth of its recruitment pool.

Cavalry forces could be devastating. The early sixteenth century is generally seen in terms of the triumph of gunpowder forces, most obviously with a series of spectacular Ottoman victories over Persia, Egypt and Hungary in 1514–26, and also with the role of firepower in defeating Swiss pikemen and French cavalry during the Italian Wars. Yet, it is also necessary to give due weight to the triumphs of cavalry forces. Cavalry provided mobility, and that was crucial for strategic, logistical and tactical reasons. It enabled forces to overcome the constraints of distance, to create equations of numbers, supplies and rate of movement that were very different to those of infantry, and also to force the pace of battle in a very different fashion to that of infantry.

Cavalry was not incompatible with firepower. The horse archers of Central Asian origin had shown this effectively in the twelfth and thirteenth centuries in combating the Crusades. Mounted archers remained important outside Europe in the sixteenth century, as in the Mughal victory over a large Indian insurrectionary force at the Second Battle of Panipat in 1556. Ming Chinese advances against both Mongols and Manchus were defeated by the mobile mounted archers of their opponents. Mounted archers were also effective in co-operation with foot musketeers and cannon, as in the Ottoman victories of Chaldiran (1514) and Mohács (1526), those of the Mughals at First Panipat (1526), Kanua (1527) and Haldighati (1576), and that of the Safavids over the Uzbeks at Jam (1528).

It is all too easy to concentrate on infantry gunpowder weaponry, and to present it as the paradigm of progress, ignoring the continued role of cavalry, whether armed with bows or gunpowder firearms. Cavalry forces could make the transition to gunpowder weaponry, as shown to devastating effect at Alcazarquivir, and also with pistoleers in mid-sixteenth-century Europe, although that transition was not necessary to their effectiveness.

The proportion of cavalry fell in the Spanish and French armies in the period covered by this book, although cavalry remained important and demonstrated its value on the European battlefields of the mid-seventeenth century; and, in the later stages of the Thirty Years' War the percentage of cavalry in the armies competing in Germany rose. In Ireland in the 1640s, the 'crucial weakness' of the Catholic Confederacy was in cavalry, not infantry, and this led to the defeat of the army at Dungan's hill in 1647, which caused an irreparable loss of trained manpower.[31]

At the sociological level, if cavalry is not seen as necessarily anachronistic (a powerful check to implicit or explicit Eurocentric views), then this has consequences for assumptions about whether particular governmental-social systems were better suited to military success. This issue and, more generally, those of the military dimensions of state-building, and the governmental and social contexts of military change, need to focus on the question of military purpose. Some systems were not suited to the maintenance of substantial standing forces. Such systems succumbed in the eighteenth and, still more, nineteenth centuries, most obviously with the Russian conquest of peoples such as the Crimean Tatars, Kazakhs and Uzbeks. Yet, to read back from that failure to the early modern period is problematic. It is not simply that it entails a nineteenth-century perception of infantry and artillery firepower, and of the attendant relationship between disciplined, well-drilled and well-armed permanent firepower forces and those that were not so armed. There is also the related perception of the governmental dimension, namely the increased effectiveness and apparent potency of states able to mobilise and direct resources, and to support permanent forces.

Methodologically, however, this approach fails to address adequately the controverted and contingent nature of governmental strength, which appear clear in any close reading of political history, administrative processes and practice, and such branches of military life as recruitment, logistics, and control and command.

There is also the problem of extrapolation. The degree of organisation required to create and support a large, permanent, long-range navy, or large, permanent armies, was not required to maintain military forces fit for purpose across most of the world. In addition, there is a problematic empirical dimension. In the early modern period, administrative sophistication did not suffice for victory, as the Chinese discovered with their defeats at Mongol and, more completely, Manchu hands in the mid-fifteenth and mid-seventeenth centuries respectively.

In terms of both government and weaponry, there were similarities, but also differences between the European powers and those of other states deploying gunpowder forces, although it is important to note differences in military systems among the latter.[32] Indeed, the term 'gunpowder empires' was coined to describe Islamic states: those created by the Ottomans, Safavids, Mughals and the Sa'dids of Morocco.[33] Thanks in part to the Europeans, but with important other areas of origin as well, the use of gunpowder weaponry spread markedly in the period 1494–1660.[34] Furthermore, it would be misleading to suggest that other powers made less effective use of such weaponry than the Europeans, although this was certainly true at sea. For example, recent work has corrected the earlier view that the Ottomans concentrated on large cannon, rather than larger numbers of more manoeuvrable smaller cannon, and has instead emphasised that their ordnance was dominated by small and medium-sized cannon. It has also been shown that they were able to manufacture an adequate supply of gunpowder.[35] Again, there is a danger of reading back from the eighteenth and, even more, nineteenth centuries, when the Ottoman artillery was clearly weaker, to the period of this book.

Instead, it is worth noting that, in Europe and elsewhere, the armies of this period were mixed infantry/cavalry forces and, for both infantry and cavalry, involved troops that used firearms and those who did not. Thus, the response to gunpowder weaponry varied, and this variety has to be understood not in terms of military progress, or administrative sophistication or cultural superiority, but rather as a response to the different tasks and possibilities facing the armies of the period, within a context in which it was far from clear which weaponry, force structure, tactics, or operational method were better.

Political contexts were different, but again it would be mistaken to distinguish Europe from the other powers. If the Ottoman, Mughal and Chinese states were far-flung empires that contrasted with France or even Spain (at least in so far as their European possessions were concerned), the contrast was much less clear if Russia or Poland were compared to Persia or Morocco.

In Europe, states sought to monopolise organised, large-scale violence, but with the co-operation of their social elites who controlled command positions.

These elites were willing to co-operate with military change, including the organisation of armies around a state-directed structure, but only on their terms and, more particularly, because they saw the state in terms of their relations with the sovereign. Non-European rulers sought the same monopolisation, although the scale of states such as the Ottoman empire made this a formidable task.

This monopolisation was linked to the more general internal dynamic of the socio-political systems of the period. If war was a forcing house of change, it was also designed to prevent it, certainly in terms of challenges to prevailing political, social and ideological practices and norms. Armies suppressed rebellions and maintained, or strengthened, social and spatial patterns of control. Although the New Model Army of the Parliamentary side in the English Civil War was a revolutionary force, and the Huguenot forces of the French Wars of Religion had a radical potential, in general armies did not act in this fashion. Thus, the army of the Dutch Republic did not act as a socially radicalising force, although, under the Princes of Orange, it challenged the power of the urban oligarchies of Holland.

Instead, it was the need to provide for armies and to retain their capacity to resist political, social and territorial change that caused political and administrative pressures, and can therefore be seen as a potential source of radicalisation. The relationship between military demands and governmental change[36] was not restricted to Europe. Other important examples include the Songhay Empire on the middle Niger under Askia Muhammad (r.1493–1528).[37]

To return to the theme of the relative effectiveness of the European military, on land there had been no revolution in capability in 1494–1660 comparable to that on sea. Indeed, there is a need for considerable caution in running together this period with that down to 1800, as in Geoffrey Parker's deservedly influential *The Military Revolution 1500–1800: Military Innovation and the Rise of the West* (1988). The two together suggest a continuing process of success, but this impression can be greatly qualified. For example, is it more important to emphasise the Portuguese loss of Muscat in 1650 or the Dutch establishment of a base at Cape Town in 1652? For the seventeenth century as a whole, how far are European gains in North America to be counterpointed by Dutch failure on Formosa (Taiwan) or Russian in the Amur valley? These points are important for any evaluation of relative capability as they set the parameters of the questions that are asked.

No European power faced a crisis comparable to that of Ming China in the mid-seventeenth century (when it was overthrown by the Manchu), or, indeed, of Safavid Persia in the 1720s, when it was conquered by the Afghans. The general crisis that afflicted Spain was far more modest in its course and consequences, and the same was true of France. Yet this contrast does not argue a greater strength for European militaries but rather a different political context, both domestically and internationally. After the reign of Suleiman the

Magnificent (r. 1520–66), when the Ottoman threat ebbed, no major European state was threatened by an external challenge from outside or within Christian Europe comparable to that of the Manchu, although Gustavus Adolphus in 1631 appeared an inexorable force, and there was talk of him advancing on Vienna the following year.

As another example of a comparative approach that should be considered, successful conquest involved incorporation and the winning over of local elites, as the Mughals showed in India and the Manchu in China. This was also possible in Europe, as the Swedes showed in the eastern Baltic, but the ideological division and hatred stemming from the Protestant Reformation made this far less easy if confessional divides had to be overcome. As a consequence, incorporation could involve conversion or expulsion, as in the case of both Moslem Spain and Protestant Bohemia after their conquest.

The overthrow of Ming China and the lack of anything comparable in Europe does not demonstrate the superiority of European military systems. Instead, it is more pertinent to argue that no such superiority had been demonstrated on land over other 'gunpowder states', and, in the case of the conflict between Portugal and Morocco, the very opposite was the case. There had been success in clashes with less 'developed' militaries and less organised states, although there had also been many failures, as in sub-Saharan Africa. However, such success could also be seen in the case of other 'gunpowder states'. Rather than assuming any European superiority, whether based on (or amounting to) a military revolution or not, it is more appropriate to note the more complex, contingent and varied nature of relative military capability; and also to give due weight to the non-military factors for differential regional success.[38]

# 10

# CONCLUSIONS

War powerfully contributed to a mental world dominated by chance and a frequently malign fate. It encouraged a providentialism in which the world appeared outside human control. War was presented as one of the curses or plagues of life, and, indeed, as one of the four deadly horsemen of the Apocalypse.[1] This forms an ironic counterpoint to the scholarly emphasis on a growing bureaucratisation of war in early modern Europe. The gap between intention and impact is common to war, but it is worth considering how far the bureaucratisation has been exaggerated. John Nolan's description of the 'militarization of the Elizabeth state' in terms of a 'centralized administration of local resources, supplemented by entrepreneurial enterprise' is not really one of military revolution. In England and elsewhere, 'most of the innovations were created by elaborating or modifying traditional institutions'.[2] It is necessary to stress that this was done by societies whose ethos, social assumptions and political practice were conservative, certainly in so far as emphasis on lineage and social prominence were concerned.

As a related point, it is also unclear that war led to the development of more 'modern' state forms, although the changes of the period have been presented as leading towards such forms; and these changes have been seen as war related, if not driven. In the United Provinces, the serious financial strains caused by military expenditure helped to sustain a political system based on provincial particularism and the power of urban oligarchies,[3] although the Dutch were able to support a formidable military effort. More generally, these financial strains threatened to overwhelm both established governmental and political practices and attempts to create new ones more favourable to a powerful state.

The analysis of war also leads to a reconceptualisation of the chronology of the period. The Roberts thesis of the Military Revolution is commonly linked with the view that developments in the following century (1660–1760) were of considerably less importance and that the pace of military change resumed in the closing revolutionary period of the eighteenth century, with the outbreak of the French Revolutionary War in 1792. The thesis is therefore related to the generally dominant view of early modern

Europe, one that sees a resolution of a period of crisis that culminated in a mid-seventeenth-century general crisis, such that between 1660 and the French Revolution there was relative stability within states and only limited wars between them. Indeed the Military Revolution has been employed to help explain and define the period of stability, which is described as the age of absolutism.

This approach can be questioned, and it can be suggested that changes after 1660, especially the growth of larger standing armies and the tactical impact of the development of socket bayonets and the replacement of the pike, were more important than those over the previous century.[4] As a related issue, it is possible to reinterpret absolutism in order to emphasise the need to win elite support. This, however, does not preclude the argument that an important development in military-politico organisation took place in some countries, with the foundation of what are known as 'fiscal–military states', most obviously, in the early seventeenth century, the Dutch Republic and Sweden.[5]

The suggestion that, in 1494–1660, the Europeans used the opportunity presented by firearms to invent a new way of war that was radically different, at least on land, to non-European use of firearms can also be questioned. It can be suggested that it was only in Europe that there was a sustained transformation of the culture of war, whereas elsewhere, firearms were adopted as useful force multipliers without altering the underlying culture of war. However, the extent and effectiveness of any European transformation of the culture of war in this period should not be exaggerated. Instead, it can be argued that, on land, the Europeans had not by 1660 made a major transformation, opening up a capability gap with other gunpowder cultures, akin to that which was to exist by 1760.

This issue is difficult to analyse. For example, it is not clear how far organisational effectiveness in this period can be assessed in a comparative context. It has been argued that European superiority in gunpowder weaponry rested on cultural–organizational factors, specifically drill and discipline,[6] on firing on command and on operating as units, an approach that avoids the critique of technological determinism associated with the emphasis on weaponry. This approach can also be related to changes in military institutions and methods of raising troops, and although these have been seen as stemming from shifts within the West, they have been presented as affecting its global capability: 'there *were* distinctly Western ways of constructing an army…the emphasis on discipline, drill, and ability to suffer losses without losing cohesion would also appear to be a Western trait. Because the Western military style rested upon certain political, social, economic and cultural foundations…Western states produced particular kinds of military institutions'.[7]

Thus, it has been suggested that European forces acquired an edge in retaining cohesion and control in battle, and that this permitted more sophisticated and effective tactics. This analysis rests, however, on limited knowledge of non-European capabilities. For example, it is unclear, certainly in this

213

period, that Ottoman war-making was less organised or effective.[8] Furthermore, the organisational sophistication of European armies should not be exaggerated. Most, for example, lacked standardisation in their artillery, and attempts to standardise weaponry had only limited success. It was also very difficult to standardise the quality of gunpowder. Within Europe, the pressures of war frequently proved too much not only for political harmony and administrative structures but also for military practice. For example, in the Thirteen Years' War of 1593–1606 between Austria and the Ottomans 'the annual campaigns forced both sides to use increasing numbers of irregular troops, since trained men and financial resources were in ever short supply'.[9]

Like technology, organisational factors, and an assessment of their effectiveness, should be set in the context of the purposes of conflict, specifically, but not only, of why wars were fought. This does not entail a demilitarisation of military history, nor a neglect of the contingent, the conjunctural and the operational dimension. Nevertheless, a cultural interpretation that focuses on reasons for conquest, or for the avoidance of aggressive warfare, rather than on technological or organisational enablers of military capability, directs attention to moods as well as moments; ideological factors as well as political and military contingencies. It is unclear that any revolutionary change occurred under this heading. Such an interpretation also focuses on the methodological difficulties of devising a general theory of military capability and change.

Aside from this, the debate over European military developments in the period specifically relates to the issue of modernisation, its definition, cause, course and consequence. If modernisation is seen in terms both of a change in Europe's position in the world and of European state formation then their extent in this period and their relation to military causes both require qualification.

The use of vocabulary is instructive, but can be misleading. References to military revolution and state-building employ terms associated with modernisation, although much that is being discussed was very long-established in character, and this makes the use of the term revolution questionable. For example, monetarisation and the spread of a money economy permitted the raising of revenues in cash rather than kind, and this was important to the development of expensive projects of enhanced military capability, such as standing armies and navies, and improved fortifications. However, this spread had been going on for centuries. The availability of New World bullion in the sixteenth century encouraged the money economy, but so also did the growth of markets and fairs in the twelfth and thirteenth centuries and the weakening of feudal controls over labour after the Black Death plague epidemic of the 1340s. Similarly, it is possible to point to the long term when considering such military developments as trained infantry able to resist cavalry on the battlefield and, later, the spread of gunpowder firearms.

Economic change was long-term, but political developments in 1490–1534 increased the pressure to use the opportunities of a more commercialised economy. The sudden availability of New World bullion and of trade routes to the Indian Ocean controlled by Europeans was important, and also ensured that the purposes of naval capability were radically transformed for the Atlantic powers. In Western Europe, the confrontation between Valois and Habsburg, in the Baltic the break-up of the Union of Kalmar, and in Eastern Europe the advance of Suleiman the Magnificent, all led to military demands that put pressure on existing governmental and military structures. However, although, for example, the confrontation between Valois and Habsburg was greater in scale than the Hundred Years' War between England and France, while Ottoman pressure was far more consistent and further reaching in Europe than that of the Mongols in the thirteenth century (and also had a naval dimension), these demands were not revolutionary.

Most authors seek to emphasise the importance of their subject, and for many decades it has been customary to do so by stressing its revolutionary character and consequences. This has a symbolic quality in academic life, and it is not inappropriate to underline this point in a book that has asserted the need to appreciate that the symbolic nature of military actions encompassed issues of organisation, command, force structure, tasking and strategy. It may appear doubly perverse to take a different approach in the case of a period generally described in terms of a Military Revolution. The most recent generalist account claims that Roberts was 'correct in suggesting that European warfare in this period had undergone fundamental systemic changes' and goes on to present 'anticipatory RMAs [Revolutions in Military Affairs] of the Middle Ages and early modern era – longbow, offensive–defensive strategy, gunpowder, new fortress architecture' followed by 'Military revolution 1: the seventeenth-century creation of the modern state and of modern military institutions'.[10]

In contrast, this study does not deny the existence of important changes, but it seeks to qualify them, and thus to challenge the notion of such a Revolution. The general conclusion is that the military realities were both too complex (geographically) and too much dependent on previous experiences (political, cultural and economic) to make the term Military Revolution useful as a phrase to encapsulate military changes in the period. There were changes, in technologies, organisations and attitudes, but they were neither revolutionary nor universal. Instead, the emphasis is on continuities, not least in terms of reasons for conflict, and of limitations, especially in tactical, operational and strategic military effectiveness, administrative structures and support, relative capability with regard to non-European military systems, and European trans-oceanic impact on land. To stress continuity entails, in part, noting continuities between the warfare of the late fifteenth century with that of the mid-seventeenth. Battles were changed by the greater role of firepower, but sieges remained a mixture of bombardment, blockade and storming, while the role of cavalry and light forces in raiding territory and denying opponents the opportunity to raise supplies remained crucial in operational terms.

Cavalry also continued to play a major role in battles, contributing to their character as combined arms actions, and thus to the need for commanders able to co-ordinate forces successfully.

There is also a stress on variety, not only in conflict, force structure and political context within Europe, but also between land and sea developments, and also in overseas European effectiveness. To stress variety in conclusion is not a 'cop out', but rather a pointed reminder of the flaws of schematic interpretations, and an attempt to recreate the uncertainty and confusion within which people lived their lives and in which choices and changes occurred.

# NOTES

For all books listed below, the place of publication is London unless otherwise noted.

## PREFACE

1   C. Duffy, *Siege Warfare: The Fortress in the Early Modern World, 1494–1660* (1979). This work did not employ the term military revolution.

## 1 INTRODUCTION

1   J.M. Hill, 'Gaelic Warfare 1453–1815', in J.M. Black (ed.), *European Warfare 1453–1815* (1999), pp. 201–23.
2   A. Santosuosso, 'Anatomy of Defeat in Renaissance Italy: The Battle of Fornovo in 1495', *International History Review*, 16 (1994), p. 226.
3   R. Hellie, *Enserfment and Military Change in Muscovy*, (Chicago, 1971), p. 161; C. Finkel, 'French Mercenaries in the Habsburg-Ottoman War of 1593–1606', *Bulletin of the School of Oriental and African Studies*, 55 (1992), pp. 451–71.
4   D. Ditchburn, *Scotland and Europe. The Medieval Kingdom and its Contacts with Christendom, c. 1215–1545* (East Linton, 2000), p. 201.
5   G.E. Rothenberg, 'Venice and the Uskoks of Senj: 1537–1618', *Journal of Modern History*, 33 (1961), pp. 155–6; R.A. Stradling, *The Spanish Monarchy and Irish Mercenaries: the Wild Geese in Spain 1618–68* (Dublin, 1994).
6   W.R. Thompson and K. Rasler, 'War, the Military Revolution(s) Controversy, and Army Expansion. A Test of Two Explanations of Historical Influences on European State Making', *Comparative Political Studies*, 32 (1999), pp. 14, 25–6.
7   M.R. Smith and L. Marx (eds), *Does Technology Drive History? The Dilemma of Technological Determinism* (Cambridge, MA, 1994).
8   K. DeVries, 'Catapults Are Not Atomic Bombs: Towards a Redefinition of "Effectiveness" in Premodern Military Technology', *War in History*, 4 (1997), pp. 475–91.
9   H. Kleinschmidt, 'Using the Gun: Manual Drill and the Proliferation of Portable Firearms', *Journal of Military History*, 63 (1999), p. 629.
10  C. Oman, *A History of the Art of War in the Middle Ages* (1924, 2 vols) II, 356.

## 2 CULTURAL, SOCIAL AND POLITICAL CONTEXTS

1 S.J. Gunn, 'The French Wars of Henry VIII', in J.M. Black (ed.), *The Origins of War in Early Modern Europe* (Edinburgh, 1987), pp. 34–40; P.S. Fichtner, 'The Politics of Honor: Renaissance Chivalry and Hapsburg Dynasticism', *Bibliothèque d'Humanisme et Renaissance*, 29 (1967), pp. 567–80; E.H. Dickerman and A.M. Walker, 'The Choice of Hercules: Henry IV as Hero', *Historical Journal*, 39 (1996), pp. 315–37.

2 On which, see G. Richardson, *Renaissance Monarchy: The Reigns of Henry VIII, Francis I and Charles V* (2002).

3 P. Russell, *Prince Henry 'The Navigator': A Life* (New Haven, CT, 2000).

4 G. Parker, *The Grand Strategy of Philip II* (New Haven, CT, 1998), and 'The World is Not Enough: The Imperial Vision of Philip II of Spain', Charles Edmondson Historical Lecture Series, Number 22 (Waco, TX, 2001), p. 50.

5 D. Parrott, 'Richelieu, the *Grands*, and the French Army', in J. Bergin and L. Brockliss (eds), *Richelieu and His Age* (Oxford, 1992), pp. 135–73.

6 B. Donagan, 'The Web of Honour: Soldiers, Christians, and Gentlemen in the English Civil War', *Historical Journal*, 44 (2001), pp. 365–89.

7 F. Billacois, *The Duel: Its Rise in Early Modern France* (New Haven, CT, 1990).

8 S. Anglo, *The Martial Arts of Renaissance Europe* (New Haven, CT, 2000).

9 R. Hellie, *Enserfment and Military Change in Muscovy* (Chicago, 1971); D. Moon, 'Reassessing Russian Serfdom', *European History Quarterly*, 26 (1996), pp. 483–526.

10 G. Hanlon, *The Twilight of a Military Tradition. Italian Aristocrats and European Conflicts, 1560–1800* (1998), pp. 97–9; T. Barker, *Army, Aristocracy, Monarchy: Essays on War, Society and Government in Austria, 1618–1780* (Boulder, CO, 1982); F. Redlich, *The German Military Enterpriser and his Workforce* (2 vols, Wiesbaden, 1964–5).

11 S. Anglo (ed.), *Chivalry in the Renaissance* (Woodbridge, 1990); L.O. Fradenburg, *City, Marriage, Tournament: Arts of Rule in Late Medieval Scotland* (Madison, WI, 1992).

12 M. Keen, 'The Changing Scene. Guns, Gunpowder and Permanent Armies', in M. Keen (ed.), *Medieval Warfare: A History* (Oxford, 1999), p. 291.

13 J.R. Mulryne and M. Shewring, *War, Literature and the Arts in Sixteenth-Century Europe* (New York, 1989); J.R. Hale, *Artists and Warfare in the Renaissance* (New Haven, CT, 1990); M. Murrin, *History and Warfare in Renaissance Epic* (Chicago, 1994).

14 M. Greenshields, *An Economy of Violence in Early Modern France: Crime and Justice in the Haute Auvergne, 1587–1664* (University Park, PA, 1995).

15 N.Z. Davis, 'The Rites of Violence: Religious Riot in Sixteenth-Century France', *Past and Present*, 59 (May 1973), pp. 51–91.

16 G. Philipps, 'To Cry "Home! Home!": Mutiny, Morale, and Indiscipline in Tudor Armies', *Journal of Military History*, 65 (2001), p. 333.

17 D.J.B. Trim, 'Ideology, Greed, and Social Discontent in Early Modern Europe: Mercenaries and Mutinies in the Rebellious Netherlands, 1568–1609', in J. Hathaway (ed.), *Rebellion, Repression, Reinvention: Mutiny in Comparative Perspective* (Westport, CT., 2001), p. 52.

18 M. Mallett, *Mercenaries and their Masters: Warfare in Renaissance Italy* (1974).

19 G.J. Millar, *Tudor Mercenaries and Auxiliaries, 1485–1547* (Charlottesville, VA, 1980).

20 D. Potter, 'Les Allemands et les armées françaises au XVIe siècle. Jean-Philippe Rhingrave, chef de lansquenets: étude suivie de sa correspondance en France, 1548–1566', *Francia*, 20 (1993), pp. 1–20 and 'The International Mercenary Market in the Sixteenth-Century: Anglo-French Competition in Germany, 1543–50', *English Historical Review* (1996), pp. 24–58. For an international comparison, D. Kolff, *Naukar, Rajput and Sepoy: The Ethnohistory of the Military Labour Market in Hindustan, 1450–1850* (Cambridge, 1990).

21 C. Bayley, *War and Society in Renaissance Florence* (Toronto, 1961).

22  J. Lindegern, 'The "Swedish Military State" 1560–1720', *Scandinavian Journal of History*, 10 (1985), pp. 305–36.

23  F.J. Baumgartner, *Louis XII* (Stroud, 1994), pp. 110–11.

24  R.W. Hoyle, *The Pilgrimage of Grace and the Politics of the 1530s* (Oxford, 2001), pp. 283–6.

25  R.I. Frost, 'Confessionalisation and the Army in the Polish-Lithuanian Commonwealth 1550–1667', in J. Bahlcke and A. Strohmeyer (eds), *Konfessionalisierung in Ostmitteleuropa* (Stuttgart, 1999), pp. 139–60.

26  J.R. Hale, 'Brescia and the Venetian Militia System in the Cinquecento', in *Armi e Cultura nel Bresciano, 1420–1870* (Brescia, 1981), pp. 97–119.

27  G. Parker, *The Army of Flanders and the Spanish Road, 1567–1659: the Logistics of Spanish Victory and Defeat in the Low Countries Wars* (Cambridge, 1972), pp. 185–206.

28  R.G. Asch, '"Wo der soldat hinkömbt, da ist alles sein": Military Violence and Atrocities in the Thirty Years' War Re-examined', *German History*, 18 (2000), pp. 291–309. On the sources, J. Theibault, 'The Rhetoric of Death and Destruction in the Thirty Years' War', *Social History*, 27 (1993), pp. 272–90. For a contemporary source, H.J.C. von Grimmelshausen, *An Unabridged Translation of Simplicius Simplicissimus*, translated by M. Adair (Lanham, MD, 1986). See, more generally, J.R. Ruff, *Violence in Early Modern Europe 1500–1800* (Cambridge, 2001), pp. 52–66.

29  S. Porter, *Destruction in the English Civil Wars* (1994).

30  P.H. Wilson, 'German Women and War, 1500–1800', *War in History*, 3 (1996), pp. 127–60 and 'The Military and Rural Society in the Early Modern Period', *German History*, 18 (2000), pp. 217–23.

31  B.S. Hall, *Weapons and Warfare in Renaissance Europe* (Baltimore, MD, 1997), p. 149.

32  H. Zmora, *State and Nobility in Early Modern Germany: The Knightly Feud in Franconia, 1440–1567* (Cambridge, 1997).

33  W. Monter, *Frontiers of Heresy: The Spanish Inquisition from the Basque Lands to Sicily* (Cambridge, 1990); J. Edwards, *The Spanish Inquisition* (Stroud, 1999).

34  J. Tedeschi, *The Prosecution of Heresy: Collected Studies on the Inquisition in Early Modern Italy* (Binghampton, NY, 1991); B. Gregory, *Salvation at Stake: Christian Martyrdom in Early Modern Europe* (Cambridge, MA, 1999).

35  R. Bonney (ed.), *The Rise of the Fiscal State in Europe, c. 1200–1815* (Oxford, 1999).

36  For example, J.U. Nef, *War and Human Progress: An Essay on the Rise of Industrial Civilization* (New York, 1950), pp. 23–41; W.H. NcNeill, *The Pursuit of Power: Technology, Armed Force, and Society since A.D. 1000* (Chicago, 1982), pp. 65–95; G. Parker, *The Military Revolution: Military Innovation and the Rise of the West, 1500–1800* (Cambridge, 1988), pp. 67–9.

37  J.R. Hale, *War and Society in Renaissance Europe, 1450–1620* (1985), pp. 248–51; K. DeVries, 'Gunpowder Weaponry and the Rise of the Early Modern State', *War in History*, 5 (1998), pp. 127–45.

38  D. Potter, *War and Government in the French Provinces: Picardy, 1470–1560* (Cambridge, 1993).

39  For deficiencies, see for example Mallet, 'Art of War', pp. 551–2; Potter, *War and Government in the French Provinces: Picardy, 1470–1560*, p. 158; J.B. Wood, *The King's Army. Warfare, Soldiers and Society during the Wars of Religion in France, 1562–1576* (Cambridge, 1996), pp. 305–10; R.W. Stewart, 'Arms and Expeditions: the Ordnance Office and the Assaults on Cadiz (1625) and the Isle of Rhé (1627)', in M. Fissel (ed.), *War and Government in Britain, 1598–1650* (Manchester, 1991), p. 126; Parrott, 'French Military Organization in the 1630s: the Failure of Richelieu's Ministry', *Seventeenth Century French Studies*, 9 (1987), pp. 156–67 and 'The Military Revolution in Early Modern Europe', *History Today*, vol. 42 (December 1992), p. 25.

40  G. Perjés, 'Army Provisioning, Logistics and Strategy in the Second Half of the 17th Century', *Acta Historica Academiae Scientiarum Hungaricae*, 16 (1970), pp. 1–51.

41  A.J.S. Nusbacher, 'Civil Supply in the Civil War: Supply of Victuals to the New Model Army on the Naseby Campaign, 1–14 June 1645', *English Historical Review*, 115 (2000), pp. 145–60, esp. pp. 159–60.

42  For a positive view, Mallet and J.R. Hale, *The Military Organisation of a Renaissance State: Venice, c.1400–1617* (Cambridge, 1984), pp. 101–52; J.S. Wheeler, 'The Logistics of the Cromwellian Conquest of Scotland 1650–1651', *War and Society*, 10 (1992), pp. 1–18, and 'English Financial Operations during the First Dutch War', *Journal of European Economic History*, 23 (1994), pp. 329–43.

43  C.R. Phillips, *Six Galleons for the King of Spain: Imperial Defence in the Early Seventeenth Century* (Baltimore, MD, 1992).

44  G. Rothenberg, *The Military Border in Croatia, 1740–1881. A Study of an Imperial Institution* (Chicago, 1966).

45  T. Kaiserfeld, 'Chemistry in the War Machine: Saltpetre Production in 18th Century Sweden', paper given at the Dibner Institute, April 1999.

### 3  A MILITARY REVOLUTION?

1  M. Roberts, *The Military Revolution, 1560–1660* (Belfast, 1956).

2  G. Parker, *The Military Revolution: Military Innovation and the Rise of the West, 1500–1800* (1988; 2nd edn, Cambridge, 1996), pp. 1–2.

3  ibid, pp. 24, 26; Parker, 'Warfare', in P. Burke (ed.), *The New Cambridge Modern History: vol. XIII Companion Volume* (Cambridge, 1979), p. 201; see also, for the development of Parker's thought, 'The Military Revolution, 1550–1660 – a Myth', *Journal of Modern History*, 47 (1976), pp. 195–314, and 'In Defence of *The Military Revolution*', in C.J. Rogers (ed.), *The Military Revolution Debate* (Boulder, CO, 1995), pp. 337–65, and, in a slightly different form, as the afterword in Parker, *Military Revolution* (2nd edn, Cambridge, 1996), pp. 154–75 and pp. 235–45. See also for fortifications, J.R. Hale, *Renaissance Fortification: Art or Engineering* (1977); C. Duffy, *Siege Warfare: The Fortress in the Early Modern World 1494–1660* (1979).

4  J.A. Lynn, 'The *Trace Italienne* and the Growth of Armies: The French Case', *Journal of Military History*, 55 (1991), pp. 297–330; M.S. Kingra, 'The *Trace Italienne* and the Military Revolution during the Eighty Years' War', *Ibid.*, 57 (1993), pp. 431–46.

5  M. Roberts, 'Gustav Adolf and the Art of War', in Roberts, *Essays in Swedish History* (1966), pp. 56–8.

6  It is possible to approach the debate through B.S. Hall and K. DeVries, 'The "Military Revolution" Revisited', *Technology and Culture*, 31 (1990), pp. 500–7; D.A. Parrott, 'The Military Revolution of Early Modern Europe', *History Today*, 42/12 (Dec. 1992), pp. 21–7; See also M. Duffy (ed.), *The Military Revolution and the State 1500–1800* (Exeter, 1980).

7  K. DeVries, *Medieval Military Technology* (Peterborough, Ontario, 1992), pp. 143–68, 'The Impact of Gunpowder Weaponry on Siege Warfare in the Hundred Years War', in I.A. Corfis and M. Wolfe (eds.), *The Medieval City under Siege* (Woodbridge, 1995), pp. 227–44, and 'The Use of Gunpowder Weaponry by and against Joan of Arc during the Hundred Years War', *War and Society*, 14 (1996), pp. 1–15; M. Mallett, 'Siegecraft in Late Fifteenth-Century Italy', and B.S. Hall, 'The Changing Face of Siege Warfare: Technology and Tactics in Transition', in Corfis and Wolfe (eds.), *Medieval City*, pp. 245–76; A. Ayton and J.L. Price, 'The Military Revolution from a Medieval Perspective', in Ayton and Price (eds.), *The Medieval Military Revolution: State, Society and Military Change in Medieval and Early Modern Europe* (1998), p. 16.

8 T. Esper, 'The Replacement of the Longbow by Firearms in the English Army', *Technology and Culture*, 6 (1965), pp. 382–93; Hall, 'Weapons of War and Late Medieval Cities: Technological Innovation and Tactical Changes', in E.B. Smith and M. Wolfe (eds.), *Technology and Resource Use in Medieval Europe* (Aldershot, 1997), pp. 189–90.

9 B.S. Hall, 'The Corning of Gunpowder and the Development of Firearms in the Renaissance', in B. Buchanan (ed.), *Gunpowder: The History of an International Technology* (Bath, 1996), pp. 87–120, quote p. 107.

10 M. Prestwich, *Armies and Warfare in the Middle Ages: The English Experience* (1996).

11 C.J. Rogers, 'Tracing the Changes in Gunpowder Recipes through the Early Fifteenth Century', paper given at Dibner Institute, 23 April 1999.

12 T. Richardson, 'Ballistic Testing of Historical Weapons', *Royal Armouries Yearbook*, 3 (1998), pp. 50–2; P. Krenn, P. Kalaus and B.S. Hall, 'Material Culture and Military History: Test-Firing Early Modern Small Arms', *Material History Review*, 42 (1995), pp. 101–9.

13 Guicciardini, *History of Florence*, edited by J.R. Hale (1964), p. 20.

14 S. Pepper, 'Castles and Cannon in the Naples Campaign of 1494–95', in D. Abulafia (ed.), *The French Descent into Renaissance Italy, 1494–95: Antecedents and Effects* (Aldershot, 1995), pp. 263–93.

15 K. Wiggins, *Anatomy of a Siege: King John's Castle, Limerick, 1642* (Woodbridge, 2001).

16 G. Phillips, *The Anglo-Scots Wars 1513–1550* (Woodbridge, 1999), pp. 17–18.

17 J.B. Wood, *The King's Army. Warfare, Soldiers and Society during the Wars of Religion in France, 1562–76* (Cambridge, 1996).

18 M. Vale, *War and Chivalry* (1981), pp. 114–19.

19 G. Parker and L.M. Smith (eds.), *The General Crisis of the Seventeenth Century* (1978).

20 J.R. Hale, 'Gunpowder and the Renaissance: An Essay in the History of Ideas', in Hale, *Renaissance War Studies* (1983), pp. 389–90.

21 See, for example, W. Beik, *Absolutism and Society in Seventeenth-Century France: State Power and Provincial Aristocracy in Languedoc* (Cambridge, 1986); A. Calabria and J. Marino (eds), *Good Government in Spanish Naples* (New York, 1990); T. Astarita, *The Continuity of Feudal Power. The Caracciolo Di Brienza in Spanish Naples* (Cambridge, 1991); G.W. Bernard (ed.), *The Tudor Nobility* (Manchester, 1992); L. Nussdorfer, *Civic Politics in the Rome of Urban VIII* (Princeton, NJ, 1992); J.M. Ferraro, *Family and Public Life in Brescia, 1580–1650: The Foundations of Power in the Venetian State* (Cambridge, 1993).

22 R.B. Litchfield, *Emergence of a Bureaucracy: The Florentine Patricians 1530–1790* (Princeton, NJ, 1986); C. Cipolla, *Miasmas and Disease: Public Health and the Environment in the Pre-Industrial Age* (New Haven, CT, 1992). For the Low Countries, see J.D. Tracy, *A Financial Revolution in the Habsburg Netherlands: Renten and Renteniers in the County of Holland, 1515–1565* (Berkeley, CA, 1985).

23 J.K. Brackett, *Criminal Justice and Crime in Late Renaissance Florence, 1537–1609* (Cambridge, 1992); J.C. Waquet, *Corruption: Ethics and Power in Florence 1600–1770* (Oxford, 1991).

24 A. Calabria, *The Cost of Empire: The Finances of the Kingdom of Naples in the Time of Spanish Rule* (Cambridge, 1991); D. Potter, *War and Government in the French Provinces: Picardy 1470–1560* (Cambridge, 1993), p. 232.

25 S. Carroll, *Noble Power during the French Wars of Religion: the Guise Affinity and the Catholic Cause in Normandy* (Cambridge, 1998), pp. 188–92.

26 B.S. Hall, *Weapons and Warfare in Renaissance Europe* (Baltimore, MD, 1997).

27 C.J. Rogers, 'The Military Revolutions of the Hundred Years War', in Rogers (ed.), *The Military Revolution Debate: Reading on the Military Transformation of Early Modern Europe* (Boulder, CO, 1995), p. 77.

28 J.I. Israel, *Conflicts of Empires: Spain, the Low Countries and the Struggle for World Supremacy, 1585–1713* (1997), pp. 45–62.

29 Parrott, *Richelieu's Army*, pp. 164–222, quote p. 220. See, for an earlier view, J. Lynn, 'Recalculating French Army Growth During the *Grand Siècle*, 1610–1715', *French Historical Studies*, 18 (1994), pp. 881–906.

30 J. Lindegren, 'Men, Money, and Means', in P. Contamine (ed.), *War and Competition between States* (Oxford, 2000), p. 130.

31 Phillips, *Anglo-Scots Wars*, p. 4.

32 R.H.C. Davis, *The Medieval Warhorse: Origin, Development and Redevelopment* (1989), pp. 110–15.

33 E. Furgol, 'The Civil Wars in Scotland', in J. Kenyon and J. Ohlmeyer (eds), *The Civil Wars* (Oxford, 1998), p. 46.

34 M.D. Pollak, *Military Architecture, Cartography and the Representation of the Early Modern European City* (Chicago, 1991).

35 J.R. Hale, 'Printing and Military Culture of Renaissance Venice', *Medievalia et Humanistica* (8 (1977), pp. 21–62; C. Wilkinson, 'Renaissance Treatises on Military Architecture and the Science of Mechanics', in J. Guillaume (ed.), *Les Traités d'architecture de la Renaissance* (Paris, 1988), pp. 467–76.

36 M.C. Fissel, *English Warfare 1511–1642* (2001), p. 285; D.A. Neill, 'Ancestral Voices: The Influence of the Ancients on the Military Thought of the Seventeenth and Eighteenth Centuries', *Journal of Military History*, 62 (1998), pp. 487–520. For valuable discussion about Machiavelli's use of the Classics and of Renaissance military thought, F. Gilbert, 'Machiavelli: The Renaissance in the Art of War', in P. Paret (ed.), *Makers of Modern Strategy: From Machiavelli to the Nuclear Age* (Princeton, NJ, 1986), pp. 11–31; M. Mallett, 'The Theory and Practice of Warfare in Machiavelli's Republic', in G. Brock, Q. Skinner and M. Viroli (eds), *Machiavelli and Republicanism* (Cambridge, 1993), pp. 173–80; T.R.W. Dubik, 'Is Machiavelli's Canon Spiked? Practical Reading in Military History', *Journal of Military History*, 61 (1997), pp. 7–30.

37 A.W. Crosby, *The Measure of Reality. Quantification and Western Society, 1250–1600* (Cambridge, 1997); B. Steele, 'Muskets and Pendulums: Benjamin Robins, Leonhard Euler and the Ballistics Revolution', *Technology and Culture*, 34 (1994), pp. 348–82.

38 J. Bennett and S. Johnston, *The Geometry of War 1500–1750*, catalogue of exhibition at Museum of the History of Science (Oxford, 1996), quote p. 16.

39 M.R. Smith and L. Marx (eds.), *Does Technology Drive History? The Dilemma of Technological Determinism* (Cambridge, MA, 1994).

40 S. Pepper, 'Siege Law, Siege Ritual, and the Symbolism of City Walls in Renaissance Europe', in J.D. Tracy (ed.), *City Walls: The Urban Enceinte in Global Perspective* (Cambridge, 2000), pp. 573, 601.

41 R.I. Frost, *The Northern Wars 1558–1721* (2000), pp. 310–12. See also W. Majewski, 'The Polish Art of War in the Sixteenth and Seventeenth Centuries', in J.K. Fedorowicz (ed.), *A Republic of Nobles: Studies in Polish History to 1864* (Cambridge, 1982), pp. 179–97.

42 O. Chaline, *La bataille de la Montagne Blanche: Un mystique chez les guerriers* (Paris, 2000).

## 4 EUROPEAN EXPANSION AND THE GLOBAL CONTEXT
### 1490–1578

1 E.W. Bovil, *The Battle of Alcazar* (1952); W. Cook, *The Hundred Years War for Morocco. Gunpowder and the Military Revolution in the Early Modern Muslim world* (Boulder, CO, 1994).

2 An excellent introduction is provided by G. Ágoston, 'Ottoman Warfare in Europe 1453–1826', in Black (ed.), *European Warfare 1453–1815* (1999), pp. 118–44. For the sixteenth century, M. Kunt and C. Woodhead (eds), *Süleyman the Magnificent and His Age: The Ottoman Empire in the Early Modern World* (Harlow, 1996). See also K. Çiçek (ed.) *The Great Ottoman-Turkish Civilisation* III (Ankara, 2000), pp. 719–60.

3 K. DeVries, 'Gunpowder Weapons at the Siege of Constantinople, 1453', in *War, Army and Society in the Eastern Mediterranean, 7th–16th Centuries* (Leiden, 1996).

4 F. Babinger, *Mehmed the Conqueror and his Time* (Princeton, NJ, 1978).

5 C.M. Kortepeter, 'Ottoman Imperial Policy and the Economy of the Black Sea Region in the Sixteenth Century', *Journal of the American Oriental Society*, 86 (1966), pp. 86–113.

6 A.C. Hess, 'The Evolution of the Ottoman Seaborne Empire in the Age of Oceanic Discoveries, 1453–1525', *American Historical Review*, 75 (1970), pp. 1892–1919, and 'The Ottoman Conquest of Egypt and the Beginning of the Sixteenth Century World War', *International Journal of Middle East Studies*, 4 (1973), pp. 55–76; P. Brummett, *Ottoman Seapower and Levantine Diplomacy in the Age of Discovery* (New York, 1994).

7 J.F. Guilmartin, 'The Military Revolution: Origins and First Tests Abroad', in Rogers (ed.), *Military Revolution Debate* (Boulder, CO, 1995), p. 308.

8 P. Fodor, 'Ottoman Policy towards Hungary, 1520–1541', *Acta Orientalia Academiae Scientiarum Hungaricae*, 45 (1991), pp. 285–305; G. David and P. Fodor (eds.), *Hungarian-Ottoman Military and Diplomatic Relations in the Age of Suleyman the Magnificent* (Budapest, 1994); G. Ágoston, 'Habsburgs and Ottomans: Defense, Military Change and Shifts in Power', *Ottoman Studies Association Bulletin*, 22 (1998), pp. 126–30.

9 S. Soucek, 'The Rise of the Barbarossas in North Africa', *Archivium Ottomanicum*, 3 (1971), pp. 238–50; A.C. Hess, *The Forgotten Frontier. A History of the Sixteenth-Century Ibero-African Frontier* (Chicago, 1978).

10 N. Housley, *The Later Crusades, 1274–1580 from Lyons to Alcazar* (Oxford, 1992).

11 C.R. Boxer, *The Portuguese Seaborne Empire, 1415–1825* (1969); B.W. Diffie and G.D. Winius, *Foundations of the Portuguese Empire, 1415–1580* (St. Paul, MN, 1977); M.N. Pearson, *The Portuguese in India* (Cambridge, 1987).

12 D. Ayalon, *Gunpowder and Firearms in the Mamluk Kingdom: A Challenge to a Medieval Society* (1956), p. 113.

13 H. Inalcik, 'The Socio-Political Effects of the Diffusion of Firearms in the Middle East', in V.J. Parry and M.E. Yapp (eds.), *War, Technology and Society in the Middle East* (1975), pp. 203, 205; S. Özbaran, 'The Ottoman Ottomans and the Portuguese in the Persian Gulf, 1534–1581', *Journal of Asian History*, 6 (1972), pp. 45–87.

14 S. Subrahmanyam, *The Portuguese Empire in Asia 1500–1700: A Political and Economic History* (Harlow, 1993).

15 G. Raudzens, 'Why Did Amerindian Defences Fail?', *War in History*, 3 (1996), pp. 331–52.

16 P. Powell, *Soldiers, Indians and Silver: The Northward Advance of New Spain, 1550–1600* (Berkeley, CA, 1952).

17 M.J. MacLeod and R. Wassertrom (eds), *Spaniards and Indians in Southeastern Mesoamerica: Essays on the History of Ethnic Relations* (Lincoln, NB, 1983); G.D. Jones, *The Conquest of the Last Maya Kingdom* (Stanford, CA, 1998).

18 L. de Armond, 'Frontier Warfare in Colonial Chile', *Pacific Historical Review*, 23 (1954), pp. 125–32; R.C. Padden, 'Cultural Change and Military Resistance in Araucanian Chile, 1550–1730', *Southwestern Journal of Anthropology* (1957), pp. 103–21.

19 I.K. Steele, *Warpaths: Invasions of North America* (New York, 1994), pp. 7–13, 33.

20 J. Thornton, *Africa and Africans in the Making of the Atlantic World, 1400–1680* (Cambridge, 1992), pp. 40–1.

21 P. Boucher, *Cannibal Encounters: Europeans and Island Caribs, 1492–1763* (Baltimore, MD, 1993).

22 J. Hemming, *Red Gold: The Conquest of the Brazilian Indians, 1500–1760* (2nd edn, 1995), pp. 70–96.

23 L.A. Newson, *Aboriginal and Spanish Colonial Trinidad: A Study in Culture Contact* (1976); F. Moya Pons, 'The Tainos of Hispaniola', *Caribbean Review*, 13 (1984), p. 47; N.D. Cook, *Demographic Collapse: Indian Peru, 1520–1620* (Cambridge, 1981).

24 A. Crosby, *The Columbian Exchange: Biological and Cultural Consequences of 1492* (Westport, CT, 1969) and *Ecological Imperialism: The Biological Expansion of Europe, 1500–1900* (1986); J.D. Daniels, 'The Indian Population of North America in 1492', *William and Mary Quarterly*, 49 (1992), pp. 298–320.

25 J.L. Phelan, *The Hispanization of the Philippines. Spanish Aims and Filipino Responses 1565–1700* (Madison, WI, 1967).

26 The literature on this subject can be approached via R. Hassig, 'War, Politics and the Conquest of Mexico', in Black (ed.), *War in the Early Modern World* (1999), pp. 27–35.

27 N. Wachtel, *The Vision of the Vanquished. The Spanish Conquest of Peru through Indian Eyes, 1530–1570* (Hassocks, 1977).

28 C. Hudson *et al.*, 'The Tristán de Luna Expedition, 1559–1561', in J.T. Milanich and S. Milbrath (eds), *First Encounters: Spanish Explorations in the Caribbean and the United States, 1492–1570* (Gainesville, FL, 1989), pp. 119–34.

29 M. Syarfl *et al.*, 'Sultan Mahmudsyah I and his Struggles against Portuguese Colonialism, 1511–1528', paper presented at Asian Historical Conference, 1998, p. 8.

30 Cook, 'The Cannon Conquest of Násrid Spain and the End of the Reconquista', *Journal of Military History*, 57 (1993), pp. 43–70, esp. 50–1, 69–70; A.D. McJoynt (ed.), *The Art of War in Spain: The Conquest of Granada* (Mechanicsburg, PA, 1995).

31 G. Ostrowski, *Muscovy and the Mongols: Cross-Cultural Influences on the Steppe Frontier, 1304–1589* (Cambridge, 1998), pp. 187–8.

32 J. Pelenki, *Russia and Kazan: Conquest and Imperial Ideology, 1438–1560s* (The Hague, 1974).

33 H. Inalcik, 'The Origin of the Ottoman–Russian Rivalry and the Don-Volga Canal, 1569', *Annales de l'Université d'Ankara*, 1 (1947), pp. 47–110; C. Lemercier-Quelquejay, 'Co-option of the Elites of Kabarda and Daghestan in the Sixteenth Century', in M.B. Broxup (ed.), *The North Caucasus Barrier: The Russian Advance towards the Muslim World* (1990), pp. 22–3, 39–40.

34 B.L. Walker, *The Conquest of Ainu Lands: Ecology and Culture in Japanese Expansion 1590–1800* (Berkeley, CA, 2001), pp. 27–47.

35 D.H. Peers (ed.), *Warfare and Empires: Contact and Conflict Between European and Non-European Military and Maritime Forces and Cultures* (Aldershot, 1997), p. xviii.

## 5 EUROPEAN WARFARE 1494–1559

1 M. Mallett, *Mercenaries and their Masters* (1974), p. 158.

2 A. Curry and M. Hughes (eds), *Arms, Armies and Fortifications in the Hundred Years' War* (Woodbridge, 1994).

3 G. Phillips, *The Anglo-Scots Wars 1513–1550. A Military History* (Woodbridge, 1999), p. 41.

4 M. Mallett, 'The Art of War', in T.A. Brady, H.A. Oberman and J.D. Tracy (eds), *Handbook of European History 1400–1600. Late Middle Ages, Renaissance and Reformation. I. Structures and Assertions* (Leiden, 1994), p. 535; S. Pepper, 'Castles and Cannon in the Naples Campaign of 1494–95', in D. Abulafia (ed.), *The French*

*Descent into Renaissance Italy 1494–95. Antecedents and Effects* (Aldershot, 1995), pp. 264, 290; M. Mallett and J.R. Hale, *The Military Organisation of a Renaissance State: Venice, c. 1400–1617* (Cambridge, 1984), pp. 81–7.

5 A.D. McJoynt (ed.), *The Art of War in Spain: The Conquest of Granada, 1481–1492* (1995), pp. 36–7.

6 G. DeGaury, *The Grand Captain, Gonzalo de Cordoba* (1955); D.M.R. Esson, 'The Italian Campaigns of Gonsalvo De Cordoba', *Army Quarterly*, 80 (1959–60), pp. 235–46, and 81 (1960–61), pp. 105–20; P. Stewart, 'The Santa Hermandad and the First Italian Campaign of Gonzalo de Córdova, 1495–1498', *Renaissance Quarterly*, 28 (1975), pp. 29–37.

7 Mallett, *Mercenaries and their Masters*, p. 110.

8 D. Miller, *The Landsknechts* (1976).

9 For a short recent introduction, W. Blockmans, *Emperor Charles V 1500–1558* (2001).

10 B.S. Hall, *Weapons and Warfare*, p. 181; A. Konstam, *Pavia 1525* (1996).

11 E.G. Gleason, 'Confronting New Realities. Venice and the Peace of Bologna, 1530', in J. Martin and D. Romano (eds), *Venice Reconsidered. The History and Civilization of an Italian City State, 1297–1797* (Baltimore, MD, 2000), pp. 168–84.

12 B.S. Hall, 'The Changing Face of Siege Warfare: Technology and Tactics in its Transition', in I. Corfis and M. Wolfe (eds), *The Medieval City under Siege* (Woodbridge, 1994), pp. 260–2. On fortifications see also J.R. Hale, 'The Early Development of the Bastion: An Italian Chronology, *c.*1450–*c.*1534', in J.R. Hale, J.R.L. Highfield and B. Smalley (eds), *Europe in the Late Middle Ages* (1965), pp. 644–94; C.J. Duffy, *Siege Warfare: The Fortress in the Early Modern World, 1494–1660* (1979); and S. Pepper and N. Adams, *Firearms and Fortifications: Military Architecture and Siege Warfare in Sixteenth-Century Siena* (Chicago, 1986).

13 C. Cruickshank, *Army Royal: Henry VIII's Invasion of France* (Oxford, 1971).

14 N. Barr, *Flodden 1513* (Stroud, 2001).

15 M. Merriman, *The Rough Wooings: The Struggle for the Marriage of Mary Queen of Scots* (Edinburgh, 2000), and G. Phillips, 'Strategy and its Limits; The Anglo-Scots Wars 1480–1550', *War in History*, 6 (1999), pp. 396–416.

16 Phillips, 'In the Shadow of Flodden: Tactics, Technology and Scottish Military Effectiveness, 1514–1550', *Scottish Historical Review*, 77 (1998), pp. 162–82.

17 B. Scribner and G. Benecke, *The German Peasant War of 1525 – New Viewpoints* (1979); P. Blickle, *The Revolution of 1525: The German Peasants' War from a New Perspective* (Baltimore, MD, 1981); T. Scott and Scribner (eds), *The German Peasants' War: A History in Documents* (1991).

18 E. Muir, *Mad Blood Stirring: Vendetta and Factions in Friuli during the Renaissance* (Baltimore, MD, 1993).

19 J.M. Stayer, 'Christianity in One City: Anabaptist Münster, 1534–1535', in H.J. Hillerbrand (ed.), *Radical Tendencies in the Reformation: Divergent Perspectives* (Kirkville, MO, 1988), pp. 117–34.

20 M.L. Bush, *The Pilgrimage of Grace: A Study of the Rebel Armies of October 1536* (Manchester, 1996); M.L. Bush and D. Bownes, *The Defeat of the Pilgrimage of Grace: A Study of the Postpardon Revolts of December 1536 to March 1537 and Their Effect* (Hull, 1999).

21 D. Loades, *The Mid-Tudor Crisis, 1545–1565* (1992).

22 Robertson, *History* (1782 edn.), I, 134–5.

23 T.F. Arnold, 'Fortifications and the Military Revolution: The Gonzaga Experience, 1530–1630', in Rogers (ed.), *Military Revolution Debate*, p. 206.

24 J.M. Black, *Western Warfare 1882–1975* (2002).

25 J.B. Wood, *The King's Army* (Cambridge, 1996), pp. 41–2.

## 6 EUROPEAN WARFARE 1560–1617

1 M.P. Holt, 'Putting Religion Back into the Wars of Religion', *French Historical Studies*, 18 (1993), pp. 523–51.

2 Earlier work can be followed through M.P. Holt, *The French Wars of Religion 1562–1629* (Cambridge, 1995) and R.J. Knecht, *The French Civil Wars, 1562–1598* (Harlow, 2000). On the warfare, J.B. Wood, *The Army of the King: Warfare, Soldiers, and Society during the Wars of Religion in France, 1562–1576* (Cambridge, 1996). On the crucial regional and local dimension, P. Benedict, *Rouen during the Wars of Religion* (Cambridge, 1981), B. Diefendorf, *Beneath the Cross: Catholics and Huguenots in Sixteenth-Century Paris* (Oxford, 1991) and P. Roberts, *A City in Conflict: Troyes during the Wars of Religion* (Manchester, 1996). For primary sources, I. Roy (ed.), *Blaise de Monluc: The Habsburg-Valois Wars and the French Wars of Religion* (1971) and D. Potter (ed.), *The French Wars of Religion: Selected Documents* (1997).

3 M. Wolfe, *The Conversion of Henry IV: Politics, Power and Religious Belief in Early Modern France* (Cambridge, MA, 1993); S.A. Finley-Croswhite, *Henry IV and the Towns: The Pursuit of Legitimacy in French Urban Society, 1589–1610* (Cambridge, 1999).

4 H.A. Lloyd, *The Rouen Campaign, 1590–1592: Politics, Warfare and the Early Modern State* (Oxford, 1973).

5 D. Buisseret, *Henry IV* (1984); M. Greengrass, *France in the Age of Henry IV: The Struggle for Stability* (2nd edn, 1994).

6 G. Parker, *The Dutch Revolt* (2nd edn, 1984), *Spain and the Netherlands* (2nd edn, 1990), and *The Grand Strategy of Philip II* (New Haven, CT, 1998); M.V. Gelderen, *The Political Thought of the Dutch Revolt 1555–1590* (Cambridge, 1992); M.C. Waxman, 'Strategic Terror: Philip II and Sixteenth Century Warfare', *War in History*, 4 (1997), pp. 339–47.

7 G. Parker, *The Army of Flanders and the Spanish Road, 1567–1659* (Cambridge, 1972).

8 P.C. Allen, *Philip III and the Pax Hispanica, 1598–1621: The Failure of Grand Strategy* (New Haven, CT, 2000).

9 F. González de León and G. Parker, 'The Grand Strategy of Philip II and the Revolt of the Netherlands, 1559–1584', in P. Benedict, G. Marnef, H.V. Nierop and M. Venard (eds.), *Reformation, Revolt and Civil War in France and the Netherlands 1555–1585* (Amsterdam, 1999), pp. 215–32, and also in G. Darby (ed.), *The Origins and Development of the Dutch Revolt* (2001), pp. 107–32, quote p. 125.

10 J.M. Hill, *Celtic Warfare, 1595–1763* (Edinburgh, 1986), 'The Distinctiveness of Gaelic Warfare, 1400–1750', *European History Quarterly*, 22 (1992), pp. 323–45, and 'The Origins and Development of the "Highland Charge" *c.*1560 to 1646', *Militärgeschichtliche Mitteilungen*, 53 (1994), pp. 295–307.

11 C. Falls, *Elizabeth's Irish Wars* (1950).

12 H. Kamen, *Philip of Spain* (New Haven, 1997), pp. 175–6.

13 B.L. Davies, 'The Development of Russian Military Power 1453–1815', in Black (ed.), *European Warfare 1453–1815* (1999), pp. 158–9, and 'The Foundations of Muscovite Military Power, 1453–1613', in F.W. Kagan and R. Higham (eds) *The Military History of Tsarist Russia* (2002), pp. 10–30.

14 M. Roberts, *The Early Vasas: A History of Sweden 1523–1611* (Cambridge, 1968), pp. 369–84.

15 R.I. Frost, *The Northern Wars 1558–1721* (2000) has superseded S.P. Oakley, *War and Peace in the Baltic 1560–1790* (1992). See also C. Dunning, *Russia's First Civil War: The Time of Troubles and the Founding of the Romanov Dynasty* (Penn State, 2001).

16 Kamen, *Philip of Spain*, p. 288.

17 M. Perrie, *Pretenders and Popular Monarchism in Early Modern Russia. The False Tsars of the Time of Troubles* (Cambridge, 1995).

18 N.T. MacCaffrey, *Elizabeth I: War and Politics, 1588–1603* (Princeton, NJ, 1992); J.B. Wood, 'The Royal Army During the Early Wars of Religion, 1559–1576', in M.P. Holt (ed.), *Society and Institutions in Early Modern France* (Athens, GA, 1991), p. 31.

19 Hall, *Weapons and Warfare*, p. 213; F.J. Baumgartner, 'The Final Demise of the Medieval Knight in France', in J. Friedman (ed.), *Regnum, Religio et Ratio: Essays Presented to Robert M. Kingdon* (Kirksville, MO, 1987), pp. 9–17; R. Love, 'All the King's Horsemen: The Equestrian Army of Henri IV, 1585–1598', *Sixteenth Century Journal*, 22 (1991), pp. 516–20.

20 I would like to thank Gervase Phillips for letting me read his unpublished paper, 'Of Nimble Service': Technology, Equestrianism and the Cavalry Arm of Early Modern Western European Armies'. For a detailed examination of Dutch infantry and cavalry tactics, J.P. Puype, 'Victory at Nieuwpoort', 2 July 1600, in M. van der Hoeven (ed.) *Exercise of Arms: Warfare in the Netherlands, 1568–1648* (Leiden, 1997), pp. 69–112.

21 E.H. Dickerman, 'Henry IV and the Juliers-Cleves Crisis: The Psychohistorical Aspects', *French Historical Studies*, 8 (1974), pp. 626–53; E.H. Dickerman and A.M. Walker, 'The Choice of Hercules: Henry IV as Hero', *Historical Journal*, 39 (1996), pp. 315–37.

22 P. Brightwell, 'The Spanish System and the Twelve Years' Truce', *English Historical Review*, 89 (1974), pp. 270–92.

## 7 EUROPEAN WARFARE 1618–60

1 The best short introduction is R.G. Asch, *The Thirty Years' War: The Holy Roman Empire and Europe 1618–1648* (Basingstoke, 1997). See also G. Parker *et al.*, *The Thirty Years' War* (2nd edn, 1997), pp. 35–9. For earlier works, see, in particular, S.H. Steinberg, *The 'Thirty Years' War' and the Conflict for European Hegemony, 1600–1660* (1967); J.V. Polisensky, *The Thirty Years' War* (1971); and G. Benecke, *Germany in the Thirty Years' War* (1978). For the account of an officer who served Christian IV and Gustavus Adolphus, W.S. Brockington (ed.), *Monro: His Expedition with the Worthy Scots Regiment Called Mackeys* (Westport, CT, 1999).

2 G. Mortimer, 'Did Contemporaries Recognize a "Thirty Years' War"?', *English Historical Review*, 116 (2001), p. 135.

3 G. Parker, 'In Defense of *The Military Revolution*', in C.J. Rogers (ed.), *The Military Revolution Debate* (Boulder, CO, 1995), p. 337.

4 R.J.W. Evans, *The Making of the Habsburg Monarchy 1550–1700: An Interpretation* (Oxford, 1979).

5 P. Brightwell, 'Spain and Bohemia: The Decision to Intervene, 1619', *European Studies Review*, 12 (1982), pp. 117–41 and 'Spain, Bohemia and Europe, 1619–21', ibid., pp. 371–99.

6 G. Mann, *Wallenstein* (1976).

7 P.D. Lockhart, *Denmark in the Thirty Years' War 1618–1648* (Cranbury, NJ, 1996), p. 148.

8 S.P. Oakley, *War and Peace in the Baltic 1560–1790* (1992).

9 M. Roberts, *The Swedish Imperial Experience* (Cambridge, 1979), pp. 28–36.

10 A. Aberg, 'The Swedish Army from Lützen to Narva', in Roberts (ed.), *Sweden's Age of Greatness* (1973), p. 283; Roberts, *Gustavus Adolphus* (1992), p. 106.

11 R.F. Weigley, *The Age of Battles: The Quest for Decisive Warfare from Breitenfeld to Waterloo* (Bloomington, IN, 1991).

12 W.C. Fuller, *Strategy and Power in Russia, 1600–1914* (New York, 1992), p. 31.

13 D. Croxton, 'La Stratégie et La "Révolution Militaire" dans La Guerre de Trente Ans: une Révolution Manquée?', in *Nouveaux Regards sur la Guerre de Trente Ans*, Actes du colloque international, École militaire, lundi 6 avril 1998. Centre d'études d'histoire de la Défense, p. 31.

14 R.G. Asch, 'Warfare in the Age of the Thirty Years' War 1598–1648', in Black (ed.), *European Warfare 1453–1815* (1999), pp. 58–9.

15 D. Croxton, 'A Territorial Imperative? The Military Revolution, Strategy and Peacemaking in the Thirty Years' War', *War in History*, 5 (1998), pp. 266–72 and *Peacemaking in Early Modern Europe: Cardinal Mazarin and the Congress of Westphalia, 1643–1648* (Selinsgrove, 1999), pp. 59–71.

16 Y.N. Harari, 'Strategy and Supply in Fourteenth-Century Western European Invasion Campaigns', *Journal of Military History*, 64 (2000), pp. 297–334, esp. p. 333.

17 For an English abridgement of the terms, G. Symcox (ed.), *War, Diplomacy and Imperialism, 1618–1763* (1974), pp. 39–62.

18 T. McIntosh, *Urban Decline in Early Modern Germany: Schwäbisch Hall and its Region, 1650–1750* (Chapel Hill, NC, 1997).

19 J. Theibault, *German Villages in Crisis. Rural life in Hesse-Kassel and the Thirty Years' War, 1580–1720* (Atlantic Highlands, NJ, 1995), and 'The Demography of the Thirty Years' War Re-visited: Günther Franz and His Critics', *German History*, 15 (1997), pp. 1–21.

20 M.P. Gutmann, *War and Rural Life in the Early Modern Low Countries* (Princeton, NJ, 1980), pp. 200–8.

21 A.D. Lublinskaya, *French Absolutism: the Crucial Phase, 1620–1629* (Cambridge, 1968); D. Parker, *La Rochelle and the French Monarchy: Conflict and Order in Seventeenth-Century France* (1980); J. Bergin, *The Rise of Richelieu* (New Haven, CT, 1991); C. Desplat, 'Louis XIII and the Union of Béarn to France', in M. Greengrass (ed.), *Conquest and Coalescence* (1991), pp. 68–83; A. James, 'Huguenot Militancy and the Seventeenth-Century Wars of Religion', in R.A. Mentzer and A. Spicer (eds), *Society and Culture in the Huguenot World 1559–1685* (Cambridge, 2002), pp. 209–23.

22 D. Parrott, 'The Mantuan Succession, 1627–1631: A Sovereignty Dispute in Early Modern Europe', *English Historical Review*, 112 (1997), pp. 20–65, and 'A *prince souverain* and the French Crown: Charles de Nevers, 1580–1637', in R. Oresko, G.C. Gibbs and H.M. Scott (eds), *Royal and Republican Sovereignty in Early Modern Europe: Essays in Honour of Professor Ragnhild Hatton* (Cambridge, 1997), pp. 149–87.

23 D. Parrott, *Richelieu's Army: War, Government and Society in France, 1624–1642* (Cambridge, 2001), p. 95.

24 R.A. Stradling, 'Olivares and the Origins of the Franco-Spanish War, 1627–1635', *English Historical Review*, 101 (1986), pp. 68–94; D. Parrott, 'The Causes of the Franco-Spanish War of 1635–59', in Black (ed.), *The Origins of War in Early Modern Europe* (Edinburgh, 1987), pp. 72–111.

25 R.A. Stradling, *Spain's Struggle for Europe* (1994), pp. 197–212.

26 O. Ranum, *The Fronde: A French Revolution 1648–1652* (New York, 1993).

27 J.H. Elliott, *Revolt of the Catalans* (Cambridge, 1963).

28 D. Parrott, 'Strategy and Tactics in the Thirty Years' War: the "Military Revolution"', *Militärgeschichtliche Mitteilungen* 18 (1985), reprinted in C.J. Rogers (ed.), *The Military Revolution Debate*, pp. 227–51, p. 95.

29 G. Raudzens, 'Military Revolution or Maritime Evolution? Military Superiorities or Transportation Advantages as Main Causes of European Colonial Conquests to 1788', *Journal of Military History*, 63 (1999), p. 641.

30 J.I. Israel, 'Olivares, the Cardinal-Infante and Spain's Strategy in the Low Countries (1635–1643): the Road to Rocroi' in R.L. Kagan and G. Parker (eds),

*Spain, Europe and the Atlantic World. Essays in Honour of John H. Elliott* (Cambridge, 1995), pp. 267–95, and *Conflicts of Empires. Spain, the Low Countries and the Struggle for World Supremacy, 1585–1713* (1997), pp. 682–91.

31  M. Bennett, *The Civil Wars in Britain and Ireland 1638–1651* (Oxford, 1997).

32  M.C. Fissell, *The Bishops' Wars: Charles I's Campaigns Against Scotland, 1638–1640* (Cambridge, 1994).

33  For example, J. Wroughton, *An Unhappy Civil War* (Bath, 1999).

34  C. Carlton, *Going to the Wars: The Experience of the British Civil Wars, 1638–1651* (1992).

35  R. Hutton and W. Reeves, 'Sieges and Fortifications', in J. Kenyon and J. Ohlmeyer (eds), *The Civil Wars. A Military History of England, Scotland and Ireland, 1638–60* (Oxford, 1998).

36  J.S. Wheeler, *Cromwell in Ireland* (Dublin, 1999).

37  J. Ohlmeyer (ed.), *Ireland from Independence to Occupation 1638–1660* (Cambridge, 1995), and 'The Wars of religion, 1603–1660', in T. Bartlett and K. Jeffery (eds), *A Military History of Ireland* (Cambridge, 1996), pp. 163–87.

38  E.J. Cowan, *Montrose for Covenant and King* (1977).

39  I. Gentles, *The New Model Army in England, Ireland and Scotland, 1645–1653* (Oxford, 1992).

40  R. Hainsworth, *The Swordsmen in Power: War and Politics under the English Republic, 1649–1660* (Stroud, 1997).

41  This period can best be approached through R.I. Frost, *After the Deluge: Poland-Lithuania and the Second Northern War* (Cambridge, 1993) and *The Northern Wars*, pp. 156–91. For the important Cossack dimension, C. O'Brien, *Muscovy and Ukraine: From the Pereiaslav Agreement to the Truce of Andrusovo 1654–1667* (Berkeley, CA, 1963), J. Basarab, *Pereiaslav 1654: A Historiographical Study* (Edmonton, 1982), and M. Hrushevsky, *History of Ukraine-Rus'. VII. The Cossack Age to 1625* (Edmonton, 1999). For an important battle, Y. Tys-Krokhmaliuk, 'The Victory at Konotop', *Ukrainian Review*, 613 (1959), pp. 34–45.

42  G. Hanlon, *The Twilight of a Military Tradition. Italian Aristocrats and European Conflicts, 1560–1800* (1998), pp. 134–42.

43  J. Chagniot, *Guerre et Société à L'Époque Modern* (Paris, 2001), p. 83.

44  Y.-M. Bercé, *History of Peasant Revolts: The Social Roots of Rebellion in Early Modern France* (Ithaca, NY, 1990).

45  Parrott, *Richelieu's Army*.

46  P. Lenihan, *Confederate Catholics at War, 1641–49* (Cork, 2001).

47  C. Tilly, *Coercion, Capital and European States, AD 990–1990* (Cambridge MA, 1990).

48  W. Beik, *Urban Protest in Seventeenth-Century France: The Culture of Retribution* (Cambridge, 1997).

49  For an argument for indecisiveness, R.F. Weigley, *The Age of Battles: The Quest for Decisive Warfare from Breitenfeld to Waterloo* (Bloomington, IN, 1991).

50  Black, *European Warfare, 1660–1815* (New Haven, CT, 1994), pp. 67–86; Croxton, '"The Prosperity of Arms Is Never Continual": Military Intelligence, Surprise, and Diplomacy in 1640s Germany', *Journal of Military History*, 64 (2000), p. 1003.

## 8  NAVAL DEVELOPMENTS

1  The best introduction to the subject, particularly good on shifts in the maritime power structure, is J. Glete, *Warfare at Sea, 1500–1650. Maritime Conflicts and the Transformation of Europe* (2000). For the statistical background, see J. Glete, *Navies and Nations: Warships, Navies and State Building in Europe and America, 1500–1860* (Stockholm, 1993).

2 Yet again, G. Parker, *The Grand Strategy of Philip II* (New Haven, CT, 1998) is an important work.
3 B. Lavery, *The Arming and Fitting of English Ships of War, 1600–1815* (1987).
4 J.D. Tracy (ed.), *The Rise of Merchant Empires: Long-Distance Trade in the Early Modern World, 1350–1750* (Cambridge, 1990) and J.D. Tracy (ed.), *The Political Economy of Merchant Empires* (Cambridge, 1991).
5 R. Gardiner and J. Morrison (eds), *The Age of the Galley: Mediterranean Oared Vessels Since Pre-Classical Times* (1995).
6 R. Gardiner and R.W. Unger (eds), *Cogs, Caravels and Galleons: The Sailing Ship, 1000–1650* (1994).
7 C.R. Boxer, *The Portuguese Seaborne Empire, 1415–1825* (1973).
8 C. Cipolla, *Guns and Sails in the Early Phases of European Expansion 1400–1700* (1965).
9 N.A.M. Rodger, *The Safeguard of the Sea: A Naval History of Britain, Vol. I, 660–1649* (1997).
10 A. de Silva Saturnino Monteiro, 'The Decline and Fall of Portuguese Seapower, 1583–1663', *Journal of Military History*, 65 (2001), pp. 19–20.
11 L. Levathes, *When China Ruled the Seas: The Treasure Fleet of the Dragon Throne, 1405–1433* (Oxford, 1994).
12 G. Parker, 'The *Dreadnought* Revolution of Tudor England', *Mariner's Mirror*, 82 (1996), pp. 269–300.
13 K. DeVries, 'The Effectiveness of Fifteenth-Century Shipboard Artillery', *Mariner's Mirror*, 84 (1998), pp. 389–99, esp. p. 396.
14 R.W. Unger, *The Art of Medieval Technology: Images of Noah the Shipbuilder* (New Brunswick, NJ, 1991); I. Fried, *The Good Ship: Ships, Shipbuilding and Technology in England, 1200–1520* (Baltimore, MD, 1995).
15 A.B. Caruana, *The History of English Sea Ordnance, 1523–1875. I, The Age of Evolution, 1523–1715* (Rotherfield, 1994). For the list see Parker review of D. Loades's 'The Tudor Navy', *Sixteenth Century*, 24 (1993), p. 1022.
16 N.A.M. Rodger, 'The Development of Broadside Gunnery, 1450–1650', *Mariner's Mirror*, 82 (1996), pp. 301–24.
17 J.F. Guilmartin, *Gunpowder and Galleys: Changing Technology and Mediterranean Warfare at Sea in the Sixteenth Century* (Cambridge, 1974).
18 S. Rose, 'Islam Versus Christendom: The Naval Dimension, 1000–1600', *Journal of Military History*, 63 (1999), p. 577.
19 F.C. Lane, 'Naval Actions and Fleet Organisation, 1499–1502', in J.R. Hale (ed.), *Renaissance Venice* (1973), pp. 146–73.
20 J.H. Pryor, *Geography, Technology and War: Studies in the Maritime History of the Mediterranean, 649–1571* (Cambridge, 1988).
21 A.C. Hess, 'The Evolution of the Ottoman Seaborne Empire in the Age of the Oceanic Discoveries, 1453–1525', *American Historian Review*, 74 (1970), pp. 1892–1919.
22 Guilmartin, *Gunpowder*, pp. 42–56.
23 E. Bradford, *The Great Siege* (1961); Guilmartin, *Gunpowder*, pp. 176–93.
24 Guilmartin, *Gunpowder*, pp. 221–52, and 'The Tactics of the Battle of Lepanto clarified: The Impact of Social, Economic, and Political Factors on Sixteenth Century Galley Warfare', in C.L. Symonds (ed.), *New Aspects of Naval History* (Annapolis, MD, 1981), pp. 41–65. For recent Turkish work, see I. Bostan, 'Inebahti Deniz Savasi', in *Türkiye Dinayet Vakfi Islam Ansiklopedisi* vol. 22 (Istanbul, 2000), pp. 287–9. I owe this reference to Gabor Ágoston.
25 C. Imber, 'The Reconstruction of the Ottoman Fleet after the Battle of Lepanto', in Imber, *Studies in Ottoman History and Law* (Istanbul, 1996), pp. 85–101.
26 Guilmartin, *Gunpowder*, pp. 253–73.

27  C. Imber, *The Ottoman Empire, 1300–1650: The Structure of Power* (2002).

28  Glete, *Warfare at Sea*, pp. 120–4.

29  J.D. Tracy, 'Herring Wars: The Habsburg Netherlands and the Struggle for Control of the North Sea, *c.* 1520–1560', *Sixteenth Century Journal*, 24 (1993), pp. 267–71.

30  C. Martin and G. Parker, *The Spanish Armada* (1988); M.J. Rodríguez-Salgado, *Armada, 1588–1988* (1988); F. Fernandez-Armesto, *The Spanish Armada: The Experience of War in 1588* (Oxford, 1988); M.J. Rodríguez-Salgado and S. Adams (eds), *England, Spain and the Gran Armada, 1585–1604* (Edinburgh, 1991); Rodger, *The Safeguard of the Sea*, pp. 254–71.

31  D. Loades, *The Tudor Navy: An Administrative, Political and Military History* (Aldershot, 1992); K.R. Andrews, *Elizabethan Privateering: English Privateering during the Spanish War, 1585–1603* (Cambridge, 1964); R.T. Spence, *The Privateering Earl: George Clifford, 3rd Earl of Cumberland, 1558–1605* (Stroud, 1995).

32  J.R. Bruijn, *The Dutch Navy of the Seventeenth and Eighteenth Centuries* (Columbia, SC, 1993).

33  C.R. Phillips, *Six Galleons for the King of Spain: Imperial Defence in the Early Seventeenth Century* (Baltimore, MD, 1992); D. Goodman, *Spanish Naval Power, 1589–1665: Reconstruction and Defeat* (Cambridge, 1996).

34  J.I. Israel, *Dutch Primacy in World Trade* (Oxford, 1989).

35  R.A. Stradling, *The Armada of Flanders: Spanish Maritime Policy and European War, 1568–1668* (Cambridge, 1992).

36  Israel, *The Dutch Republic and the Hispanic World, 1606–1661* (Oxford, 1982).

37  A. James, *The Ship of State: Naval Affairs in Early Modern France, 1572–1661* (Woodbridge, 2002).

38  K.R. Andrews, *Ships, Money and Politics: Seafaring and Naval Enterprise in the Reign of Charles I* (Cambridge, 1991).

39  B. Capp, *Cromwell's Navy: The Fleet and the English Revolution* (Oxford, 1989).

40  S.C.A. Pincus, *Protestantism and Patriotism: Ideologies and the Making of English Foreign Policy, 1650–1685* (Cambridge, 1996).

41  J.R. Jones, *The Anglo-Dutch Wars of the Seventeenth Century* (1996).

42  R. Harding, *Seapower and Naval Warfare 1650–1830* (1999), pp. 73–5; W. Maltby, 'Politics, Professionalism and the Evolution of Sailing Ships Tactics', in J.A. Lynn (ed.), *Tools of War: Instruments, Ideas and Institutions of Warfare, 1445–1871* (Chicago, 1990), pp. 53–73, quote p. 53; M.A.J. Palmer, 'The Military Revolution Afloat: The Era of the Anglo-Dutch Wars', *War in History*, 4 (1997), pp. 123–49.

43  C. Imber, 'The Navy of Süleyman the Magnificent', *Archivum Ottomanicum*, 6 (1980), pp. 211–82.

44  Glete, *Warfare at Sea, 1500–1650*, e.g. pp. 186–7; C.R. Phillips, review of Glete, *Warfare at Sea, 1500–1650*, in *Journal of Military History*, 64 (2000), p. 1144.

45  Bruijn, 'States and Their Navies from the Late Sixteenth to the End of the Eighteenth Centuries', in P. Contamine (ed.), *War and Competition between States*, part of the series 'The Origins of the Modern State in Europe: 13th to 18th Centuries' (Oxford, 2000), pp. 78–9.

46  James, *Ship of State*, conclusion.

47  A. Pérontin-Dumon, 'The Pirate and the Emperor: Power and the Law on the Seas, 1450–1850', in Tracy (ed.), *Political Economy*, pp. 196–227.

48  P. Earl, *Corsairs of Malta and Barbary* (1970); W. Bracewell, *The Uskoks of Senj: Piracy, Banditry and Holy War in the Sixteenth Century Adriatic* (Ithaca, NY, 1992); A. Tenenti, *Piracy and the Decline of Venice, 1580–1615* (Berkeley, CA, 1967).

49  V. Ostapchuck, 'Five Documents from the Topkapi Palace Archive on the Ottoman Defence of the Black Sea Against the Cossacks', *Journal of Ottoman Studies*, 2 (1987), pp. 49–104; C. Imber, *The Ottoman Empire, 1300–1650: The Structure of Power* (2002).

50  See also K.R. Andrews, *The Spanish Caribbean: Trade and Plunder, 1530–1630* (New Haven, CT, 1978); D.D. Hebb, *Piracy and the English Government, 1616–1642* (Aldershot, 1994).

51  J.H. Ohlmeyer, *Civil War and Restoration in the Three Stuart Kingdoms: The Career of Randal MacDonnell, Marquis of Antrim, 1609–1683* (Cambridge, 1993), p. 230.

52  Palmer, '"The Soul's Right Hand": Command and Control in the Age of Fighting Sail, 1652–1827', *Journal of Military History*, 61 (1997), pp. 679–706.

## 9 EUROPEAN EXPANSION AND THE GLOBAL CONTEXT
### 1578–1660

1  G. Parker, *Military Revolution* (2nd edn), p. 175.

2  G. Ágoston, 'Habsburgs and Ottomans: Military Change and Shifts in Power', *Ottoman Studies Association Bulletin*, 22 (1998), pp. 126–41.

3  C. Duffy, *Siege Warfare: The Fortress in the Early Modern World* (1996), p. 195.

4  G.E. Rothenberg, 'Christian Insurrections in Ottoman Dalmatia 1580–96', *Slavonic and East European Review*, 40 (1961), p. 141.

5  C. Finkel, *The Administration of Warfare: Ottoman Campaigns in Hungary, 1593–1606* (Vienna, 1988) and 'The Costs of Ottoman Warfare and Defence', *Byzantinische Forschungen*, 16 (1990), p. 96.

6  H. Inalcik, 'The Socio-Political Effects of the Diffusion of Firearms in the Middle East', in V.J. Parry and M.E. Yapp (eds), *War, Technology and Society in the Middle East* (1975), pp. 199–200; G. Ágoston, 'Ottoman Gunpowder Technology and War Industry in the Ottoman Empire, 1450–1700', paper given at Dibner Institute, 24 April 1999; C. Imber, *The Ottoman Empire, 1300–1650: The Structure of Power* (2002).

7  P. Brummett, 'The River Crossing: Breaking Points (Metaphorical and "Real") in Ottoman Mutiny', in J. Hathaway (ed.), *Rebellion, Repression, Reinvention. Mutiny in Comparative Perspective* (Westport, CT, 2001), pp. 222–3.

8  K.M. Setton, *Venice, Austria, and the Ottomans in the Seventeenth Century* (Philadelphia, 1991).

9  G.D. Winius, *The Fatal History of Portuguese Ceylon: Transition to Dutch Rule* (Cambridge, MA, 1971).

10  M. Ricklefs, 'Balance and Military Innovation in Seventeenth-Century Java', *History Today*, 40 (1990), pp. 40–6.

11  G.A. Lantzeff and R.A. Pierce, *Eastward to Empire: Exploration and Conquest on the Russian Open Frontier, to 1750* (Montréal, 1973); T. Armstrong, *Yermak's Campaign in Siberia* (1975); J. Forsyth, *A History of the Peoples of Siberia: Russia's North Asian Colony 1581–1990* (Cambridge, 1992), pp. 26–83.

12  D.J.B. Shaw, 'Southern Frontiers of Muscovy, 1550–1700', in J. Bater and R.A. French (eds), *Studies in Russian Historical Geography I* (1983), pp. 122–6; C.B. Stevens, *Soldiers on the Steppe: Army Reform and Social Change in Early Modern Russia* (De Kalb, IL, 1995). More generally, see W.H. McNeill, *Europe's Steppe Frontier, 1500–1800* (Chicago, 1964).

13  P.M. Malone, *The Skulking Way of War: Technology and Tactics among the New England Indians* (Lanham, MD, 1991); B. Given, 'The Iroquois and Native Firearms', in B.A. Cox (ed.), *Native Peoples, Native Lands. Canadian Indians, Inuit and Metis* (Ottawa, 1987), pp. 3–13; T.B. Abler, 'European Technology and the Art of War in Iroquoia', in D.C. Tkaczuk and B.C. Vivian (eds), *Cultures in Conflict: Current Archaeological Perspectives* (Calgary, 1989), pp. 273–82.

14  J.P. Puype, 'Dutch Firearms from Seventeenth Century Indian Sites', in Puype and Mivan der Hoeven (eds), *The Arsenal of the World: The Dutch Arms Trade in the Seventeenth Century* (Amsterdam, 1996), pp. 52–61.

15 R. Law, "'Here is No Resisting the Country": The Realities of Power in Afro-European Relations of the West African "Slave Coast"', *Itinerario*, 18 (1994), pp. 51–2.

16 J. Thornton, *Warfare in Atlantic Africa 1450–1800* (1999).

17 R. Gray, 'Portuguese Musketeers on the Zambezi', *Journal of African History*, 12 (1972), pp. 531–3; M. Newitt, *Portuguese Settlement in the Zambezi* (1973), pp. 1–73.

18 C.R. Boxer and C. de Azvedo, *Fort Jesus and the Portuguese in Mombasa 1593–1729* (1960).

19 C.R. Boxer, *Portuguese Conquest and Commerce in Southern Asia, 1500–1750* (1985).

20 L. Blussé, 'The Dutch Occupation of the Pescadores, 1622–1624', *Transactions of the International Conference of Orientalists in Japan*, 18 (1973), pp. 28–43; E. van Veen, 'How the Dutch Ran a Seventeenth-Century Colony. The Occupation and Loss of Formosa, 1624–1662', *Itinerario*, 20 (1996), pp. 59–77.

21 E. Winius, 'Portugal's "Shadowy Empire in the Bay of Bengal"', *Camoes Center Quarterly*, 3, nos. 1 & 2 (1991), pp. 40–1.

22 R.D. Bathurst, 'Maritime Trade and Imamate Government: Two Principal Themes in the History of Oman to 1728', in D. Hopwood (ed.), *The Arabian Peninsula. Society and Politics* (1972), pp. 99–103.

23 A. Disney, 'Goa in the Seventeenth Century', in M. Newitt (ed.), *The First Portuguese Colonial Empire* (Exeter, 1986), p. 87.

24 J.I. Israel, *Dutch Primacy in World Trade, 1585–1740* (Oxford, 1989).

25 K. Glamann, *Dutch-Asiatic Trade, 1620–1740* (2nd edn, The Hague, 1981).

26 C.R. Boxer, *The Dutch in Brazil, 1624–1654* (Oxford, 1957).

27 S.G.A. Taylor, *The Western Design: An Account of Cromwell's Expedition to the Caribbean* (Kingston, Jamaica, 1965).

28 B. Stein, *The New Cambridge History of India. I. 2. Vijayanagara* (Cambridge, 1989), p. 125.

29 M. Ricklefs, *A History of Modern Indonesia* (2nd edn, 1993), p. 28.

30 Parker, *Military Revolution*, pp. 118–19; W.H. McNeill, 'European Expansion, Power and Warfare since 1500', in J.A. de Moor and H.L. Wesseling (eds), *Imperialism and War. Essays on Colonial Wars in Asia and Africa* (Leiden, 1989), pp. 19–20; J. Keegan, *A History of Warfare* (1993), pp. 187–92; A. Reid, *Europe and Southeast Asia: The Military Balance* (Townsville, Queensland, 1982), pp. 1, 5; A. Hirsch, 'The Collision of Military Cultures in Seventeenth-Century New England', *Journal of American History*, 74 (1987–8), pp. 1187–212; Forsyth, *Peoples of Siberia*, pp. 19, 51.

31 P. Lenihan, *Confederate Catholics at War, 1641–49* (Cork, 2001), pp. 228, 220.

32 R. Matthee, 'Unwalled Cities and Restless Nomads: Firearms and Artillery in Safavid Iran', *Pembroke Papers*, 4 (1996), pp. 389–416.

33 M.G.S. Hodgson, *The Venture of Islam. III. The Gunpowder Empires and Modern Times* (Chicago, 1974); W.H. McNeill, *The Age of Gunpowder Empires 1450–1800* (Washington, DC, 1989).

34 S. Morillo, 'Guns and Government: A Comparative Study of Europe and Japan', *Journal of World History*, 6 (1995), pp. 75–105.

35 G. Ágoston, 'Ottoman Artillery and European Military Technology in the Fifteenth and Sixteenth Centuries', *Acta Orientalia Academiae Scientarum Hungaricae*, 47 (1994), pp. 32–47, and 'Gunpowder for the Sultan's army', *Turcica*, 25 (1993), pp. 75–96.

36 Important recent work includes S.A. Nilsson, 'Imperial Sweden: Nation-Building, War and Social Change', in Nilsson (ed.), *The Age of New Sweden* (Stockholm, 1988), pp. 8–39.

37 See also, for example, M. Haneda, 'The Evolution of the Safavid Royal Guard', *Iranian Studies*, 21 (1989), pp. 57–86.

38 For the latter, W.R. Thompson, *The Emergence of the Global Political Economy* (2000), pp. 74–99, also in 'The Military Superiority Thesis and the Ascendancy of Western Eurasia in the World System', *Journal of World History*, 10 (1999), pp. 143–78.

## 10 CONCLUSIONS

1 A. Cunningham and O.P. Grell, *The Four Horsemen of the Apocalypse: Religion, War, Famine and Death in Reformation Europe* (Cambridge, 2000), pp. 92–199.

2 J.S. Nolan, 'The Militarization of the Elizabethan State', *Journal of Military History*, 58 (1994), pp. 418–19.

3 M.C. 't Hart, *The Making of a Bourgeois State: War, Politics and Finance during the Dutch Revolt* (Manchester, 1993).

4 Oman, *History of the Art of War*, II, 435; Black, *European Warfare 1660–1815* (London, 1994).

5 J. Glete, *War and the State in Early Modern Europe: Spain, the Dutch Republic and Sweden as Fiscal-Military States, 1500–1660* (2002).

6 D. Showalter, 'Caste, Skill, and Training: The Evolution of Cohesion in European Armies from the Middle Ages to the Sixteenth Century', *Journal of Military History*, 57 (1993), pp. 407–30; H.C. Kleinschmidt, 'Using the Gun: Manual Drill and the Proliferation of Portable Firearms', *Journal of Military History*, 63 (1999), pp. 601–29.

7 J.A. Lynn, 'The Evolution of Army Style in the Modern West, 800–2000', *International History Review*, 18 (1996), pp. 505–45, quote p. 508.

8 G. Ágoston, 'Habsburgs and Ottomans: Defense, Military Change and Shifts in Power', *Turkish Studies Association Bulletin*, 22 (1998), pp. 126–41; R. Murphey, *Ottoman Warfare 1500–1700* (1998), esp. pp. 85–129; J. Grant, 'Rethinking the Ottoman "Decline": Military Technology Diffusion in the Ottoman Empire, Fifteenth to Eighteenth Centuries', *Journal of World History*, 10 (1999), pp. 179–201.

9 G. Barta *et al.*, *History of Transylvania* (Budapest, 1994), p. 297.

10 W. Murray and M. Knox, 'Thinking About Revolutions in Warfare', in Knox and Murray (eds), *The Dynamics of Military Revolution 1300–2050* (Cambridge, 2001), pp. 2, 13.

# INDEX

Made in the USA
Middletown, DE
12 May 2015